23 April 2012

Dear John

fondly truth admiral

Meander

HARVARD HISTORICAL STUDIES • 174

Published under the auspices
of the Department of History
from the income of the
Paul Revere Frothingham Bequest
Robert Louis Stroock Fund
Henry Warren Torrey Fund

Empire and Underworld

Captivity in French Guiana

Miranda Frances Spieler

Harvard University Press

Cambridge, Massachusetts · London, England

2012

Library of Congress Cataloging-in-Publication Data

Spieler, Miranda Frances, 1971–
Empire and underworld : captivity in French Guiana / Miranda Frances Spieler.
p. cm.
Includes bibliographical references and index.
ISBN 978-0-674-05754-8 (alk. paper)
1. French Guiana—Politics and government—To 1814.   2. French Guiana—Politics and government—1814–1947.   3. French Guiana—Social conditions.   4. Captivity—French Guiana—History.   5. Power (Social sciences)—French Guiana—History.   6. Political violence—French Guiana—History.   7. Minorities—French Guiana—History. 8. Marginality, Social—French Guiana—History.   9. French Guiana—Colonial influence.   I. Title.
F2462.S69 2012
988.2—dc23   2012017838

In memory of my grandmothers

Tillie Friedberg and Fanny Spieler

Contents

Empire and Underworld

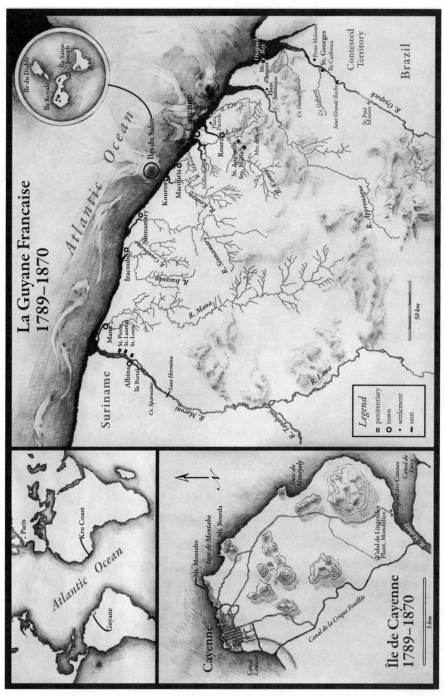

La Guyane Francaise
1789–1870

Atlantic Ocean

Ile du Diable
Ile Royale
Ile Saint-Joseph

Îles du Salut

Suriname

Albina
Ile Portal
Mana
St. Pierre
St. Laurent
St. Louis
Saut Hermina
Cr. Sparouine
R. Maroni
R. Tapahony
R. Lawa
R. Mana
Iracoubo
Sinnamary
Cr. Counamama
R. Iracoubo
R. Sinnamary
Kourou
Macouria
Macouria
Montsinéry
R. Kourou
R. Tonnegrande
Cayenne
Plant. Factoù
R. Oyac
Roura
St. Augustin
Ste. Marie
Mts. des Chevaux
R. Comté
R. Approuague
Cr. Oumari
Plant. Jamaïque
R. Kaw
Oyapock
Mt. d'Argent
Anse d'Argent
Ile Cailstoca
St. Georges
Poste Malouet
Cr. Gabaret
Saut Grande Roche
St. Paul Mission
R. Oyapock
Contested Territory
Brazil
R. Comté

50 km

Legend
▬ penitentiary
○ town
• settlement
▮ saut

Paris
Kru Coast
Atlantic Ocean
Guyane

N

Cayenne
Mt. Montabo
Anse de Montabo
Mt. Bourda
Anse de Montjoly
Vidal de Lingendes
Plant. Mondélice
Degrad des Cannes
Canal de Torcy
R. Mahury
Canal de la Crique Fouillée
Canal Laussac

Île de Cayenne
1789–1870

5 km

French Guiana, 1789–1870

Introduction

M ARC BLOCH'S POSTHUMOUS WORK, *Apologie pour l'histoire* (1949), insists often on the value of traces that mark the ground including buildings, field structures, and archaeological remains. Unwritten traces have the same importance for Bloch that footprints, fingerprints, or cigar ash would for a detective. Yet he also imagines vestiges on the land to have a moral and aesthetic value that is distinct from their usefulness. In physical remains, the past touches the land of the living and invites the touch of the historian.[1]

This is a book about French Guiana in the eighteenth and nineteenth centuries, a sparsely peopled slip of South America about the size of Maine (or Austria) that strikes the newcomer for the scarceness of traces indicating a history of human settlement. Ninety percent of the land to date remains primary forest. Looking out from a plane, you would see an expanse of green mounds of the same altitude and shape that give the impression of undulating green velour. And you might conclude that not much has changed there since the French arrived in the seventeenth century. In 1803, the colonial administrator Pierre-Victor Malouet described Guiana as land untouched by the hand of man that preserved "the native form of the globe and its original traits."[2] When the colonial era formally ended in 1947, Guiana's new civilian prefect noted "vast blanks on the map" at the time of his arrival.[3]

Guiana was not a place where human history had yet to begin, but one where human traces on the land tended to vanish. The disappearance problem began, though did not end, with the emergence of the colony in the late seventeenth century as a venue for schemes by later-day conquistadors that caused French settlers and native peoples to die and to scatter. In 1695, voyaging from Cayenne to Brazil, Governor Pierre-Éléonor de Férolles reported encountering "one hut of languishing Indians" as he journeyed eastward, whereas in Brazil "during the nine other days there are a multitude of Indians from different nations." Explorers of the late seventeenth and early eighteenth centuries walked down Indian footpaths. They relied on Indian villages for provisions and guides. With the death and flight of Indians, settlers lost contact with the interior. The explorer La Haye, a sergeant in the colony's garrison, visited the Camopi River, an influent of the Oyapock, in 1728.[4] He discovered new tribes there. They were gone by the end of the decade. When the villages and the footpaths disappeared, the colony became unmappable. Guiana offers the rare example of a colony that became unknown during the Enlightenment as a result of colonial settlement.[5]

Vanishing also marked the history of Guiana as a late-arriving slave colony, where few plantations existed in 1789. The dispersed pattern of settlement along riverbanks and the encircling vastness of the forest gave slaves much opportunity for flight.[6] Escape efforts peaked at the turn of the nineteenth century, when slaves liberated during the French Revolution were forced back into bondage under Napoleon. The government responded with military expeditions to torch the abodes of runaways and burn their fields.[7] The tables turned in 1848 after the second emancipation of the slaves. Vines wrapped the big houses, which rotted into forest.[8] Not a single planter's house remains today, even as a ruin.

The problem of disappearance, as a product of human history, equally defined the history of Guiana as a land of punishment and exile. Beginning in the late eighteenth century, the colony served as a depository for political and common criminals. In 1797 and 1798, the government sent 264 priests and a handful of royalists to French Guiana, who fled, died, or evacuated the colony under Napoleon. Fifty years later, following the coup d'état of President Louis-Napoleon Bonaparte, the navy founded a penal colony in Guiana for hard labor felons. The convict venture carried more than seventy thousand men and a few thousand women to Guiana over the next century. In contrast to convict settlers in Australia, however, Guiana's prisoners did not create families and settle down; their descendants (with extremely rare exceptions) are nowhere to be found. Apart from a few architectural remnants, the convicts left little mark on the earth.

The historian Michel de Certeau devoted his life to the study of traces that marked sites of death, displacement, and symbolic violence. Whether addressing New World discovery literature, mystical depictions of divinity, or popular culture, he read with the notion that "any autonomous order is founded upon what it eliminates." Certeau's reverence for this principle makes it all the more curious that he should have ignored the lack of people in the later discourse of colonialism. Instead, in an essay on Jules Verne, he evoked colonialism as a harmless sequence of events that began with exploratory travel, the naming of places, and the mapping of land. These preliminary acts of appropriation prepared the way for future "scientific and industrious activity."[9]

The idea of colonialism as the technocratic mastery of vacant earth has turned the history of Guiana into a misleading chronicle about colonial failure. Of the convict system, one scholar writes: "original intent and promises notwithstanding, it did little to further the economic development of the region. Land was cleared, trees were cut, but no lasting agricultural presence emerged."[10] When depicted as a system of modernizing conquest, colonialism encourages a view of European power over non-European land that drives the human subject out of history while misrepresenting rule over men as rule over things. Seen through the lens of colonialism, the disappearance of people and erasure of places become setbacks on the production schedule, abortive efforts, and hence reversals of history rather than historical situations.

During the roughly eighty-year period covered in this book, from 1789 to 1870, more than thirty thousand people came to Guiana, including slaves, convicts, political criminals, and immigrants. All of these people, whether they lived in a forest nook, a rural parish, a prison, or a house in Cayenne, inhabited a modern, manmade, interconnected world full of technical ingenuity. Yet the modern features of life in Guiana were largely invisible because they were legal in character. Law functioned there as what Henri Lefebvre calls a code of space, in the sense of providing a language for representing the colony symbolically, for structuring Guiana as a living space, and for shaping sensibilities and spatial practices.[11] As a code of space, law did not simply organize an existing world but instead produced a new world for humans by inventing new ways of being, seeing, and suffering.

The legal approach that guides this study began with a decision—originally a thought experiment—to use Marc Bloch's notion of the unwritten trace as a guide to Guiana with the idea that everything including primary forest, secondary forest, and abandoned lots on the edge of Cayenne should count as elements of a manmade world and not of a world that man failed to constitute. If it is true, as Bloch presumes, that humans shape the way that nature shapes society, then human vanishing must be a form of manmade change to the earth. "Does the physical world ever act on the social world without its action being prepared, aided or permitted by factors that originate with man?"[12] I decided to treat human absence as a wordless trace. I redefined places where people no longer lived as human inventions (rather than places man failed to make a mark). I also opted to introduce a few conceptual, yet visualizable adjustments to Guiana as a historical site. Bloch provides an especially apt interpretive model for Guiana in the course of his textual saunter through northern France, when he notes the importance of "strange field design" (l'étrange dessin des champs).[13]

To reproduce my thought experiment, I propose to move Guiana out of South America (we will move it back) in order to reconstitute the colony, for analytical purposes, as a French region where the ground is marked by unusual patterns. Calling Guiana a place in France marked by strange field design has many practical benefits, not least for being accurate on at least one point. After the Second World War, Guiana became an overseas French department, as did Martinique, Guadeloupe, and Réunion. At present, the currency in Guiana is the Euro note (there is a picture of Guiana on the Euro note). In 1947, law redefined the bond between Guiana and France so that land in South America could become the equivalent of metropolitan French territory.

The provisional relocation of Guiana to domestic France makes it newly possible to see how law functioned there. In a place with few institutions, one newspaper (published by the government), and fragmentary archives, law alone makes it possible to fold the human subject back into the narrative of Guiana's colonial past. This book's legal approach arose from the need to interpret archival documents in which people are hardly visible. I have used the law to magnify their presence by connecting acts that I can barely see to contemporaneous acts of symbolic violence against their second selves as legal subjects, which can be described with considerable precision. I have also sought (in the rare cases where this is possible) to track law-related spatial maneuvering by disadvantaged groups. The dire situation of convicts has hindered my ability to reconstruct their lives archivally, as has the institutional barrenness of nineteenth-century Guiana and the despotic character of its government. The instruments of social history do not work for people who are not members of society. Most felons did not live in civilian areas and could not marry, exercise property rights, or even sign legal documents. They were not the clientage of a notary.

To call Guiana a place in France marked by strange field design is to adopt a model of historical change that is exactly opposite what colonialism proposes. There could not be strange field design in a world where human history followed the dictates of technocratic rationality. Bloch observes: "man passes his time raising mechanisms of which he becomes a more or less voluntary prisoner."[14] Strange patterns do not result from strange people or express preternatural oddity of place. Strange patterns are also not failed attempts to create perfect field design. Bloch understands design oddity to arise from the universal human tendency toward accretion: one-time experiments become habits, and new experiments likewise disappear into the evolving shape.

Moving Guiana into Europe, at least provisionally, makes it possible to question the logic of colonialism in a spatial sense. How were colonies distinct from France? What structures intervened to delineate the empire in general and Guiana in particular from domestic territory? By questioning the distinction between metropolitan and colonial land, it becomes newly possible to understand the framing principles that created the empire as a particular domain of state in the New Regime. Those framing principles structured power relations in Guiana and hence played a central role in events there.

This thought experiment cancels the myth of Guiana as virgin earth while making it possible to pull Guiana out of the exoticism in which it has long languished. Revisualizing Guiana as a land inside France makes this a case to puzzle over within the context of European history. This is not the end but the beginning, however, which I nuance by looking to the particularities of the region, to political contingencies—maritime war, for example—and to the larger context of colonial history.

The people whose presence I have tried to restore lived in situations of extreme disadvantage. Because of my reliance on law (and hence on changes to the law), the moment I am able to access the presence of a particular group is usually the moment of that group's unmaking. While it is possible to resituate people in Guiana in a narrative about law and power, it is not possible to constitute them as empowered legal subjects. There simply are no materials to support a narrative of this sort, whereas documents of quite a different character abound.

When Europeans moved into new colonial spaces, law moved with them. Two general sorts of law supplied a framework for inventing imperial spaces. The first defined the personal status of individuals and therefore created symbolic legal selves; the second created a symbolic version of the earth (overlapping with the real one) by creating boundaries and shaping institutions.[15] Guiana is not distinct from other domestic or imperial territories because law shaped living space, personal identity, and spatial practice. Nonetheless, law intervened there in an unusual way because of the colony's double identity as a land of exile and a land of slavery and emancipation. Most newcomers to Guiana from 1789 to 1870 arrived there in a state of extreme incapacity. This was the predicament of slaves, convicts, immigrants, and political criminals. As for the land, Guiana invariably consisted of an extra-constitutional zone. In the nineteenth century the colony was even further divided to create internal zones of abnormality.

Albert Memmi describes colonized people as *hors de la cité* (outside the city), which aptly captures the predicament of people in Guiana.[16] The phrase *outside the city* harks back to a Europe of walled towns and summons a mental picture of municipal expulsion. Yet the predicament of a person who lives outside the city is rather different from that of someone closed out of town. To live outside the city means you are stuck. You must be under the city's authority to be defined as other by its laws. You need to be in to be out. You cannot enter and you cannot leave.

As a place to live in and to topple from, the city or polis is at the center of Hannah Arendt's reflections on the conditions that enable distinctly human life. She understands law as a framework through which people enact their will for freedom and realize personal distinctiveness in community. For reasons that appear essential to her worldview, Arendt cannot define the law as a cause of human unmaking. As George Kateb observes, "Arendt's hard truth, perhaps her hardest truth, is that when many if not most of the awful events in political life happen . . . the leading perpetrators do not feel . . . that they are doing or even intending wrong." What Arendt cannot acknowledge is the role of law as a maker of what Kateb calls "mental constructions," which clear the conscience and hence make it all the more possible for bad things to happen.[17] Arendt contrives the polis as an ideal that stands for the possibility of mutual transparency and human flourishing. The polis, the only hope, cannot be allowed to become a contrivance that degrades people.

Arendt's version of the legal order is a sealed utopia. She models the nation-state after a Greek polis "physically secured by the wall around the city and physiognomically guaranteed by its laws."[18] Life inside the walls begins with second birth, or what Arendt calls natality, by which people will themselves out of the nothingness of biological life into "the space of appearance," which she also calls Being.[19] In word and deed, they cause themselves to be reborn as actors in a theater-like world that is real life.

Arendt refuses to taint the law by associating it either with structures of violence or with people she takes for natural men—savages of different sorts. It is striking that she feels obliged, when writing of interwar refugees, to attribute their predicament to "the decline of the nation-state" rather than seeing their misfortune to arise from the nation-state. Similarly, she insists that refugees live outside the law as people unknown to it rather than being victims of a legal situation. Whether during the French Revolution or during the interwar years, her ex-citizen lives "outside the range of the law and the body politic of the citizens, as for instance a slave—but certainly a politically irrelevant being."[20] While resembling slaves, people who lose citizenship also descend to the level of "savage tribes" whose tragedy (in her view) is to "die without leaving any trace, without having contributed anything to a common world."[21] Arendt uses the slave to sharpen the poignancy of the ex-citizen's predicament and likewise invokes the barbarian to indicate how low the citizen has fallen. She also makes instrumental use of the slave when depicting second birth as exit from the unspeakable domain where humans appear to each other as specimen-like "physical objects."[22] Yet Arendt cannot allow the law to help the slave whom the ex-citizen resembles. The slave exists in a fictionally distinct zone of life that is dedicated to production and reproduction. This region of existence can only (in her scheme) contaminate the domain of Being if allowed to become visible to it. Arendt's citizen becomes the slave when he is thrown from the polis, but Arendt's polis cannot touch the slave without defiling itself.

Arendt excludes criminals irreversibly from the city as men "against all men." For criminals to become visible in the polis heralds an age of decadent immorality. Criminals are "marginal figures who usually enter the historical scene in times of corruption, disintegration, and political bankruptcy."[23] Since they do not inhabit the space of Being, there is only one place they can live: outside the walls. Yet when citizens are uprooted and fall out of the legal order, they do not meet criminals there. Instead, in Arendt's narrative, as citizens fall, criminals ascend. Thus, for instance, she imagines that a refugee "can become almost a full-fledged citizen because of a little theft. Even if he is penniless he can now get a lawyer, complain about his jailers, and he will be listened to respectfully. He is no longer the scum of the earth but important enough to be informed of all the details of the law under which he will be tried. He has become a respectable person."[24]

The people whom I consider as legal subjects in this book are the very ones whom Arendt locates outside the law in a debased state of nature. By examining the overlapping lives of criminals, slaves, so-called savages and political criminals, it becomes possible to understand how law, while providing a framework for human flourishing, also enables violence and masks it. The predicament of people in the colony who might not seem to have much in common resulted from quite similar legal configurations. To the extent that ex-citizens resembled colonial subjects, this arose not from living outside the law in vile nature but from living inside the law as inventions of human artifice.

Samuel Beckett's final novel, *The Unnamable* (1953), is acutely relevant to the situation of people in this study because of what his fiction suggests about the way inscription defines the margins of the legal order. Beckett's first-person narrator embodies what it means to assume voice and existence under someone's pen as an invention of writing. In his case, language creates subjection rather than self-mastery. The only hope of Beckett's narrator is to pass through the door that recurs frequently in the text. At the end of the tale, the narrator observes: "they have carried me to the threshold of my story, before the door that opens on my story, that would surprise me, if it opens, it will be I, it will be the silence."[25] For Beckett's character, the door stands for the edge of language. For someone who lives outside the city, the threshold that cannot be crossed is also language (law in particular), which constitutes the outsider without allowing him to pass beyond its reach.

Beckett's novel (or autobiography) inverts the common idea of the non-citizen as someone who lacks inscription—who stands outside the law because he has yet to be written into it. That inexact yet conventional notion, which survives in contemporary ideas of illegal immigrants, may have originated with the exclusion of unbaptized heretics from state records under clerical control. The old idea of inscription assumed a new character in France when the state took over recordkeeping from the clergy in 1792. When describing the significance of the new *état civil* or secular civil rolls, the legislator Louis-Jérôme Gohier observed: "slaves have no civil status. Only the free man has a city, a fatherland; only he is born, lives and dies a citizen. All the documents relevant to his birth, his marriage, and his death should therefore declare this great character."[26] In this instance, Gohier is likely to have used the word slaves to mean followers of the Church, not colonial slaves.[27] Yet soon, as we shall see, inscription in the civil roll assumed symbolic importance in the colonial world; having a name to the law distinguished the legal person from the legal thing.

Where Beckett suggests marginal identity to originate with inscription as opposed to its lack, Maurice Blanchot identifies life outside the city with erasure. In the novel *Le très haut* (1948) he addresses the European notion of legal inscription as a mechanism that enables people to become visible and hence shielded from violence. The novel's protagonist is a delirious official who keeps the civil rolls. The man so identifies himself with the law that jotting down details of his insipid life promises to yield "the fulfillment of a supreme verity." Soon the official meets a man in the underground who tells him about the rising number of deleted people living in attic rooms in the form of a "class without name and without right." These are people whom the delirious public servant has learned to regard as nonexistent. Early in the novel he tells a photographer that she and he practice versions of the same métier: to inscribe is to make someone appear to the eyes of law (to himself). "Thanks to us, individuals have a juridical existence; they leave a durable trace, one knows who they are; I wanted to show to her that to the eyes of the law, we fulfilled similar functions."[28]

To fix the archival problem in French Guiana has been quite a research project. In addition to drawing on records from French Guiana's departmental archives in Cayenne and multiple document series from the colonial archives in Aix-en-Provence, I use materials from several navy depositories in France, from the archives of the Jesuits, from four departmental archives in metropolitan France, and from numerous series at the National Archives in Paris. The legal materials that guide my reading of those documents come from elsewhere: I develop scattered hints in archival documents by looking to legal codes, legal treatises, debates of the Conseil d'état, and parliamentary records.

The scope of this research project draws attention to what I have not managed, after all that, to turn up. The slaves who obtained freedom during the Revolution are not accessible from an archival standpoint until just before their return to slavery under Napoleon: this perversity is not lost on me. Many of the priests and laypeople who survived their deportation to French Guiana in the 1790s published accounts of their misadventures. In contrast, not one of the roughly twenty thousand hard labor criminals and ex-convicts transported there from 1852 to 1870 published a memoir. The four accounts by detainees from this period are by political deportees who had no contact with common criminals during their time in the colony. Scarcely any convict letters survive from this period. Convicts, ex-convicts, and non-European immigrants do not speak in the documents I have been obliged to use and make the best of. Freed slaves after 1848 bought and sold property, recognized children, and contracted marriage before notaries while being closed out of politics, having no press, and being excluded from public life. There are no novels in this period. The most expressive published material, other than the laws in Second Empire Guiana, are liquidation sale notices. Had the people spoken, this would be a different book.

Broadly similar principles define what a legal subject is, which people can embody differently without ceasing to be universal in what they stand for. They can live in a region marked by odd legal design while the design, on scrutiny, is recognizably part of a common cultural patrimony. The story of Guiana is a tale about people reduced by law, who could not speak as we are used to hearing people speak in France and in other postemancipation societies. The analytical method I employ to bring that story to light is guided by a cosmopolitan sensibility, in the sense that I approach Guiana as a kind of world city. Everyone here exists in relation to the citizenry; they live under the law as it threatens and unmakes them. As described by Kwame Anthony Appiah, a cosmopolitan approach, whether to the past or the present, requires analytical categories that allow people to be recognized as universal in their distinctness. Here that principle finds expression in a legal approach that has made it possible to see structural resemblances between disparate lives and to treat metropolitan and colonial territory as a unity.[29]

My approach departs in important respects from that of Michel Foucault in *Surveiller et punir* (1975) (*Discipline and Punish*, 1978), though I have tried to extend and refine a number of his suggestions. In that book, Foucault disputed conventional explanations for the apparently humane penal reforms that replaced torture, mutilation, and spectacular execution in the nineteenth century. Foucault identified the modern era with the subtilization of violence rather than its disappearance. In his account, the penitentiary acts as an impersonal machine of mind control that arose when general surveillance and disciplinary retraining gained acceptance as norms within mainstream society.

In the final phase of Foucault's history, during the 1840s, the enclosed and silent world of the reformatory overtook the city. With the advent of what Foucault called the carceral archipelago on domestic soil, prison-like structures began popping up everywhere in the form of youth reformatories, almshouses, orphanages, and even workers' estates.[30]

In Foucault's understanding of modernity, coercive structures that originally served to enclose and exclude contaminated groups—symbolized by the leprosarium—moved from the periphery to the center of life. With the rise of new notions of social dangerousness, the contaminated group became indistinct from the citizenry. In a sense, the disease crept inward.[31]

To represent the new mode of exercising power over the suspect masses, Foucault frequently looked to the model of a plagued city under quarantine.[32] In the plagued city, everyone is under watch as a source of infection. Everyone is shielded from infection by the solicitude of the state. No one goes in. No one goes out. Houses are subject to routine search by village health inspectors as a service to the inhabitants. In the plagued city, the self and the other are the same figure. It is a situation of complete collapse between interdiction and inclusion. But the plagued city in its modern form is immeasurably more insidious than it once was, because the epidemic is permanent and cure is impossible.

Of the carceral archipelago, Foucault wrote: "it does not cast the unassimilable into a confused hell; there is no outside."[33] Life and incarceration became indistinguishable. It is no wonder that Foucault could not take scope of the overseas penal colony: the idea would seem ludicrous, even impossible, after the formation of the carceral archipelago. There was, he suggested, already a gulag inside the country. Why create another one? Whom to drag there? What group seemed distinct enough, vile enough, to want removing? In *Surveiller et punir* Foucault so closely identified the actual prisoner with someone who might become one in the future—the masses are suspect—that there was no room to address the particularity of an other who might be destroyed, or subjected to extreme cruelty, rather than watched carefully.

Violence continued unabated after the eighteenth century, and new forms of barbarism arose then. In *Surveiller et punir,* Foucault wrote of modern uses of power that subjected the populace to an intrusive, all-encompassing gaze. In contrast, this study is concerned with uses of power that were frequently understood to flout the norms of society and that seemed to require not looking and not knowing.

Did Foucault believe there was no outside? He modeled the plagued city after modern France as he pictured it: a state under permanent emergency rule by the police. He watched people being hauled off. In 1977, after a confrontation with the police at the Santé prison, Foucault observed: "from now on, police are above the law. Power wanted to show that the juridical arsenal is incapable of protecting citizens."[34] In November of that year he returned to the extra-legality of the modern state; its "exceptional and extra-legal character cannot be allowed to appear as a sign of arbitrariness or excessive power, but rather in the form of solicitude."[35] Since the plagued city stood for permanent emergency rule, as these remarks suggest, it was not really a domain of subtle violence and invasive watchfulness. A city under permanent emergency rule had to be a war zone.

To Foucault, the modern state and the modern legal order internalized war and waged what he called "race war" (the enemy race is socially constructed and historically variable). He analyzed this problem in his 1975–76 lectures at the Collège de France. On 17 March 1976, Foucault spoke to forms of death that became possible with the advent of what he called biopower. In place of the old sovereign power to kill, this new power concerned collective species management—the power to "make live" and "let die." Addressing himself to lethal uses of biopower, Foucault noted practices such as "exposing someone to death, increasing the risk of death for some people, or quite simply, political death, expulsion, rejection, and so on."[36]

In light of Foucault's 1976 analysis of internal war and biopower, the problem with *Surveiller et punir* is all the more striking: when writing of punishment, Foucault committed to the view that the prison enveloped the world and absorbed the outside. One year later he depicted society as the setting of permanent internal war against outsiders marked for different kinds of death.

Foucault devoted half a page to convict transportation and wished it away in an essay he wrote prior to publishing his book on punishment. "Deportation disappeared rather quickly."[37] In fact, the punitive innovation of the era that began in the 1850s, where *Surveiller et punir* leaves off, was convict transportation.[38] André Zysberg, an historian of the galleys during the Old Regime, suggests that the treatment of convicts in French Guiana "was as inhumane as that of galley slaves in the time of Louis XIV, and perhaps more so."[39] In such circumstances, one could hardly claim there was no outside.

Foucault's analysis of the carceral archipelago is still of use to under-standing élan for the penal colony in the nineteenth century. How could a society that celebrated unending confinement accept the idea of criminal release? In a world where everything became prisonlike, what place re-mained for the liberated man? The figure who menaced French society of the early nineteenth century more than any other was the ex-convict. Lib-erated felons elicited panic and repulsion among officials and members of the public. From the 1820s forward, ex-convicts became the object of le-gal and administrative procedures of rising complexity. Artful police mea-sures arranged for their expulsion from towns and whole departments. Law acted in conjunction with police power to shape an underclass of hunted and placeless vagabonds. The internal war against ex-convicts that began in the 1820s led to the founding of Guiana's penal colony in 1852. Within the colony, the persistence of that internal war created a new militarized world of punishment.

Nineteenth-century Guiana was the scene of two internal wars: one against liberated felons and the other against liberated slaves. At the end of the French Revolution, the internal war against freed people climaxed with the reenslavement of black citizens in 1803 with assistance by militia-men and garrison troops, cued by the metropolitan government. During the early nineteenth century, the struggle against liberation left an endur-ing mark on the colony. Guiana emerged during the 1820s as a depository for Africans seized aboard slave ships after the abolition of the slave trade whom neither the French navy nor the local administration imagined lib-erating. Legal innovations that would shape Guiana's later history arose from that impasse, as officials angled to render these people invisible while withholding freedom from them indefinitely. Years later, the second emancipation of the slaves in 1848 inspired so violent an elite response that officials and planters hoped, in 1852, to annex the new free black so-ciety to the penal colony.

Internal war of a prolonged sort shall always depend on legal mecha-nisms. Modern critics of sovereign violence look to the German legal scholar Carl Schmitt to understand the nature of emergency law and the structure of internal war zones. Schmitt's works of 1921 and 1922 offer dis-tinct yet uniformly admiring depictions of sovereign omnipotence as it inter-venes in the legal order. In *Diktatur* (1921), Schmitt explores suspensions of the constitution (with constant reference to French history) that shield the state without damaging the legal order.[40] In *Political Theology* (1922), Schmitt argues that normal law cannot authorize its own nonapplication. In the later work, he treats the laws of the state as laws of nature and depicts the exception as a form of miracle. Viewed this way, it becomes impossible to imagine law turning law off, just as gravity cannot shut itself down. Instead, Schmitt locates authority over the exception in a sovereign who stands outside the legal order as God stands outside creation. Only a sovereign who creates the law without being bound by it can make miracles. "Sovereign is he who decides the exceptional situation."[41]

What remains steady in Schmitt's thought is his idea of rule and exception as completely distinct yet interdependent realities. Miracles cannot exist without laws of nature. A patternless world of virgin births and talking shrubs, where water burst from rock at random intervals, would be a meaningless world, not a miraculous one. The sovereign lives in the normal law as much as he lives in the exception. "It is necessary for a normal situation to be created, and the sovereign is he who decides definitively whether this normal situation exists."[42]

In France during the eighteenth and nineteenth centuries, the empire did not lie outside the domestic legal order but instead comprised a region of state marked by the suspension of domestic constitutional law.[43] In the same period, on domestic soil and in the empire, legal experiments that arose during states of emergency wound up as norms with marked frequency, only to be outdone by stranger novelties that vanished in their turn. This ongoing, accretive cycle of invention and absorption profoundly altered life in domestic as well as colonial France during the eighty years traversed by this book (1789–1871). Nasser Hussain distinguishes the legal regime of Victorian Britain from that of nineteenth-century British colonies by noting the high degree of entanglement between legal norms and exceptional practices in the empire.[44] It is impossible to call recourse to emergency law an imperial particularity in the French case. During the years after 1789, the French people experienced a prolonged epoch of insurrection, revolution, regime change, multiple dictatorial interludes, and street-sweeping phases of violent reaction. Domestic law, and not merely imperial law, accreted emergency structures.

Walter Benjamin observes: "the tradition of the oppressed teaches us that the 'state of emergency' in which we live is not the exception but the rule. We must attain to a conception of history that is in keeping with this insight."[45] The philosopher Giorgio Agamben looks to this maxim when developing a dialectical reading of Carl Schmitt, nuanced by mysticism, which climaxes with the merging of rule and exception in a world of constant miracles: the apocalypse.[46] In Agamben's account, law remakes the city into a scene of what he calls bare life. The world of biological humanness that Arendt cordons off from law and Being in the walled polis overtakes the city as legal artifice disintegrates. When this occurs, there is only one thing left for the sovereign to suspend, which is life.

Notwithstanding the brilliance of this approach to Schmitt, it presents several problems for the historian. The first results from the frequency with which exceptions became rules in the late eighteenth and nineteenth century. How to know when we have reached the end of history? Imperial law routinely absorbed the weapons of crisis law. Both the Civil Code and the Criminal Code incorporated legal mechanisms that began as emergency decrees. The merging of exception and rule happened all the time. Empirically it is impossible to see that there can be an end to this process.

A second problem with Agamben's eschatology results from the way he brackets the prison from bare life. In this respect, he would appear to be indebted to Hannah Arendt, who went out of her way to define the history of the oppressed against the criminal. Similarly, Agamben invokes the prison to define the space of apocalyptic suffering by opposition. He writes: "while prison law only constitutes a particular sphere of penal law and is not outside the normal order, the juridical constellation that guides the camp is . . . martial law and the state of exception."[47] Agamben's definition of the prison as lying inside the normal order is not consistent with his claim that the state of exception "gradually comes more and more to the foreground." If the state of exception corrodes legal normality by a continuous process, and the two become ever less distinct, there is no normal order for the prison to belong to. Far from being untouched by a general shift of such consequence, the prison will be among the first areas of the state to go off the rails.

CHAPTER 1

Leaving the Republic

IN THE SUMMER OF 1795, the tone-deaf vaudevillian Louis-Ange Pitou moved his act from the Armed Man, a royalist tavern, to the public squares of Paris. He stood with a shapely fiddler on a table near the Louvre and insulted the government in verse that he made obscene through his talent for physical comedy.[1] He was arrested for the sixteenth time in August 1797 and sentenced in October. Pitou used his chilly months in the Bicêtre prison to write his memoirs, *Analysis of My Woes and Persecutions*.[2] But the real misery lay ahead. In January he set off with a gendarme escort on his long journey to French Guiana.

Three weeks later Pitou joined the mixed group of deportees who were then imprisoned in the Saint Maurice convent at the port of Rochefort. In mid-March, at the sound of a drum roll, Pitou and a column of priests, hairstylists, nobles, cobblers, and two legislators carried their satchels to the shore, past broken ships. Pitou remembered a sexagenarian clerk, "dressed as a traveler, who seemed to be emigrating to another world."[3]

Pitou's arrest occurred days before a detachment from Lazare Hoche's army dissolved the legislature on orders from the Executive Directory— the steering panel of the executive branch. At dawn on 18 fructidor year V (4 September 1797), fifteen hundred soldiers surrounded the Tuileries Palace, the hall of the assemblies, to preempt an ill-planned coup by royalist deputies, fellow travelers, and turncoat generals who had made common cause in both houses of the new government.

The rump of the legislature met that evening at a provisional location, the Luxembourg Palace, to consider emergency measures to save the republic. Antoine Boulaye de la Meurthe spoke to his colleagues about a new punishment—deportation—that would allow for a clean sweep of the Counter Revolution. "The triumph of the Republic will not be sullied by a single drop of blood. . . . From now on, deportation must be the means of saving the Republic. Thus we will finally rid ourselves of the émigrés and the priests who refuse the reign of liberty."[4] The next day the legislature voted to annul the elections of that spring, slated fifty-four prominent men—deputies, journalists, and generals—for deportation, reactivated lapsed statutes against counterrevolutionaries and made it possible for the Executive Directory to arrest and deport suspect priests by individual warrant.

Despite the importance that Boulaye and his colleagues accorded to deportation, the rump of the legislature seemed to have no interest in the destination of the men they purged. The law of 19 fructidor swept the Counterrevolution into "the place the Executive Directory will determine."[5] The deputies' distractedness about where the deportees were going had an analogue in the directors' unconcern about how they would get there. On 22 July 1797, less than two months before the coup, the ordonnateur at Rochefort repeated his plea for financial assistance and described the dire circumstances of the port to the minister of the navy. Ragged and hungry, the workers of the admiralty lacked the strength to build new ships. Rochefort had no "pine slats and planks, irons of small dimension, multiple kinds of canvas" or money to buy them with since the collapse of the *assignat,* the republic's paper money. There were only twelve carpenters in the port. There was no old cord and no hemp to make new cord. It was becoming too expensive to chase the sailors who deserted. But the minister knew all of this. "By the forementioned letter, I informed you of how essential it was to help the miserable salaried workers of the Navy . . . The workers have received very little money and are kept alive on bread from the bakers who are paid by the republic to supply them."[6]

Fewer than four hundred deportees left Rochefort for Guiana between

October 1797 and August 1798. The ships that carried them disappeared or returned shredded by British cannon fire. Pitou's ship, *La Charente,* delayed its scheduled departure, on 14 March 1798, when three English ships blocked the harbor. Two weeks later, the *Charente* set sail, only to encounter the same three ships near Bordeaux. To escape, the captain beached the *Charente* on a mud embankment near the mouth of the Gironde River.[7] The replacement convoy, *La Décade,* deposited its 193 passengers, including 162 priests, in Cayenne and then fell to the British almost immediately after reembarking.[8] The final ship, *La Bayonnaise,* delivered 109 deported priests and 11 laypeople to the colony. Nearing home in the Bay of Biscay, the ship encountered the *Embuscade,* a captured French warship under British command, and fought what became the most celebrated French sea battle of the Revolution at the cost of sixty French sailors, an equal number of British lives, and *La Bayonnaise.*[9]

The apparent failure of this attempt to deport thousands of counter-revolutionaries to French Guiana did not actually result from unforeseeable contingencies related to the maritime war. Instead, it resulted from a refusal on the part of the political elite to entertain any known obstacle to the execution of this punishment, including the maritime war.

The legislature and the directors had every reason to know the significance of those obstacles. Revolutionaries made use of deportation in a remarkable number of decrees since the early 1790s. Through that history the word *déportation* acquired a new significance. It came to mean punitive exile from metropolitan France followed by indefinite confinement to land remote from the nation yet under its sovereignty. Before 1789, it had been a specialized term used by jurists as a synonym for banishment; by the new system, deportees needed both to live outside the boundaries of metropolitan France and to remain in the custody of the French government.[10]

The accelerated use of the guillotine between fall 1793 and summer 1794 has distracted attention from the widespread use of banishment and deportation before, during, and after the period of the Terror. In fact, the removal of political enemies to somewhere outside national frontiers and the liquidation of political enemies inside those limits had an unexpectedly intimate connection to one another. Many of the people who were imprisoned or killed on national soil during the 1790s were first defined legally as deportees who could be summarily executed if they crossed back into France. The illicit wandering of counterrevolutionaries was, at least in part, a legal construction. Among the people affected by revolutionary laws of proscription were people called émigrés and deportees who never left the country.

During the Old Regime, civil death was an auxiliary punishment to permanent banishment from the realm. Civil death began as a contrivance of medieval canonists, who twisted metaphorical comparisons between deportation, slavery, and death in Justinian's *Digests* to elaborate a worldly punishment that duplicated the effects of mortal excommunication, or anathema.[11] Later French jurists rehearsed the same interpretation of Roman law when describing the status of banished criminals. To justify the link between civil death and banishment, they suggested that banishment was a modern substitute for Roman deportation to an island and cited passages from the *Digests* likening *deportatio ad insulam* to death.[12]

Seventeenth-century natural law theory, which reached France mainly through translations of Hugo Grotius,[13] helped to produce a new understanding of civil death that made the old glosses of Roman law superfluous. In *De Jure Belli ac Pacis* (1625) (*The Rights of War and Peace*), Grotius had envisaged that internal enemies—"enemies of the human race"—who waged what he called "informal war" against the sovereign would lose all their rights and undergo either execution or enslavement along with the confiscation of their belongings.[14] Likewise, in *Traité de la mort civile* (1755) by François Richer, civil death punished rebels against a sovereign called the nation with the seizure of their bodies and their property, which both became the property of the state.

In his 1755 treatise on civil death, François Richer described political society in terms that resembled the 1789 Declaration of the Rights of Man and Citizen. In common with later revolutionaries, he understood the nation as a legal community that a man entered on being born and that existed for the purpose of conserving species life. Nonetheless, in spite of that affinity, Richer did not describe the individual as a bearer of rights; in his account, rights belonged exclusively to the nation as a collective entity.

The whole nation works to maintain the rules that it establishes for its security, tranquility and convenience, and to protect each of its members so long as he deserves it, by his unwavering submission to the duties that he is assigned at birth. . . . Upon being born, every man contracts tacitly with society. From the moment he comes into the world, he is required to do more than avoid harming others and undermining the public good. He must also do the utmost for them that he is capable of.[15]

Because Richer regarded humanness as life in conformity with national laws, he wrote of people who defied the law as though they had exited the human species. The civilly dead were actually less than dead, because they were no longer men.

It is the absolute proscription of the citizen; it is an extraction one makes from civil society; it is a member one rips from it; it is the state of a man whose forehead is printed with public infamy; it is the state of a citizen with whom one prohibits all commerce, engagement and alliance; it is the state of a man who one removes from the catalogue of the living; it is the state of a man whom society is warned not to recognize as such, to look upon as already in the class of the dead, whom one reduces to having neither homeland nor family.[16]

Missing from Richer's list of what civil death removed—honor, civil bonds, filiation, humanness, recognition of existence, a birthplace to defend and belong to—was any reference to membership in the nation. Although a person struck with civil death might lose his share in sovereignty, exit the citizenry, and undergo irreversible withdrawal from the domain of civil and natural law, he could not exist as nothing without retaining a connection to the laws of the nation that punished and hence defined him.

During the French Revolution, the soil and geographical limits of France became symbolic expressions of the regenerated French people. Prior to then, under the monarchy, the nation referred to an abstract collectivity, not to a territorialized group.[17] Later, revolutionaries infused the nation with new spatial meaning as they crafted a new world of politics. In 1789 and 1790, the Constituent Assembly abolished the provinces and divided the country into new units, called departments; this remaking of French legal space annulled regional identities while putting the citizenry within range of new, uniform institutions.[18] At the popular level, the French nation acquired a new spatial identity through symbolic acts of territorial conquest, beginning with the liberty trees and poles that insurrectionary peasants planted in 1790.[19] Mona Ozouf identifies popular revolutionary celebration with "the beating down of gates, the crossing of castle moats, walking at one's ease in places where one was once forbidden."[20] During the dechristianization campaign of 1794, the conquest of space involved renaming places to expunge saints' names from memory. It meant melting down bells, dancing around auto-da-fés of relics, and reconsecrating the stripped churches as temples of reason.[21]

Revolutionary understandings of national space harked back to the monarchy to a considerable degree, nonetheless. Patriotic discourse from the 1790s concerning undesirables on French soil recalled a prerevolutionary controversy concerning the status of slaves in France. In the eighteenth century, as Sue Peabody has shown, Old Regime jurists rediscovered the French legal adage, "Let all servitude become freedom." This maxim supplied the legal basis for descriptions of France as "free soil." Slaves from French colonies could (and did) sue for freedom after setting foot in metropolitan France. Yet the dramatic rise of Caribbean plantation economies in the eighteenth century helped to create a backlash against the freedom principle among French administrators. Official efforts to block the passage of colonial slaves onto metropolitan "free soil" climaxed in 1777 with a ban on blacks entering France. If discovered there without authorization, black people including slaves risked being sent to the colonies to be sold at auction or used as slaves of the king.[22]

The Old Regime controversy over the meaning of free soil lefts its mark on revolutionary culture. During the period of the Terror, enemies of state who refused to abide by the people's laws figured in republican rhetoric as slaves on the soil of liberty. On 14 March 1794, the popular society at Longwy complained about "the hordes of slaves and barbarians surrounding and menacing us. . . . Let them no longer defile the sacred land of liberty."[23] The same day, the citizens of Loudon congratulated the legislature for the decree of 4 February 1794, emancipating colonial slaves and promised, in the service of the same cause, to behead *liberticides*. "The soil of liberty must not be inhabited except by free men. . . . Liberty or death!"[24] On 14 April 1794, the popular society at La Rochelle thanked the Convention for emancipating colonial slaves and for a second decree deporting counterrevolutionaries. Both deportation and abolition seemed to extend from the same principle. "In decreeing Revolutionary Government, the liberty of men of color, and the exportation of suspects, you continue to be just . . . in purifying the soil of the republic."[25] On 23 May 1794, the popular society at Josselin in Morbihan ordered the Convention to "purge the territory of the republic of all interior enemies. . . . Send this execrable cargo of suspects to Madagascar. The land of free men must not be defiled by the presence of slaves."[26] On 5 July 1794, the popular society at Oradour-sur-Vayres in Haute-Vienne asked for a decree deporting "all fanatical priests including the sexagenarians. Let us include the fathers, mothers, and wives of émigrés . . . purge the soil of liberty of the impure remains that deface this blessed land."[27]

Punishments that affected counterrevolutionaries during the 1790s resembled earlier measures affecting the legal status and treatment of vagabonds and common criminals. Revolutionaries were quick to approve the deportation of nonpolitical offenders and the stripping of their civic rights. The jurist Louis-Michel Le Peletier de Saint Fargeau described the need for a revolutionary form of anathema in a speech of May 1791 explaining the new Criminal Code: "We propose that you adopt . . . this salutary and terrible thought, *society and the laws pronounce anathema against whomever defiles it by a crime.*"[28] The new punishment, civic degradation, entailed the ceremonial removal of citizenship from felons. Criminals would lose their citizenship in a public ritual that replaced convict branding, which revolutionaries abolished. A clerk of the court would lead a convict to the town square and declare: "Your country has found you guilty of an infamous action. The law strips you of your French citizenship."[29] The convict would remain bound and on display for between two and six hours with a placard over his head indicating his name and crime.[30] Felons were also subject to another punishment, legal interdiction, which suspended all "civil rights" (unspecified in the code) during their prison sentence.[31]

Moderates in the Constituent Assembly imposed limits on the enjoyment of citizenship that made nonsense of civic degradation. The 1791 constitution created three categories of citizens. The first, including domestics, men without property, women, and children, were passive citizens and could not vote. The second, composed of propertied men, were active citizens and could vote. The third, a small group of wealthier active citizens that included fewer than half of all adult males, could stand for election.[32] Addressing the Jacobin Club in October 1791, Camille Desmoulins used the term civic degradation to evoke the disenfranchisement of poor men in metropolitan France and of free colored men in the colonies. The refrain of this speech was "I CALLED THEM PASSIVE CITIZENS AND THEY THOUGHT THEY WERE DEAD."[33]

When presenting the new code, Le Peletier described the ostracism of ex-convicts by Old Regime society. Released men from the galleys were "horrifying to all men, excluded from all human commerce, from all professions and from all industries."[34] Le Peletier credited their status as pariahs to the brands imprinted on their bodies. In fact, however, these ex-convicts were outcasts for other reasons. During the eighteenth century, when the navy began freeing galley prisoners with limited sentences, men who left those facilities lived as fugitives on French soil. In a sense, they became criminals by the fact of their release.[35] Each released man received a certificate called a *congé*. For an ex-convict to lack this certificate was punishable with two years in the galleys.[36] Unfortunately, even an ex-convict with a *congé* did not have the two documents that distinguished authentic travelers from criminal vagabonds. The first was a passport from his native village stating his purpose and destination. The second was an *aveu,* an attestation of good character from a parish priest, from a municipal government, or from the *marechaussée* [constabulary]. "There is no one who does not at least have a domicile of origin, except vagabonds and *gens sans aveu.*"[37] Wanderers without travel documents had no legally recognized place of birth. They were strangers distinct from people born elsewhere. In contrast to foreigners, they were people without a provenance. A 1722 ordinance excluded released galley prisoners [*forçats libérés*] from Paris, from Marseilles (then the site of the galleys), from towns with royal residences, and from the jurisdiction of the courts that originally sentenced them.[38] In Lyon, a local ordinance of 1777 subjected *forçats libérés* to such rigorous requirements for entering the town that it effectively banned them; other towns would follow Lyon's example.[39]

While the legislature discussed the new Criminal Code, the Committee on Beggary laid plans to deport all *gens sans aveu* to Africa. The chair of that committee, Charles-Antoine-Joseph Leclerc de Montlinot, described them as an un-Christian horde of wolf equivalents with their own language: argot.[40] To distinguish the envisaged sweeping purge of vagabonds from criminal banishment, Montlinot used the term *transportation* and not *déportation*. The latter term implied civil death, whereas the vagabonds had no rights and no property to remove.

When the Constituent Assembly discussed the deportation of recidivist ex-convicts it became obvious that the projected colonial scheme would not resemble the occasional, purgative removal of urban riffraff, galley prisoners, prostitutes, and *mauvais garcons de bonne famille* to Canada, to the islands, and to Cayenne under the monarchy.[41] Under the new scheme, deported criminals were not to mix with, and hence to contaminate, the colonial citizenry. Pierre-Victor Malouet, a career navy bureaucrat, wanted a promise from his fellow deputies that convicts would not besmirch the empire. "Since the assembly has the intention of including deportation among the punishments, I insist on the exclusion of all places except deserted islands."[42] Agreeing to this request, Lepeletier followed Montlinot in recommending that beggars and recidivists be sent to a new colony in Africa.[43]

Lepeletier imagined that recidivists slated for deportation, after serving their sentences in France, would die civilly upon liberation. "It seems that deportation must result in civil death, because the guilty man who is removed from his homeland must remain apart from it for the rest of his days." In compensation, the deportees might earn privileges in the new colony that would allow them "a sort of existence."[44]

The mandate of the Committee on Beggary expired in September 1791 without any legislation resulting from its deliberations.[45] The site for ex-convict recidivists was speculative in the 1791 Criminal Code and would remain so for the future. Under title II (On Recidivism), article 1, after serving a second sentence in a French prison or a work camp, the recidivist "[will be] transferred, for the rest of his life, to the *place fixed for the deportation of malefactors.*" In 1798, the commissar to the criminal court in Doubs wrote the minister of justice to ask where the recidivists were being sent; the minister forwarded the note to his counterpart at the navy. "Since the matter concerns your administration, I ask that you reply [to him] and inform me of the results."[46]

In 1807, the navy began emptying recidivists scheduled for deportation from the citadel of La Rochelle and nearby Ré and Oléron Islands into *depôts de mendicité* [depots for the indigent]. There they joined the poor, the mad, and the venereal prostitutes. The police soon arranged for their transfer to an abandoned charterhouse on the Rhône. The island of deportees mentioned in the Criminal Code had existed inside the country for more than a decade and it would remain there.[47]

In October and November 1791, the Legislative Assembly addressed the punishment of émigrés—fugitive counterrevolutionaries—by examining legal structures of violence, ancient and modern, including martial law in France, the suspension of habeas corpus in England, and Roman dictatorship. Deputies understood all three of these mechanisms as weapons for extraordinary times that existed to save the state.[48] Eventually, however, legislators in 1791 came to view the stripping of rights from émigrés as a normal way of punishing breaches of the social compact that did not involve recourse to emergency law. The problem of émigré soldiers and officials led deputies to theorize civil death as a modern political punishment. The legislator Mathieu Dumas quoted from article 4 of the 1789 Declaration of the Rights of Man and Citizen: "the exercise of natural rights has no limits except those which guarantee the enjoyment of those rights to other members of society. Those limits can only be fixed by law."[49] Dumas argued that a man could be stripped of all natural rights without violating this article. To support this claim, he invoked Montesquieu: "sometimes it is necessary to throw a veil over the statue of the law."[50] The deputy Pierre-Victorin Vergniaud argued that there was no contradiction between honoring the rights of citizens and removing those rights from enemies of state. On entering political society, "man alienates not only a portion of his liberty but also, in a sense, his right to life."[51]

The émigré seemed to be divided from the citizen by a territorial frontier that stood for a new kind of community, even a new kind of nature. Yet the frontier rapidly developed an entirely different character. It became possible to exit the country as an émigré without moving. Legislation against émigrés, from 1791 forward, worked on the basis of several fictions. First, émigrés who lived outside the country were presumed to live inside French sovereign limits. Second, the counterrevolutionary suspect who lived inside the country was treated as though he had left the country illegally. Finally, the émigré who lived inside France and might never have left it did not have a domicile—a legal address—in the state. Decrees against émigrés made it possible to exist simultaneously as absent from one's domicile and as a vagabond suspect (an *homme sans aveu*) without ever leaving home. To go missing from one's domicile as a fugitive was to exit the citizenry and to lose one's natural rights. The stranger of no provenance, who lacked a legal address in France, was the unnatural remainder of the man he once was.

All deputies who participated in debates in November 1791 referred to the soldiers, officials, and civilians who were then pouring over the actual frontiers as absent. This was a legal designation of the Old Regime, which described the status of criminal fugitives as well as that of soldiers, pilgrims, and people who disappeared.

> The absent person is not merely a non-present person, whose existence is not in doubt. . . . A deeper analysis of the situation reveals that the "absent" or according to the customary expression . . . the "dépaysé," or "forpaysé," is a person engaged in a distant adventure whose return, whose existence even, seems uncertain.[52]

Because such people were at unknown coordinates and might or might not exist, they could not be presumed to live in another state. Speaking for the Committee on Legislation, Jean-Baptiste-Louis Ducastel refused to acknowledge that the émigrés had exited France. He suggested that the term most commonly used to describe them—émigré—was a misnomer.

> Emigration occurs when a citizen really abandons his country and adopts another. . . . Man can change his *patrie* whenever he wishes. . . .

> But the French people who leave the realm while retaining their domiciles here and without renouncing their citizenship are either by an express declaration, or by effective naturalization, absent and fugitive Frenchmen and not émigrés. Since they remain French, they do not cease to be under the laws of France.[53]

The legal mechanism of absence made it possible to treat people who lived in foreign countries as though they were nowhere in particular. In the fall of 1791 it seemed essential to distinguish the traitor who left the realm from the harmless emigrant. Abstractly, deputies still believed in the natural right of all humans to leave their place of origin and to live under a government of their choosing. To believe otherwise would have been to reject a founding myth of the Revolution. The capacity of each individual to choose his own sovereign, through the right to emigrate, made it possible to view political society as founded on a social contract.

Ducastel suggested that fugitive traitors had declared their desire to remain French citizens before fleeing the country. He referred to the oaths sworn by soldiers and by public officials. But Ducastel's allusion to the "effective naturalization" of other émigrés demonstrates that ordinary civilians of French birth had the same status as men who defaulted on their civic oaths. They all remained under French law, which meant that the legislature could remove their citizenship and condemn them to death.

The frontier functioned in this discussion as an ideological line of demarcation that defined the citizen against the political enemy. But it is clear that deputies did not regard the actual territorial frontiers as the limits of French sovereignty. They hoped to adopt measures for punishing people who lived outside the country and whose crime was to leave it. Most recommended military tribunals that would condemn and execute soldiers who left the realm. Jean-Antoine-Nicolas Condorcet wanted to require a civic oath of French expatriates on foreign soil for the purpose of removing their citizenship and confiscating their property should they refuse. The deputy Cécile-Stanislas Girardin alone noted the oddness of Condorcet's desire to apply French law to foreign soil. "By what means can one compel French people residing in foreign territory to an oath? Does your power have other limits than your territory?"[54]

In this discussion, as in Richer's treatise, an enemy of the people might lose his citizenship, his *patrie,* and his legal character as a human (an absent person is neither alive nor dead), but he could not exit what contemporaries understood as the nation. This is the meaning of Ducastel's assertion that naturalization, or the fact of being born in France, meant that a national who defied the sovereign could never cease to be French or cease to live under French law.

In mid-December 1791, the Legislative Assembly decreed that government officials could not receive salaries or annuities without furnishing "a certificate attesting that the person . . . actually lives on French territory and has lived there without interruption for the last six months." These certificates would be issued by municipalities and needed to be renewed every month. This measure was explicitly directed against émigrés who were returning to acquire certificates of residence and thus avoid a punitive triple tax on their property, which the Constituent Assembly imposed in June 1791.[55]

The new law made it possible for a municipality to refuse residential certificates to suspect individuals. Someone who lived in his usual home could now be reclassified as a person without a legal domicile. This mechanism made possible the sequestration of émigré property that winter. A decree of 9 February 1792 put the "property of the émigrés under the control of the nation under the surveillance of administrators."[56] The return to the full version of civil death, as practiced during the Old Regime, had begun.

Revolutionaries understood the émigré as both a fugitive outside the country and as an internal enemy. A decree of 9 April 1792 instructed municipalities to make inventories of the "property belonging to persons who are not currently domiciled in the department" (art. 6). The same decree threatened municipal officers who furnished false certificates of residence "without procuring the attestation of two active and domiciled citizens" (art. 10). It also punished citizens who gave false testimony in their own favor (art. 11). Later articles addressed émigrés inside the country. Those who returned after the February sequestration law would lose their active citizenship for two years. Those who returned more than a month after the promulgation of the 9 April decree would lose their citizenship for ten years (art. 24).

On 27 July 1792, the legislature suspended foreign travel. All such travel after that date became illegal, because passports ceased to be issued. The next day, the Committee on Legislation submitted a new bill to punish illegal travelers, whom the ban on travel of the day before would call into existence. The bill assimilated people who traveled without passports or under false names and were "ascertained to have left the realm" to émigrés. A person suspected of leaving the country without a passport or in disguise who then returned to his usual address or to some other place inside France would have the same status as a person who left the country definitively without travel documents.[57] This device eliminated the difference between a vagabond who is known to be alive at a particular site and an absent person, who might or might not exist at a site that remains a mystery.

The Convention banished all émigrés from the realm in October 1792 at pain of death for returning.[58] A decree of 26 November 1792 dealt with the émigrés who remained "in the frontier towns or the interior of France" or who were "returned émigrés." The latter were supposed to leave Paris and any other town of more than twenty thousand inhabitants within twenty-four hours and to leave the republic within fifteen days or be "deemed to have broken the law of banishment and punished with death." A person who had never left the country could now be killed as an émigré who had returned to France illegally.[59]

On 28 March 1793 the Convention banished émigrés and declared them civilly dead. That apparently redundant measure concerned both émigrés outside the country and people in France who lacked residency certificates, which had become impossible to obtain. In December 1792, the Convention nullified past residency certificates and imposed new conditions for acquiring them. For a so-called *prévenu d'émigration*—émigré suspect—to prove a legal domicile in France had originally required two witnesses. After December 1792 it required the testimony of eight citizens who could not be "relatives, allies, tenants, domestics, debtors, creditors, or agents of the certified."[60] It required a pledge by complete strangers; and strangers, while incorruptible, could not verify a person's whereabouts.

Under the heading *De ce qu'on entend par émigrés* (what we mean by émigrés), the March decree listed (1) a person of either sex who had left France since 1789 and returned as requested by the decree of April 1792; (2) a person of either sex who was absent from his or her legal domicile and unable to justify continual residence in the country in keeping with the decree of 9 April 1792; (3) a person of either sex, "in spite of being present," who had absented himself, or herself, and could not justify continual residence since 9 May 1792; (4) people who left the country without papers; (5) government officials who did not return three months after recall; (6) people who crossed the frontiers during an invasion to live on enemy land and who might or might not have returned to France since; (7) naturalized foreigners with two legal domiciles who could not justify their continual residence in France since 9 May 1792.[61]

Though banished from the country and threatened with death if they appeared on French soil, the domestic émigrés could not obtain passports for leaving France. The decree of 28 March 1793 was a writ of execution. "The émigrés who will return, the émigrés who have returned, those who remain on the territory of the Republic against the disposition of the laws will be conducted before the criminal tribunal of the department of their last domicile in France." Two witnesses of recognized civism would identify the émigré, upon which judges would decide either for death or for deportation, "if the suspect is a women between fourteen and twenty-one years of age."[62]

The definition of an émigré developed out of a conflation of the frontiers of the realm with a legal boundary defining adhesion to the new contractual society. To cross the frontier was to break the social contract. But the reverse was also true, as the case of internal émigrés demonstrates. To break the social contract or to be suspected of having done so meant transfer across the frontier of the law, whether or not one exited the country.

The early debates in 1791 and 1792 about the status of émigrés overlapped with discussions about priests who held posts in the new national church but refused loyalty oaths to the regime. Originally, refusal of those oaths was supposed to result in the removal of a priest from his official post. Nonetheless, deputies of the Legislative Assembly would retroactively interpret those oaths as manifestations of the social contract. In November 1791, they began describing nonjuring priests as political deviants worthy of banishment. Pierre-Anastase Torné, a bishop who pledged loyalty to the New Regime, asked the assembly to treat the nonjurors as naturalized foreigners in an effort to protect them. "In the eyes of the constitution, they are not, it is true, active citizens; but by law they are *régnicoles* [natives of the king's realm]; by assimilating them to foreigners, the homeland would deny them the honor of serving it without banishing them."[63]

The king vetoed a November decree banishing nonjurors from their parishes and imprisoning them in the administrative seat of their department. The more radical measures that deputies proposed that fall, while missing from the final decree, resurfaced when debates on the clergy reopened in the spring of 1792. After the outbreak of war, heightened alarm over internal enemies prompted new passport legislation in April 1792. Travelers without passports were to be arrested and interned. On 5 May 1792, the deputy Français compared nonjurors to vagabonds and émigrés. "By the law of passports, you subject people without domiciles to detention when no one will pledge on their behalf. . . . Here it is a question of men who do not enjoy the rights of citizens . . . because they do not wish to; of men who not only lack a legal domicile in the place they live, but who do not even have one in the state, because they do not want to obey the laws."[64]

The priests were aliens of a special type. The deputy Louis-Jérôme Gohier called them "neither foreigners nor citizens."[65] As the equivalent of traitors who had fled the realm, priests were at war with the state, and measures against them were a matter for the executive branch. "It is not a question of making either general laws or particular laws against refractory priests. It is a question of a political measure to save the state."[66] Lecointre-Puyraveaux demanded that the priests be declared *hors la loi* [outside the law], which meant they might be killed with impunity.[67]

An unimplemented decree of 27 May 1792 banished not only priests who lost their cures by refusing oaths but also monks and lay priests who were not required to take those oaths in the first place.[68] As the terms of the social contract became more elusive, the contractual rhetoric of deputies developed a new stridency. On May 24th, Pierre-François-Joachim

Henry-Larivière read aloud the passage from Jean-Jacques Rousseau's *Social Contract* (1762) concerning the oath of all citizens to a civil religion. According to Rousseau's text, whoever refused that oath would be banished as an unsociable being. The deputy Jacques-Joseph Filassier said, "I convert the proposition of Jean-Jacques Rousseau into a motion and I demand that it be put to a vote."[69] The king vetoed this decree as he had the earlier one.

With the elimination of the monarchy, deputies broke with their earlier restraint and embraced overseas deportation as a punishment for recalcitrant nonjurors. A decree of 26 August required that priests who refused or recanted on the oath of November 1790 or of April 1791—the latter being required of priests who taught school—would need to leave the country within fifteen days or face deportation to Guiana. The monks and lay priests who were not subject to either of those oaths would be deported like the others if denounced.

It was ideology and not expediency that led deputies to replace detention, which they approved in November 1791, with banishment in May 1792 and then to opt for overseas deportation that August. Had they been guided by expediency, they would never have abandoned detention in the first place. After declaring war on the Habsburg Crown in April 1792, they embraced a solution that only extremists had sought the previous autumn. The change from banishment to deportation between May and August had other causes. The popular insurgency of 10 August nullified the constitution by deposing the king. In the aftermath, deputies were no longer bound, as they had been, by legal scruples.

When rare deputies doubted the practicability of deporting fifty thousand clergymen, they were met with patriotic indignation. In late July 1793, Georges-Jacques Danton asked that the Convention reroute the priests to the beaches of Italy as a prudent compromise with felicitous symbolism. Jean-Baptiste Drouet, Jean-Jacques Bréard-Duplessis, and Jean-François Delacroix insisted on shelving deportation altogether, at least until peacetime.[70] Maximilien Robespierre responded by attacking the motives of the speakers. "It is said that there are transport difficulties. I am not at all aware of this problem. It must be proved in order to outweigh urgent considerations. I demand the execution of the decree."[71]

The effective equivalence between the nonjuror and the émigré justified increasingly radical measures against the clergy. Lecointre-Puyraveau
got his wish for a decree putting the priests *hors la loi* when the Convention adopted new measures against counterrevolutionary elites in the
spring of 1793 after civil war erupted in the Vendée. On 18 March, the
Convention decreed that all citizens were obliged to denounce, arrest, or
cause to be arrested émigrés and priests with the nominal status of deportees who were discovered on domestic soil. Once captured, they were
to be judged by military tribunals and put to death within twenty-four
hours.[72] That fall, on 17 September 1793, the Convention formally assimilated deported priests to émigrés, which meant that civil death applied to
them. Priests who had been rounded up on domestic soil and lived in
state custody became identical to traitors banned from the republic who
would be killed if discovered there.

The legislature and Committee of Public Safety tinkered with the destination for refractory priests in measures of late 1793 and early 1794. A
decree of 22–23 October 1793, deported them to Africa, between the
twenty-third and the twenty-eighth parallels (Namibia). On 13 February
1794, the Committee of Public Safety changed their destination to Madagascar, which the Convention had already selected for vagabonds by a
decree of 1 November 1793.

People began to speak as though the priests were actually living in a
distant and mythical country. On 2 April 1794, Pierre-Laurent Monestier,
representative on mission to Lot-et-Garonne and Landes, wrote to the
Convention of his success in cleansing France of refractory priests. "The
bad citizens here are all reduced or incarcerated. Others who are even
worse, the priests, leave the soil of liberty. There is not a day that there are
not embarkations to their apostolic mission in Madagascar. . . . Vive la
République! Only inflexibility on her part! Ça ira et ça va! S[alut] et
F[raternité]."[73]

The most notorious atrocities of the Revolution were perpetrated
against stationary deportees in the winter and spring of 1794. Two Nan-
tais Jacobins invented a sinkable ship to dispose of priests who had been
rounded up in the Vendée and transferred to a "vessel on the Loire . . .
waiting to be transported to the colonies." All but three of the ninety

priests underwent "vertical deportation"—were drowned—in the first use of the vessel. There were probably six more uses of the drowning ship that winter and spring.[74] The events at Nantes permanently colored French understandings of deportation in the 1790s. At the time of his arrest, Ange Pitou recalled: "I was persuaded, as were many, that deportation was drowning under another name."[75]

The deportation of priests and the banishment of émigrés inspired a one-act comedy, *Les émigrés aux terres australes ou le dernier chapitre d'une grande révolution,* which debuted in late November 1792. Gamas, the author, published the script in year II (1794). Its topical interest had increased in the interval. In the play, remnants of the Old Regime are stranded in the future on a fictional island populated by Jacobin Indians. On arrival, one of the deportees, Prince Fier-à-Bras, spots an obelisk whose inscription (in the published text) reads: "In year III of the Republic, free and triumphal France in concert with all of Europe deported the rebels it toppled here."[76] This cheerful fantasy of a clear, spatial separation between the free citizenry and their enemies, like the benign fate of the men on the island, obscures the truth about this type of country. Whatever its name—*terra australis*, French Guiana, Namibia, or Madagascar—it lay inside domestic France. Of the thousands of priests slated for deportation, only six were deported to French Guiana under the Convention and fewer than three hundred reached the colony during the revolutionary decade.

After the coup d'état of 18 fructidor year V (4 September 1797), local Jacobins, the legislature, and the directors hoped to capture counterrevolutionary priests who had sworn false oaths of loyalty—so said local republicans—or who conducted clandestine religious ceremonies while pretending not to be priests anymore. The law of 19 fructidor allowed the directors to issue individual warrants for the deportation of seditious priests and religious. They made enthusiastic use of that privilege, and all signed vague and often identically worded warrants for the arrest of 2,135 French and 875 Belgian ecclesiastics on advice from the police, who sifted through denunciations that poured in from local administrators.[77] Only two-fifths of the priests who were named in the warrants ever made it to Rochefort. The *administrations centrales* of the departments sent a completely different group of nine hundred priests to the port. In all, nearly fourteen hundred priests collected at Rochefort or on nearby Ré Island. Less than 20 percent of them were deported to French Guiana.[78]

The roundup of royalist conspirators in the legislature after the coup of 18 fructidor worked by quite different principles than from the expansive crackdown on the underground church. The directors Louis-Marie La Révellière-Lépeaux, Jean-Francois Reubell, and Paul-François-Nicolas Barras had ample time to prepare for a general sweep of royalist deputies in the capital and an army with which to accomplish it. Instead, the troops arrested even core conspirators with reluctance. In a sense, the seventeen men who ended up in French Guiana, out of the fifty-four named in the law of 19 fructidor, were volunteers. On discovering an all-night gathering of plotters inside the Tuileries Palace, Hoche's troops told them to disperse. But a small group, including General Jean-Charles Pichegru and the Jacobin apostate François-Louis Bourdon de l'Oise refused to budge. Pichegru still hoped to provoke a violent confrontation with the army. He baited the troops, demanding that they shoot him or leave. They did not shoot and did not wish to arrest the regicide Bourdon. He insisted, "My colleagues, you have heard the proposition that has been made to me. I beg that you not underestimate me. I am not paying the slightest attention to it."[79]

The directors who launched the coup were uneasy about deporting their colleague, the director François Barthélemy. He refused two requests to resign, warnings to flee, and chances to do so from the Luxembourg Palace, the official residence of the directors. "It was evident that they were asking for my resignation to dishonor me and make me commit an act of cowardice. Whatever happened, I absolutely refused to explain myself or be party to this resignation until they removed the bayonets from around me."[80] Barthélemy instructed his valet Le Tellier to pack his trunks for the journey into exile. The servant, a companion for twenty years, refused to abandon him. Lazare Carnot, the second purged director, the rest of the deputies, and the purged journalists fled or went into hiding in France, as they were meant to.[81]

Three days after the coup, the remaining three directors invited the legislature to treat deported deputies as émigrés. The Council of Five Hundred buried the matter in committee.[82] The question resurfaced in fall 1798. Against the recommendation of the committee and the inclinations of the assembly, the deputy Jean-Henri Rouchon urged that the government make no effort to hunt down deputies who remained in the country and he asked for the recall of men in French Guiana. He wanted only the deputies who had fled to England to be declared émigrés. His colleagues met this suggestion with scorn and rose in unison to cheer the republic and the 1795 constitution.[83] On 9 November 1798, the legislature resolved that deported deputies, including those who had remained in the country, should identify themselves to local administrators for removal to a site other than Guiana or become the equivalent of émigrés. One month later, the Executive Directory authorized them to resettle on Oléron Island, off the coast of La Rochelle. The substitute for overseas deportation was an offshore municipality. To get onto the island, they needed to make a declaration of submission to the law and live under the surveillance of the local government.

CHAPTER 2

Strange Dominion

D EPORTATION DURING THE 1790s combined the removal of rights with notional long-distance travel. This form of exile did not require going anywhere. It meant crossing a threshold of law that represented the edges of the rights-bearing French community. Whether they fled abroad, remained in France, or wound up in Guiana, enemies of state lived under the sovereignty of the French government in an unusual sanctum of its authority. Revolutionaries projected this dominion for traitors onto the edges of the world, as they pictured it. Madagascar, Namibia, *terra australis*, and French Guiana were the same place. They were abstract destinations off the map of the citizenry.

The practice of banishing counterrevolutionaries to the overseas empire, in word if not in deed, raises the question of how the political elite understood the relationship between the colonies and domestic soil during these years. If crossing out of France into some colony or other signified irreversible removal from the civic order, how did revolutionary legislators define the legal status of imperial soil and the people who lived there? The story of revolutionary exile, notwithstanding the relatively small number of people who actually left for Guiana, suggests that legislators understood the colonies as zones of legal oddity.

Historians of the French empire during the Revolution suggest, to the contrary, that the French civic order grew ever more inclusive during the 1790s. According to this interpretation, slaves in revolutionary Saint Domingue (modern Haiti) helped to redefine the boundaries of the French nation. The 1791 Saint Domingue slave revolt helped to "smas[h] juridical and political separation between metropole and colony," and made the republic consistent with its myth. Laurent Dubois observes, "France and its colonies had become one, legally consistent, a nation-state."[1] The conquest of freedom by insurgent slaves helped bring about what Bernard Gainot calls "complete fusion" between imperial and domestic territory.[2]

The idea of revolutionary France as an inclusive transatlantic polity dates back more than a century to the Third Republic. In 1907, the political economist Arthur Girault described revolutionary colonial rule as *assimilation violente, à outrance*.[3] By *assimilation*, Girault meant the legal fiction by which colonial territory assumed the status of domestic territory and colonial people assumed the status of citizens of France. For Girault as for historians of our own day, the case for France's "extreme, violent assimilation" of the overseas empire during the revolutionary period rests on two documents: (1) the 1794 decree of the National Convention emancipating slaves in the empire and (2) the 1795 constitution, which declared the colonies to be "integral parts of the Republic" and "under the same constitutional law."[4]

The history of deportation in the 1790s has another significance in the imperial context that speaks directly to the assimilation question. Speeches and petitions calling for the deportation of deviants of various sorts in the revolutionary years all suggested that metropolitan undesirables needed to be settled somewhere remote from free soil and ordinary colonial society. The un-French wilderness under metropolitan sovereignty, whether in the form of French Guiana, the once and future colony of Madagascar, or the wishful imperial hinterland of Namibia, would make possible this double quarantine. The 1795 constitution transformed not only French Guiana but also Madagascar into French departments. The purged deputies, priests, and petty undesirables who embarked in 1797 and 1798 for "a location that the Executive Directory will determine" left the republic for the republic.

No colony in the empire had closer formal ties to domestic France than Guiana, which was one of only two colonies, with Guadeloupe, where slaves obtained freedom through the 1794 abolition decree. As for the other colonies, people in Saint Domingue exited slavery by virtue of a 1793 local act, issued by the republican commissar under conditions of military encirclement.[5] The Committee of Public Safety made no attempt to free the slaves in Mauritius or Réunion thanks to maneuvering by deputies from those colonies, who then enjoyed impeccable Jacobin credentials.[6] The decree never went into effect in Tobago or Martinique, because these colonies fell to the English.[7] People in Saint Lucia experienced an interlude of emancipation in 1795, ending with the recapture of the island by the British in 1796.[8]

Guiana was one of two colonies, with Saint Domingue, where the 1795 constitution actually went into effect, in the sense that the agent of the Directory in Guiana promulgated the document. Victor Hugues, the republic's envoy to Guadeloupe, declined to apply the constitution to keep the forced labor of freed people from becoming illegal.[9]

The August 1791 rising of ten thousand slaves in northern Saint Domingue unleashed a series of events that later obliged the Convention, on 4 February 1794, to decree the abolition of slavery. It is true that slaves helped to refashion the legal structure of colonial rule after 1794. The new empire of black liberty was also an exclusionary place, however. Legislators relied on rhetorical and legal devices to withhold rights, to suspend laws, and to legitimate extraordinary forms of power on overseas territory.

Throughout the revolutionary decade, the French overseas empire consisted of a domain of suspended norms. Yet the abolition of slavery gave a new direction to legal maneuvering by the political elite. At the beginning of the Revolution, legislators sought to avoid tampering with slavery and devised legal instruments aimed at screening imperial territory from the new rights culture. At the same time, men on the left embraced the cause of free men of color overseas, to whom they hoped to grant private and public equality. Robespierrre, while advocating for the enfranchisement of free people of color, urged that slavery remain behind "the sacred, terrible veil that the decency of legislators led them to throw upon it."[10]

In the wake of abolition, revolutionary law withheld from emancipated slaves the very rights that deputies had earlier sought for free people of color.[11] Here Robespierre's remarks again reflect the ideological contradictions that shaped colonial policy during the 1790s. In September 1791, he underscored the inability of slaves to understand liberty when defending the political rights of freeborn people of African descent. "You will never persuade anyone that either the decrees of this assembly, or the relationship between those decrees and the rights of citizens, could give such clear ideas to men rudened [abrutis] by slavery, who have very few ideas— whose only ideas are alien to the matter at hand—so as to cause them to break all of a sudden with their old habits and chains."[12] In November 1793, Robespierre described the revolutionary project of liberty and that of slave liberation as contrary enterprises. He attacked the fallen faction of the Girondists for having desired "to liberate and arm all the negroes to destroy our colonies."[13]

Before abolition, legislators sought to veil colonial slavery from the new French law; after 1794 they devised a new form of unfreedom for people their law had liberated. Revolutionaries impeded French law from reaching the colonies in order to flatten the distinction between freedom and slavery and to withhold citizenship from emancipated people. This feature of colonial rule after 1794 makes it necessary to connect Jacobin overseas policy to the enormities of Napoleon. The refusal of deputies in the 1790s to construct a legal framework for colonial freedom helped to enable the revival of slavery in 1802.

The planter and jurist Médéric-Louis-Élie Moreau de Saint Méry remarked in 1791: "Well! If you want the declaration of rights, as far as we are concerned, there will no longer be any colonies."[14] Even slave owners in the Constituent Assembly recognized that people of African descent were men and eligible, at least abstractly, for the same rights being extended to white metropolitans.[15] The need to preserve slavery in spite of the humanness of the African and the illegality of slavery according to the new rights charter lay at the heart of the colonial question in the first years of the Revolution.

The first question to confront the National Assembly after the union of the clergy, nobility, and third estate, was whether to admit colonial deputies. That nine deputies for Saint Domingue took the Tennis Court Oath on 20 June 1789, pledging with other deputies "not to separate . . . until a new constitution is established" did not assure the success of their campaign for admission to the assembly; nor did the recognized importance of West Indian plantations to the French economy provide sufficient grounds for including them. The admission of colonial deputies could not be justified by mere political convenience or economic calculation. On 4 July 1789 Le Peletier de Saint Fargeau spoke as a jurist in setting forth the principle: "In the question before us, so that it may be set on secure footing, it is necessary to begin with a principle: that we regard Saint Domingue as a province of France."[16]

The idea that France and the colonies were fused in a single regenerative enterprise inspired Louis-Alexandre, duc de La Rochefoucauld d'Enville, to call for an end to colonial slavery on the night of 4 August 1789, during the abolition of privileges, feudal and otherwise.[17] There may have been many more demands to abolish slavery that night. The Saint Domingue deputy Louis-Marthe de Gouy d'Arsy later recalled, in an ironic mea culpa, "I accuse myself of obstinately refusing repeated demands made from all parts by philanthropic colleagues to consent in the name of my constituents to the liberation of the blacks, and to immortalize myself at their expense, in placing, in my turn, this small sacrifice on the altar of debris."[18]

The fusion of the colonies with the revolutionary domestic state acquired new significance when the assembly adopted the Declaration of the Rights of Man and Citizen. The Declaration was not part of the constitution, which does not diminish its importance. The document called an end to the Old Regime in a geographically unlimited manner. It traced a new order of things for a territory whose limits had yet to be determined. It beckoned toward a new public law that might apply on all of French territory indistinctly and which was incompatible with colonial slavery.[19] Colonial deputies, for their part, were struck with "a type of terror, when we saw the Declaration of the rights of man posed as the basis of the new constitution, absolute equality, identity of rights, and liberty of all individuals."[20] On 20 August 1789, when the National Assembly finalized the text of the Declaration (formally adopted on 26 August), the

French Colonial Corresponding Society, later known familiarly as the Club Massiac, convened for its first meeting. Its members aimed to disavow the colonial deputies; to keep colonial matters out of the legislature; and to assure that the colonies might exist as a separate legal order beyond reach of the National Assembly's decrees.[21]

The need to redivide the colonies from domestic soil shaped the efforts of the Colonial Committee in March 1790 to formulate a new model of colonial rule. Antoine-Pierre-Joseph-Marie Barnave explained: "Your committee thinks that the different laws, decreed for French provinces, are not applicable to the regime of our colonies."[22] The decree approved on 8 March 1790, which aimed to initiate a colonial constitution-writing process through local assemblies, called the colonies "a part of the French empire." Behind this deceptively anodyne phrase lay an intricate mode of colonial rule. While colonial assemblies had the power of legislative initiative, those texts—including legislation related to slaves—could not become law before being discussed and approved by the National Assembly, transformed into decrees, and submitted for approval by the king.[23] This was not a system of indirect rule: it was a means of ruling over a fused metropolitan-colonial entity through a bicameral legislature whose upper and lower chambers were divided by an ocean.

Revolutionary legislators understood the contradiction between slavery and the New Regime. They knew what self-consistency required of them: it was being enacted before their eyes. "People are posted along the streets to stop negroes and men of color, conduct them to notaries, make them protest against their servitude and reclaim the rights of man."[24] But deputies did not strive to create a morally consistent universe. The decree of 8 March 1790 not only fashioned an ersatz form of local rule for the colonies; it also appeased merchants and slave owners in a rhetoric of avoidance. Deputies sought "a turn of phrase which does not put the assembly into obvious contradiction with its principles." It was impossible to "call things by their real name," or to discuss the question openly; the decree was approved with near unanimity (five people voted against it) and without debate.[25]

The fusion of metropolitan and colonial soil survived these early efforts to screen slavery from the law. According to a buried article of the

1791 constitution, "the colonies and the French possessions in Asia, Africa, and America, although they are part of the French empire, are not included in the French constitution."[26] This article declared the empire to lie outside the constitution; yet the constitution would need to apply in the colonies for this article to take effect there. The bracketing of the colonies from the new metropolitan legal order by the 1791 constitution required that the colonies lie within that order in the first place; it also meant that the colonies would remain within that order for the future, in the form of an empty place.

The completion of the constitution did not call an end to tinkering with the colonial empire. In late September 1791 as the assembly prepared to disperse, the structure of colonial rule became the object of fresh debate. Earlier, on 15 May 1791, deputies had approved a decree granting political rights to men of color in the colonies who were born of free parents; the narrow scope of the decree arose from compromises during its drafting.[27] Through this decree, deputies extended the Declaration of the Rights of Man and Citizen overseas, albeit selectively; they also asserted their power of legislative initiative in colonial internal matters in defiance of earlier promises. The histrionic response of whites in Saint Domingue to the May decree led deputies beholden to planters and merchants to seek its repeal at the close of the legislative session, in late September 1791. In reply to Barnave's appeal, a decree of 24 September set forth new so-called constitutional articles—though never inserted into the constitution—by which the metropolitan legislature forbade itself to meddle "in the status of persons unfree and the political status of free persons of color and free negroes."[28]

The slave revolt in Saint Domingue that began on 22 August 1791, of which legislators learned that October, called forth a radical remaking of the colonial legal order. This event made it possible for philanthropically minded men to demand equal rights for free persons of color in a new register. Colonial racial equality ceased to be a mere question of conscience and became a practical adjustment to the circumstances. Enfranchising free men of color would help contain a slave insurgency that Jacques-Pierre Brissot and his allies took for a counterrevolutionary maneuver by royalist whites in league with the king: it was a pretext for drawing royal troops to the colony, whose presence would enable colonists to break off with the metropole.[29]

The enfranchisement of free men of color overseas required a law in breach of the constitutional articles of 24 September, which forbade the National Assembly to meddle in the status of persons. In consequence, deputies allied with Brissot were forced to square their political program with the constitution they had sworn to uphold. To enfranchise free men of color, they needed to prove that the decree of 24 September was not a constitutional document—that it was even an unconstitutional document. In result, the debate over a law of circumstance aimed at restoring peace in Saint Domingue became an occasion for ardent musings about the relationship between the metropole and the colonies in a general sense. The decree of 28 March 1792 that resulted from those discussions, sanctioned by the king on 4 April, applied to all the Atlantic colonies.

Deputies centered their argument against the constitutional articles of 24 September on the indivisibility of national sovereignty. According to the Declaration of the Rights of Man and Citizen, "the source of all sovereignty resides essentially in the nation. No body, no individual, can exercise authority that does not emanate from it explicitly." Brissot and his followers used the Declaration to attack white assemblies that were empowered, by the decree of 24 September, to decide matters relating to slaves and people of color without the consent of the National Assembly; these assemblies became schismatic usurpers of metropolitan legislative power. Jean-Philippe Garran-Coulon remarked: "It is the unity of the state that is divided; national sovereignty is destroyed at its foundations."[30]

The officials whom Brissot and his allies wished to empower to dissolve the white assemblies, to repress the uprising, to round up and deport suspects, to enfranchise free men of color, and to convoke new mixed race assemblies would command powers of an unprecedented magnitude. The officials were called civil commissars *(commissaires civils)* in the decree of 28 March 1792 establishing a new mode of colonial rule for the Atlantic colonies. The earlier envoys had enjoyed narrower powers. The task of these earlier envoys, whom the Constituent Assembly sent to Martinique, Saint Domingue, and French Guiana, was to restore the prerevolutionary status quo, to annul legal innovations of refractory white assemblies, and to assist the existing royal administration.[31] In contrast, the commissars of the Legislative Assembly were superior to colonial governors, whom they might—and did, in Saint Domingue— remove from office.

The new commissars might "resort to public force at all times they judge necessary, either for their proper security or for the execution of the orders they will be given." At hearing this article read aloud, the deputy Salvador-Paul Leremboure, son of the mayor of Port-au-Prince, asked when that power would cease and proposed the amendment "until the legal organization of the constituted powers." Yet for Brissot and his allies, civil commissars needed to act without formal legal constraints while enjoying indefinite terms of appointment. "The assembly decrees that there is no place to deliberate on the amendment."[32]

The deputy Antoine-Christophe Merlin (of Thionville) cautioned deputies against assuming the "terrible responsibility" of appointing commissars; in his view, the assembly would need to suspend the constitution on domestic soil to bestow repressive powers of the desired scope on these officials. He recommended that the assembly keep its hands clean by forcing the executive branch to assume emergency powers on its behalf. To Merlin, formal limits to the power of royal officials could not be a hindrance overseas, because the constitution did not apply there. "We must not follow the rules of the French constitution in America, because [the constitution] does not yet exist for the colonies." Where the constitution did not apply, meddling in elections by royal appointees could not be illegal.[33]

During the summer of 1792, French Guiana became unexpectedly central to a new round of discussions over enlarging commissarial power in the empire. For reasons that at first seemed specific to the hinterland, a decree of 14 June sent a civil commissar there with a mandate that did not involve rebuilding local institutions or overseeing the drafting of a local constitution. "The former royal courts, the admiralty, the superior council, and the ordonnateur will resume their functions until the organization of tribunals and administration in the colony of Guiana have been statuted, but they will not be able to make any regulation."[34] Pierre-Léon Levavasseur, speaking for the Colonial Committee, wanted old royal officials restored to their posts to oversee the colony's judiciary and the budget until the National Assembly, one day, reorganized the administration and courts of Cayenne. The commissar in Guiana would not need to bother building institutions of political life in the colony. Saint Domingue was in flames. Civil war raged in Martinique. Yet the commissar of French Guiana, after dissolving the colonial assembly and annulling local laws, was to hunt down savages in the wilderness, lure them to the coast by friendly inducements, group them in new villages, and rule them by laws unknown to the French. Levavasseur's model for revolutionary Guiana was the Jesuit *reducionne*—the New World missionary settlement that became a symbol of the clergy's temporal power during the eighteenth century. He also desired the commissar to choose an isolated site and make recommendations, concerning security, for a future deportation colony. "What would prevent a quarter of this vast continent from being a site of deportation?" Guiana figured in the minds of legislators as a vast uncivic dominion, where the institutions of revolutionary public life would never take shape.

The June decree was in a sense superfluous, because the decree of March had named a commissar to Guiana as an afterthought. The new arrangements, however, reflected the changed assumptions of this assembly. Guiana, a wilderness that no one had ever visited, allowed extra-constitutional rule by metropolitan envoys to appear uncontroversial, a mere adjustment to the strangeness of the surroundings. The next day, on 15 June 1792, deputies amended the decree of March. What had been a deviation for the hinterland became the new model for imperial rule everywhere.[35] The decree of 15 June granted commissars the power to dissolve refractory municipalities and to nullify local laws without reaffirming the earlier commitment to new elections and the drafting of colonial constitutions. Disobedience to the commissar became an act of high treason, punishable according to the rigor of the laws—metropolitan laws—on being shipped back to the France for trial (art. 5). While granting imperial commissars indefinite emergency powers, the decree of 15 June dressed them up as embodiments of legal normality. The officials whose powers exceeded those of the legislature and the king would wear "a tri-colored ribbon across the chest, from which a gold medal marked *la nation, la*

loi, le roi on one side, *commissaire civil* on the other, will be suspended"
(art. 6).

The 1793 constitution outlawed the ownership of bodies in its preamble.
"Every man may contract for his service and his time but he may neither
sell himself nor be sold; his person is not alienable property."[36] In contrast, there was no reference to colonies in the new constitution. In February 1794, an unidentified deputy attempted to silence the reading of the
emancipation proclamation by remarking, "It is decreed," to which another unidentified member replied, "Yes, on the continent but not for the
colonies."[37]

Had deputies wished to break with the imperial policy of earlier assemblies, the time to abolish colonial slavery would have been in June
1793 during the drafting of the new constitution, which would have allowed them to include explicit language to that effect in the document.
That month, a group of men and women of color, including the venerable
Jeanne Odo (age 114), marched around Paris with a musical band and a
petition demanding the abolition of slavery. Two accounts describe the
visit of the abolitionists to the Jacobin Club on 3 June. Neither suggests
much support for their cause among members. According to an incom-
plete reconstruction of club minutes by the historian François-Victor-
Alphonse Aulard, the "colonial battalion" marched in, at which the
ex-Capuchin François Chabot declared, "The Jacobins must swear to
free men of color, and I swear in my own name!" Members responded
with applause and a change of subject. The Aulard account does not indicate a general oath by the club to free the slaves, contrary to what
Florence Gauthier has suggested.[38] The second account of this event,
from the *Journal de la Montagne* (the club newspaper), does not mention an oath by Chabot or anyone else. According to the *Journal,* three
men including the club president, François-René-Auguste Mallarmé,
greeted the abolitionists warmly. After debate (unrecorded), the club refused to admit them as honorary members and bestowed that favor on
Odo only.[39]

The deputation paraded into the Convention the next day, where the
president of the session received their leader with a fraternal kiss. That

would have been an excellent time to announce the abolition of slavery. Instead the abbé Henri Grégoire, alone among the deputies, spoke in support of the militants to demand "that this petition . . . not remain buried in committee, like so many others . . . that you respond with an expeditious report in which you pronounce the liberty of the blacks."[40] The petition was not only buried in committee but expunged from memory. Newspapers suppressed the petitioners' demand and Grégoire's remarks to varying degrees; at the extreme end of the spectrum, the *Journal de la Montagne* mentioned neither. The journalist Claude-Louis-Michel Milscent informed the deputation that "journalists were paid to silence your demand."[41]

It was a time of insurrection in the capital. On 2 June 1793 perhaps twenty thousand sans-culottes from the Paris sections and the National Guard blockaded the assembly in the Tuileries Palace; with 150 cannons pointed at the Convention, the crowd demanded a tax on the rich, a restriction of the right of suffrage to the poor, the formation of a revolutionary army of sans-culottes to round up suspects, and the arrest of the Gironde faction, which they accomplished.[42]

The abolitionists threw in their lot with Parisian insurgents and briefly became symbols of the sans-culotte movement. Where the abolitionists had encountered an unfriendly reception at the Jacobin Club and in the Convention, they were embraced by the insurrectionary municipality. This outbreak of radical chic among leading figures of the Parisian uprising may have served a tactical purpose. The purged Girondists were known for supporting racial equality and the abolition of the slave trade, though the trade remained off limits as a topic of legislative discussion. The slogan on the standard of the colored deputation, "Men of color you shall be free," had been an informal motto of Brissot and his followers, whom the insurrectionists conspired to destroy.

After a rally on the Champs de Mars, on 8 June, the insurrectionary commune promised to accompany their colored brethren on a sortie to the Convention to demand the abolition of slavery for a second time.[43] That second appearance of the petitioners, bolstered by the authority of municipal envoys, would have occurred on Saturday, 15 June 1793. It never happened. Instead, the commune fell back on the politics of spectacle. On 12 June, the prosecutor-general, Pierre-Gaspard Chaumette, appeared with what he called a slave child before municipal councillors to conduct what he called a baptism of liberty and announced his intention to educate the boy if the town agreed to adopt him. "This child is a slave; there should not be slaves on free soil; this child has no father, the council should serve him as a father; I promise to teach him a trade."[44] Rather than press for the abolition of slavery, Chaumette now contented himself with emancipating one young person (who could not have been living in Paris of 1793 as a slave in the first place).[45]

Florence Gauthier recalls the circulation of the colored deputation and their battle standard through Paris in early June as evidence of unambiguous enthusiasm for abolition among the Jacobins. She has also interpreted the silence of the 1793 constitution as proof of deeper conviction; to mention colonies would be colonialist while to omit them communicates plans to decolonize and "establish new relations between peoples, former colonists and colonized, by a federative link constituted by the declared rights of man and citizen."[46] But the missing emancipation decree of that month and the absence of constitutional language about colonies suggest that we should interpret these events otherwise. Chaumette and the insurrectionists should not be confounded with Robespierre and the National Assembly. Chabot, the ex-religious who vowed to free the blacks on 3 June, belonged to the *enragés,* the radical faction that organized the insurrections of 31 May and 2 June.[47] Chabot survived the purge of the *enragés* in September 1793 after a second, ill-planned uprising.[48] Chaumette was arrested on 18 March 1794 and executed on 24 March as an English spy in yet another sweep of sans-culotte leaders.[49]

The abolition of slavery by the Convention on 4 February 1794 did not arise from a longstanding Jacobin commitment to abolition but instead announced a break with the policy of earlier months. The advent of new crisis measures in the fall of 1793 made possible that reversal. The circumstances that gave rise to abolition, the decree that proclaimed it, and the meaning of colonial citizenship in its aftermath were shaped by legal structures associated with the Terror. On 10 October 1793, Louis-Antoine Saint Just proposed that the Convention not disperse as envisaged after completing the new constitution. Instead, deputies should suspend the application of the constitution and vest the Committee of Public Safety with dictatorial powers on a national scale to address the food crisis and the war needs. "The provisional government of France is revolutionary until the peace."[50] The resulting system, called Revolutionary Government, supplied a legal framework for the Terror. It also had the inadvertent effect of giving new prominence to slave emancipation as a national political question. When three deputies from Saint Domingue belatedly took their seats in the Convention on 4 February 1794, they conveyed news of abolition in the colony and asked the assembly to approve the local measure.[51] The 1793 constitution made no provision for admitting colonial deputies to the French legislature. Only the Convention, which extended its term as an emergency measure, included them.[52]

Revolutionary Government helped to supply colonial deputies with a national stage that would not necessarily have been available to them under conditions of legal normality. Revolutionary Government also furnishes a context for interpreting peculiarities in the emancipation decree. "The National Convention declares negro slavery to be abolished in all the colonies. In consequence, it decrees that all men without distinction of color who are domiciled in the colonies are French citizens and will enjoy all the rights guaranteed by the constitution. This decree is referred to the Committee of Public Safety, which will report immediately on measures for its execution."[53] The decree did not acknowledge the suspension of the constitution. It defined the freedom of former slaves through the rights they would enjoy under a law whose suspension defined French political life at the time. The suspension of the constitution gave members of the Convention the power to govern after their mandate expired; it was the raison d'être of that assembly.

The reference to the constitution in the emancipation decree did not appear in an earlier draft and may have been added for reactionary ends. The insertion of this phrase followed an attempt by Georges-Jacques Danton to stall emancipation by moving the question off the floor of the Convention and into the Committee of Public Safety; the last sentence of the decree resulted from that maneuver. Several newspaper accounts of Danton's remarks suggest that he attempted to revive gradual emancipation as a political option during the debate on abolition. According to the *Journal de la Montagne,* he observed: "Too abrupt a passage from slavery to emancipation has its dangers and needs to be directed by a clever hand. Let the committees of Public Safety and the Colonies make a prompt report so that the truth can be launched into the colonies with the means of allowing them to enjoy it without inconvenience."[54] Danton's speech inspired a new round of "debates on the drafting of the decree" that were suppressed by every newspaper.[55] The decree of emancipation was modified after Danton's speech and the ensuing unrecorded conversation.[56] In this context, it is possible that the inserted phrase "will enjoy all the rights guaranteed by the constitution" sought to obscure rather than amplify the rights of former slaves.

On 5 February, opponents of abolition contested the official record of the proceedings, disputed the existence of an emancipation decree, and proposed deceptively worded, alternate versions as though the question were undecided. In consequence, one day after emancipation, the cowed assembly voted to entrust the very drafting of the decree to the Committee.[57]

Opposition to abolition in the Committee of Public Safety did not produce an alternative version of the emancipation proclamation.[58] But it influenced the committee's handling of the existing decree. The official charged with emancipating the slaves in those colonies—who succeeded in retaking Guadeloupe from the English because of the decree—was Victor Hugues, a former merchant from Port au Prince. In France, he became public accuser before the Revolutionary Tribunal at Brest and an agent of the pro-slavery lobbyists Pierre-François Page and Théodore-Claude Brulley.[59] On learning of Hugues's appointment as commissar, two free men of color from Saint Domingue waited for two hours without success for an audience with the Committee of Public Safety. They hoped to expose Hugues's racism and his activities as "agent of colonists." They added: "Such a man . . . can only do harm and a large number of citizens can attest to what we advance here."[60] The choice of Hugues to implement emancipation in Guadeloupe indicates great laxity in the "dismantling of the pro-slavery lobby" in March 1794.[61] His appointment also indicates resistance, at the highest level, to the incorporation of freed slaves into the republic as citizens.

The 1795 constitution took over the formula that the emancipation decree projected into the future by turning the empire into an extension of metropolitan soil under the same constitutional law. Yet it is unlikely that the framers of the constitution imagined the colonies would ever be ruled in that manner. They drafted the document so as to make constitutional rule overseas impossible.

There was no mention of the colonies in the complete draft of the constitution that François-Antoine Boissy d'Anglas presented to the legislature in June 1795.[62] The belated addition of articles on the colonies followed a report by Jacques Defermon speaking for the Committee of Public Safety. In July 1795 Defermon praised black republican troops for recapturing key points of Saint Domingue from the British. He underscored the need to include the colonies in the 1795 constitution to assuage the anxieties of emancipated people fighting for France, who feared the government would restore slavery.[63] The framers had no choice but to revise the document. They did not, however, assent to constitutional rule overseas in a normal sense. Instead they presented an anomalous legal regime as constitutional articles.

Commissarial rule, which deputies of the Legislative Assembly contrived as an extra-legal measure, became a legal norm in the 1795 constitution, which prescribed the appointment of colonial envoys by the executive branch at the initiative of the legislature; these officials, called agents of the Directory, would command "the same functions as the Directory" (the executive) in time of internal war. They might remain at their posts for an unlimited period and had the power to name all public functionaries until the peace.[64] These arrangements resembled procedures for administering places undergoing military pacification, as in the Vendée region of western France and in the Rhone Valley, beset by royalist murder gangs and brigands.[65] Boissy d'Anglas understood the absorption of the colonies by the domestic state as a way of magnifying sovereign power in the empire so as to quash men whom he deemed unfit to govern or to vote. Of the slave revolt in Saint Domingue, he observed: "Those savages, tormented by the burden of liberty, did not delay in giving themselves chiefs."[66]

The 1795 constitution turned each overseas colony into one or more French departments, or seemed to. Yet the department is not defined by the mere existence of an outer boundary line. This administrative unit, which replaced the province in 1791, is distinguished from any other patch of delimited earth by an interior jurisdictional map that fixes the location of courts, electoral assemblies, and administrative bodies. According to the 1795 constitution, however, the colonial departments were blank. The third article of the first title of the constitution began: "France is divided into" and then listed the departments of metropolitan France. The fifth article described the division of those departments: "Each department is distributed into cantons, each canton into communes. The cantons preserve their present circumscriptions." This prior division of metropolitan departments supplied the foundation for all institutions described in the constitution (as in "primary assemblies are composed of citizens domiciled in the same canton").[67] Only after describing the organization of domestic soil did the constitution address the colonies: "The French colonies are integral parts of the Republic, and are subject to the same constitutional law." A contextualized reading of this celebrated article reveals that the 1795 constitution defined the colonies as institutionless, vacant units of the metropolitan state.[68]

The undivided character of imperial departments became a matter of acute political significance after an attempt by the minister of the navy, Admiral Laurent-Jean-François Truguet, to carry republican law to the empire. At his insistence the Executive Directory sent commissars to Saint Domingue and to French Guiana, who promulgated the new constitution and called elections. The French legislature responded by annulling the election results. Two-thirds of those deputies had been members of the Convention, which approved the 1795 constitution and also approved the abolition decree.[69]

On 23 November and 14 December 1796 the lower and upper houses of France's legislature voided the elections for French Guiana on the grounds that French constitutional law neither could nor should apply to any colony, including that one. The deputy Jean-François-Auguste Izoard accused the Directory's agent in Guiana, Nicolas-Georges Jeannet-Oudin, of picking a list of candidates for Guiana's seats in the Council of Five Hundred (the lower house) so that former deputies to the Convention from the Aube, Jeannet's home department, could return to politics as colonial representatives. Izoard used this controversy as a pretext for advancing a general reinterpretation of constitutional articles relevant to colonies.

In common with all other colonies, Guiana did not have the internal spatio-legal character of a French department. Since there were no territorial divisions, there could not be election districts. Without municipalities there could not be any municipal officers to preside over electoral assemblies. Without these things, there could not be an electorate. "How can there be a primary assembly composed of domiciled citizens in the same canton where there are no circumscribed cantons?" The 1795 constitution could not apply in the colonies in the absence of a legal division of space. "Nearly all of the essential dispositions [of the constitution] suppose this division and refer to it." Yet Izoard urged the assembly not to repair this situation and abolish what he called the *régime particulier* of the colonies. The French civic order should not take shape on land thronged with unsuitable candidates for public life. "In the colonies, the brigand can still take the place of the proprietor, the public thief that of the taxpayer; the vagabond and stranger that of the domiciled man."[70]

In describing the challenge of distinguishing between criminals, vagabonds, and domiciled citizens in colonial settings, Izoard might appear to have been concerned by the presence of those noncitizen deviants whom successive revolutionary governments drove beyond the speculative frontiers of France into Guiana. But Izoard based his portrait of undomiciled strangers, thieves, and brigands on rebel slaves in Saint Domingue. "It is from the most important of the colonies that monsters have burned one thousand fires, spilled torrents of blood, and chased out most of the domiciled citizens, proprietors, and merchants, who were obliged to flee their rage."[71]

The central colonial question during the royalist onslaught of spring and summer 1797 was not whether to roll back constitutional rule but whether to apply the constitution in the first place. Deputies allied with colonial planters sought to place the colony of Saint Domingue under an indefinite state of siege to enable a new militarized regime of plantation labor. As the question of constitutional rule became the object of faction fighting, the directors abandoned their earlier silence and urged the legislature to divide the colonial departments to enable constitutional rule overseas. Boissy d'Anglas, who framed constitutional articles relevant to the colonies, retorted that the overseas departments were empty on purpose and ought not to be tampered with. "The intention of the constitution is that these matters be adjourned until the peace."[72]

While the attack on constitutional rule for the colonies coincided with the period of royalist ascendancy, the rhetoric of that attack extended from the logic of militant Jacobinism. Admiral Louis-Thomas Villaret-Joyeuse observed: "Have you forgotten that the war in the Vendée worsened while we multiplied the proconsuls . . . it is to the wisdom and firmness of a clever general invested with enormous powers and surrounded by an important force that you owe the extinction of that great political volcano."[73] The comparison between blacks in Saint Domingue and peasant rebels in the Vendée region of western France first surfaced among proslavery Jacobins of the Convention, led by André Amar of the Committee of General Security.[74] In mid-1797, the comparison between the Vendée and Saint Domingue served as a justification for placing the island under a state of siege. On 21 June, Bourdon de l'Oise, a former deputy to the Convention, who did a brief stint as a representative on mission to the Vendée until his recall for incompetence, demanded that General Gabriel Hédouville, the pacifier of the Vendée, replace the agents of the Directory in Saint Domingue.[75]

After the purge of royalists and fellow travelers, the republican rump approved two laws erecting a framework for the application of the constitution to the Atlantic colonies. The law of 26 October 1797 created a map of administrative and judicial circumscriptions in French Guiana, Guadeloupe, and Saint Domingue. The law of 1 January 1798 defined the terms of colonial membership in the nation and, for a narrower group, in the citizenry, which was a status enjoyed by propertied men and soldiers in the 1795 constitution. By the latter law, the colonial citizenry included soldiers as well as men who were at least twenty-five years old and paid taxes equal to three days of agricultural labor.[76]

The drafting and discussion of what became the law of 1 January reflected the enduring ambivalence of metropolitan deputies toward extending French nationality and political rights to former slaves. According to this text, "black or colored individuals removed from their fatherland

and transported to the colonies are not reputed to be foreigners; they enjoy the same rights as an individual born on French territory if they are involved in agriculture, if they serve in the armies, if they exercise a profession or trade."[77] Rather than encourage a view of colonial people of color as French nationals, this article depicted them as aliens who were to benefit from a benevolent legal fiction. The text contained equally ambiguous language about the status of slaves who fled to French colonies in search of freedom or arrived there aboard confiscated slave ships after 1794. (In the next chapter, I shall address the legal problem of newly arrived Africans as it inflected the history of French Guiana during the revolutionary decade.)

Even deputies who felt obliged to advocate for colonial constitutional rule expressed disquiet at the enfranchisement of freed slaves. Louis-Antoine-Esprit Rallier observed: "People who have seen blacks recently arrived from the coast of Africa (and the number is still quite large in our colonies) know that they are generally little apt to exercise the function of French citizens."[78] The man charged with implementing the January law in Saint Domingue was Hédouville, whom reactionaries had tapped that summer to govern as a military dictator. There was no man in France more identified with the suspension of the constitution and with military rule than Hédouville, the pacifier of the Vendée rebellion.[79]

Bonaparte's regime for the empire opened directly from the evolving principles of revolutionary imperial rule. Under the 1799 constitution, "the regime of the French colonies is determined by special laws."[80] As for the relationship of those special laws to the new constitutional order, the next article in the document is suggestive. "In case of armed revolt, or troubles menacing the security of the state, the law can suspend the application of the constitution."[81] In placing the colonies under special laws, article 91 enacted the procedure described in the next article.

The colonies were no less "integral parts of the republic . . . and subject to the same constitutional law" in 1799 than in 1795. To declare the colonies outside the constitution within the text of the document meant they were under that law in the first place; it meant that the constitution, while applying overseas, would be suspended there. This mechanism—

the suspension of the constitution—became associated during the Consulate with uses of political siege on domestic soil.[82] The French empire at the beginning of the nineteenth century should be understood as an appendage of metropolitan soil subject to permanent siege rule.

At the time of Bonaparte's coup d'état, French public law was a dead letter in the empire. The apparently novel style of colonial rule traced in the 1799 constitution repudiated the abstract commitment of the republic to the extension of constitutional government overseas. Yet the actual legal structure of the empire departed absolutely from those normative principles as a consequence of the 1795 constitution and not as a deviation from it. Revolutionaries furnished Bonaparte with a template for colonial rule that he raised to the status of a new norm.

By the law of 30 floréal year X (20 May 1802), the Consulate revived slavery where it had not been abolished and replaced exceptional laws with executive regulations.[83] Months later, the Constitution of 16 thermidor year X (4 August 1802) empowered the Senate to make law for the colonies in the form of an "organic sénatus-consulte." A sénatus-consulte was an act voted by the Senate. Yet it could not be written by the Senate. "Organic Sénatus-Consultes and Sénatus-Consultes are deliberated on by the Senate on the initiative of the government."[84]

Bonaparte's Council of State made room for slavery's revival during the drafting the Civil Code. According to the code's introductory chapter, "on the application and effects of law in general," laws became executable *on all French territory* on being promulgated by the first consul—the chief of the executive branch. Did French territory include the colonies? In September 1801, Jean-Etienne-Marie Portalis, the principal author of the code, addressed the absence of any reference to the overseas empire in the Civil Code. Portalis had his own views on the nature of *lex*, which he understood as the voice of a simulated divinity; the word of that being, who was neither Bonaparte nor Portalis but rather the sovereign they comprised, needed to go into effect instantly on promulgation.[85] To reconcile this idea of sovereignty with the need to notify people of new laws, Portalis proposed a scheme for legal travel that invites comparison with boulevard shows involving mechanical dolls, levers, and magic lanterns. The law would "be said to be known" within the jurisdiction of Paris in twenty-four hours. From there, the *vive voix du législateur* (the voice of the legislator) would spread to the provinces by courier at a rate of one hour for every myriameter (ten kilometers). This fantastical proposition drew the interest of Antoine-François Fourcroy, who noted the hardship of moving around with such speed and precision. Portalis explained: "It is less a question, in effect, of finding a means of making the law known than of fixing a period when it will be regarded as known."[86]

This device for making laws known did not apply to the colonies or to islands just off the French mainland, which were then full of displaced people, especially deportees. Portalis represented the colonies and these European islands as equally hard to reach, because of the weather. "The delay in the publication of laws in the colonies and on the islands of Europe is to be determined by a regulation. Circumstances and natural causes render travel to those countries too uncertain for a delay to be fixed invariably by the law." When Michel Regnauld de Saint Jean d'Angély insisted that he "express the exception" that pertained to colonies and nearby islands, Portalis returned to the problem of weather. He observed that "the contrariness of winds and seasons" made it impossible to know at what point metropolitan law would reach the colonies, when it would be published there, and when it would apply. But Portalis, when addressing legal travel in the republic, had no interest in the practical conditions by which laws became known. François-Denis Tronchet closed the discussion. "He leaves the colonies aside, for which a separate regulation is indispensable."[87]

CHAPTER 3

Free Soil

O N 13 APRIL 1793, the mayor of Cayenne faced the sea, the town's mud wall behind him, and waited to greet the new commissar, Nicolas-Georges Jeannet-Oudin, at the gates of the city. Later that day, Jeannet joined the regiment, the militia, and local worthies to pay "homage to the fatherland on its altar." The patriot mass ended with the song that people still called "The Hymn of the Men from Marseille." At the words "Sacred Love of the Fatherland, Liberty, Sweet Liberty," everyone fell to his knees.[1]

When reporting his arrival, Jeannet confessed to a flicker of unease as he knelt, singing of liberty, before enslaved onlookers. "For an instant I feared the effect of this trait of the *tableau* on the *cadre* [frame] of slaves who surrounded it." The slaves were not quite outside what Jeannet likened to a painted or theatrical scene. Watching them watch him heightened the unreality of the spectacle. "I too, knelt as though I were on the happy soil of France." When Jeannet joined townsmen in worshipping the ground beneath him, he was pretending.

In contrast to the commissar, local men did not imagine the soil they adored to be elsewhere. The tricolored flag over the fort, the scarves of municipal officers, and the patriot hymn paid tribute to a fatherland that was both near and far. The colonists were slave owners who expected to rule by practices unknown in metropolitan France. Yet they insisted on the unity of the republic. They pictured themselves as living inside France and under its law.

More than any other official, Jeannet shaped the meaning of revolution in Guiana. During his four years in the colony, from April 1793 to November 1794 and from April 1796 to November 1798, he freed the slaves, devised a new regime of liberty, and arranged for the settlement of deported politicians and priests. While contriving these two apparently contrary modes of life, he looked to the methods and principles of white Jacobins, whose worldview merged with his own.[2]

White radical belief in the unity of Guiana and France arose in a solitary outpost that stood apart from other slave colonies because of its poverty, its smallness, the insignificance of plantation agriculture, the infrequency of ships traveling to and from France, and the lack of an elite with any history. In 1788, there were 10,430 slaves, 253 white children, 483 free colored people, 763 white male settlers, 330 white women, and 350 soldiers.[3] The colony had virtually no commercial bond to the metropole. The Crown did not bother imposing mercantile restrictions on a colony that had nothing to sell and no money to buy with.[4] Statutes that regulated slave treatment applied there only selectively before the Revolution. Instead of requiring masters to grant slaves a weekly day of rest, administrators deemed one Saturday every two weeks sufficient, "given the state of misery of the colony."[5] French slave law ceased to apply there altogether in 1790, when Guiana's colonial assembly repealed the Code Noir.[6] The deliberate nonapplication of laws emanating from France defined colonial life in Guiana before and after 1789; this colonial world of law doubled as a world of lawlessness.

The experiences of marginal people in Guiana during the revolutionary era depended to a remarkable extent on the legal character of the ground they stood on. Local understandings of Guiana as a legal space shaped the lives of slaves, emancipated slaves, and political exiles. When analyzed in light of changing legal notions of imperial land, the experiences of all three groups offer distinct yet overlapping perspectives on a single problem. Slaves, freed people, and deported counterrevolutionaries encountered novel forms of violence in Guiana that unfolded from the unity of the French republic as a white colonial idea.

Where the previous two chapters focused on languages of legal exception, here I explore legal sameness as a doctrine that shaped imperial space and marginal identity from the beginning of the Revolution to the revival of slavery under Napoleon. The importance of legal sameness opens from the meaning that former slaves attached to this principle. Freed people in Guiana as elsewhere viewed the unity of the republic as a doctrine that enabled their metamorphosis into rights-bearing French people.[7] The idea that metropolitan and colonial soil comprised one land under one law had other applications in this period, however. This doctrine was also an instrument of coercion, even of lethal force. As a principle with diverse uses and surprising effects, the oneness of Guiana and France was both the making and the unmaking of colonial legal subjects.

The legal fusion of the empire and the metropole, as a white colonial idea, depended on slavery's persistence and became associated with a revolutionary language of racial exclusion. The French 1791 constitution indicated, in a late article, that it did not apply to overseas colonies. By the law of 8 March 1790, colonial assemblies were supposed to draft their own constitutions. Guiana's assembly fulfilled this instruction by declaring the colony a department of France—an appendage of the metropolitan state. The fusion principle first surfaced in October 1790, when the assembly applied French municipal law to the colony at the invitation of the metropolitan government. Guiana became "a single department with a single municipality." Guiana's 1792 constitution declared in its first article that "the colony belongs to the French empire." The text also called Guiana a "department, which will be divided into as many cantons as there are parishes."[8] Through that document Guiana assumed a double identity as both imperial and domestic land. In consequence, there could be one law for free men and one for slaves. Free men lived on national soil in a French department. They were bound by the French constitution and lived under the authority of the national legislature. Slaves lived in another country under a different sovereign.

The French constitution and the laws decreed by the Constituent Assembly and by the Legislative Assembly and those that will be decreed by the National Convention are and will be recognized and accepted for men who are free in the colony. The colonial assembly puts the property of citizens under the protection of the law of 13 May 1791 sanctioned the first of June by which, "The National Assembly decrees as a constitutional article that no law on the status of unfree persons will be made by legislature except on the formal and spontaneous demand of the colonial assemblies."[9]

The law of 13 May 1791 to which the local constitution alluded promised colonists that metropolitan legislators would not tamper with slavery. A text of 29 May 1791 explaining that law referred to slaves as a "foreign nation who by their ignorance, their unhappiness at expatriation, in their own best interest and by the imperious law of necessity cannot hope for a change in their condition except with time and the progress of the public spirit of enlightenment."[10] The foreignness of the slave was a convenient fiction that enabled lawyerly men to locate slaves outside the sovereignty of the National Assembly just as people living in Spain or England fell under the power of another prince.

Although white Jacobins in Guiana wrapped themselves in the laws of the metropole, the French legislature viewed their creed as a dangerous constitutional heresy. The commissar sent to the colony by the Constituent Assembly, Frédéric Guillot, spoke against white Jacobin insistence on the unity of the French republic. "The laws made for the interior of France are not those which must rule the colonies."[11] To apply the laws of the revolutionary state overseas would incite slave insurrection. "What have you done? Or rather what have you not done to bring upon yourselves the afflictions that menace the most beautiful, the richest, and the most important of our colonies."[12] In 1792, Guiana seemed poised to become another Saint Domingue.

In 1789, most of the nine hundred free residents of Cayenne, the seat of the government in Guiana, lived *extra muros* in the so-called new town. For white Jacobins, the most conspicuous symbol of the enmity dividing the government and the people was the dirt rampart that split the new town from the old city, the gate that sealed the wall at night, and the insect clouds rising from moat-like pits around the wall. The quarrel over the ramparts, which patriots wanted destroyed, offers a revealing glimpse of the local controversy over the relationship between slave insurrection and the new language of liberty.

In Guiana, the outbreak of the French Revolution heightened an existing administrative fear of mass murder by slave rebels. The warning to readers of Abbé Raynal's *Histoire des deux Indes* (1770–1781) that slaves would "break the sacrilegious yoke of their oppression" with "vengeance and slaughter" did not rate as sensationalist prophecy in French administrative circles.[13] Guiana lay adjacent to Dutch colonies that were the principal theaters of slave insurrection in the Americas.[14] Guiana's governor in 1787, Pierre-François de Mareuil, comte de Villebois, defied instructions from Paris to demolish the walls of Cayenne because "when the revolt happened at Berbice . . . those who could not lock themselves up were assassinated and their women were taken by the negroes."[15]

After 1789, royal officials in Guiana warned of a slave rising stimulated by local Jacobins and by news arriving from France. Far from being a time to raze walls, the Revolution signaled a need for higher and thicker bastilles. In April 1790, Governor Jacques-Martin de Bourgon proposed to encase Cayenne's old city in massive fortifications. "Twelve or fifteen years would seem sufficient to carry it to perfection."[16] In February 1791, after a slave revolt on the Approuague River, the acting governor, Henri Benoist, defied the colonial assembly by refusing to destroy the walls. "The spirit of independence that is manifest among the blacks should awaken us from a false sense of security; we have seen that such a revolution is in no sense impossible."[17]

On 14 January 1793, the curate Moranville, who was president of the colonial assembly, wrote the ministry to renew his demand for the razing of the rampart. He again complained of the locked gate and the vile trenches.[18] Knocking down the wall had ceased to be a matter of urban improvement, of course. For officials of the old city, the wall stood for the lethal danger that attended new political ideas; the rampart was a shield against black and white Jacobins. For the colonial assembly, to insist on the demolition of the wall was to scoff at royalist warnings of revolt.

As with Robespierre, so with men in Cayenne: the imperviousness of the slave to the message of liberty emerged as a founding tenet of a strain of radical thought that found adherents on both sides of the Atlantic. According to the white patriot creed, the slave could make war on liberty, but he could not rise up in its name. The slave rebel became a political deviant—a royalist fanatic. In December 1790, slaves revolted on the Approuague River because they interpreted an oath-taking ceremony by soldiers and the colonial assembly as a pact to keep them unfree.[19] Troops who suppressed the rising appeared on 7 January 1791 at the bar of the colonial assembly to receive thanks for "your courage, your patriotism," in quashing "perfidious slaves."[20] The soldiers might as well have been hunting aristocrats. Two years later, a former member of that assembly likened slaves to royalist peasants in an official publication of the Convention.[21] In 1796, Jeannet noted the importance of banning dances by emancipated people after ten at night for fear that drums would convoke the Counterrevolution. "What the sound of [church] bells are in countries of superstition, the sound of the negro drum can be in the colonies."[22]

The slave stood outside the laws of nature unless he happened to be waging war against them. That notion survived emancipation and became part of what the unity of the republic came to mean. The motto of Guiana's government in 1798, *travail ou la mort* (work or death), a variant of the French wartime motto (liberty or death), conveyed the only idea of black freedom that ever dawned on the colonial master class.[23] At the end of the revolutionary era, on 24 October 1801, Jeannet distilled this idea of freedmen in a memoir to Bonaparte describing black people as machines. "That the liberty of the blacks is desired by nature I shall not bother to prove or to deny; but it is permitted to consider men in general as instruments of work, as causes of production, and the negroes can be classed as such."[24] The notion of France as a transatlantic polity bound by a common law developed alongside an idea of the slave—and later of the freedman—as an existential incongruity on free soil.

The deportation of priests and politicians in 1797 and 1798 opened the question of whether metropolitan legal categories would move with the men and command significance overseas. In practice, the status of deportees and hence their treatment opened from local notions of place and belonging. The identity of the exiles depended on how people with power in the colony defined the citizen, the noncitizen, and the legal relationship between metropolitan and colonial land.

Years before, white Jacobin belief in the sameness of Guiana and France turned nonjuring priests into enemy suspects in the land of liberty. By a decree of 15 June 1791, missionaries in Guiana were obliged to swear to "maintain with all my power the constitution decreed by the National Assembly and accepted by the king." In contrast, priests in Saint Domingue pledged "fidelity to the nation, the law, and the king."[25] There was no reference to the constitution in the Saint Domingue oath, because the document did not apply there, just as it was not supposed to apply in Guiana. Three men took the oath and three refused. In September 1791, Guiana's assembly voted to strip the three nonjurors of their pensions and to send them back to France.[26] The missionaries remained in Guiana until 1793. That February, news reached the colony of the August 1792 decree deporting nonjurors to Guiana. The assembly responded by banishing the colony's own nonjurors, who soon left for New York.[27]

In March 1793, with the arrival of the abbé Amalric, the first deportee from France, Guiana's assembly decreed that future deported priests would be sent to a region they called Macary in the bay of Maraca in current Brazil.[28] France retained a claim to land there, between the Oyapock and the Amazon, because of a disagreement with the Portuguese over the meaning of words in the Treaty of Utrecht (1713), which fixed the border between the two colonies. At the time of the Revolution, the French presence in the contested zone amounted to a few Indian missions, which closed by order of the colonial assembly in 1792.[29]

Guiana's deputy to the Convention, André Pomme called L'Américain, was the first to propose sending nonjurors to the abandoned missions. He submitted this advice to the minister of the navy on 31 August 1792 and later developed his ideas in a 1793 published report for the ministry of finance (with cost studies).[30] Pomme suggested placing the priests "under the command of a practical man of the country, acclimatized, of recognized civism."[31] L'Américain was a habitué of the Amazonian borderland. In 1786, at age thirty, he left the priesthood and became a herdsman in the contested zone, which Guiana's government had hoped to fill with cattle and poor settlers "whose means did not permit them to cultivate the land."[32]

The priests were no less a threat to the colonial citizenry than to the metropole; they needed to be kept apart from the noncitizen fanatics whom Pomme called blacks, not slaves, in his report. Anything short of total isolation, Pomme declared, would cause the loss of Guiana for France. By exploiting the piety of the blacks, the priests would become "supreme guides of their arms"; the rebel army would hoist the counter-revolutionary standard, massacre the patriots—fourteen or fifteen hundred people "of all ages and sexes"—and transfer Guiana to an enemy power. The explicit model for this uprising was the Vendée civil war in western France.[33]

The deportees would live under the surveillance of troops from the garrison in Cayenne assisted by twenty gendarmes of color. The guards, along with "a very repressive law," would prevent deportees "from spreading into inhabited portions," opening the question of what he meant by inhabited.[34] Pomme wanted to people the new settlement with "twenty-five women, taken little by little from the prisons" for every one hundred priests, and an assortment of convict tradesmen, namely "three bakers, two masons, two blacksmiths, two carpenters, two joiners, two sawyers, and two coopers."[35]

This design for a punitive dominion sealed off from the land of the citizenry was a disconcerting synthesis of revolutionary Guiana. Guiana's 1792 constitution organized land outside Cayenne as a series of cantons, each charged with patrolling and punishing slaves. To supplement the local militia, forty gendarmes would stand at the ready in each canton for "requisition by every public functionary."[36] The gendarmes would swear an oath to be "faithful to the nation and the law, to maintain liberty and equality, and zealously to obey the orders that are given them."[37] They would wear the blue and white uniforms, with gold buttons, of the new National Guard.[38] Yet the principal task of gendarmes was Maroon hunting. "The detachment will receive 12 livres for every Maroon negro stopped in the canton or nearby and 25 livres in the great wood."[39]

The chief difference between Pomme's proposed Amazonian settlement and Guiana's new cantons lay in the direction of constraint. Where gendarmes, guardsmen, and troops were supposed to stop slaves from fleeing the cantons in and around Cayenne, troops and gendarmes would restrain priests from escaping to the colonial capital. Pomme even referred to the Amazonian post as the canton of Macary in his report ("the canton of Macary abounds extraordinarily in resources for animal existence").[40] In this colonial plan, inspired by French municipal law, the priests took the place of slaves and sank to the level of their associates in the tropical Vendée.

In late November 1797 sixteen political deportees, including twelve deputies, one policeman, two Bourbon agents, and an ex-director traveling with his valet arrived in Cayenne. Georges-René Pléville-Le Pelley, minister of the navy, sent written instructions with their ship that Jeannet should settle the men "in a manner to form a bourg or hamlet near and under the surveillance of one of the military posts already established at Sinnamary and Iracoubo."[41] Provisionally, Jeannet exiled the men to the existing town of Sinnamary, a grid of huts with a church and barracks at its center. The deportees moved into the presbytery of Father Hochard, the former curate of Sinnamary, whom Jeannet deported as a nonjuror in 1793.[42]

In the Sinnamary town hall on 21 March 1798, a freedman called Sans Culotte witnessed the marriage of "Citizen Jean-Baptiste, of the Bambara nation, age thirty-seven," and "Citizen Marie-Thérèse, around twenty years old, of the Congo nation," before the mayor, Leopold Vogel, a former child bugler in the Hussars from Lorraine.[43] As an honorific, the word citizen remained in use throughout the 1790s in Guiana. Yet officials at Sinnamary did not define African villagers as members of the French nation.

"The title of Frenchman is too noble for us to share in good conscience with savage hordes of African cannibals." In July 1797, Guiana's envoy to Paris submitted a legislative petition demanding the revival of slavery and denigrating freed slaves with an openness of prejudice that is typical for this phase of the Revolution. After the September 1797 coup d'état purging the legislature, deputies linked to white colonial interests headed to Guiana as deportees and received the welcome of heroes.[44] One deportee, François Barbé-Marbois, a former intendant of Saint Domingue, wrote his American wife: "They even gave a sort of banquet for the deportees." The title of deportee was "an honorable distinction."[45] Another deported legislator, André-Daniel Laffon-Ladébat, learned that Mayor Vogel "[did] not think of refusing me the title of citizen."[46] In June, eight deportees fled in a canoe that a nearby planter commissioned, paid for and concealed for them.[47] Men who remained unwillingly—Guillume-Alexandre Tronson Ducoudray, François-Louis Bourdon, Stanislas-Joseph Rovère, Charles-Honoré La Villeheurnois, and André-Charles Brottier—died in quick succession of what Laffon-Ladébat took for fever, despair at never leaving, and grief at the deaths of their companions. Marbois and Laffon-Ladébat, who chose to remain, became the leaders of a junta that toppled Étienne-Laurent-Pierre Burnel, who succeeded Jeannet as agent of the Directory. On 29 November 1799, Laffon-Ladébat mused in his journal: "It is one of the singularities of my destiny to have seen myself deported here and to dictate acts of government."[48]

The antipathy of colonial whites toward the metropolitan government after the 1794 emancipation decree worked to the advantage of deported politicians. The hostility of former slave owners to the republic for freeing the slaves led white colonials to sympathize with royalists active on metropolitan soil during the spring and the summer of 1797. Before the coup d'état of September 1797 that restored the republic, whites in Guiana and elsewhere had expected right-wing legislators to revive slavery. The political sympathies of former slave owners helped deported politicians to become Guiana's first citizens. In this respect, the exilic fortunes of the deputies suggest quite a different relationship between land and law than does the plight of deported clergymen. Both the white radical notion of the unity of the republic and the revolutionary structure of imperial rule shaped the local treatment of priests. At the time of the priests' arrival, white colonists had deserted the revolutionary cause and many had fled Guiana. Yet the early Jacobin creed survived in the person of Jeannet and became an ideology of state.

The 1795 constitution enabled imperial officials to coerce workers by local decree, unhindered by domestic law. Government by these principles opened a breach between liberty as imagined and liberty as experienced. By the late 1790s, emancipated slaves lived in a constant state of alarm about their futures. Officials had once fretted over the prospect of a slave revolt. After emancipation, they worried about a rising of freed people to preserve their liberty from attack.

Guiana's administrators knew that their policies were among the chief causes of insurrection. In late February 1795, Governor François-Maurice

Cointet anticipated the fears of ex-slaves when he publicized the first of his work decrees. "Malicious men seeking to mislead you will present this regulation as an attack on your liberty. The men who speak this way are enemies of your peace of mind and of public order. You must denounce them to the authorities."[49] On 19 December 1795, Cointet requisitioned freed people as plantation workers on forty-seven estates that he had seized from absent proprietors.[50] One month later, on 25 January 1796, workers rose up as rumors of reenslavement swept through the colony.[51] On return to Guiana in April 1796, Jeannet sanctioned all acts of his predecessor and improved on them. That June he extended the requisitioning to private land and reduced all worker salaries.[52]

In July 1797, Jeannet blamed royalist electoral victories in France for stirring up an insurrection as rumors spread about reenslavement.[53] Yet he also viewed black revolt as a counterrevolutionary act. Faithful to the white Jacobin creed of earlier years, Jeannet feared a black uprising led by priests deported from France. That fear led him to embrace Pomme's 1793 isolation plan for clergymen, which took its model from the slave cantons of Guiana's revolutionary city.

On 13 June 1798, Jeannet received a dispatch about the settlement of deportees in Guiana from Georges-René Pléville Le Pelley, minister of the navy. The letter arrived aboard *La Décade,* which carried 193 deportees, including 162 priests.[54] Pléville Le Pelley selected the banks of the Conamama River as the site of a new bourg for deportees alone; the choice of this site probably originated with the director of colonies, Daniel Lescallier, who remembered this as a breezy savanna thronged with Indians from his short term in the colony as ordonnateur. The minister intended this settlement to contain both politicians and priests "whose backgrounds or tastes do not incline them to agriculture or commerce." Yet he did not require Jeannet to group the deportees together. "You can permit them to form agricultural or commercial establishments in all parts of the colony except Cayenne."[55]

Jeannet examined the problem of what to do with the deputies and what to do with the priests at the same time and opted to treat the two groups quite differently. He responded in two letters, written one day apart. With the deputies in mind, Jeannet dismissed Conamama as too isolated. When it came to the priests, Conamama seemed too crowded. The exiles would spur cultivators in the region to revolt. "I do not know how to keep them from using their influence to spread alarm among the blacks about the future of their liberty, or from rousing them with superstitions, either on behalf of an enemy power or for themselves. They will endanger public order and the security of persons and property. Citizen Minister, even if I could attach two armed soldiers to every deportee, this locale would make it impossible to prevent them from escaping." The priests required continuous surveillance by soldiers and total isolation. Jeannet drew the attention of the department to "the undated observations of A. Pomme, deputy for Cayenne, printed by order of the Committee on Finances."[56]

Pomme's martial canton took shape on the Conamama River. Jeannet instructed passengers who arrived aboard *La Décade* to make their own housing and living arrangements with the provision that they remain clear of the island of Cayenne. Those who failed to find a host or a plantation to rent within two weeks—the case for 82 of 162 priests—became eligible for stiffer measures. Jeannet sent Indians to build huts for them at a swamp near Sinnamary that locals called a savanna. Priests were to subsist there on the lard and beans of the sea ration while living under the guard of soldiers to prevent contact between the deportees and freed slaves of the region.[57]

With the arrival of the next convoy of deportees, *La Bayonnaise,* which reached Guiana on 29 September 1798, the rules toughened. According to Maurice Barbotin, 87 of the 120 deportees aboard the ship, including 68 priests, left for Conamama without disembarking first in the colonial capital.[58] Thirty-three sick passengers left the ship for the military hospital in Cayenne. Some invalids rented or bought properties, which delivered them to the chicanery of broke frontiersmen. Pierre Leroy, a young priest from Mayenne, leased a plantation despite his penury by agreeing to lodge, feed, and wash the laundry of Jean-Baptiste Poulin, the elderly proprietor. Leroy died in Guiana.[59]

The experiences of priests and politicians offer divergent perspectives on white colonial ideology as it mutated in the late 1790s. Deported politicians in Guiana benefited from the racism of colonial slave owners and from their rejection of domestic authority; these politicians belonged to a fallen legislative faction that had sought, in spring and summer 1797, to overturn the emancipation decree. Atrocities against priests resulted from the enduring mental association of missionaries with slaves and hence, by a fateful metonymy, of nonjurors with the local version of the Counter-revolution or slave rebellion. Their treatment also developed, however obliquely, from the white Jacobin design for a slave polity modeled on metropolitan France.

In his memoir of political exile in Guiana, Louis-Ange Pitou recalled the sounds of his arrival to the colony—cranking cables and anchors—as sailors secured the ship. "They chain up the frigate in the same way that we are prisoners in these climates."[60] In 1798, when Pitou reached Guiana, the place of his exile was also a land of deliverance. Four years earlier, with the abolition of slavery in Guiana on 14 June 1794, the colony became free soil. Until 1794, slaves were able to claim freedom on setting foot in the metropole while slavery persisted on imperial territory.[61] After the abolition of slavery, the soil of Guiana acquired the same transfiguring power as that of France.

Guiana existed simultaneously as free soil and as a site of deportation during the 1790s. The place that stood for absolute removal from the civic order was also a magic portal of sorts. Yet liberation and exile in Guiana were not so distinct as they might appear. As an applied doctrine, the free soil principle became an apparatus of human displacement, bodily seizure, and legal estrangement.

The free soil doctrine became a formal policy of Guiana's government over the objections of white notables. In fall 1794, Portuguese troops and boats began patrolling the Oyapock River on Guiana's eastern frontier for the purpose of controlling slave flight from Brazil.[62] The governor of Brazil's Para province demanded that the French government render the fugitives. On 25 October 1794, a council of war in Cayenne made up of colonists declined to pronounce on the rendition demand. Two days later, at the likely insistence of Jeannet, the council reconvened to disavow the earlier minutes as an "error of redaction." The council decreed on 27 October 1794, "relative to the desertion of slaves now said to be on French territory, [that] there can be no action with respect to them, because of the promulgation of the law concerning the abolition of slavery in the colonies, solemnly published in Guiana."[63] While conceding rhetorical support for the free soil doctrine, members of the war council nonetheless refused to enforce their declaration by sending troops to stave off Portuguese encroachment. Their inaction emboldened the governor of Para to enlarge his presence in the borderlands.

Jeannet quit Guiana in November 1794, abandoning his duties and leaving behind a colony menaced by invasion that whites refused to defend. The free soil doctrine assumed new prominence in local life after he returned in April 1796 as agent of the Directory. In August 1798, a slave woman fled an American ship anchored at Cayenne. The captain appealed to the governor of Surinam for help in recovering her. Jeannet refused to render the woman, citing "one of our constitutional laws." By the law of 1 January 1798, "any black individual, born in Africa or in foreign colonies, transferred to French islands, will be free the moment he sets foot on the territory of the French republic."[64] (In fact, the free soil principle took effect as a consequence of the emancipation decree, as the 1794 Oyapock crisis made clear.) Jeannet did not resist the demand of Surinam's governor because of a scrupulous regard for constitutional law. He took the high ground on slave rendition because of the importance of the free soil doctrine to his regime; it had become the key to his plan of colonial development.

On 3 October 1796, Jeannet wrote to Admiral Laurent Truguet, minister of the navy, about his new privateering campaign, whose "principal object will be to intercept and to direct to Cayenne the floating dungeons that carry sixteen thousand negroes from Africa to Brazil each year."[65] By hijacking slaves for delivery to free soil, Jeannet hoped to revive Guiana's moribund plantations. Most freed slaves exited the estates of their masters after emancipation and established family farms on abandoned estates or on land claimed from the forest. In the course of 1796, Guianese people were forced off newly claimed family plots to which they lacked legal title. That year, Jeannet put the number of emancipated slaves employed on plantations at four thousand out of approximately ninety-five hundred freed people in Guiana.[66] After the abolition of slavery, Africans from seized ships filled out the colony's diminished rural work force as requisitioned laborers; they comprised perhaps one-third of the colony's plantation workers at the turn of the nineteenth century. From 1796 to 1800, seven captured ships delivered 2,163 Africans to Cayenne. During roughly the same period (1795–1801), five captured vessels delivered 1,862 Africans to Guadeloupe—a colony with nine times Guiana's population.[67]

The applied history of the free soil doctrine makes it necessary to revisit the law of 1 January 1798 that Jeannet quoted when refusing a rendition request from the governor of Surinam. The 1798 law originated with Saint Domingue deputies who wanted the French government to apply the constitution to their colony; no one in the Saint Domingue delegation sought a restatement of the free soil principle by the metropolitan legislature.[68] From 1794 to the drafting of this law, 2,784 Africans had reached Guiana and Guadeloupe aboard captured Liverpool ships;[69] at least 1,515 Africans disembarked in Saint Domingue during those years under circumstances that remain ambiguous due to partial British occupation of the colony.[70] Thousands more Africans were expected to follow as spoils of war. The 1798 law did not merely restate the free soil principle; it also defined new Africans as foreigners. Although the new law could not reduce such people to slavery, the ghost of slavery was in the text because of the earlier fiction by which slaves became "individuals of a foreign nation" and ineligible for the rights of man.[71] The 1798 law resolved the question of African status following the wishes of imperial officials who saw free soil as a device for creating a colonial underclass. Daniel Lescallier, director of colonies, believed that "new negroes . . . cannot, without endangering the plantations . . . be given liberty."[72]

What set newly arrived Africans apart from other emancipated people in Guiana? The case of black soldiers illuminates the exclusionary character of Guianese civic life in the era of slave interception. The same doctrine that carried slave ships to Guiana called the black battalion into being. The occupation of Guiana's eastern frontier by Portuguese troops to stem the flight of slaves led Governor Cointet to muster 480 black soldiers in April 1795.[73] The defenders of free soil did not wear the national colors. They lived segregated from the white garrison. They were forbidden to hold any rank in the army. Outfitted in their special costume—grey toile blouses and pantaloons—they served under white corporals, sergeants, and commissioned officers. Until December 1798 they did without shoes. Jeannet warned of the danger of introducing "needs they do not have and that they could not contract without becoming less proper to colonial service . . . costume ends by becoming a part of man."[74]

The 1798 law that restated the free soil principle also enfranchised colonial soldiers and freedmen who met a limited property requirement. In Guiana, administrators applied the law as a license to seize slave ships. They declined to apply the law to empower the colonial citizenry.[75] This policy had the effect of flooding the colony with Africans called foreigners while officials effaced the distinction between the newcomers and everyone else.

Abstractly, the free soil doctrine was the fullest expression of the legal bond between the metropole and the colony; the same doctrine appeared to affirm the French commitment to emancipation. In practice, this doctrine caused the empire and the metropole to drift ever further apart. After 1794, as we have seen, Jeannet continued to view emancipated people through the prism of white Jacobin notions of the slave. Yet it was not merely vestiges of the past but new structures of law, arising from emancipation and inseparable from it, that cut freed people loose from the French nation and the legal norms of the New Regime. What is perhaps most troubling about Guiana after 1794 lies in the way the regime of liberty supplied the tools of its unmaking. When slavery revived in Guiana, newly arrived Africans were the first people in the colony to be declared chattel.[76]

The white Jacobin notion that metropolitan and colonial soil comprised a single land under a single law guided the use of force against slaves and indirectly shaped the lives of deported priests; in the hands of administrators, the legal fusion of France and Guiana turned against emancipated slaves and threatened their status. Yet the legal doctrine of sameness cannot be understood merely with reference to its use as a weapon of elites. Despite the exclusion of former slaves from politics, the 1794 emancipation decree conferred basic rights on Guiana's freed people that allowed them to enjoy a measure of freedom in highly coercive conditions during the later years of the republic. On 7 June 1797 the departmental administration of Guiana complained to the navy that "the exercise of private rights [*droits civils*] produces great evils," by which they meant the right to wed.[77] Administrators denounced the "assimilation of persons and property in this country to those [persons and property] of the metropole" and demanded "usufruct of their capital." By usufruct, they meant lifelong use of bodies belonging to people—freed slaves—who owned themselves. At the turn of the nineteenth century, rights that people received at the time of emancipation became defensive tools as slavery revived incrementally. People then sought to use the law to retain their liberty and that of relatives and friends.

By a decree of 2 July 1802 Bonaparte revived a 1777 royal edict banning black and colored people from entering France.[78] The original edict, which had never been enforced, sought to deactivate the Old Regime free soil principle by preventing colonial slaves from acceding to metropolitan territory.[79] The revolutionary history of emancipation led the 1802 racial ban to acquire a new significance. Bonaparte's decree was a writ of quarantine timed for the revival of slavery in the French empire. The travel ban affirmed the overturning of the recent past. When read against the history of the 1790s, Bonaparte's enactment of the 1777 edict performed a sweeping act of expulsion. It shrank the contours of free soil and hence evicted all emancipated people, including people in the colonies, from the land of liberty.

In proclamations of reassurance, revolutionary officials in Guiana declared the abolition of slavery to be irreversible. The same proclamations menaced slavery's return. When dangling those threats, officials alluded to slavery, or to forced labor as a criminal layabout, as though describing a form of political proscription. Idlers "will be returned to the profound ignominy that a generous and benevolent homeland has allowed you to exit."[80] Failure to comply with the law of toil annulled "all right to the protection of the law and public force."[81] In Guiana as in Guadeloupe the refractory laborer merged with the counterrevolutionary traitor.[82] In practice, when slavery returned, no one dared to justify the collective annulment of legal being by recalling those earlier threats.

Victor Hugues, the former revolutionary commissar to Guadeloupe, became the Consulat's commissar to Guiana in 1800 and in that capacity revived slavery following cues he received from the metropolitan government.[83] Hugues did not model reenslavement after the logic of the Terror. Instead he deleted the Revolution. The era of liberty perished by erasure. In a decree of April 1803, Hugues ordered civil record keepers to strike the word *citizen* in reference to black and colored people and to remove their surnames from birth, marriage, and death certificates of the revolutionary era.[84] In 1804, reflecting back on his handiwork, Hugues wrote that emancipation had ended "without an effusion of blood, without a hitch. It is as though this colony had never been revolutionary."[85]

The version of slavery that emerged in the phase of transition, which began in January 1800 and ended in June 1803, belies Hugues's claim to having erased the revolution. That transitional regime also marked a rather uncanny turning point in the history of free soil. Once Guiana had been land that made men free. Under Hugues, the land you lived on absorbed you; the person who owned that land became your master.[86] In the decree of 7 December 1802 reestablishing slavery and the slave trade in Guiana, this regime went by the name of conscription. Navy officials abandoned that euphemism when parsing drafts in internal memoranda. The decree, on Hugues's advice, "transformed the slave into immovable property [*l'immobiliserait*] completely and in perpetuity."[87] In simpler terms, the emancipated people became real estate.

Changes to the colony during the 1790s called forth the new doctrine. During the Revolution, nearly all emancipated people had abandoned the property of their former owners and wound up in town or as requisitioned workers on other rural estates. In October 1802 Hugues warned the minister of the navy that splitting up families and redistributing slaves to original owners would result in mass flight to the forest.[88] In 1800, he resolved to reenslave people where they were by incremental steps. In April 1802, slavery seemed poised to return. By November, the process was complete in fact, though not in law.[89]

With the conversion of freedmen into real estate came a second adjustment, a new free soil principle of sorts, which emerged through practice and not as doctrine, yet enjoyed recognition by the master class and by near-slaves in the colony. According to the new free soil principle, if you owned real estate, you could not be real estate. Guiana again became a colony where land made men free. Yet it was also a place where men were land.

Mothers transacted in their children's liberty under the cover of land sales. On 21 June 1801, the planter Louis-Marie Favard sold a plot in the Kaw quarter to his former slave Marie-Rose "for the sole profit of her minor children named Henriette, Lucile, and Pacifique," who were all mulattos. She paid with money "from someone who does not wish to be known."[90] On 22 July 1801, a townswoman called Dalila purchased the house where she lived and its plot, which had once belonged to her master, Labuton, who liberated her and her mulatto children François and Marie-Louise in 1792. Dalila bought the property from the new owner, the mulatto Noel Coutard, for the benefit of her young mulatto sons, Gratien and Damas, who were probably born during the Revolution and absent from the manumission act. She paid with 2,000 francs she received from "persons who do not wish to be known."[91]

It became pressing to spread land around. On 22 August 1802, Joseph called Monach transferred part of his lot near the Crique Sartine to Venus called Leclerc and her three children.[92] Six days later, on 28 August 1802, Raphael, a black soldier in the Battalion of Guiana, donated parcels of a property he shared with his cousin Marie-Louise to his son Sevrin and his goddaughter Suzette; the children became joint proprietors of a narrow vacant lot measuring 15 feet by 222 feet.[93] On 15 September 1802, a Cayenne townswoman called Marie-Catherine transferred her late mother's shack and small plot to her seven nieces and nephews.[94] Vacant lots and houses split apart and moved around as freedom came to depend on smaller and smaller pieces.

Notarial documents hint at the imminent legal death of Guiana's emancipated people. The approaching moment of collective expiry is most palpable in documents that record unsuccessful property transactions. During the Revolution, Zabeth and her daughter Marie-Charlotte-Adrienne lived on a plot in Cayenne belonging to the retired notary Rondeau where they built a house and several outbuildings.[95] Rondeau refused to part with his land. On 7 October 1802, he sold them lifelong usufruct of the house they built and the land they worked for 4,500 francs.[96]

Usufruct offered the women no security, however. Only definitive title to land was thought to secure personal status. On 10 October 1802, three days after Zabeth and her daughter acquired usufruct of Rondeau's land, the sister and brother Honorine and Noel, both mulattos, annulled an earlier transaction granting their black brother Thimoté usufruct of their house on Cayenne's Rue Jean-Jacques. In a new act, all three siblings became proprietors of the house for the manifest purpose of securing Thimoté's freedom.[97] At stake in the problem of usufruct during the revival of slavery was the reversion of property to the original owner at the legal death of the occupants. By selling usufruct rights to the women, Rondeau assured that his property would return to him if or when the women ceased to exist as legal subjects with slavery's formal return. Hugues solicited a decree to that effect on 12 October 1802, five days after this transaction.[98] On 17 October 1802 he requested a slave inventory from all masters and forbade displacements—slave sales—without his authorization.[99]

In the end, land did not make men free. By the consular decree of 7 December 1802, following Hugues's advice, "blacks or men of color not free before 1789 . . . who became proprietors since that period will be required to reimburse their old owner for the cost of their liberty based on an estimation of their personal value."[100] According to this arrangement, which took effect on 25 April 1803, proprietorship conferred the possibility of self-purchase, which French slave law did not allow.[101] Of the 215 landowners who purchased their liberty, most were black adults and black or mixed children rescued from slavery by black mothers.[102]

Suzette, who got a sliver lot from her godfather Raphael, bought her liberty from the widow Mangot on 14 May 1803.[103] As for Raphael, who entered the black battalion as a defender of free soil, he could not afford to buy his freedom or that of his son. One month after Raphael transferred property to Suzette and Sevrin, Hugues received the instruction to shrink the black battalion by transferring half its members to the fields. The former defenders of free soil who remained under arms became foot soldiers in a scorched-earth war against maroons.[104]

The legal efforts by Guiana's freed people to shield themselves and loved ones from reenslavement, whether or not those efforts proved successful, draw attention to an unexpected link between political exile in Guiana during the Revolution and slave liberation. The first tale illuminates the second. The precinct for deviant ex-citizens that Revolutionaries hoped to establish in Guiana, but largely failed to constitute, came into being during the Consulate with strange literality. It did so in the form of a colony peopled by thousands of ex-citizens who were banned from France and returned to slavery. Nearly everyone freed during the Revolution died to the law under Napoleon.

The revolutionary history of free soil closed definitively with the 1809 conquest of Guiana by Portugal, with British assistance (and perhaps with help from Hugues). Portugal would retain sovereignty over the colony until 1817. The Portuguese expeditionary force, consisting of one thousand Brazilian Indians, played no role in the French surrender. Hugues capitulated because of an internal rebellion stimulated by the enemy as slaves "armed with sabers and agricultural instruments ran through the countryside." In 1794, Hugues had recaptured Guadeloupe from the British while armed with the emancipation decree. In December 1808 he sent three hundred slave soldiers to defend the eastern frontier of slave soil, with consequences that he, of all people, could have predicted. The soldiers deserted—including Apollo, whom the British gave the title of general. In the service of Britain and Portugal, Apollo and his company traveled westward, "giving orders, cutting whips, breaking irons, and burning the properties indicated to him." They carried a standard marked with the figure of a black man and the word *liberté*. The flag (a British confection) celebrated a cause in search of a country.[105] In 1809, the revolutionary era of slave emancipation became a cynical instrument of colonial conquest; Britain and Portugal exploited Guianese slaves' memory of their lost liberty without having the slightest intention of freeing anyone. In a fitting coda to Guiana's revolutionary past, the Portuguese (at Hugues's insistence) deported Apollo and his troops to Brazil.

CHAPTER 4

Missing Persons

I N SEPTEMBER 1828, Dezailly Allongé Alexis (Artifaille, Alexis Allongé nicknamed Artifaille, Dessailly, Desalliers, Darzalier), imprisoned for vagabondage in Beauvais, petitioned the minister of the interior
to release him from yet another random imprisonment. "The little security he enjoys when traveling for his personal affairs . . . makes him the
frequent victim of false suspicions and arrests that hover over him, as a
kind of misfortune attached to his person. . . . Your Excellency, render a
citizen to society who will be eternally grateful for this good turn." Dezailly
appealed to the minister in a political vocabulary that harked back to the
Revolution, which was the era of his youth and of his vanishing. Sentenced at Douai to fourteen years of hard labor for stealing two horses, he
escaped from the navy's work prison at Brest or Lorient in 1796 or 1797.[1]

Dezailly's sense that something lay on his body was the result of measures against suspects that began to emerge in France after he fled captivity. Dezailly did not understand changes to the state that arose during his
thirty-two years on the lam, or else pretended not to. In 1827 he returned
to live under his own name at his relatives' farmhouse near Laon (Aisne),
believing himself immune to pursuit by the law for the past. He was right.
No crime could be prosecuted after a lapse of twenty years. Unable to

punish Dezailly for the past, the prosecutor of Laon turned the man over to an agency that could touch him: the ministry of the interior.

The government of Napoleon Bonaparte retreated with reluctance in the early nineteenth century from the revolutionary goal of spatializing the ideal limits of the French legal community. During the early nineteenth century, in place of mass expulsion, there arose new legal devices for defining and excluding undesirables. Napoleonic civil and criminal law created a group of outsiders to what jurists and legislators called *la cité*, which was a spatial metaphor, not an actual place: *la cité* referred to the people whom the law invested with rights and its boundaries bore no connection to the geographical limits of France. In its handling of deviants, the Napoleonic state made room for life outside the city inside the country.

In the early nineteenth century, convicts serving sentences to hard labor in the navy's prisons [*bagnes*] at Brest, Lorient, Toulon, and Rochefort and men liberated from those facilities lived in a state of extreme legal incapacity with respect to their private and political rights. They also lived outside what jurists and administrators called the common law.[2] Convicts in the naval prisons fell under royal edicts of the seventeenth and eighteenth centuries that remained in force during the New Regime. The prisons were nonetheless open-air facilities, where convicts worked out of doors in ordinary towns. The jurisdiction of the work prison was a matter of personal status, not a delineated zone, and moved where the men did.

After exiting those facilities, ex-convicts lived in an unusual legal predicament because of a new system of surveillance that developed at the turn of the nineteenth century for them alone to later encumber many other lawbreakers. Surveillance transformed ex-convicts into a new category of suspect. It banned them from their home villages and towns. It transformed peasants and tradesmen into perpetual wanderers, for whom France resembled a rather inhospitable foreign country.

In the nineteenth century, the infamous criminal replaced the émigré as the absolute stranger through the extent of what law removed and of what it authorized. Nonetheless, jurists and administrators who organized the treatment of criminals in the nineteenth century poached from the history of political persecution by incorporating techniques that had arisen as extraordinary measures of repression against enemies of state during the revolutionary period. Those devices became normal features of the legal order for use against ordinary deviants. The predicament of common criminals in the nineteenth century was thus subtly linked to the recent history of political persecution. In turn, the fate of future enemies of state— of the republican opposition, in particular—would prove inseparable from that of common criminals. In the nineteenth century, political dissidents, conspirators, and rebels were rhetorically confounded with infamous criminals and handled by similar means. The conflation of political enemies with criminals had the further effect of rendering felons and even petty offenders vulnerable to retributive violence against revolutionaries.

Forçats libérés, released men from the navy's work prisons at Rochefort, Toulon, and Brest, came to exemplify social dangerousness in the first half of the nineteenth century. In the discourse of civic leaders and administrators, the figure of the ex-convict tended to glow with particular malevolence whenever the state laid claim to new repressive powers at times of political upheaval. Amid clamor for the elimination of ex-convicts from the country, in the wake of the 1848 Revolution, the French government laid plans to empty the navy's prisons into the colony of French Guiana. With the founding of the new convict settlement there in 1852, the legal incapacities affecting convicts and ex-convicts, the special jurisdiction of the work camp, and the surveillance system traveled from the metropole to the empire with the bodies of these men to become the invisible architecture of a new society.

During the revolutionary period, the journey from the Bicêtre prison in Paris to the navy's prisons at Brest and Lorient was a month-long traipse in the custody of Citizen Vié and his mother, entrepreneurs of the convict march.[3] The men walked while chained together by metal neck clamps. Each wore wooden clogs and a toile blouse and trousers whatever the season. They slept in stables and churches. They were sustained (with some luck) on a daily ration of six ounces of beans or meat in a liquid called soup, a pound and a half of bread, and a bowl of cider or wine in the evening.[4] The Vié family chain grew as new men were hooked on from local prisons and shrank as men fled, perished, and collapsed.[5]

The men in the Vié chain lost more than their liberty. Nineteenth-century jurists and legislators defined the legal status of prisoners and ex-convicts by stripping away powers that enabled masculine authority in private and public life. The felon was the anti-patriarch, the anti-citizen, the obverse of civic and domestic ideals. The Civil Code (1804) substituted the criminal for the counterrevolutionary in defining the edges of the new legal order. In the new code, civil death applied only to people who lost their civil rights by judicial convictions and not—as during the Revolution—by virtue of legislation against political enemies. All drafts of the code defined the legal status of émigrés in a manner distinct from revolutionary governments. Rather than being civilly dead, fugitive traitors now lost their civil rights through the removal of their nationality.[6]

For jurists who drafted the code, the interest of civil death lay in what it revealed about the world-making and world-destroying power of the law. As Jean-Étienne-Marie Portalis observed, "legislative power is human omnipotence. Law establishes, conserves, changes, modifies, perfects; it destroys what is; it creates what is not yet."[7] In obliterating the legal subject, civil death seemed to announce the power of law to institute and sustain identity. What law created, it might also annihilate. Civil death also stimulated reflections about the link between legal metaphor and reality. As the councillor of state Jean Grenier explained to the Tribunate, "civil death is a fiction by which one looks upon those who have undergone it as naturally dead." And yet in law there were no fictions. "The principle of fiction is always raised against objections, because fiction, for law, is reality."[8]

As an affirmation of what law could withhold, civil death at the turn of the nineteenth century dissolved more than it ever had.[9] The new form of civil death nullified the marriage bond and the bond between children and a civilly dead parent. In the final version of the Civil Code, civil death rendered the wife of a civilly dead man a type of widow; children born before civil death took effect were orphans, while those born afterward were bastards. In contrast, during the Old Regime, marriage was a sacred bond recognized by the state that the state's laws could not cancel. Although marriage ceased to be a religious act in 1792, revolutionary jurists and legislators understood the conjugal bond as an act of natural law that was indissoluble by the state.[10] After the Civil Code went into effect, nineteenth-century courts would interpret the dissolving effects of civil death with reference to different legal times. When confronted with cases that dealt with the revolutionary period, courts upheld the validity of émigré marriages despite the civil death of a spouse. In contrast, courts affirmed the capacity of women to remarry after the civil death of their husbands once the Civil Code took effect.[11]

At Bonaparte's insistence, the 1801 draft of the code included an article (later deleted) that applied civil death to convicts sentenced for unspecified crimes to "perpetual deportation in a French dependency outside the continent."[12] Revolutionary criminal law, which was still in force, punished all recidivist felons with overseas deportation after they completed their second prison term in France; the only type of deportation addressed in existing codified law concerned nominally free people who were banned as irredeemable deviants from reentering society. The new draft article was not meant to apply to this narrow group. Rather, Bonaparte hoped that revised criminal statutes would apply deportation quite expansively. He observed to the Council of State: "We have six thousand individuals in prison who do nothing, who cost a lot, and who escape daily. . . . Deportation is a prison, but one with more than thirty square feet."[13] The first consul and those around him envisaged perpetual deportation during the drafting of this text as a punishment for convicts with criminal sentences of varied lengths. In the end, however, nineteenth-century law applied these measures far more narrowly than jurists had originally envisaged. The 1810 Criminal Code applied civil death to people with lifelong sentences to forced labor and to deportation, while the latter became a punishment for lesser political crimes. The practical impossibility of founding an overseas penal colony turned deportation into detention in a prison of state.[14]

In 1802, France's inability to found an overseas convict settlement inspired the government to seek the revival of the convict brand as a punishment for forgers and recidivists; the latter group then awaited deportation according to yet unmodified revolutionary law. The notion of the convict brand as a substitute for deportation survived into the Bourbon Restoration (1814–1830) and would figure in debates on penal reform in the 1819 Chamber of Peers. The Napoleonic Criminal Code punished forgers, recidivist felons, and arsonists with the brand until legislators abolished the practice altogether in 1832.[15]

The framers defined civil death in the final version of the code while expecting to reintroduce life sentences through the revision of criminal law. In the 1810 Criminal Code, civil death resulted from life sentences to forced labor. It also struck people sentenced to deportation (art. 18), which punished lesser political crimes and in practice meant detention in a prison of state.

Convicts with limited sentences underwent diluted versions of civil death during and after their terms of punishment. While serving sentences to forced labor in one of the navy's work prisons, or to less grueling labor in a closed prison, convicts were subject to legal interdiction.[16] According to the 1810 Criminal Code, "whoever is sentenced to the punishment of forced labor for a limited term or to reclusion will be . . . in a state of legal interdiction; a trustee will be named to manage and administer his property."[17] The terseness of this text led some jurists to argue that convicts could not buy or sell property during their internment but remained free to marry, to exercise paternal power over children, and even to draft a will.[18] Against this view, other jurists interpreted legal interdiction to suspend every civil right including marriage by analogy with legal handicaps affecting the mad and otherwise mentally incompetent.[19]

The lifelong punishment of civic degradation overlapped with legal interdiction and outlasted it. Though civic degradation affected women and men alike in theory, it was conceived with men in mind and emasculated them in a legal sense. By the 1810 Criminal Code, civic degradation excluded felons from "all public employment or functions"; it prohibited them from sitting on juries, from serving as witnesses to legal acts, and from testifying "except to give simple information." Finally, civic degradation made it impossible for a man to be the guardian or trustee of a child, including his own child, except with the assent of a family council.[20]

Legal interdiction, civic degradation, and civil death summoned an ideal image of the patriarchal citizen silhouetted against a figure defaced for moral unworthiness. Yet the being reduced by such practices was not quite a human, or not directly one; it was rather an anthropomorphic legal representation, the *personne* or legal persona, which shaped the life of an actual man by determining his capacities. The French legal historian Jean Carbonnier insists that the *personne* in civil law is not a body. "Man is treated essentially as a will; this is not a fleshly being, subject to frailty, prey to needs, broken by economic forces; it is a will that is always strong, enlightened, tending toward a goal, and free."[21] This putatively incorporeal being derives its particular character, and very life, from the actual body to which it is linked by legal documents, especially the *état civil*—the civil records of births, marriages, and deaths that indicate the name, sex, age, lineage, and legal domicile of individuals. The *personne* is born and sexed by the archive and endowed with powers that are known collectively as the legal personality.[22] In the nineteenth century those powers varied between men and women, children and adults, the sane and the mad, and further depended on marital status, criminal record, and bodily presence. (The personalities of missing people were deactivated.) Because of the importance of physical data to the legal personality, it will never be possible to separate the human body and its history from the "will that is always strong" evoked by Carbonnier.

In September 1796, the convict chain to Brest stopped for inspection near Versailles. "A number of them had already cut their irons; we found files, and wigs they would use to disguise themselves, their hair being cut short."[23] The following day, surrounded by two gendarme brigades, the convoy reached Dreux in the wake of a violent attempt at mass escape. Forty convicts awaiting transport from Dreux had "knock[ed] down several walls, breaking their irons." Eight had fled.[24] After the chain departed Dreux, officials learned that women tracking the caravan had "sought to purchase small files in the shop of an ironmonger at Lamballes."[25]

Jurists who drafted the Civil Code defined the criminal as the absolute stranger at a moment when the distinction between convicts and citizens was coming to pieces, in part because of the large number of men who fled the naval prisons at Rochefort, Lorient, Brest, and Toulon at the end of the revolutionary decade. In December 1801, Claude-Ambroise Regnier, councillor of state and future minister of justice, spoke of the ease with which convicts escaped and assumed false identities when arguing for the revival of the convict brand.[26]

The distinction between the convict and the citizen drawn by legal texts of the Napoleonic period had little connection to the texture of French life in these years for reasons other than convict flight. The naval prisons that in theory gathered the country's worst criminals were full of soldiers, deserters, and draft evaders who enjoyed public sympathy at a time of widespread disaffection with conscription.[27] In 1813, a commissioner at

Boulogne described the customary local treatment of convicts sentenced for "theft, desertion, and all other offenses." Accompanied by a few soldiers, convicts paraded around town, dragging a ball and chain, and collecting alms. The commissioner had just spotted "three sailors convicted for theft and desertion circulat[ing] in the town" who drew sympathy and contributions from peasants at the marketplace. "This always occasions declamations against the severity of the law and the repression of desertion."[28]

The naval prisons of France were unusual legal enclaves—islands of the Old Regime inside the New Regime in the form of special jurisdictions. A law of 20 September–12 October 1790 invigorated royal regulations on the punishment of galley slaves, many originating from the reign of Louis XIV. In the era of the Declaration of the Rights of Man and Citizen, the beating of hard labor convicts enjoyed the sanction of revolutionary law.[29] Napoleonic jurists conferred new legitimacy on those texts in the final article of the 1810 Criminal Code. "In all matters that have not been regulated by the present code, and which are ruled by special laws and regulations, the courts and tribunals will continue to observe them."[30] As a result of this article, hard labor convicts of the nineteenth century were said to live "outside the common law"[31] under "laws of exception."[32]

Although Old Regime regulations for galley slaves remained valid in the New Regime, the regime of hard labor convicts did not follow the letter of those texts. Punishments in the nineteenth-century naval prisons short of execution came to consist of internment in dungeon cells or of blows of the *bastonnade* (invariably a cord) that were administered to the back of a convict strapped to a wooden bench—the bench of justice—on which the man, while being beaten, was called the patient.[33]

The normal juridical system sustained these special enclaves. On multiple occasions in the nineteenth century, the Court of Cassation confirmed the right of special maritime tribunals to judge convicts without appeal.[34] In 1842, under pressure from the ministry of the navy, the Court of Cassation struck down a judgment by the special maritime tribunal at Brest. The military court had sentenced a convict who killed another inmate to three years of imprisonment by invoking article 463 of the revised French Criminal Code relevant to extenuating circumstances. The Court of Cassation chastened the Brest tribunal for violating the principle that "general laws must not be applied in cases that are regulated by special laws." The special maritime tribunal ought to have applied the ordinances of 16 December 1686 and 4 April 1749 and sentenced him to death, regardless of the circumstances.[35]

The special maritime jurisdiction that enveloped hard labor convicts in the nineteenth century had spatial peculiarities that did not exist before the Revolution. By a regulation of 1749, men who rebelled during their journey into prison were punished with death. In contrast, nineteenth-century convicts did not fall within the purview of the old edicts and could not be punished in light of them until crossing into the arsenal prison. While traversing the country, they remained under the jurisdiction of normal courts.[36] Nonetheless, the special maritime jurisdiction that applied to convicts in the nineteenth century defied mere spatial definition. Escapists from the *bagnes* could not be tried before normal courts for acts they committed while on the loose in the country. Once a convict crossed into the arsenal prison, the special maritime jurisdiction ceased to be a spatial zone and moved wherever he did.[37]

The journey of convicts to the ports changed in the decades after the fall of Napoleon. The shackled men traveled chiefly by open cart in 1832, though some agreed for a small fee to make the journey on foot.[38] During the 1820s and 1830s they traversed the country as objects of prurient amazement, or so it seemed to bourgeois onlookers.[39] An 1830 letter to the *Gazette des Tribunaux* from a middle-class felon reproached crowds at the Bicêtre prison for taking pleasure in observing convict bodies and brands. The men were shackled in the courtyard before their journey in front of "a crowd of free persons who are lured to this horrible festival by the unique desire to satisfy their cruel curiosity." The crowd "search[es] every naked shoulder avidly to spot the imprimatur of atrocious laws, and applauds, smiling, the moment they have seen it."[40]

Parisians in the chain responded to oglers by mugging for the audience. They became burlesque performers, singing and declaiming lewd couplets, mocking their chains, and bidding adieu "in the dialect of argot." Yet most men confronted crowds with impassive expressions that seemed to betoken moral numbness. "What chills the heart in this sorry spectacle is not the misery of the convicts; it is their indifference, their apathy, their gaiety even."[41] In 1835 the Paris prefect of police banned crowds from watching the shackling of convicts at Bicêtre. That year, the official who oversaw the convict chain urged the minister of the interior to implement further restrictions. An appetite for spectatorship had overtaken rural gendarmes and garrison troops, who abused the privilege of their uniforms by escorting wives and friends into convict resting places. "In some localities . . . one often finds a member of the local authority, the captain or lieutenant of the gendarmerie, the officers of the garrison, arriv[ing] alone or accompanied by friends and wives to observe the convicts resting peacefully on beds of straw . . . the mere sight of these strangers . . . irritates them to the point of revolt, which the guards must punish to maintain order."[42] On 9 December 1836, the government abolished the chain, prescribing that new wagons with barred windows would replace the open carts. Thereafter, men would travel in silence and haste, screened from the suspect public.[43]

In his 1828 petition seeking release from prison in Beauvais, Dezailly noted his sense that suspicion followed him everywhere as "a kind of misfortune attached to his person." That uncanny bodily sensation resulted from new police procedures for monitoring suspects that began to take shape in France at the turn of the nineteenth century. The system, called *surveillance de la haute police* (surveillance of the high police), originally targeted men from the port prisons. Later it affected thousands of other offenders including petty criminals, vagabonds, and republican militants. The surveillance system had a twofold effect on the predicament of ex-convicts of various description in this period. First, it rendered them conspicuous pariahs and, second, it set them apart as a group whose very bodies might be moved about at the convenience of the police. Surveillance defined the social question of the ex-convict during the first half of the nineteenth century by making it possible to invoke a large and diverse group of free people as an administrative category, to discuss the hazards of the category, and to propose that the category be removed.

In the first years of the nineteenth century, men exiting the port prisons were simply obliged to choose a future place of residence, as they had done for years, without constraints. Soon, however, complaints by prefects about the inconvenience of such people in Paris and frontier regions of France led the administration to impose spatial interdictions. By a decree of 10 March 1805, felons from the ports were banned from living in Paris, in towns with imperial residences, in places that lay within three kilometers of the frontier, near theaters of war, and from all towns that were the site of naval work prisons.[44] An imperial decree of 18 July 1806 repeated those spatial rules while enabling administrators to move the men around and to ban them from wherever they wished. Ex-convicts from the naval prisons were also forbidden to leave their assigned residences without receiving approval from the prefect of the department where they were living and from the prefect of the department where they wished to go.[45]

The new ex-convict tracking system combined earlier banning practices of the monarchy with novel tactics that arose during the revolutionary and Napoleonic era for tracking the movement of soldiers and monitoring political suspects. In the state's handling of criminals, practices that originated with extraordinary state necessity—war and counterrevolution—became permanent administrative norms for the handling of a different group.

In the early nineteenth century, ex-convicts exiting the navy's camps received internal passports called *feuilles de route* that were modeled on the traveling papers of soldiers in the army. In the case of a man leaving prison, the *feuille de route* indicated the distinguishing physical characteristics of its bearer, his past criminal record, his destination, and his itinerary. This document needed to be stamped by mayors in all the towns he passed through on his way to the assigned location. The *feuille de route* also accorded the traveler a small sum—30 centimes per kilometer—to subsidize the journey. In the case of blind and lame men, the *feuille de route* might confer the right to a horse or coal cart for the journey.[46]

The system of assigned residence that applied to ex-convicts from naval prisons during the Napoleonic period borrowed from police measures that were then in use against other provisionally tolerated suspects, who included village scoundrels, foreigners, and people removed from the émigré list. The sénatus-consulte of 26 April 1802, a sweeping writ of amnesty for émigrés, subjected all those who returned by virtue of it—approximately fifty thousand people—to a minimum of ten years of special surveillance; the government might also "oblige individuals subject to this special surveillance to distance themselves from their usual places of residence by up to twenty leagues; and they can be distanced further if circumstances require it."[47] An 1810 chart of people under surveillance in the cathedral town of Laon included several priests, erstwhile deportees, who had resumed their old livelihoods, now as government functionaries. Also listed was the nobleman D'Y de Résigny, whose occupation in 1810 was mayor.[48] In Laon of the First Empire, the distinction between the government and the people under special government surveillance was indeed a hazy one.

The 1810 Criminal Code transformed the system of ex-convict surveillance from an administrative measure into an element of the rule of law. As defined by the code, surveillance of the high police entailed living "at the disposition of the government, which has the right to order either the distancing of an individual from a particular place, or his continuous residence in a specific place in one of the departments of the empire."[49] Conquered lands annexed to France in the Napoleonic era—in Germany and Italy—thus received surveillance of the high police as a French legal inheritance. Under the 1810 Criminal Code, felons who served sentences to hard labor were subject to lifelong surveillance of the high police as an automatic effect of their punishment that judges could not modify. So, too, were vagabonds, who remained after their release from prison "at the disposition of the government for a period that it will determine, depending on their conduct."[50] The code further attached surveillance of the high police for a limited period to a number of lesser offenses, such as inciting minors to debauchery, administering hazardous substances, writing death threats, sequestering persons, begging, associating illegally, manufacturing weapons, wrecking crops, poisoning animals, manipulating stock prices, and all kinds of stealing.[51] The predicament of ex-convicts from the naval prisons nonetheless differed from that of other surveyed people. Men from the ports remained subject to the spatial bans and auxiliary administrative constraints set forth in the 1806 decree, which applied only to them and remained part of French administrative law after the fall of Napoleon.

There were two means of avoiding surveillance. The first was payment and the second, flight. In theory, ex-convicts might pay a fee fixed at the time of their sentencing and avoid surveillance altogether. In 1812, the

Council of State decided that a court could opt not to set the fee, which made it impossible to escape the system.[52] As for flight, it was common and harshly punished. In the case of a surveyed person who broke his ban—who fled an assigned town, or strayed from a prescribed travel itinerary—"the government will have the right to arrest and detain the convict for an interval of time that can extend over the full period of special surveillance."[53] Men from the ports and vagabonds, for whom surveillance was lifelong, risked open-ended administrative detention.

In elaborating surveillance of the high police, the Criminal Code opened a trap door into what jurists of the period understood as a special dominion of state authority that lay outside the law. When presenting an early draft of the Criminal Code to the Tribunate in 1804, Gui-Jean-Baptiste Target, councillor of state, evoked surveillance of the high police as the abandonment of suspect bodies by the law to the police. "As for their personal liberty, they are transferred from the empire of law to the empire of administration." The administration would assume a power over the body of surveyed felons that Target compared to slavery. "The old republics believed themselves capable of maintaining the liberty of citizens only by reducing their number and by delivering an immense population of slaves to the despotism of masters. . . . We propose an idea that is happier and more humane; it is to abandon—not to despotism, but to the enlightened vigilance of the government—the guilty people who are judged according to the law."[54]

Despite the restrictions placed on men from the naval prisons during the Napoleonic era, the ministry of general police resisted pressure from prefects to meddle further in the selection of ex-convict residences. Prefects complained that men from the ports were living in departments other than the ones where they were born. In response to such a complaint by the prefect of Allier in 1810, an official at the ministry of general police observed in marginalia: "The law leaves them the master of choosing their place of retreat. This arrangement can only be changed by a law and is paternal. A *forçat libéré* would generally be too poorly viewed by his compatriots and certainly by his family to find resources, and a peaceable existence, in his birthplace or habitual domicile."[55] After the fall of Napoleon, when the central government became more responsive to regional elites, the convict's freedom to choose where he lived disappeared.

During the reign of Louis XVIII (1814–1825), local governments and departmental prefects demanded the removal of ex-convicts unknown to the region, whom they depicted as unemployable, repugnant, and a burden on public funds.[56] In response to such complaints, the choices of men leaving the port prisons became irrelevant, though their preferences continued to be solicited officially. The process of assigning an ex-convict a residence began when a prison official recorded the preference of an inmate nearing his release date. On receiving these details, officials in Paris opened an inquiry into the man's personal life—the sexual habits of his wife, the income and repute of his parents and siblings, and the fears of his former neighbors. The ministry of general police would then reply to the prison official by indicating an entirely different site and by inviting the man to choose again. The fiction of choice was no less essential to this system than the constraints imposed on those who always chose unwisely.

Departmental councils insisted that ex-convicts from the navy's camps were choosing to live where they did not belong. To placate such objections, birthplaces became a frequent default site of residential assignment. Birthplaces that were not hometowns were ideal from the high administrative standpoint. Local authorities could not object that a man was a stranger there; they could also not complain of the danger he posed to friends, neighbors, relatives, and spouses. In 1830 François Lefebvre, a convict awaiting release from Toulon, hoped to return to his wife after an absence of twenty years. Instead the ministry wanted him assigned to Saint Victor (department unknown), a town that Lefebvre had left as a child of eight, never to return, and "where he knows no one . . . where he cannot earn a living."[57]

The birthplace was the default site of residential assignment except when a man asked to return there, at which officials discovered reasons for sending him someplace else. Men from the ports could rarely return to birthplaces where they might rejoin their families. Louis-Alexandre Droulin, awaiting release from Brest, was refused permission to return to Villantrois (Indres) because "his parents who are indigent will be upset by his return."[58] The convict Raynaud, imprisoned at Toulon, was banned from his hometown because his family "enjoys a despicable reputation and lives chiefly by stealing." Jacques Bareron could not rejoin his wife and children in Vitteaux (Côte d'Or), because "they live off alms."[59]

The ministry of the interior gathered intimate details about the wives of convicts, sometimes with the participation of the women themselves. Marie-Marguerite d'Heinville notified the prefect of Seine-Inférieur that she was sleepless with worry at the thought of her husband's return. "Her lodgings are in poor shape. The doors and the walls are not at all solid."[60] Yet the prospect of domestic violence was merely one among a great number of reasons that administrators used to keep men from rejoining their wives. A native of the Vaucluse awaiting release from Toulon in 1830 wished to return to his wife in Pertuis; the director general of police observed that "[she] has left the town and one is assured that she leads a disorderly existence in Lyon. Considerations of public order further oppose his return to the department of the Vaucluse."[61] In another example of foiled homecoming, François Donguy, a carpenter, was banned from returning to Montpont (Saone et Loire), where he was born and where his wife lived. She had conceived a child during his time at Toulon. "The information transmitted by the prefect does not make it possible to know whether [he] is aware of this circumstance. It is necessary to avoid revealing the reason we are refusing his choice of place, and to make him choose somewhere not too close to it."[62]

Because of the still-active 1806 decree, Parisian ex-convicts from the navy's prisons could not return home. That prohibition made it impossible to oblige the wishes of local governments and prefects by sending ex-convicts back where they belonged. In the face-to-face world of nineteenth-century commerce, that ban also meant that Parisians with urban livelihoods, whether they were masons, bibelot hucksters, wine merchants, furniture makers, or locksmiths, could not work without slipping back into the capital. The case of Antoine-Nicolas Landeux, who served five years of hard labor as an accomplice to burglary, is a particularly vivid example (with a surprise ending) of the way surveillance of the high police generated continuous illegal movement (see map, p. 96). It is a case that also demonstrates the little interest of village officials in keeping surveyed people from wandering off.

Landeux never appeared in Laon after his release from Brest in January 1817; arrested in Paris that September, he spent two months in the Bicêtre prison before reaching Laon under gendarme escort in December 1817. At

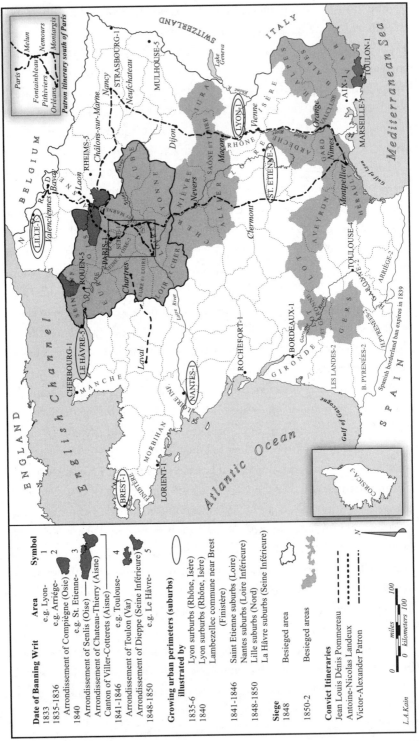

Date of Banning Writ **Area** **Symbol**
1833   e.g. Lyon-   1
1835–1836   e.g. Arriége-   2
Arrondissement of Compiègne (Osie)
1840   e.g. St. Etienne-   3
Arrondissement of Senlis (Oise)
Arrondissement of Chateau-Thierry (Aisne)
Canton of Viller-Cotterets (Aisne)
1841–1846   e.g. Toulouse-   4
Arrondissement of Toulon (Var)
Arrondissement of Dieppe (Seine Inférieure)
1848–1850   e.g. Le Hâvre-   5

**Growing urban perimeters (suburbs)
illustrated by**
1835-6   Lyon surburbs (Rhône, Isère)
1840   Lyon surburbs (Rhône, Isère)
   Lambezellec commune near Brest
   (Finistère)
1841–1846   Saint Etienne suburbs (Loire)
1848–1850   Nantes suburbs (Loire Inférieure)
   Lille suburbs (Nord)
   La Hâvre suburbs (Seine Inférieure)

Siege
1848   Besieged area
1850-2   Besieged areas

Convict Itineraries
Jean Louis Dénis Pommereau
Antoine-Nicolas Landeux
Victor-Alexander Patron

L.A.Kain

Surveillance of the high police, 1830–1848

his arrival, Laon's mayor wrote the ministry of police that "this individual, knowing no one, being a simple laborer, and having no means of existence," should be reassigned to Paris, his birthplace. The youngster disappeared from Laon days later. He was back in Bicêtre in the winter of 1818 and then returned to Laon, again under gendarme escort, on 30 April 1818. The mayor put Landeux to work repairing a promenade in town, an activity that would seem ideal for surveillance purposes. Landeux was gone days later. Learning of his disappearance from other sources, the prefect of the Aisne, for whom Landeux had become an embarrassment, complained to the mayor that he had "reason to believe you were not observing the prescribed measures for this class of men with the desired exactitude." When asked to furnish a description of the man, the mayor gave his age as thirty-three (he was twenty-six), his eye color as blue (his eyes were brown), and his face as thin and heavily lined (*fortement grâvé*), whereas his release papers describe a man marked by smallpox, missing an eyebrow, with a large scar above the right eye, and the right side of his face "entirely scarred by burns" that extended to his arm.[63]

Landeux could not get lost in a crowd. Approximately one year later, in April 1819, he was again returned by gendarmes to Laon after a stay in Bicêtre. Back in Paris in May, he was arrested and returned to Laon by gendarmes in June 1819. After quitting Laon for Paris later that month, he was arrested in September 1819 and detained for six months in familiar surroundings: the Bicêtre prison. He continued to move between Laon and Paris, with stints in Bicêtre, from 1822 to 1824. Yet at some point he found work and companionship in Laon. A document of 1836 listing the names, livelihoods, and addresses of surveyed people in the town mentions "Landeux, Antoine-Nicolas, stone-cutter [*équarrisseur*] in Laon, age forty-eight, supports himself, married in Laon."[64]

Local officials had a strong incentive, and the bureaucratic means, of thwarting the system of residential assignment and delivering themselves of burdensome strangers.[65] Such was the unlucky fate of Jean-Louis Pommereau, a former priest who was assigned in 1823 to the town of Gallardon, near Chartres, after serving one year and a day in the Poissy prison for begging and vagrancy (see map). The elderly Pommereau had no cure and it is not clear where he lived in Gallardon. In July 1825, he was discharged from a hospice for paupers in Chartres, where he had been living for some time. Soon gendarmes seized him on the road in Gallardon and conducted him out of the department. "Having a passport delivered by the mayor of Chartres to go to Laval by a fixed route . . . he was arrested going in the opposite direction." Questioned in Laval by the prefect of Mayenne, Pommereau observed "that he had done nothing contrary to the laws that might motivate his expulsion from the department."[66]

Surveillance of the high police sought to transform postrevolutionary France into a tidy world of static and watched people with files. Instead, the system produced errancy and anonymity. In 1830 the director of the Gaillon prison wrote the prefect of the Eure about the indefinite internment of ban-breakers there. "Almost none of the orders in question [for detention] indicate the nature of the punishment which resulted in surveillance, or its length." The prisoners were going mad from the hopelessness of their circumstances. "They support the first year of their detention rather well, but after this, tormented, irritated, knowing not what to do, to whom to appeal, what authority to petition to recover their liberty, they surrender to ennui and die."[67]

Women under surveillance became the object of harassment by administrators who used their surveillance power as a way of getting at prostitutes. The sale of sex was legal, but breaking the ban was not. In September 1824, Marie-Louise Rayenoire, or Renouard, age twenty-three, left the Gaillon prison, where she had spent five years for an unspecified crime. She was assigned to the village of Beville-le-Comte, the home of her parents; she soon received permission to resettle in nearby Chartres, the home of her mother's sister Françoise, a seamstress. In December 1824, the mayor of Chartres complained to the prefect that Marie-Louise "had just augmented the number of women of ill repute in the town." After the seamstress denounced her niece as a jezebel, the girl was reassigned to Béville and sent there under gendarme escort. She returned to Chartres two days later. On 3 January 1825, gendarmes arrested her on the stoop of a lodging house with Manuel, gardener to the mayor of Ouville. The girl told her captors, "This is my *pays,* you cannot keep me from coming here; you will put me back in prison and you will see, I will always return. Prison does not scare me." Nearly one year later, in December 1825, the police commissioner of Chartres arrested her for breaking her ban; she was "notably engaged in the most complete prostitution."

She landed in the Chartres prison "to be retained there administratively," at which her trace vanishes.[68]

Surveillance of the high police shaped the purge mentality that developed in France during the 1820s and 1830s. The power exerted by the state over surveyed bodies made it possible for officials and members of the public to imagine a general sweep of ex-convicts. The idea of gathering up surveyed bodies and depositing them outside the country extended from the logic of the existing surveillance system. Administrators throughout France would not have pressed for the deportation of thousands of former inmates—people who were not serving sentences—had there not been an extant framework for moving surveyed bodies around at the state's convenience.

Ministers of the interior in 1819 and 1827 called for the deportation of *forçats libérés*.[69] In Loiret, where such people were banned from public works *(ateliers de charité)*, the general council suggested in 1821 that forced colonization offered the "sole effective means" of guaranteeing ex-convicts a means of subsistence.[70] In 1826, forty-one departmental councils voiced support for the deportation of *forçats libérés* at ministerial prompting.[71] In 1829 and 1834, councils in the Nord and in Finistère adjusted to the impossibility of an overseas venture by proposing "sites of refuge" for the internment of surveyed people on domestic soil.[72] Legislative petitions of 1830, 1839, and in 1841 called for the deportation of ex-convicts. The petitioner in 1841, a Dr. Bréon, judged French Guiana "eminently appropriate for the undertaking."[73]

Changes to the surveillance system during the revision of the Criminal Code in 1832 altered the relationship between administrators and surveyed people. Ex-convicts then acquired the ability to move from their assigned towns after notifying the police three days in advance.[74] The new freedom of surveyed people to move around raised the question of what sort of passport and what funds they would use on their journeys. At the time, the state accorded traveler's aid *(secours de route)* to poor travelers during compulsory trips—men leaving prison, paupers forcibly returned to hometowns, and foreigners expelled from France.[75] Yet in the case of paupers soliciting funds for voluntary travel, prefects were urged to be miserly. "It does not suffice for the person seeking travel funds to be really indigent to obtain *secours de route*. It is necessary that affairs of personal interest call him to the place that he desires to go, that the displacement be judged necessary, that it be useful to him, that it offer the possibility of an amelioration of his condition." The food stipend should not be accorded to people whose lives were sure to be as miserable at their destination as at their point of departure.[76]

In 1833, the minister of the interior forbade prefects from granting surveyed people traveler's aid: they became a subclass among the indigent whose lack of future prospects and past transgressions made them undeserving of state support when they journeyed to new assigned locations.[77] They were destitute, pointless wanderers who were forbidden to eat at state expense while begging remained illegal.

After 1832 the ministry of the interior shifted its tactical approach to surveyed bodies. Before the reform, these people were assigned residences, constrained to reside there, and banned from the rest of the country. The 1832 reform called an end to that individualized banning system. Thereafter the administration would apply a list of spatial interdictions to the whole of the surveyed population to control their movement (see map, p. 96).[78] Only men from the ports had hitherto negotiated categorical spatial bans, because of the still-active 1806 Napoleonic decree. After 1832, all surveyed people and not merely one category among them contended with a forbidden zone that grew immensely, to swallow every major French city, many industrial centers, and whole departments over the next two decades.

In 1833, the region banned to surveyed people included not only Paris but also the whole surrounding department of the Seine; it included the cities of Lyon, Marseille, Bordeaux, Lille, Strasbourg, and Nantes and the ports of Brest, Toulon, Rochefort, Lorient, and Cherbourg.[79] Two years later, the forbidden zone widened to include Aix-en-Provence and six Lyon suburbs (La Guillotière, La Croix Rousse, Vaise, Caluire, Sainte Foy, and Oullins). Beginning in 1835 and for the duration of the civil war in Spain (1835–1839), surveyed people were forbidden to reside in five southeastern departments near the Spanish border.[80] In 1836, the ministry of the interior widened the cordon around Paris by banning surveyed people from the adjacent departments of Seine-et-Oise and Seine-et-Marne. That year, surveyed people were banned from living near the palaces of Versailles, Fontainebleau, and Compiègne in the absence of special administrative authorization.[81] In 1840 the forbidden zone increased to include Corsica, but only for Corsicans; the commune of

Lamberec near Brest in the department of Finistère; several communes in the Department of Isère that seemed too close to Lyon; the mining town of Saint Etienne in the Department of the Loire; the arrondissement of Chateau-Thierry and the commune of Senlis, which were near the royal hunting lodge at Compiègne.[82] In 1841, the ministry of the interior created a safety perimeter around the mining town of Saint Etienne by banning three suburbs—Valbonite, Montaud, and Outrefurens—to surveyed people.[83] By April 1846 the forbidden zone had absorbed Toulouse, an additional suburb of Saint Etienne (Beaubrun), four suburbs of Nantes, greater Toulon, and all of Algeria (for the French and Maltese).[84]

As the forbidden zone expanded, administrators in other towns and departments pressured the administration to widen the ban.[85] In 1845 the chamber of commerce in Le Havre put its case to the minister of agriculture and commerce in the hope that he would raise the matter with the interior minister. The building of a railway from Rouen to Le Havre "will cause many thousands of English and French workers to crowd into Le Havre; among this unenlightened population, who are susceptible to obeying evil impulses, the presence of *forçats libérés* cannot fail to carry a dangerous ferment—all the more so, because the communes that surround Le Havre are without a means of surveillance and policing."[86] Among the more remarkable elements of this petition is the asymmetry between the alleged peril and the merchants' request. Here the danger is said to lie with the presence of *forçats libérés,* ex-convicts from the naval prisons, who would insinuate evil among a crowd of alien workers including people from other parts of France and Englishmen, who were regarded by the town's elite as foreigners in equal measure. But the chamber of commerce did not seek to ban *forçats libérés* from entering Le Havre and surrounding towns; rather, the merchants sought to ban the whole category of surveyed people. Surveillance of the high police created a single category out of a diverse group whose actual offenses might be republicanism, labor organizing, vagabondage, or attempted murder. Yet in its petition the chamber of commerce reduced all surveyed people to a single figure, the *forçat libéré,* who was a pastiche of elite anxieties.

The growth of the forbidden zone did not arise merely from a desire to rid cities of irredeemable riffraff. During the monarchy of Louis-Philippe

(1830–1848), surveillance became a weapon against political militants. The 1830s and 1840s in France were years marked by worker insurrections, the founding of republican societies, violent plots against the government, and attempts to kill the king. It was after the rising of silk workers in April 1834, after linked revolts in Paris and other towns, and following an attempt on the life of the king by Giuseppe-Marco Fieschi, a ban-breaker residing illegally in Paris, that the forbidden zone expanded so dramatically.

Surveillance became a tool for destroying the republican opposition by dispersing its members and by subjecting militants to amplified police scrutiny over a period that might endure the whole of their lives. From August 1835 to January 1836, the Chamber of Peers, acting as a court of last resort, used surveillance of the high police against dozens of members of the Society of the Rights of Man, who were convicted of attempting to overthrow the government in Lyon and other towns as part of a coordinated revolt. In most cases, the court imposed lifelong surveillance on defendants with prison terms ranging from five to twenty years. In August 1836, after the discovery of a clandestine gunpowder factory run by affiliates of Auguste Blanqui's communist club, the Society of Families, the criminal court in Paris sentenced club members to prison terms ranging from four months to two years, fined them, and imposed two years of surveillance on most.[87] Participants in the attempted coup d'état of May 1839, organized by the Society of Seasons, the new clandestine army of Blanqui and Armand Barbès, received prison sentences ranging from seven to fifteen years, followed by lifelong surveillance.[88] During the monarchy of Louis-Philippe, surveillance became a calvary of the left, from which amnesty offered no relief. Amnestied prisoners were arrested in May 1837 for breaking their bans when they tried returning home to Lyon.[89] Blanqui, who was sentenced to death, then to deportation, and amnestied in 1844, described his life as a surveyed person in Blois as "the lot of a leper in the Middle Ages."[90]

As a measure unworthy of political dissidents, surveillance aroused indignation among deputies on the left and right during the 1834 debate in the Chamber of Deputies about the law on associations. The law subjected meetings of fewer than twenty people to retractable police authorization, toughened existing criminal law against participants in illicit gatherings, and transferred jurisdiction over "plots against the security of the state" by such groups (without defining what a plot was) to the Chamber of Peers.[91] Both traditional royalists who remained attached to the Bourbons and republicans protested the use of surveillance to punish crimes of opinion. The poet Alphonse de Lamartine insisted unsuccessfully that "surveillance of the high police be effaced from article 1. This would create a political inquisition [and] . . . legitimate quotidian ostracism; it would invent a new mode of existence for citizens, an intermediary status between liberty and prison! It would assimilate political crime to one of those infamous crimes that is branded by surveillance." The deputy Justin Laurence denounced this measure as "nothing other than simple banishment as it existed in the past, the interdiction to live in some portion of the country," to which another member replied, "It is a type of deportation."[92]

The republican opposition exposed the voluntary method of residential assignment as a hoax. In 1836 the prisoner Eugène Rixain, a republican from Clermont, refused to comply with the demand of the minister of the interior that he choose a residence for himself; at his refusal, the administration brought criminal charges against him for breaking his ban. Rixain became a vagabond without moving. When prosecuted before the correctional tribunal in Troyes, and later before the royal court in Paris, the twenty-seven-year-old former law student explained his refusal to choose. "I chose my home town [Clermont], where my family is. That residence was forbidden to me, in addition to eight departments, and three arrondissements. I took this freedom to choose for a bad joke, a legal mystification, and I did not want to submit to it." In refusing to choose, he wished to "oblige the courts to pronounce on an interpretation of the law that degenerates for many of my comrades into veritable persecution."[93]

After the reforms of 1832, surveyed people contended with a forbidden zone that might include every place they had ever known. Large towns, the most likely places of finding work and anonymity, were barred to them. Chased from village to village, they moved in and out of prison and changed their names to escape the system for a while. Victor-Alexandre Patron was a teenager of unknown parents living in Paris with his guardian, the widow Loiseau, when his surveillance troubles began (see map, p. 96). In October 1836, the boy wrote to the widow about his misadventures. He then awaited expulsion from Nemours, southeast of Paris. The prefect had just learned of the new decision to exclude surveyed people from departments around the capital.

> I am again forced to wander and choose a new residence, again without traveler's aid, without a cent or a suitcase . . . after being tossed [*saladé*] from town to town, from Paris to Montpellier, from Montpellier to Nancy, from Nancy to Meaux and from Meaux to Nemours. Now I am forced to leave Nemours. . . . Everywhere I go I am received—dare I say it—like a *forçat libéré,* expelled, chased, and even escorted out of town by the gendarmerie in places. . . . I am going to Montargis where I expect to be received in the same manner.[94]

Patron's letter of October 1836 illustrates the combined effect of the widening spatial ban, the reformed passport system, and the withholding of traveler's aid. The modified surveillance system had evolved into a method of instantaneous expulsion. The granting of free passports without a subsidy allowed mayors to shunt undesirables to new destinations the moment they appeared. Freedom of movement on request had become compulsory movement at the will of officials, who secured their administrative terrain by keeping these people moving, and making them someone else's problem.

Surveyed people became so indistinct from actual inmates to administrators that they began receiving matriculation numbers on exiting prison. Patron, "the liberated convict inscribed at your ministry under the number 2225," vanished in 1838 to escape the system.[95] Under a new name, he lived on Paris's Rue de Mouffetard until he ran afoul of the law six years later and resumed life as a surveyed person. As Charles-Emile Vérard, he was sentenced in 1845 to three months in prison and five years of surveillance for vagabondage. In the La Force prison, he gave his occupation as cobbler.[96] It was an apt livelihood for a man who walked 450 leagues through thirty-two departments during the eight months he spent out of prison in 1836, when he began life under surveillance.[97]

The forbidden zone, in a period of rapid expansion during the 1830s and 1840s, entered a new phase of development with the revolution of 1848. In March, the ministry of the interior banned surveyed people from

Rheims and Mulhouse as a temporary measure aimed at containing popular insurrection.[98] In June the ministry responded to "grave events that have recently afflicted the town of Rouen" with a similar provisional ban.[99] When Paris was placed under a state of siege in late June 1848, the cordon around the capital widened to include a thirty-kilometer perimeter, swallowing parts of Picardy and Normandy.[100] In October, the industrial town of Lille, already banned to surveyed people, acquired a safety cordon that enveloped the suburbs of Wazemmes, Les Moulins, Fevis, la Madeleine, and Saint André.[101] A decision of November 1848 banned "*forçats,* reclusionary prisoners, and correctional convicts subject to surveillance" from Le Havre, presumably to the euphoria of leading citizens.[102] Soon French courts began applying surveillance of the high police to minor offenders with unprecedented zeal. In 1848, correctional courts applied surveillance of the high police to 1,786 people; the same courts applied it to another 2,358 in 1849 and 3,540 more in 1850.[103]

Beginning in June 1848, with the suppression of the workers' rising in Paris, the government of the Second Republic used the state of siege as a frequent weapon against rebels, potential and actual. Paris and the eleven departments comprising the capital's territorial military division—the Seine, Seine-et-Oise, Oise, Loiret, Loir-et-Cher, Eure-et-Loire, Seine-et-Marne, Seine-Inférieure, Eure, Yonne, and Aube—were placed under a state of siege on 13 June 1850. Two days later, the town of Lyon and the five departments within its military division—Isère, Drôme, Ain, Rhône, and Loire—were placed under a state of siege that endured until March 1852.[104] In September and October 1851 the departments of Ardèche, Nièvre, and Cher were placed under a state of siege.[105] Through these declarations, the government aimed to destroy the burgeoning social democratic movement with the expeditious mass arrest of alleged militants by the army, the banning of newspapers, and the dispersal of public gatherings.[106]

The state of siege, a weapon that was supposed to preserve the republic, became the instrument of its demise. The coup d'état of 2 December 1851, launched by then president Louis-Napoleon Bonaparte, opened with the declaration of a state of siege in Paris and in the eleven departments of the first military division; the same decree dissolved the National Assembly and the Council of State. In the weeks that followed, thirteen other departments were placed under a state of siege. The use of the army to put down armed opposition to the coup had the effect of expanding the rural revolt in southeastern France, as peasants took up arms in response to news of repression elsewhere. Though the state of siege gave momentum to the peasant rising, it led to the arrest of 26,885 people by the army, wrecked socialist village networks, and benumbed peasant radicals, who abandoned their struggle in the face of such reprisals.[107]

The state of siege had the effect of subjecting every pauper, unemployed laborer, and person with a criminal record to a version of surveillance of the high police. Ministerial circulars of February and April 1850 forbade prefects and mayors to issue passports "to Lyon and other departments under the state of siege to people who are denuded of resources, without work, or suspect." *Forçats libérés* who had paid a fee and hitherto avoided surveillance were banned from besieged regions.[108]

The state of siege emboldened reactionary journalists and civic leaders to call for broader regional bans against surveyed people and to clamor for their deportation overseas. In late June 1848, the provisional government passed an extraordinary decree sending barricade fighters who survived the slaughter of the June Days in Paris to Algeria. In response, an unsigned editorial in the *Courrier du Havre* approved heartily of the purge but regretted its limited scope. "We have only one regret, which is that the introduction of this penalty to our Codes [*sic*] is only provisional and limited to the June insurgents. Why is it not permanent? Why should it not replace police surveillance for ex-convicts? . . . The June Days have showed beyond a doubt that ex-convicts should be expelled from European society."[109]

Reactionary discourse of this period, whether it originated with the administration or with ordinary citizens, frequently confounded ex-convicts and revolutionaries. From the standpoint of officials, the equation of socialist militants with ex-convicts discredited the former politically while recasting violent repression against such people, whether they were armed or not, as a proportional response to rapine maniacs.[110] This discourse had other consequences, however. In this editorial from the *Courrier du Havre,* the depiction of the June insurrectionists as ex-convicts was not mere slander, but also justified a demand for transporting the whole category of surveyed people to Algeria——tens of thousands of people, who were for the most part ordinary offenders, and included extremely minor offenders. After the legislature of the Second Republic resolved to transport Parisian insurrectionists, whom the panicked bourgeoisie depicted as (and believed to be) criminal riffraff, the transportation of ex-convicts who had no known involvement in revolutionary happenings could seem a rational response to current events.

Shortly after assuming emergency powers, President Louis-Napoleon Bonaparte issued a decree on 8 December 1851 calling for the arrest of members of secret societies and surveyed people who broke their bans. Both groups were to be punished with transportation for up to ten years to Algeria or French Guiana, where they would live under martial law and a hard labor regime while "deprived of their civil and political rights."[111] This decree supplied the government with a framework for handling the 26,885 people arrested by the army after the coup d'état of 2 December. The mixed commissions of soldiers and administrators that judged prisoners in 1852 sentenced 9,581 people for political offenses to transportation to Algeria and another 329 to French Guiana. The newfangled courts also made expansive use of surveillance of the high police. Of people sentenced to transportation to Algeria, 5,032 were to live as surveyed people in assigned Algerian towns; another 4,549 were to be imprisoned in fortresses; 5,194 were sentenced to surveillance in domestic France at locations of their (alleged) choosing; and 2,827 were placed under surveillance in France at sites assigned to them outright. In 1853 the revision of sentences decreased the number of people in Algeria while enlarging the number under domestic surveillance. At the end of September 1853, there were 3,006 transportees in Algeria of one sort or another and 8,875 militants under surveillance in France.[112]

The decree of 8 December 1851 that helped to organize these punishments also introduced a long-awaited and permanent change to the surveillance system that acquired new urgency in the struggle against socialist militants. The December decree struck down the surveillance reform of 1832 and revived the Napoleonic system of assigned residence, now backed by the threat of transportation. By this decree, 3,076 people who broke their bans disappeared into Algeria and French Guiana from 1851 to 1870.[113] Jurists during the reign of Napoleon III (1852–1870) depicted the new mode of exercising surveillance as a prudent reform, without noting that it originated with an emergency decree following the dissolution of the government by the former president and actual emperor. In his commentary on the Criminal Code, Antoine Blanche remarked: "It was not until the month of December 1851 that the government had the happy inspiration to replace [the system of 1832] with measures more rational and in conformity with the exceptional situation of convicts subject to surveillance of the high police."[114] In a similar spirit, the legal scholar Henri Pascaud presented the new manner of punishing ban-breakers—transportation under conditions of martial rule—as consistent with the past meaning of surveillance. "The punishment of surveillance is independent of the manner in which it is exercised."[115]

Felons of the nineteenth century and many others endured what the horse thief Dezailly described as "a sort of misfortune attached to his person." Dezailly's person was his experience of his own body, because of the dread he inspired when strangers looked at him, and because of the many captivities he underwent, notwithstanding his talent for flight. Dezailly exhorted the minister of the interior to "render a citizen to society," implying that he thought of himself as a citizen and knew of a society to which he belonged. Society was Etreux, his hometown, among a group of relatives and friends that included the mayor. Featureless depictions of men belonging nowhere and "denuded of all pecuniary resources" in administrative directives and ex-convict files fail to capture the complexity of the lives that the archive occasionally hints at. What is certain, however, is that the entry of a convict into one of the work prisons of France, and even the journey there, marked passage into an unusual dominion of state authority that cannot be defined spatially, because it moved with the man and followed him into freedom.

Leaving prison meant crossing into a version of free life that administrators choreographed so as to estrange people from the world they knew and where they were known. The system hinged on removing people from contexts where friendships and allegiances might overrule the state identity paper. From the perspective of the surveyed person, the system withdrew the *pays,* the local geography of belonging, in the words of the Renouard girl. So completely did surveillance subordinate the world to the paper certificate that a man could be arrested while walking home, as was case for the elderly Pommereau, because the document he carried required travel in another direction. There was a further element of this system. The bodies of watched people belonged to the police. Target had suggested as much when comparing surveillance and slavery. The same assumption underlay plans to move these people around, to gather and disperse them, to impede their travel, and to run them out of town.

Although the surveillance system began with ex-convicts from the ports in mind, the experience of surveyed people with minor criminal records suggests that the dread associated with the *forçat libéré* in early nineteenth-century France resulted from administrative procedures rather than from moral taint associated with particular types of crime. As a conjuration of the surveillance system, the identity of the *forçat libéré* proved highly transferable. In 1836 the petty thief and vagabond teenager Patron noted his treatment everywhere "as, dare I say it, a *forçat libéré*," with surprise. The application of surveillance to dissidents and insurrectionists in the 1830s and 1840s—who thereby became *forçats libérés* in a sense—coincided with the envelopment of many thousands of poor people by the same measure for petty offenses, who thus acquired the same generic identity.

The coda to the entangled nineteenth-century history of republicans and ex-convicts took the form of a ringing silence on the part of advocates for transported political prisoners about the fate of transported felons. The protagonist of Victor Hugo's novel, *Les Misérables* (1862), Jean Valjean, is an ex-convict from the work camp of Toulon during the Restoration and the July Monarchy. In the preface to the novel, written from the present day, Hugo does not mention that such people and such places had moved out of France and into the empire. The shipment of hard labor convicts to Guiana, as we shall see in the next chapter, began in 1852, a decade before Hugo published his book. The same silence about criminals recurs in Emile Zola's novel, *Le Ventre de Paris* (1882), which chronicles the transportation of a political prisoner who escapes from Devil's Island and returns to Second Empire Paris. In Zola's version of Guiana, one decade before the Dreyfus Affair, Devil's Island is the exclusive scene of punishment, while the mainland, through which his hero escapes, is wild and empty of people. Concern about the conflation of political prisoners with felons hardened into a memory of Devil's Island that screened the continent, where events passed without criticism.

Jurists at the turn of the nineteenth century became infatuated with the power of law to deactivate the legal person by canceling filiations and conjugal bonds. Changes to the status of criminals short of civil death—whether the change was provisional, in the case of legal interdiction, or permanent, in the case of civic degradation—equally impeded the capacity of a man to speak, to choose, and to enter into agreements. Surveillance of the high police duplicated the effects of the other punishments. He who is banished forever from his wife and family cannot be a patriarch; he who is a stranger everywhere cannot function as a citizen. Yet surveillance achieved these ends by different means and in a different idiom. While severing bonds and scattering people through the manipulation of bodies in space, administrators insisted that people submit to the system as an expression of choice. It was in the capacity of a volitional subject that surveyed people appeared to the authorities of the random village and (when the system changed) moved on the next day to another one. Patron's voyage through thirty-two departments was voluntary travel in official protocol, even when he walked from place to place under gendarme escort. In the case of Patron and others like him, the supposedly elective nature of the journey made it possible to withhold traveler's aid and hence sustenance. The system presumed that the bodies of surveyed people did not belong to them. Yet it moved those bodies around by simulated acts of will, animating each with the voice of freedom.

CHAPTER 5

Idea for a Continent

"A FTER HAVING OCCUPIED OURSELVES so intently with making the races of animals better and more beautiful . . . is it not shameful to have so neglected the race of man?"[1] For the legislator and physician Pierre-Jean-Georges Cabanis, the aim of studying man was to remake him. In 1796 he proposed to revamp the national project of human regeneration. What began in 1789 as a legal and political project should become a scientific one.

Under the influence of Cabanis, a motley assortment of scientists including linguists, zoologists, and physicians founded the Society for the Observation of Man under the Consulate.[2] In 1800, the group launched the applied science of *anthropologie* with an exploratory voyage to the South Seas. Preparations for the voyage were in tune with the society's Baconian ambitions. The two geographers, two astronomers, three botanists, six zoologists, two mineralogists, five gardeners, five artists, three physicians, and one pharmacist aboard the *Géographe* and the *Naturaliste* could avail themselves of every imaginable scientific instrument. As floating versions of the Institut national, the country's new learned society, the ships each carried a library of major scientific works and travel accounts.[3] Heavy with reference volumes, *anthropologie* sailed under Captain Nicolas Baudin for Australia and disaster.[4] The sailors died of scurvy while aboard ship, dysentery when they left it. The captain died on Mauritius in 1803, never returning to France.

Although Captain Matthew Flinders reached Tasmania before the French, scientists at the Institut still regarded the Baudin mission as a successful voyage of discovery. Experts who reviewed the expedition's findings especially praised the work of François Péron, a one-eyed sergeant from the Army of the Rhine and a doctor-zoologist in training. While Péron showed astonishing pluck as a specimen collector, his greatest gift to science lay elsewhere. During his convalescence in Sydney from June to November 1802, Péron encountered a new model of colonial society—convict New South Wales—that rose to the aims of the new human science.

"On this distant soil . . . all races are improved."⁵ The antipodes enhanced imported humans and animals by different means. The air and soil beautified the horses and merino sheep while violence refined the human organism. Péron noted with approval that convicts faced hundreds of blows of the lash "without trial and on the simple order of an agent of police." Every form of brutality that existed in New South Wales figured in Péron's account as a technique of species betterment. The young *anthropologiste* especially admired an official he called the chief of police, who relied on garrison troops and a network of convict spies to maintain discipline and repress revolt.

Like Cabanis, Péron understood physiology and law as affiliated fields of inquiry. In his account, the omnipotence of imperial officials and the legal incapacity of Australian convicts were indispensable to the British regenerative experiment. In praise of Péron's work, an expert panel of scientists from the Institut observed: "Never perhaps was there a more shining example of the powerful influence of laws and institutions on the character of individuals and peoples . . . such is the touching spectacle that these new English colonies present."⁶

While the Baudin mission ransacked the South Seas, French legislators debated the future of convict deportation. The antipodean adventures of Péron coincided with debates in the Tribunate over the first book of the Civil Code, "On Persons." The text included an article expressing the government's intention to deport civilly dead criminals. The legislative committee that examined the new code for the Tribunate expressed alarm at the envisaged imperial settlement. According to the government plan, convicts would not be able to exercise basic legal capacities, including the right to marry, in their place of exile. The former revolutionary legislator and criminal prosecutor Nicolas-François Thiéssé observed: "In making them die civilly, [the code] strips them of all they possess . . . in dissolving marriage, it deprives them of the most legitimate and natural means of securing morality and the spirit of family . . . if in the colony they are only given civil rights by exception, the largest number will live in dissolution and debauchery."[7]

The divergent views of Thiéssé and Péron on overseas convict settlements make it possible to recognize unspoken assumptions that animated French blueprints for the penal colony in years to come. Navy officials, legislators, and pundits who promoted convict transportation all described an isolated settlement where convicts as well as liberated men were stripped of their civil and political rights. This was the formula that Thiéssé and other members of the Tribunate refused to countenance in 1801. It also resembled Péron's Australia, which scientists at the Institut praised as an enlightened system of colonization. Ideas that seemed repugnant at the turn of the nineteenth century became untroubling in later decades. The same ideas later inflected decrees and laws from the early 1850s that created the penal colony in French Guiana.

In the view of the Australian historian Colin Forster, French enthusiasts of convict transportation sought a benevolent alternative to the penitentiary under the inspiration of Australia. In Forster's assessment, convict colonies in French Guiana and New Caledonia began with lofty intentions. If French efforts to create a new Australia proved unsuccessful, this arose by accident due to poor soil and a shortage of women. "It proved impossible to find a penal site with anything like the economic potential of the Australian settlements."[8]

It is true that advocates of convict deportation often referred to Australia as their inspiration. But the French imperial model bore no resemblance to the British colony at any moment in its history. The few French travelers who visited Australia saw what they chose to see there. The musings of François Péron offer a characteristic glimpse of wild inaccuracies in French depictions of Australian convict life. Péron's police chief, whom he extolled as an enlightened despot, was drunk Judge-Advocate Richard Atkins, "the ridicule of the community," according to Governor William

Bligh. "Sentences of death have been pronounced in moments of intoxication; his determination is weak, his opinion floating and infirm; his knowledge of the law is insignificant and subservient to private inclination."[9]

What defined early British Australia was not the natural bounty of the earth but instead the legal structure of colonial society, without which no economy could have existed there. In 1801 the legislator Thiéssé spoke presciently about the problem of convicts' legal status when he opposed the founding of a penal colony; as a lawyer, Thiéssé understood that the convicts' legal powers would define the character of any overseas settlement peopled exclusively by such people. Similarly, historians of New South Wales underscore the importance of convicts' legal rights to Australian economic, social, and political life from the moment of the First Fleet's arrival in 1788. In principle, felons in Australia lived under various forms of attaint. According to Blackstone's *Commentaries on the Laws of England,* felons with commuted death sentences (usually for crimes against property) were civilly dead. Transported felons with noncapital sentences were struck with infamy, which meant they could not bring suit or bear witness.[10]

Since the legal handicaps of British felons resembled those of French convicts and ex-convicts, one might expect the structure of early Australian colonial society to resemble French blueprints for overseas convict ventures and later penal settlements in French Guiana and New Caledonia. In practice, however, the legal disabilities of convicts were ignored in Australia until 1820 and circumvented in New South Wales thereafter. In contrast, all French plans for pseudo-Australian ventures viewed the legal incapacity of convicts as a necessary and even highly desirable element of the system.

Historians look to the changing legal structure of British imperial rule, to the legal status of Australian territory, and to eighteenth-century notions of the rule of law when accounting for the breach between antipodean practice and Blackstone's *Commentaries.* To David Neal, Australia's status as *terra nullius*—undiscovered earth, untouched by law—helped the common law of England to take root there as the birthright of all British subjects, including felons.[11] The importance of the rule of law to eighteenth-century ideas of Britishness also helped transported people to recover rights in the colony. Where Neal interprets convict legal rights as a mark of Australia's bond to the imperial center, Bruce Kercher treats the

divergence between Australian and British law as the sign of a loose imperial structure that tightened after the Napoleonic Wars. Against Kercher
and Neal, Alan Atkinson and Christopher Bayly evoke early British rule
in Australia as part of a larger trend toward despotic imperial power. In
this reading, the body of local practices that Kercher calls the "custom of
the country" arose from the extraordinary discretionary authority vested
in military governors by the Crown.[12]

French enthusiasts of the penal colony treated the idea of a felon with
civil and political rights as unthinkable. Yet their stance on the question
cannot be reduced to a mere national quirk. The story of Australia, set
against the French case, suggests that the rights of felons on overseas territory depended on the structure of imperial rule; as that structure tightened, the rights of felons shrank. For the eighteenth-century lawyer
William Eden, British convicts sent to America had been "transferred to
a new country," though Virginia and Maryland remained under the authority of the Crown. (His brother, Robert Eden, was governor of
Maryland.)[13] In the early nineteenth century, Britain moved toward a direct style of imperial rule and thus grew to resemble France in its mode
of governing overseas territory. It ceased to be possible for officials
and members of the public to envisage prospective convict settlements
as detached worlds of law or new countries, following Eden's turn of
phrase.

The French habit of direct imperial rule does not suffice to account for
the character of early nineteenth-century French designs for overseas
convict settlements. Cultural developments within France shaped those
blueprints, as did French imperial legal culture.

First, élan for the penal colony opened from a desire to rid the country
of nominally free people—liberated felons. French plans for convict settlements did not merely project convicts' existing legal handicaps onto
imperial territory. Instead, those plans invariably worsened the legal predicament of ex-convicts to the point of merging the liberated man with
the inmate and subjecting everyone to civil death indistinctly.

Second, a new medical conception of power marked these projects.
Rather than depict the stripping away of rights as a punitive arrangement,
French advocates of the penal colony presented legal handicaps as a form
of moral therapy. Just as Péron imagined human regeneration to require a

police state, so later imperial plans presented the subjugation of convicts as a way of releasing curative administrative power.

Third, the authors of these settlement plans conceived of the empire as a legally exceptional dominion. Convicts, as they moved overseas, would carry law with them; yet new law would transfigure them on arrival. The legal specificity of colonial earth made it possible to imagine ignoring judicial sentences and effacing judicial categories. Only then did it become possible to annex the free man permanently to prison.[14]

François Barbé-Marbois (1745–1837) emerged in the 1820s as the leading opponent of deportation in France. It is tempting though mistaken to assume that his ordeal in Guiana was responsible for this. The bourgeois from Metz who began as Barbé and became Barbé de Marbois on the advice of his protectress, Barbé of the Revolution, Barbé-Marbois of the Directory, imperial Count Barbé-Marbois and finally Marquis de Marbois during the Restoration, served every sovereign from Louis XV to Louis-Philippe. After deserting Napoleon for the Bourbons, he holed up during the Hundred Days in his new chateau in Normandy and wrote a quick book about the plot against George Washington by Benedict Arnold.[15] Thomas Jefferson praised the book for its insight into Arnold's treason.[16] Marbois became the first minister of justice of the Second Restoration government. In October 1815 he launched the White Terror with a sedition bill that punished speech offenses with deportation. The *ultras* in the Chamber fought to punish offenses like displaying the tricolor flag or verbally abusing the royal family with death. Marbois replied by "pictur[ing] the horrors of his own exile in Guiana so vividly that the Chamber was induced to permit deportation, rather than the death penalty, for more offenses than it had intended originally."[17] During the reading of that bill, he drafted another emergency measure reviving provostal courts, military-style tribunals that judged civilians during the Old Regime and again during the reign of Napoleon had judged civilians in regions of France under political siege rule.[18]

In 1816, the king smoothed his dismissal with a marquisate. The provostal courts were suppressed on 16 May 1818. Within months, the spry seventy-three-year-old discovered himself as a liberal peer.[19] Once, Marbois had filled the prisons. Later, as a prison philanthropist, he made a show of tasting the bread of inmates on his inspection tours.

In April 1819, Marbois moved to abolish deportation and replace it with imprisonment. "Condamnation illusoire!"[20] The 110 people sentenced to deportation by the law he wrote and the courts he resurrected were in the Mont Saint Michel fortress anyway. Deportation was too expensive, too lethal, and too impractical. Marbois's initiative in the Chamber of Peers had the double aim of clearing his conscience and of preempting the efforts of high-ranking officials in the navy to create a penal colony in southwestern Australia. It was a fanciful idea that would have required amending the Criminal Code to apply deportation to hard labor convicts. Marbois quoted from Jeremy Bentham to refute Péron and his adepts in the navy; the penal colony could neither rehabilitate the deportees nor deter future crimes. "The hopes of M. Péron have been completely disappointed." He ridiculed the navy for choosing a destination to which it had no claim and which it lacked the sea power to defend: "To indicate New Holland amounts to saying that deportation is impossible."[21]

Ten years later, at the age of eighty-three, Marbois again battled rising support for the penal colony. The idea of deporting *forçats libérés* baffled him. He had never heard of such people. No one he knew had heard of them either. "The name *forçat libéré* is hardly known. . . . I often travel on foot and interrogate other pedestrians . . . most people have never heard the name *forçat libéré.*" To rectify what he took for confusion, Marbois cited statistics for the year 1826 to show that ex-convicts from the port prisons were responsible for a mere 179 of 6,988 cases before the Assizes. Most criminals were first offenders or petty offenders, whom it seemed unthinkable to deport, at least to Marbois. "There are ills to which the best organized society must resign itself when there is no remedy."[22]

What Marbois knew of Australia came from the report of a Tory lawyer, Thomas Bigge, whom the British government sent to New South Wales in 1821 to make recommendations about toughening the system. In common with Bigge, Marbois emphasized the imprudent generosity of Governor Lachlan Macquarie toward ex-convicts. In consequence, liberated felons had overrun the colony and imperiled the free emigrants.

"Freed except for some restrictions . . . insolent and arrogant, they torment the honest and peaceful inhabitants."[23]

To Marbois, a former imperial administrator, the question of the penal colony was most of all an imperial matter. He had been intendant of Saint Domingue until 1789, when planters ran him out of the colony. The destruction of the world's wealthiest slave colony—the birth of Haiti—turned Marbois into an expert on imperial disaster. With Haiti's past and French Guiana's future in mind, Marbois warned in 1828 of a bloody revolt should the French government send convicts anywhere near West Indian slave plantations. A lack of political realism had destroyed the first French empire, and there could not be a second one. A French version of Australia would be militarily insecure, useless at reforming the convicts, repugnant to free settlers, and impossible to administer, except by the most violent means.[24]

In 1830, the naval administrator Basterot responded to Marbois in a series of memoranda to the Dauphin, the country's leading prison philanthropist, about creating a French penal colony in southwestern Australia near the Port of King Georges. "The work of a few English criminals sufficed to conquer for civilization a fifth part of the world and to lay the foundation for an immense empire!" While Basterot hoped to repeat British colonial success, he rejected the centerpiece of the Australian convict system, which was the private employment of convicts by free immigrants and ex-convicts. He answered Marbois's objection to the unwholesome exposure of upright settlers to convicts and ex-convicts by turning the harshest work detail in the British system into the norm of the envisaged French settlement. He praised the mobile frontier work gangs of second offenders in Australia. "As soon as they completed an establishment, the convicts pushed forward to make new conquests in the wilderness. This system was as admirable in its politics as in its philosophy."[25] While seeming to celebrate the rehabilitation of felons, Basterot wrote against those elements of the Australian system that opened onto free life and even prosperity for at least a portion of transported people.

Marbois had hoped that a review of what he took for Australia's defects would dim the enthusiasm that Britain's penal colony seemed to inspire among his countrymen. He miscalculated. If ex-convicts and free people could not live together in Australia, they surely could not coexist in metropolitan France. French critics of Australia inspired deportation fantasists to clarify their objectives. If the problem in Australia lay with a group of ex-convicts who enjoyed excessive freedom, the solution was to reduce it. If ex-convicts and free immigrants could not mix, then felons should be isolated completely.

Nineteenth-century utopian doctrine proved influential to all plans for the settlement of felons overseas. Both Pierre Rosanvallon and Michèle Riot-Sarcey have suggested that it is fruitless to distinguish the aims of so-called utopian socialists from those of the French political and industrial elite in the first half of the nineteenth century. During the Restoration, the legitimating principle of French administrative power, including police power, became social regeneration.[26] The idea of regeneration owed much to early nineteenth-century science, which the philosopher Claude-Henri de Saint Simon (1760–1825) adjusted and popularized. To Riot-Sarcey, the attraction of elites to the creed of Saint Simon developed out of contemporary anxiety about the collapse of the old society of orders and the resulting emergence, during the Revolution, of a mass of individuals free of traditional allegiances.

Saint Simon aimed to reinvent society along the lines of what is recognizably a modern corporation, which he called *société industrielle,* by subordinating individuals to the commands of inspired experts who drew the religious reverence of the populace. He promoted a social ideal that developed in reaction to the legal foundations of postrevolutionary France. The framers of the Civil Code presumed that self-actuating patriarchs would create and perpetuate society through the social bonds they forged between one another, which the law would mediate from the instant of their birth onward. Saint Simon instead pictured society as a machine-man, in which individuals were wheels or springs while a small group of experts acted as mind. To Saint Simon the notion of civil society as a zone of contractual exchange between self-directed individuals was retrograde and harmful. So, too, were the chartered public rights granted by nineteenth-century kings.

> The maintenance of liberty was bound to be an object of primary concern as long as the feudal and theological system retained some of its force. . . . Now, if the vague and metaphysical idea of liberty current

today continued to be taken as the basis of political doctrine, it would tend severely to impede the action of the mass on individuals.[27]

Crucial to the progressive creed of Saint Simon was the notion that "the metaphysical idea of liberty" belonged to a prior phase of history, one of resistance to traditional authorities. The new wisdom, which he regarded as an adjustment to the forces of history, involved maximizing "the action of the mass on individuals." This seemed for good reason to be incompatible with the metaphysical idea of liberty, since that idea became concrete in the legal powers of individuals. By metaphysical liberty he apparently meant all powers vested in the individual either in the form of public rights or civil capacities.

Auguste Comte (1798–1857), who briefly served as the secretary of Saint Simon, applied the scientific language of regeneration to the collective social body. To study the social body became physiology. To act upon it became hygiene. To act freely within it became an anatomical malfunction. "Disorder results promptly whenever some perturbing cause viciously augments the activity of some at the expense of others."[28]

When it became possible to view metaphysical liberty as an impediment to social regeneration, it also became possible to speak of the legal handicaps that expressed a convict's excommunication as the key to his moral recovery. Stripped of those legal capacities, the hygienists might go to work on him unhindered.

This was the explicit program of *La Ville des expiations* (*The Town of Expiations*), a blueprint for a jail town by the mystic Pierre Ballanche (1776–1847), who was a chief influence on Saint Simon.[29] Ballanche began the book in 1820 and never completed it. Fragments appeared in *La France littéraire* between 1832 and 1835.[30] Contemporaries ridiculed Ballanche's town as an "Eldorado for rascals."[31]

The Town of Expiations offers a lively illustration of how French utopianism in the nineteenth century contrived a social ideal that was indistinguishable from social proscription. Ballanche drew his understanding of social regeneration from Charles Bonnet, who invented the term *palingénésie* to describe the regeneration of beings out of divine seeds after predetermined catastrophes that he called revolutions. *Palingénésie* also described the final sprouting of the seeds in heaven, where all organic life attained formal and spiritual perfection.[32]

To Ballanche, there was no possibility of collective regeneration without a long period of penance for a regicide people. With the execution of Louis XVI, the social body died; but it died a criminal. "Thus the contemporary history of man begins with the history of expiation."[33] He understood the Town of Expiations as an instrument of human progress, although his notion of progress seemed to begin with descent to purgatory and in a sense to end there.

Ballanche discovered a method for perfecting society in the legal incapacity of convicts and in the Code pénal des bagnes, the special law of the arsenal prison. In the force of its commands and in its general opaqueness to the public, naval prison law struck Ballanche as a secret code resembling the laws of Egypt under the ancient hierophants, who were the keepers of unwritten divine commands.

> The evildoers in the prisons and the work camps have a code that governs them alone, which they obey blindly, at the instigation of the power that punishes them. So great is the human social instinct and the need for law! Plato once noted the tendency of malefactors to unite as a social body. . . . The unfortunate men among us who have passed outside the laws they have violated fall under other laws that they sanction with their consent; the unknown code that rules them from in the shadows of the prisons and the work camps is also a divine institution, in the sense that it is not the result of a convention, of a contract, but has been founded instead on a primordial law of human nature. . . . Should the tight grip that holds these corrupt men in irons be relaxed little by little, the crude rudiments of a kind of society would be capable of improving and perfecting them. Do not forget that Cain was the founder of the first town. (*PS*, 241–243)

To Ballanche, law was always contrary to nature and thus punitive. "Savage man is not primitive man but degenerate man" (*PS* 296). The Code des bagnes of the arsenal prisons resembled a divine code because it was ancient, nonnegotiable, apparently secret, connected to absolute humiliation, backed by force, and extrinsic to modern life. The law of the prison and the absolute authority of officials there also inspired Ballanche to hope that he might contrive a secret enclave of the same sort.

To accomplish the regeneration of inmates of the Town of Expiation,

Ballanche wanted the French legislature to declare everyone civilly dead on arrival. This seemed to make it possible to subject the townspeople to an exceptional legal code that the legislature would draft and that village authorities, wielding a style of commissarial power, would adjust when occasion demanded (*VE* 73).

Ballanche turned civil death into the basis of social palingenesis in the new town. Village penitents would be initiated to life there with simulated death in an isolation cell called the Tomb. On leaving the Tomb for the Desert—Ballanche's term for the lower town—they would be congratulated for choosing "social excommunication" over "civil liberty, to enter into the fullness of their moral liberty" (*VE* 28–29). To symbolize their exit from the world, all inmates would lose their *état civil*—their family names—on arrival and receive new names for local use. The secret of their old life would be confided to an armband they received on leaving the Tomb and to the roll books of *le dictateur,* who governed the town from inside a skylit granite cube. Ballanche modeled the renaming practice and many other elements of village life on monastic rituals, but the rituals assumed an entirely different significance because of the punitive function of this settlement. Most though not all of the inhabitants would be criminals transferred there by the state. Others would be people fleeing their worldly sorrows. Still others would be the spouses of convict inmates. Whatever the circumstances at their arrival, all villagers would be treated identically. Everyone including the wives would be declared civilly dead.

Guards of the lower hamlets would send weekly reports on the moral progress of the neophytes, called nomads, to the dictator, which he would insert in a register that Ballanche compared to "the Book of Life" (*VE* 25). The book would allow the dictator to decide when a neophyte was ready for promotion to the upper town. But residents of the upper town were no less civilly dead than nomads in the lower one. Artisans would live in a walled commercial district called the *cité* (a medieval term for the commercial zone of a town and for the quarter near a church). Ballanche raised high walls around the workers, "in order to distance the noise and movement of the region," during the day; he locked them in at nightfall (*VE* 12). Because civilly dead people could not contract their labor, the choice of an occupation lay with the dictator and his auxiliaries.

Civilly dead people could not have spouses. The administration would substitute itself for the legal marital bond and regulate contact between the pair by special laws. "The [new] law . . . did not for an instant forget the natural empire of man over woman and of father and mother over children; it respects them, even in suspending them." Civilly dead parents could not claim authority over their children. Instead town administrators would seize their offspring at birth. "The children, whose parents must remain unknown, are called orphans of blood, or children of Providence" (*VE* 75–77).

Sentence lengths had no place in Ballanche's utopia. The future of the Town of Expiations seemed to require that as few people as possible ever leave it. Ballanche imagined that all the hamlets would become fixed residences one hundred years after the founding of the town. The dictator would disappear, as would the prison guards. But the special laws and thus the civil death of all the villagers remained indispensable. Should the laws lapse, the town would "not lose time in perverting itself" (*VE* 81).

In the first half of the nineteenth century, civil death was a real possibility for all the residents of a future French penal colony. Until 1850, the Criminal Code attached civil death to sentences to deportation. Deportation then punished political crimes exclusively, but the extension of this punishment to common criminals might also subject them to its traditional accompaniment. Nonetheless, it remained possible that deportees would enjoy some form of civil life. By article 18 of the Criminal Code, they might recover "the exercise of their civil rights or of some of these rights" at the discretion of the government.

No one who wrote on the penal colony in the first four decades of the nineteenth century imagined doing away with those legal restrictions. Instead, legal incapacities seemed to make possible the convicts' redemption by imperial overseers. Relatedly, sentence lengths and the eventual liberation of convicts could not be reconciled with the idea of administrative power as moral therapy.

During the French debate of the late 1840s on the merits of American-style penitentiaries, Jean-Daniel Bentzien, a merchant from Bordeaux, published *An Exposition of a New System for Penitentiary Reform Based on the Natural Law of Progress* (1846), which he dedicated to the legislature. In June 1852, Bentzien sent a copy of this text, rededicated to Louis-Napoleon Bonaparte, with notes about how his plan for a semicircular penal colony might be adapted for either French Guiana or Algeria. He thought it would be necessary to build at least two such structures, with one for political transportees and another for common criminals. The original semicircular shape might be slightly altered, to become a circle or an ellipse, without weakening the regenerative effects of the architecture.[34]

The creation of a penal colony for hard labor convicts was just one element of a larger reform plan, which in this case evolved under the direct influence of Ballanche's *Town of Expiations* and the work of Charles Fourier. Bentzien wanted all French convicts to lose their *état civil,* their last names, on conviction, which he described rather cheerfully as baptism (under one's first name) by the magistrate. Ex-convicts would recover their last names on release, as surveyed people; the names and the details of their internment would appear on special passports for which Bentzien devised a special administrative cipher.

Not everyone would get their names back. Bentzien wanted hard labor convicts and all recidivists sent to the Atlas Mountains, the unconquered homeland of the Kabyls. In Eugène Sue's novel, *Les Mystères de Paris* (1842–1843), Rudolphe, the savior-prince, rewards an ex-convict called The Slasher for saving his life with one-way travel to the Algerian hinterland as a settler-soldier.

> A person who possesses some extensive allotments in Algeria will make over to me, for you, one of two extensive farms. The lands attached to them are extremely fertile, and in full cultivation; but I must not conceal from you that they are situated at the base of Mount Atlas—that is to say, at the furthermost outposts—and exposed to frequent Arab raids.[35]

There were no French farmers in the vicinity of "Mount Atlas" in 1840. The pioneer whom Rudolphe packs off to Algeria would expiate his crime by fighting locals beyond the last outpost of the French army.

Bentzien grouped the *hommes sans nom* in a semicircular penal farm on a plain radiating from a mountain base, with three surveillance forts on the hills overlooking the settlement. The convicts would be sorted into three arcs, each with a uniform of a different color, to make them easy to track from the mountain forts. Each group would sleep together in a central prison and clear the empty wilderness around them. The first arc, closest to the forts, would contain "the most culpable convicts"—those doing fifteen years to life as well as "the worst subjects of the different work camps." The second and third arcs would contain convicts with lesser sentences. He surrounded the whole settlement with "a cordon of surveillance troupes aided by blockhouses . . . charged with preventing escapes by convicts night and day."[36] Bentzien did not imagine liberating the prisoners. After serving their sentences, ex-convicts would move into *champs d'asile pour les libérés* (fields of refuge for ex-convicts) that lay inside each of these arcs. They would live encircled by blockhouses like the other men. To the extent that the law of progress announced in the title of the work would be active there, inmates could win the favor of building a "little house and garden at certain conditions, to form a small village under the surveillance of a chief," while still inside the penal arcs.[37] Exemplary convicts might move to better arcs "with a certain ceremony," while others slid in the wrong direction.

In his *Notes du Voyage* (1841), Aléxis de Tocqueville described an Algeria covered with blockhouses (always spelled in the German manner). In all cases but one, these were small wooden huts at the periphery of military installations in unconquered regions. In a sole instance, in Philippeville (modern Skikda), then in transition from a military camp to a settler village, Tocqueville found a blockhouse that served as a prison. The town's commander boasted of pinning the head of an Arab to the door of nearby Constantine; he requisitioned the settlers' horses to humble them; and he threatened to send anyone who questioned the order "to the blockhouse *des Singes* (it is an isolated blockhouse on an arid and scorched mountain)."[38] This building, too, probably began as an army outpost.

Bentzien did not bother with the problem of conquest. His frontier beyond the law was not an outside region populated by Arabs and Kabyls. It lay inside the lines of a new martial jurisdiction. The merchant from Bordeaux remade the imperial frontier as an enclosure and pointed the guard posts inward.

Louis-Napoleon announced his intention to found a penal colony for hard labor convicts in a public address of November 1850 while the minister of justice, Eugène Rouher, prepared a bill to accomplish it and formed a commission to choose a site. In February, Prosper de Chasseloup-Laubat, minister of the navy, convened a commission under Admiral Ange-René-Armand de Mackau to choose a location and make recommendations about the organizing principles of the new colony. In July, Mackau's commission chose French Guiana over New Caledonia by a narrow margin.[39]

The commission resolved to create a single convict enclave under government direction that would be impenetrable to outsiders. "During at least the first few years, no element foreign to the penal population should be authorized to mix with this population." Early Australian society informed this plan only as a cautionary tale.

> Although enlightened by the example of the English penitentiary colonies, and disposed to admit the usefulness of dividing convicts into categories . . . the commission is of the opinion that . . . the diverse categories of convicts should be united in the same sphere of action and under a single direction and surveillance in the penitentiary colony.

The commission did not wish to base the new colonial economy on the private ownership of land or on the employment of convicts in private enterprise. In Australia, convicts with special abilities or crafts had been sought out as workmen on arrival. The French commission seemed to acknowledge the wisdom of sorting convicts by their abilities, but the state alone would make use of their labor. The new isolated settlement, consecrated to the use of convicts for public works alone, would remedy the defects of Australian convict society that French writers, following British sources, had singled out for criticism. French Guiana seemed an acceptable site for the new venture because there was sufficient land and few enough people to "accord to the penal establishment a compact territory isolated from the free population."

In only one respect did members of the commission wish to imitate British Australia; they believed it necessary to create a penal out-station equivalent to Norfolk Island. This would be "an additional site, in an insular position, where no colonist will be authorized to reside."

Ex-convicts should be "solicited, by all means at the disposal of the legislator and the administration," to remain in the colony. Since government officials had manifestly ample means at their disposal to adjust the whereabouts of ex-convicts, it is worth assuming that the commission intended all liberated felons to remain in Guiana.

The commission thought there would need to be a modification to civil death. A colony full of people incapable of acquiring property or marrying seemed inconsistent with the activity of "moral amelioration," which the commission equated with "the very spirit of colonization."[40] Yet civil death, in the summer of 1851, was no longer the problem, at least not the principal one. In June 1850, the legislature expanded the number of political crimes subject to deportation and replaced civil death with civic degradation as the auxiliary punishment. At the time this commission convened, in the summer of 1851, civil death applied to hard labor criminals with life sentences, a fraction—25 percent—of the convicts they hoped to deport. But no one on the commission mentioned either legal interdiction or civic degradation, which applied to convicts with limited sentences.

In November of 1851, Antoine-Marie Demante, professor of law at the University of Paris, spoke to the legislature about the meaning of civic degradation and legal interdiction and the magnitude of the rights they removed. He did so to support his argument in favor of abolishing civil death. On that occasion, Demante fondly recalled the Old Regime version of civil death. What troubled him about the new version was the nullification of past marriage bonds, "whose indissolubility is an article of faith for the Christian conscience."[41] Demante would have been content with civil death in its Old Regime form. To this jurist, the existence of civic degradation and legal interdiction made the abolition of civil death possible. Otherwise one might have feared "a regrettable lacuna" in criminal legislation, "to the great prejudice of the social order." These punishments assured that "the good citizens are protected from impure contact with gangrenous members in the exercise of their rights."[42]

That the Mackau Commission bothered to ask "Will the work of the Commission comprehend the entirety of forced labor convicts or just future ones?" is a clue to the administrative culture in which its members operated. To deport men who had not been sentenced to deportation was to violate the dictum that no law should apply retroactively. But the administration in the nineteenth century was legally inviolable.[43] Hence it was reasonable to wonder whether the law should be observed or circumvented. In the end, the commission recommended that the navy lure those convicts who had been sentenced before the new law to volunteer for deportation to Guiana.[44]

After the coup d'état of December 1851 and the publication of the decree transporting ban-breakers and members of secret societies, the navy embraced the principle of voluntary deportation on new terms. Where the Mackau Commission had looked forward to a new law that opened convict volunteer rolls, the navy under Theodore Ducos, Chasseloup's unscrupulous replacement, began enrolling volunteers in anticipation of a new law that the minister did not think would apply to them.[45]

At Toulon, 1,560 men signed up for voluntary deportation to Guiana.[46] The convict Van Neuvetz (no. 4215), sentenced to twenty years for fraudulent bankruptcy, wanted permission to leave with his unwitting accomplice, his mother, who was then serving a fifteen-year sentence in a work prison. "The old woman wants to accompany her only son. She has no support, no relatives in the world. Her three brothers, who might have helped her, have long ceased to exist." Her brother Charles died at the battle of Iéna (1806). Her brother Jean died at the battle of Elchangen (1805). Her brother Antoine died in the hospital, one day after the battle of Montereau (1814) from the amputation of his leg. Her husband died at the battle of Dresden (1813) when a shot blew through both legs. "The supplicant begs you again, Monsieur le Ministre, to let him leave by the next ship."[47] The old woman, despite her entreaties, remained behind. The men boarded the ships without chains, wearing secondhand clothing that the navy bought from dealers in the ports.[48] They wore new metal rings (500 grams) around their ankles that were half the weight of the rings used in the port prisons. There were plenty of old rings in the hold. Each of the first eight ships carried "300 single chains, 100 rings of one kilogram, 100 junction bars, 400 rivets, 1 collection of metal instruments." This continued until early 1854, when the governor of Guiana, Admiral Louis-Adolphe Bonard, announced that he had adequate supplies. The early convoys also carried a few dozen of the old uniforms, which Ducos pictured "[as] a means of repression during the crossing and even in the colony."[49]

The navy evacuated the volunteers with remarkable speed. According to statistics compiled by Jesuit priests, 1,561 men from the camps at Brest, Toulon, and Rochefort arrived in Guiana between March and September 1852 aboard five convoys, along with 194 ex-convict ban-breakers and 174 members of secret societies (see Tables 1 and 2, pp. 227–228). Ducos kept up this pace with an informed indifference to the health risk. He convened a commission in December 1851 to examine questions related to the removal and resettlement of ban-breakers and members of secret societies who were slated for transportation. None of the participants, except Ducos, suspected that convicts from the work camps were soon to be emptied into the empire. At the time, the minister suggested sending six thousand men at once, to which General Defitte, inspector general of the marine infantry, responded by insisting on the certainty of a medical catastrophe. "Every time we send many soldiers at once there is an epidemic. There certainly will be one with two thousand deportees." The confidential minutes of this meeting were read by four people.[50]

In late March 1852, the prince-president promulgated a decree spelling out the conditions of life in the new penal colony. He timed the decree for the departure of the *Allier,* the first convoy of 303 convicts. It became law two years later with minor changes that made explicit what the earlier decree merely implied. The work camps in the metropole would close. Convicts sentenced to hard labor would in the future perform the "most arduous labor of colonization and at all other work of public utility."[51] The new law did not mention French Guiana, but instead made it possible for convicts to be sent there or to any other colony that seemed desirable, with the exception of Algeria.[52]

Every mechanism that had served during the past fifty years to define the convict and the ex-convict against a thing called the *cité,* variously defined as Paris, towns in general, the nation, the citizenry, and life in the sight of the law, would travel with them overseas and organize life in the new settlement. The special maritime tribunal and the Code pénal des bagnes, the special laws of the work camp, would remain in effect there. "The infractions foreseen by articles 10 and 11 [on evasion] and all crimes and misdemeanors committed by the convicts will be judged by the First Council of War of the colony, *functioning as the Special Maritime Tribunal.*"[53]

In keeping with the rules for convicts in French work prisons, the punishment for attempting to escape from the penal colony was two to five years of additional forced labor on top of the original sentence. Convicts with life sentences would face two to five years in double chains instead (art. 10).

The 1852 decree turned civil death, legal interdiction, civic degradation, and surveillance of the high police into the architecture of the new settlement. By the mid-nineteenth century, what had seemed outrageous to the political elite in 1801, a colony of dead men, had come to look like generosity.

> After serving at least two years of their sentence, whether in France or in the colony, convicts of both sexes who make themselves worthy of indulgence by their conduct and repentance can obtain:
>
> —Authorization to work, under conditions to be determined by the administration, either for the inhabitants of the colony, or for the local administration.
>
> —Authorization to contract marriage.
>
> —Land concessions and the ability to cultivate them for their own profit. The concessions will not become definitive except after ten years of occupancy.
>
> A regulation will determine: (1) the conditions under which the concessions will be given, either provisionally or definitively; (2) the extent of the rights of third parties, of surviving spouses and heirs of the recipients of concessions.[54]

Convicts required authorization to contract marriage because they could not marry as a result of either civil death or legal interdiction. They required authorization to farm land for their own profit, because neither civilly dead convicts nor convicts under legal interdiction could exercise property rights or handle money.

The decree seemed to promise some concession of civil rights. "The convicts can obtain, partially or integrally the exercise of their civil rights in the colony. They can be authorized to profit or dispose of all or part of their property." But the emphasis of this decree was on the unusual nature of those concessions. The next paragraph insisted on the general incapacity of all the convicts. Unusual administrative authorizations alone would allow the settlers to make use of the money or property they had in France (art. 9).

According to this decree, land would be granted to them and retracted according to the stipulations of a local regulation that did not yet exist.

Men liberated in the colony with sentences of less than eight years would remain for the rest in exile for an equal length of time. The other ex-convicts were to remain for the rest of their lives (art. 6). Even ex-convicts who were pardoned would need special dispensation to avoid these requirements.

For ex-convicts living in exile in French Guiana, to leave the colony without authorization counted as *rupture de ban,* an infraction that in December 1851 became punishable with transportation to French Guiana. To resolve this problem, ex-convicts who broke their ban by attempting to flee the colony were to be judged by the same military courts that judged the convicts; escapists would face hard labor sentences of one to three years (art. 11).

The law that Ducos did so much to circumvent came two years later, on 30 May 1854, in a form that he could not have imagined. "In the future, the punishment of forced labor will be served in establishments created by imperial decree in one or more French possessions besides Algeria."[55] The law was phrased to legalize the transportation of everyone who had been sentenced to hard labor before its passage. Of the volunteers, the minister wrote in December 1855: "All the convicts detained in the colony know that this law affects them indistinctly, whatever their origin, whatever the date of their conviction."[56]

One day after the transportation law went into effect, the new emperor promulgated its companion piece, a law abolishing civil death, which the Legislative Corps had approved earlier that month. But it had seemed impossible to abolish civil death in France before making sure that everyone subject to it would soon be leaving for the empire.

Remarkably, the law abolishing civil death did not in fact abolish civil death. Under article 3, "the convict subject to a perpetual afflictive punishment cannot dispose of his property, in all or in part, either by donation among living persons or by testament, nor receive anything under this title, except for the purpose of feeding him. All testaments made anterior to his conviction, once it is definitive, are null."[57] Here is the text in the Civil Code that this law was supposed to modify:

> By civil death, the convict loses ownership of all the wealth that he
> possessed; his succession is opened for the profit of his heirs, to whom

his property devolves in the same manner as it would if he were naturally dead and without a will. He cannot receive any succession, nor
transfer the wealth he would have acquired. He cannot dispose of his
property, in all or in part, by donation among living persons or by testament, nor can he receive anything other than sustenance.[58]

The text describing the status of the people who were no longer civilly
dead in the decree of 31 May 1854 replicated the text describing civil death
in the Civil Code; but now the name for this punishment was legal interdiction. Never before had legal interdiction nullified a will written before
the date of a criminal's conviction. This measure, which assured that all
convicts with life sentences would die intestate, was a feature of civil death
that the law of 31 May revived.

Everyone transported before the date of this law remained civilly dead.
Those awaiting deportation sprang to life, such as it was; their spouses
remained their spouses and their children remained their children, whom
they could remember after they disappeared. The only effect of this law
was that the *past* marriage bond, a parochial obsession of the nation's jurists, remained in tact. A convict might contract a new marriage only as
a favor from the government, which might decide to return "civil rights
or some of those rights" removed by legal interdiction in the penal
colony.[59]

Even the law of 31 May abolishing civil death in these terms seemed
too radical to implement. Neither that law nor the law of the day before
emptying the work camps into some colonial hinterland or other went
into effect that year. The Legislative Corps of the Second Empire approved what became the law abolishing civil death on 2 May 1854; it then
awaited approval by the Senate. On 3 May, Napoleon III announced that
all colonies but for Martinique, Guadeloupe, and Réunion "would be
ruled by decrees of the emperor until a sénatus-consulte creates statutes
for them."[60] The colonies that became subject to rule by decree included
French Guiana, Senegal, Gorée, French possessions in India, the Mar-
quesas, the island of Mayotte, Saint Pierre et Micquelon, the island of
Sainte Marie off Madagascar (a detention site for colonials), and all territories that the French might acquire in the future.[61]

In March 1855, the moment seemed ripe, to the emperor if not to the governor of French Guiana, to implement the transportation law and its companion piece, the law abolishing civil death, albeit with certain modifications.[62] In final form, the administrations in French Africa, Oceania, and India were given the choice of deciding whether their hard labor convicts would serve time in the colony or be sent to French Guiana. In the emperor's second and final modification to the transportation law, those ex-convicts who received permission to leave French Guiana were forbidden to set foot on French colonial or metropolitan soil.[63]

The governor of Guiana, Admiral Bonard, opted to enact the transportation law but not the law abolishing civil death after a closed-door interview with the magistrate who headed the judiciary services of the colony.[64] The governor who replaced him, Vice-Admiral Auguste Baudin, implemented the law abolishing civil death two years after taking office, in April 1858, for reasons of expediency. Months earlier, in January 1858, a transportee called Vadard (no. 1346) had sought to "obtain authorization to contract marriage and to continue to reside there." He was the first to make this request out of the more than ten thousand transportees who had come to Guiana since 1852. Confused about how to reply, Baudin asked the magistrate whether he could grant this favor and whether he ought to. He was told that the concession of civil rights was akin to a pardon and that only the emperor had authority in such matters. The 1854 law on transportation specified that a "regulation of public administration will determine ... the disciplinary regime," which made Vadard's marriage a problem of high administration. There was nothing to do but wait for the promised regulation. Vadard, sentenced to forced labor for life, had his sentence commuted to twenty years in 1856. He remained subject to civil death by the old law. Baudin asked for guidance from Admiral Ferdinand-Alphonse Hamelin, minister of the navy. In a long reply, Hamelin explained that the governor might return some civil rights to convicts as a reward for good conduct, but he could not change the manner in which they were punished. Vadard could marry, but he could not live with the woman.[65]

CHAPTER 6

Local Arrangements

$\mathbf{F}$RENCH ADVOCATES for convict transportation projected sealed
nooks of punishment onto abstract stretches of empty ground. The
Mackau Commission claimed to have chosen Guiana because so much
land remained available. As an enterprise that administrators planned to
cordon from the world, the penal colony seemed to require territory that
stood outside human history.

There was, in practice, no such thing as vacant earth. It proved impossible for anyone to envisage land in Guiana without reference to the colony's past and present. The local history of slavery shaped the new convict
settlement, as did the unfolding story of the second emancipation, which
began on 10 August 1848 with the liberation of thirteen thousand people.

The reaction against ex-convicts in domestic France called Guiana's
penal colony into being. Within Guiana, the convict settlement had a different story of origins and served other purposes. It developed out of elite
resistance to slave liberation and became a weapon in that struggle. With
the selection of Guiana as a site for convicts, the legal and spatial architecture of the penal colony as an imperial idea merged with the local *nomos*
of the earth.

During the Revolution, the French political elite turned Guiana into an otherworldly place outside the civic order. In the nineteenth century, other worlds began to accrue inside the boundaries of the colony. In these years there arose a new legal structure for organizing imperial space in Guiana and elsewhere in the form of a permanent exceptional sector or special box. This new framework for imagining and acting on the world did not topple the seasoned doctrine that the whole colonial empire comprised an unusual zone where French public law—domestic constitutional law, laws relating to institutions and suffrage—remained in suspension. That earlier framework allowed special boxes to operate by making it possible for tracts of earth within a given colony to become enduring zones of legal anomaly.

The permanent exceptional sector became an active shaping tool of Guianese legal space during the main phase of Algerian conquest (1830–1847). It would be overstating matters to describe this legal structure as arising uniquely from Algerian frontier violence. As we have seen, the special box figured in unrealized schemes for isolated punitive enclaves that date from the 1820s, before the conquest of Algeria. Work camps in France under the control of the navy became permanent exceptional sectors during the Napoleonic era. Nonetheless, it is plain that Algeria had far-reaching effects on French notions of law, space, and police power well beyond North Africa (as we shall see with particular clarity in the next chapter). During the 1830s and 1840s, as Benjamin Brower observes, "extermination was in the air" to the point that legislators discussed the Algerian conquest as a war of annihilation while scholars examined Arab and Berber extinction prospects.[1] The special box crystallized as a structure of imperial rule around the time that Algeria came to exist in what Olivier Le Cour Grandmaison calls "a permanent state of emergency." In his view, law did not supplant lawlessness in Algeria; instead violence grew a legal carapace. That process began with the royal ordinance of 22 July 1834 placing Algeria under the ministry of war.[2]

During the 1830s, Guiana broke into dissonant legal realities. It became a new world of possibility—a place to scatter with legal spaces of experiment. The fracturing of Guianese legal space resulted from the opposition of legislators, imperial officials, and members of the local elite to slave emancipation. The special jurisdictions that took shape in Guiana during the first half of the nineteenth century contained unusual free people of African descent who could not be made to disappear and whose recognition by the legal order seemed impossible. Guiana stood apart from other French slave colonies because of the unusual rifts in its legal space and because of the story behind the zones that only Guiana contained.

Administrators created the boxes to enclose black people who differed from manumitted slaves and from runaways. These freedmen attained liberty without violating colonial slave law and without having recourse to it. They did not owe their status to the will of masters. They did not become free by criminal defiance. Because their liberty could not be described and hence authorized or punished by slave law, they were seen as an existential menace to the legal order that sustained colonial society. Planters and officials reacted to them as though fending off a lethal infectious disease. By the fact of living outside slave law, Guiana's unusual freedmen resembled everyone after the 1848 abolition of slavery. They were versions of people to come.

The first such group, called *noirs de traite* (blacks from the trade), came to Guiana aboard illegal slave ships that the French navy intercepted. The second group were Boni Maroons, a people descended from Dutch slaves who in the eighteenth century fled Surinam to resettle on French Guiana's western frontier. Beginning in 1836, diplomatic overtures and migratory efforts by the Boni brought them into contact with slaves, planters, and administrators in the French colony. *Marronnage*, or flight, a regular occurrence in all slave societies, counted everywhere as a punishable offense. Yet the Boni had not fled from masters in French Guiana. They were seemingly inviolable descendants of Dutch fugitives.

With the boxing of these unusual freedmen, Guiana became an anomalous world of law among French slave colonies and in the Atlantic world more generally. This occurred just as the settlement based at Cayenne became interlaced with domestic French institutions while developing new institutions of its own and acquiring a new transparency to the public, as did Martinique, Guadeloupe, and Réunion during the 1830s.[3] The French Court of Cassation emerged during the reign of Louis-Philippe as an activist final court of appeal for disputes rising from the so-called "old colonies"—lands that had been part of the French overseas empire

since the Old Regime.[4] Through the 1830 constitutional charter, the legislature acquired the power to move bills as opposed to deliberating on
whatever the king put forward.[5] Imperial affairs entered public legislative
debate for the first time since the 1789 Revolution. In a further affinity
with the Revolution, the legislature dismantled colonial race law as it
affected free people of color. That process began in September 1830 and
ended with the law of 24 April 1833.[6]

The government defined the legal status of the Boni and the *noirs de
traite* at a time when free people of African descent were no longer supposed to comprise a disadvantaged legal category in French colonies.
Guiana's unusual free people were not allowed to benefit from the legal
equality extended by the 1833 law to manumitted slaves and their descendants in Guiana as in other French colonies. Yet the Boni and the *noirs de
traite* cannot be called a new disadvantaged class within Guianese colonial society, either, because they did not exist to it.

The unusual free people were not socially marginal types. They were
taxonomical impossibilities. They belonged to the genus of unrecognized
life forms. Both the Boni and *noirs de traite* embodied a type of liberty
that imperial officials and planters refused to acknowledge. In common
with civilly dead and absent people, they needed to exist to the law to be
placed outside it. Similar nonrecognition tactics affected the two groups.
The Boni and the *noirs de traite* became nonpersons whom imperial officials assigned to remote and artfully configured administrative zones.
They lived in legally constituted time-space capsules that stood outside
what the elite took for reality.

Ira Berlin observes that "the free Negro was an incorrigible subver-
sive" whom slave owners in the United States likened to banditti.[7] Guiana's unusual free people resembled other free groups in the Atlantic
world in the sense of descending from fugitives, arriving by captured vessels, and being disadvantaged and terrifying. Their legal situation nonetheless set them apart from manumitted people elsewhere, Maroons
elsewhere, and even from the ten thousand Africans in nineteenth-century
Cuba called *emancipados,* who left intercepted slave ships to become laborers in conditions "little different than slavery."[8]

The story of special freed people in Guiana before 1848 unlocks a
number of oddities of the later period. First, the experience of people

who lived in special boxes before the abolition of slavery helps to explain why it proved impossible after abolition for administrators and planters to envisage the penal colony as an isolated jurisdiction sealed to colonial society. The same legal structure that enabled the isolation of free people of African descent in anomalous zones ought abstractly to have allowed the navy to cordon off a piece of Guianese forest for a new convict dominion just a few years later. Yet the circumstances of Guiana in 1851 made the isolation of felons unthinkable. From the perspective of the colonial elite, the 1848 decree abolishing slavery turned nearly everyone in the colony into outlaws; planters and administrators understood emancipated slaves as unauthorized creations and regarded them much as they had earlier viewed the Boni and *noirs de traite.*

Guiana's local government responded to abolition by banning emerging life patterns, by dismantling black public life, and even by annulling the family lineages of freed people. The penal colony took shape in Guiana simultaneous to the construction of this new, highly coercive postemancipation legal order. Officials in Paris, guided by planter-administrators on the ground, hoped to mold the new convict venture into a hybrid enterprise that would envelop all of Guiana after slavery; they viewed the new punishment venture as a means of encasing emancipated slaves in new zones of repression.

The early story of unusual freed people would shape Guiana's penal colony in a formal sense. Disciplinary schemes that first arose for use against black people parked in voids of law later became rehabilitative projects for felons. The early history of the unusual freed people haunted the penal colony in other respects. In May 1860 the navy transformed the region around the Maroni River, Guiana's western frontier, into an extraordinary jurisdiction "for exclusive use by the penitentiary administration." The convict fiefdom fell on top of the groups of African descent who had lived in unusual jurisdictions before 1848. Through the penal colony, Guiana's ruined elite, acting from behind the scenes, refurbished the special box.

French Guiana experienced a larger proportional increase in its slave population after France abolished the trade in 1818 than did any other

French colony.[9] Between the 1815 declaration at the Congress of Vienna banning the trade and the July Revolution of 1830, 5,060 Africans disembarked from slave ships in Guiana (perhaps thousands more) who came chiefly from the Bight of Biafra and Guinea Gulf Islands. Of these people, at least 3,215 were *noirs de traite*.[10]

In 1820, Guiana became the destination for all slave ships intercepted by the French navy in African and Caribbean waters.[11] By way of clandestine and captured vessels, the number of slaves in Guiana reached its all-time high of 19,102 in 1831, when there were 3,760 free people, both white and of color.[12] Sparsely peopled and economically irrelevant, Guiana provided an ideal depository for a troubling category of people who could not be classed as persons or sold as things and came from outside the family of nations.[13]

The slave plantation did not become established in Guiana until the nineteenth century. It developed in a political context of insecurity, threatened by slavery's approaching demise. The influx of thousands of captives aboard illegal ships in the 1820s, after France outlawed the trade, led planters to enjoy an interlude of prosperity that peaked in 1834, followed by a rapid decline. The cultivation of cacao and cloves decreased sharply in the later 1830s. Yet even in the best of times Guiana produced negligible quantities of export crops. The colony produced 2 percent of French imperial sugar. The main crop in nineteenth-century Guiana was rocou *(bixa orellana)*, a plant native to the New World. The seeds, which smeared red on the bodies of local Indians, became a yellow dye for French cheese and cloth.[14]

From a legal standpoint, the *noirs de traite* differed from contraband slaves. If you were contraband, someone could buy you. If you were called a *noir de traite*, your value was inestimable (or nonexistent). A liberated captive could not have a price. You were *res nullius*, a thing never owned.[15] According to the Civil Code, "possessions [*biens*] that have no master belong to the state" (art. 713).

The only figure in French slave law who resembled the seized African captive was the so-called *épave*. The 1835 *Dictionnaire de l'Académie française* follows earlier editions in defining *épave* as a juridical term for a lost thing, especially a living thing "with an unknown master or proprietor, said principally of horses, cows, and other beasts." The *droit d'épave* (abolished in 1789) enabled seigneurs in France to seize lost movable things on their domain, including livestock. Objects washed ashore from a shipwreck counted as *épaves maritimes* in the sense of being "thing(s) lost on the waves or tossed there without a master or guardian" and subject to the maritime law of salvage.[16] Only after the abolition of slavery did *épave* lose its original, juridical meaning to become a poetic term for rescued debris from an implied shipwreck. Baudelaire's work *Les épaves* (1866) contained salvaged remnants from his censored masterpiece, *Les fleurs du mal* (1857), a work packed with references to unearthly voyages. Émile Littré's *Dictionnaire de la langue française* (1872–1877) similarly allowed for figurative salvage. "The fortune is lost; he will be lucky to gather a few *épaves.*"

In the colonies an *épave* was a masterless slave seized by the state.[17] During the Bourbon Restoration, *noirs de traite* became slaves of the king on arriving in Guiana. They lived in a state of murderous abandonment that probably surpassed that of other slaves in the colony. In March 1827 a new governor, Vice-Admiral Louis-Henri de Saulces de Freycinet, ordered the transfer of 112 *noirs de traite* from the state plantation at Baduel to the hospital in Cayenne. The group included at least thirty children under the age of ten with dysentery. The official who ran this branch of the local service, Lagotellerie, replied with amazement. He complained about the *journées de nègres* (slave work days) lost by hospitalizing them and about the danger they would pose to the real patients. "Do you not fear, Monsieur le Gouverneur, that this scum will infect the portion of the sick who are inside the same building?"[18]

The enslavement of seized captives by the state ended officially with the law of 4 March 1831, which reiterated the ban on the trade and arranged for the liberation of intercepted Africans after a "work engagement to the government whose duration cannot exceed seven years from the moment of their introduction in the colony, or the moment of their adulthood."[19]

The choice of Guiana as a gathering place for seized Africans shaped its later history. On 6 September 1831 a legislative commission chose Guiana as the destination for all liberated captives. The shunting of *noirs de traite* to Guiana for a decade, which had seemed a boon for the colony, led the requirement of freeing such people to seem all the more calamitous. To diminish the local effect of the new law, officials in Guiana maneuvered to withhold freedom from as many people as they could manage. Not one of the twenty-four hundred captives who reached Guiana from 1818 to 1826 became eligible for release. Only a fraction of those who arrived from 1827 to 1831 attained freedom by the new law. The government in Cayenne seems to have retained everyone else as government slaves.[20]

The navy interpreted the 1831 law with a view to prolonging the Africans' terms of government service beyond the specified limit. In principle, adult captives owed no more than seven years of labor to the state after setting foot on French soil. In 1831, many people had spent years as slaves. Rather than count the toil of slaves toward the work requirement, the navy dated all indentures to the moment the law took effect in each colony. Because of this maneuver, not one of the *noirs de traite* became eligible for release before 1838.

As the moment of liberation drew near, the navy under Admiral Victor-Guy Duperré founded a reserve for *noirs de traite* on the Mana River near Guiana's western frontier and far from settled regions of the colony. From March 1836 to April 1837, the colonial government transferred 477 Africans.[21] Laws applicable to free persons in Guiana including the Civil Code and the Criminal Code did not apply there. African engagés could not exit the enclave during their terms of indenture. Anyone who remained in the zone, free or not, needed to live by the special laws of the depot.[22]

In its isolation from Cayenne, the new settlement expressed the incommensurability of African freedom, achieved without recourse to manumission, with slave society. In its extra-legal structure, it expressed the unwillingness of the imperial state to recognize the Africans as persons. The navy denied them the symbolic identity of self-actuating beings marked with human universality and individual uniqueness. Because they did not count as legal subjects under the Civil Code, the Africans did not have the power to buy, to sell, to make contracts, to transmit and receive property, or even to marry freely.

With the founding of Mana, Pierre Ballanche's Town of Expiations moved into the tropics. The colony had a structural resemblance and a spiritual kinship to Ballanche's penitential enclave. Anne-Marie Javouhey, founder of the Order of Saint Joseph de Cluny, ruled the village. As a peasant girl in the 1790s, she discovered her faith while acting as sidekick to Pierre Ballanche, a refractory abbé hiding in Burgundy. To the alarm of her father Balthazar, a municipal councillor at Seurre, the girl attached herself to the abbé as a spotter at floating masses and as the mistress of a secret religious school.[23] The abbé Pierre Ballanche was the uncle of Pierre Ballanche, the Lyonnais writer. Although the nun and the abbé's nephew do not seem to have met, both grew up in the orbit of Dom de Lestrange, founder of the Trappist monastery for émigré monks near Fribourg.[24] Both transmuted the monastic principle of elective withdrawal from the world into a compulsory model of social improvement. Both understood redemption to require living in artful bubbles and sucking people into them.

Where Ballanche planned the Town of Expiations for criminals, Anne-Marie Javouhey devised hermetic containers for Africans and children, usually in combination. During her stint in Senegal in 1822, Javouhey pressed the director of colonies in Paris for cash to buy child slaves whom she wanted to educate for liberty in adulthood. This, she said, would launch "the great project of civilizing Africa, of creating a laborious agricultural people of honest Christians."[25]

Javouhey's earlier colonial scheme in Africa shaped the Mana River settlement, despite claims to the contrary by French officials. The minister of the navy, Admiral Duperré, pitched Mana as a French version of Liberia. To the extent that Liberia existed to empty freedmen from the American South, the comparison was just. Yet the actual model for Mana was Javouhey's failed agricultural colony in Dagana (Senegal), which Anne-Marie Javouhey founded in 1822 on state funds (200,000 francs). At Dagana, the navy had hoped to submit "all negroes who have been captured or confiscated" to a fourteen-year work engagement and continuous religious instruction.[26] Precisely the same colonial model, involving extended servitude by supposed nonslaves, recurred in the Mana Village.

Guiana's elite campaigned against Mana from the date of its founding.[27] In 1838, local men sought to place the village under a disciplinary code that originated in Cayenne; they aimed to annex and to reenslave the Africans. "For these blacks, who were taken as adults from the coast of

Africa, and who come mostly from tribes of the interior, only a very long de facto slavery would guarantee security, order and work."[28]

The Mana village was not under French law, but the Africans had names, lines of descent, and spouses in a roll book kept by Louis Javouhey, the nephew of the mother superior. Cayenne's elite rejected even this minimal version of nonslavery, sent emissaries to inspect the registers, and campaigned against what they discovered there.

After being taken from slave ships, the Africans at Mana each received the name of an ancient Greek or Roman personage, as did all arriving slaves in the colony. The custom of refusing Christian names to slaves developed in the early nineteenth century, after responsibility for record-keeping passed from the clergy to the state. Later the Africans each received a new name, which was a month of the revolutionary calendar, "but the old name remained as a patronymic."[29]

Officials in Cayenne opposed alterations to the Africans' names as the nuns at Mana began pressing them into families. On 21 March 1838, the ordonnateur complained to the governor that "married blacks were given patronymics without the administration being consulted."[30] In this case, the ordonnateur referred to the new patronymics that were assigned them by the nuns and by Louis Javouhey, the officer of the civil rolls, so that husband, wife, and child shared the same last name.

The controversy over the Mana registers coincided with a crisis in Guianese colonial society over the symbolic function of civil registers, the legal genealogies of freed people, and the status of slave marriage. In 1835, Guiana's Colonial Council opposed an imperial ordinance, then in draft, that would have made it impossible to free any slave without freeing his or her spouse and children. Guiana's elite retorted that slaves could not be wives, husbands, or fathers. French slave law had never recognized paternal lineage. Religious unions had no legal significance in the New Regime. "In the case of a slave, paternity is a fact that nothing indicates, except the declaration of he who wants to call himself a father, because there is no legal bond between man and woman. The benediction that the Church gives to some unions, often without the consent and knowledge of the master, proves nothing and cannot have the same meaning for a slave as it would for a free man." In 1861, Augustin Cochin clarified the meaning of this passage in his study of abolition by observing: "A slave is not able to contract marriage before an officer of the civil rolls."[31] Only after 1792, when the state seized control over recordkeeping, did the mere fact of existing with a name and a filiation to the official archive assume such radiant significance. The civil roll book was the door between the legal person and the legal thing.

The founding of Mana coincided with a series of encounters between French colonists and the Boni Maroons (also called the Aluku). The Boni lived above the Cottica Falls on the Lawa River, an influent of the Maroni. Attempts by tribespeople to migrate eastward to the Oyapock region began after the Boni encountered Leprieur, a pharmacist who explored the Maroni in 1836.[32] The Boni wanted to deliver themselves from the Auka Maroons, who controlled traffic on the Maroni and prevented the Boni from descending to the coast.[33] Because of their isolation, they lacked manufactured things—guns, powder, lead, knives—of great practical importance to forest people.

The problem of nonpersonhood, which the people at Mana encountered within the domain of civil law, troubled the Boni as an international legal matter. The tribe made numerous formal bids for collective recognition, unable to comprehend the repeated and even murderous refusal of the French to acknowledge them. In December 1836, eight Boni traveled to Cayenne to seek permission to settle above the Camopi, an influent of the Oyapock. The governor, Laurens de Choisy, refused their demand, gave them guns, and enjoined them "never to appear on the territory of French Guiana." Months later, in April 1837, a Boni party traveled to the lower Oyapock; four were seized and shot summarily by the garrison. On 1 and 2 November 1837, the Boni hoisted a white cloth on the Oyapock cliff at Grande-Roche, above the first and most dramatic of the river's many *sauts,* or cataracts. The commander of the new fort at Casfesoca, built at the foot of the rapids to contain the Boni, responded with cannon fire. Over a year later, in early January 1839, a French bird fancier encountered eighteen Boni near the Camopi River and swore a blood pact with the group, who wrapped him in a white cloth ("their flag"), which he promised to carry as a sign of peace to the captain general of Cayenne. Several tribesmen soon appeared under the escort of local Indians at the Casfesoca fort. They wanted to travel to Cayenne and negotiate "peace with the whites"; the commander answered that "it was his duty to forbid them to venture beyond the falls." That summer, on 7 June 1839, the Boni "hoisted a white flag above the falls to parley." After the commander declined to trade with them, the Boni "expressed the desire to exchange their flag with the standard of the post," which he refused. Two years later, in mid-June 1841, a new commander of the post informed Boni who had camped above the falls that "we could not receive them, had no gifts for them, that if they appeared at the fort I would be obliged to shoot at them."[34]

For the French to treat with the Boni required that they recognize the tribe as a *personne morale,* a collective free being. International public law, whether during the Enlightenment era of natural law or afterward, opened from the analogy between nations and individuals. The eighteenth-century jurist Emerich de Vattel evoked the moral person of the nation as a body of men united "to procure mutual health and advantage." As a self-actuating being by analogy with the nature of man, the nation "is a moral person that has its own understanding and will, and which is capable of rights and obligations."[35]

The Boni embodied so potent an ideological threat to slave society that their mere appearance seemed to herald (or foment) the colony's extinction. "Emancipation obtained by force would be a dangerous example," observed the governor in 1837, Laurens de Choisy.[36] He was later stripped of his post for issuing written orders for a massacre. "If it is necessary to adopt measures to combat them and destroy them totally . . . it is necessary . . . to make every effort that not a single one be able to return to his country."[37]

Local administrators refused to include the Boni among the family of nations to the point of annexing them to French territory and making them over as brigands. The local government assigned them (by an act of mind) to a special jurisdiction inside Guiana under the menace of annihilation. The tribe's legal predicament was the work of Jean-François Vidal de Lingendes, Guiana's prosecutor-general. A planter of the gentlest sort, he hastened to Surinam in 1836 after Leprieur's return to negotiate a so-called treaty with the Dutch. The accord (of which no copy exists in the colonial archive) banned the Boni from French territory. "If the Boni Negroes of Surinam present themselves on French territory, they will be informed of the disavowal of Leprieur and summoned to withdraw onto the territory where they are tolerated under the dominion of the Auka."[38]

The agreement that forbade the Boni to set foot on French soil stipulated that Boni villages lay on French soil. On 12 June 1837, the Dutch governor wrote to his opposite number in Guiana about "the convention concluded in the name of Your Excellency with Vidal de Lingendes, by which that country is to be considered as French territory."[39] The prosecutor molded the agreement to express his understanding of their outlawry. The Boni were "fugitive rebels, unconstituted and unrecognized."[40]

The French foreign ministry refused to endorse this document; as a decree that simultaneously banished and annexed the Boni, the text lacked the reciprocal nature of an international legal accord. Yet the treaty had the force of law in the colony. Members of Guiana's privy council understood the text to justify massacring the tribe for noncompliance. Future appearances of the Boni on French soil became violations of a legal agreement backed by death. "If the Boni persist in desiring, despite everything, to engage in peaceable relations, this treaty permits no other solution in their regard than a war of extermination, extreme means, to which one ought not to resort except in the case of absolute necessity."[41]

The massacre sanctioned by the treaty occurred in July 1841. A combined force of Indians, soldiers, and Wolof Africans acting as French auxiliaries ambushed a group of Boni men, women, and children at their campsite, compelling them to flee to the water for safety. As the Boni neared the waterfall in their canoes, Oyapock militiamen sprang from a hiding place and began shooting at them. In the distorted account that survives (by the commandant), the Boni then opted for a suicidal plunge rather than surrender. In Cayenne, the slave Espérance, "who speaks their language well," translated during the interrogation of Adouba, the lone survivor. Asked whether she knew the government "forbade your tribe to communicate with inhabitants of French Guiana under any pretext," Adouba replied she had never heard of such an order.[42]

The year the Boni went over the falls, there was still no law in the village at Mana. The building called *le Gouvernement* was an infirmary. Anne-Marie Javouhey lived in an apartment upstairs.[43] Everyday life in the village gave ample clues of its extra-legal design. The Africans lived in equidistant houses in rows, white inside and out, each containing a couple of strangers, who were newlyweds.[44] The sisters matched the couples: "We make the choice of the best negress for a wife."[45] They also prized away the infants of the married pairs. "I hope in removing them from the impressions caused by bad domestic examples . . . we will be able more easily to make them acquire that . . . religious morality whose power is so effective in the civilization of peoples."[46] The children lived cloistered with the unwed girls in the nuns' sector.[47] Mismatched men who brawled in the tidy streets (there was no bar) could expect some random number of days or hours in jail or else a whipping.[48] The absence of law had yet direr consequences for the future of the village. The nuns marked the transition from whatever it was to freedom, as they pictured it, with the gift of small pieces of land to which no one—not the nuns, not the liberated people—had legal title. Some villagers wandered off for privacy and larger plots that soon turned out not to belong to them either.[49]

The nonrecognition of free Africans as legal persons by the ministry of the navy and colonies, which gave rise to the Mana Village, survived the dismantling of that enclave's special status. In 1847, Guiana's interim governor, André Pariset, noted the inaptness of Mana Africans for French law when the navy stripped the nuns of sovereignty and placed the village under his authority. "It is anomalous to apply the practices of the most civilized and advanced society in Europe to a new population that has scarcely exited slavery and barbarism . . . where what are required are the capitularies or institutions of Saint Louis or where it would be necessary to punish blasphemy and the vices of private conduct, as is done in Papeïti."[50] In 1848, the provisional government of the Second Republic entrusted Pariset, a career navy bureaucrat, with overseeing slave emancipation and gave him the new title of civil commissar.[51] Pariset's observations on Mana Africans in 1847 offered a foreglimpse of the worldview that later guided his conduct toward emancipated slaves. He so confounded Guiana's freed people with inhabitants of the nuns' village that Mana in its original form, as a void of law, became his explicit model for all of Guiana after slavery.

The 1848 decree abolishing slavery conferred legal personhood and citizenship on emancipated people; that decree also annulled the only law that planters considered valid and dismantled their authority. It is unsurprising that the problem of nonrecognition, which had earlier struck the Boni Maroons and Mana villagers, should trouble freed people after 1848. Yet opponents of emancipation faced considerable constraints to their actions in this period. They could not revoke the private and public rights that the emancipation decree conferred on freed people as a matter of personal status. Instead, they required a formula for unmaking legal subjects while allowing their rights to subsist abstractly.

Although Pariset could not strip the freed people of citizenship, he could disable its exercise. The election of deputies to the Constituent Assembly of the Second Republic took place in Martinique on 9 August and in Guadeloupe on 22 August 1848.[52] In Guiana, elections were convoked on 1 February 1849 and occurred on 4 March 1849.[53] Originally Pariset had expected the Constituent Assembly to disenfranchise colonial citizens as the Second Republic entered its reactionary phase and delayed the elections in the hope of avoiding them altogether.[54] Perhaps he also intended the colony's deputy to reach Paris at the end of the legislative session, just before the assembly disbanded.[55] Yet the government did not rescind the franchise from new citizens either in 1848 or in 1849. Soon after the March 1849 election, Pariset learned he would need to convoke a second election that summer for Guiana's representative to the Legislative Assembly (the final assembly of the Second Republic).[56]

In common with local notables, Pariset did not imagine black people or people of color as embodiments of the French nation. He also did not recognize emancipated slaves as self-directed beings with the right to will their own futures. The idea of freedmen imposing their collective will on the master class struck Pariset as a catastrophic inversion of the social order to the point that voting seemed comparable to an act of conquest—an act of war. Pariset duly staged the 1849 election as a racial struggle. He chose Vidal de Lingendes, the prosecutor-general, as the government candidate to oppose Dorville Jouannet, a Martiniquan magistrate of color who had been Guiana's substitute prosecutor until June 1848, when he returned home and became a judge in Saint Pierre.[57] Pariset charged sheriffs throughout the colony with spreading ballots printed with the name of Vidal de Lingendes in the hope of exploiting the people's illiteracy. The new sheriff of Mana, Eugène Mélinon, reported: "It was a done deal. We put bulletins marked with Vidal de Lingendes for the titulary . . . everywhere."[58] For the Jouannet network, the challenge lay in anticipating fraud by officials. Agents from Cayenne and trusted rural leaders distributed ballots marked with Jouannet's name and made "vow not to use other ones."[59] After Jouannet's electoral triumph in March 1849 (which he repeated in July), Pariset and Vidal de Lingendes accused the electorate of separatist treachery. "They have equality, liberty . . . they reject fraternity!"[60]

Through the March 1849 election, planters and administrators discovered the fullness of their calamity. For the elite, the civic rights of freedmen were weapons of racial abasement: universal male suffrage had suborned masters to slaves. The 1849 election was a turning point and inspired a violent local response. The time had come to strip land and bodies of law, to eradicate institutions, and to recapture people.

In Guiana, the offensive against colonial citizenship opened from the domestic constitution while defying the letter of the law. According to the Constitution of 4 November 1848, "The territory of Algeria and the colonies is declared to be French territory and will be ruled by particular laws until a special law places them under the regime of the present constitution."[61] Through this article, domestic legislators retreated from the colonial policy of the provisional government as set forth in the decree of 27 April 1848 abolishing slavery. Under the influence of France's leading abolitionist, Victor Schoelcher, the provisional government had granted French citizenship to freed slaves at the instant of their liberation with the idea of governing the empire as an extension of domestic soil, subject to the same constitutional law. Through the 1848 constitution, the notion that colonial people would enjoy rights common to French citizens and institutions like those of France moved out of the present into the indeterminate future.

The phrase "particular laws" assumed a meaning in Guiana that deviated from what the 1848 constitution envisaged. This phrase held two quite different significances in the first half of the nineteenth century. "Particular laws" might refer to executive orders that bypassed the legislature entirely and originated with monarchs who commanded extensive discretionary power. The same phrase during the reign of Louis-Philippe also referred to colonial legislation drafted and voted on by Parliament that violated metropolitan legal norms.[62] In 1848, the National Assembly embraced the principle of particular laws in a constitution that accorded the president of the republic no discretionary authority.[63] According to this short-lived constitutional regime, the executive branch could not issue decrees independent of the legislature, even for colonial soil.[64] Yet this formal constraint on executive power proved irrelevant overseas. In Guiana, as in the Antilles and Réunion, commissars claimed decree power for themselves. The earlier regal style of particular laws, not the parliamentary version, took hold in the colonies after emancipation.

Until the March 1849 election, Pariset made studied use of inaction to sabotage the new era of liberty. On 2 August 1848, he dissolved Cayenne's municipal council—the only one in the colony—and appointed a provisional body headed by Nicolas Merlet, the town's longtime mayor, pending future elections that Pariset never convoked.[65] Though charged with organizing a colonial militia, he declined to create one. Instead, he demanded a fourfold increase in the white garrison.[66] He opted not to replace the sheriffs [*commissaire-commandants*] who ruled the countryside to predictable effect. Those officials "continue to speak . . . of dangerous subjects to remove from their localities."[67] Sheriffs used the new police force, created at the time of emancipation, to expel people from their houses (shacks on estates) without leaving them time to harvest their crops.[68]

Jouannet's victory inspired Pariset to dispatch a profession of faith to the navy. Invoking the constitutional article about "particular laws," he argued that there should be no local elections for "the municipal council, the authorities in the [rural] quarters, [or] for the officers of the National Guard." He advised against the future election of colonial deputies to the national legislature. "Our new free population is not sufficiently enlightened to understand the exercise of political rights."[69] His quiet agenda since the founding of the republic then became his formal prescription.

Beginning in April 1849, Pariset launched an offensive against freed people with the aim of stripping them of sovereignty, annulling their collective will, and reviving the social hierarchy that slave emancipation and universal male suffrage had overturned. To quash civic engagement, he banned speech offenses "unforeseen by the Penal Code." He promulgated snippets of legislation from the 1790s concerning night gatherings and riotous assemblies.[70] He disarmed the citizenry by illegalizing the possession of sabers, rifles, muskets, carabines, bayonettes, air pistols, pocket pistols, and air guns. Here, as in the case of riotous public gatherings, Pariset rearranged pieces of lapsed metropolitan laws into a new pastiche. He ransacked expedient sentences and suppressed inexpedient ones when culling from texts reaching back several centuries. Among the bits that served to criminalize the bearing of arms in Guiana were "article 3 of title 20 of the ordinance of 1669" and "article 27 of the law of 13 fructidor year V."[71]

In June 1848, Pariset had felt powerless to stem the migration of freed people onto land belonging to no one. The next year, as people continued to clear land and cut timber, he used particular laws to ban every feature of the rural freedman's new life. The decree of 4 April 1849 "for the repression of separate facts together constituting vagabondage" did not concern idle people. Practicing a craft but lacking a steady residence, having a place to sleep but lacking a livelihood, or being fully occupied while residing in "a hangar covered with leaves called ajoupa" became punishable by fines, imprisonment, or both for recidivists.[72] The next month, on 3 May 1849, Pariset struck against the sale or peddling of "carpentry wood, rafters, boards, shingles, planks, colored wood, firewood, and wood charcoal without a certificate establishing its provenance . . . delivered by the proprietor or by the sheriff of the quarter." The only people excepted from this requirement were wood merchants with shops in Cayenne.[73] Should the timber workers or their infants be discovered scantily clad anywhere in the colony, they faced punishment for indecency, which might mean imprisonment for up to five days and a fine of 5 to 20 francs or one or the other.[74]

Pariset used decree power to ban huts, voices, defenses, manufactured things, and the bodies of their makers. Particular laws, taken together, aimed to illegalize the postemancipation moment while seizing the bodies of freed people and everything around them. Pariset's boldest maneuver, which took the general purpose of particular laws to a new extreme, was a child snatch with philanthropic packaging that began with his "decree for the tutelage of foundlings and poor and abandoned children." Rather than apply the decree of the provisional government "relative to the maintenance of the elderly, infirm, and abandoned orphans," Pariset opted to target children who, as he put it, "find themselves in an analogous position" to abandoned ones. For this measure, Pariset scavenged a definition of foundlings from an 1811 French decree by which "abandoned children are those who, born of unknown fathers and mothers, were found exposed some place."[75] Foundlings, children deemed abandoned, and others called poor orphans faced removal to a facility run by the nuns of Saint Joseph de Cluny on the state plantation of La Gabrielle.[76]

Most children in Guiana had unknown parents in 1849. Registers of the free population created during the summer of 1848 did include notes about family lineages, as the provisional government required. Months later, on 8 December 1848, Pariset stripped those indications of legal force. "Enunciations relative to the filiation and parentage contained in these registers will serve only as indications, with the parties left to prove that filiation and parentage by the religious or civil acts that furnish the basis for such statements . . . while parents may recognize their natural children should they wish, following the dispositions of the Civil Code."[77] The same problem that surfaced in the local campaign against Mana defined the conduct of the colonial government toward everyone after 1848. The abolition of slavery turned freed people's lineages into a focus of elite wrath about the unauthorized birth of black legal subjects, whose emergence defied the will and nullified the prerogatives of the master class.

The evolving legal sensibility of Vidal de Lingendes, Guiana's prosecutor-general, makes it possible to situate the postemancipation problem of legal lineages in the context of local history. A rich sugar planter descended from Saint Domingue refugees, Vidal de Lingendes spent his career perfecting Guiana's slave regime from a legal standpoint with the apparent aim of squaring the circle and marrying contraband slave trafficking and self-enrichment by lethal African toil with seigneurial benevolence. He supported the right of slaves to bear witness in court. He prosecuted masters for obstructing manumission and for barbarity.[78] The instrument of the prosecutor's munificence was invariably slave law. What looked like liberality was enforcement. When he met a challenge to the legal order that sustained slavery, he became vicious. In the 1836 pseudo-treaty, he had inserted the Boni Maroons into a capsule of oblivion that was both a place and a mobile predicament. They were people who could be killed with impunity for becoming visible.

As the official responsible for overseeing the inscription of emancipated people in 1848, Vidal de Lingendes guided the hand of Pariset in assuring that no one exited slavery with a single legal relative. The phrase Vidal de Lingendes used to describe the Boni in 1836, "unconstituted and unrecognized," perfectly sums up the state of the whole emancipated population in consequence of his handiwork: they were an anti-society. No wonder the recognition of children by parents before notaries immediately became, in his words, "a fashion." In 1851, he observed, "Under slavery, natural filiation did not exist legally."[79] Natural filiation not only existed under slavery (in slave law) but was something Vidal de Lingendes enforced and even took to the Court of Cassation. In 1845 he helped to block the sale of a slave woman and a child, resulting in the manumission of both, on the grounds that the woman's other child, Marie-Euphénie, had been manumitted by their master before he died.[80] In 1831, Vidal de Lingendes voted against the governor and the privy council to allow whites to recognize colored children.[81] At his death in 1857, he left everything to daughters he never avowed. In Guiana, "Octavie Pauline Clarence, daughter of Rose, now Dame Robert," received "a capital of 20,000 francs in annuities . . . or 900 francs at 4.5 percent," as well as his "furniture, dishes, personal effects," what remained of his silver, use of the land next to the house of her mother, and travel expenses "if Octavie is in France at the moment of my decease."[82]

By ruling on behalf of whites exclusively after emancipation, Pariset achieved political victory while assuring the colony's economic ruin. His policies helped to destroy the Guianese plantation, to which the convict system delivered the death blow. This unanticipated consequence of his white supremacist program is especially worthy of note because of the importance that Guiana's economic doom assumed in his later career. On his return to France, Pariset became a prominent expert on local affairs. In 1851 he helped to craft a scheme intended to revive Guiana's economy and advised the navy on settling deportees in Guiana the next year. On both occasions, Pariset promoted a vision of Guiana's future that he sharpened while administering the colony.

Guiana lacked the institutions and informal practices that organized work after slavery in other French colonies. In Martinique during the Second Republic, sharecropping agreements consisted of written contracts that required the sanction of municipal councils.[83] There, rural institutions called cantonal juries (abolished in 1852) enforced labor contracts and mediated between workers and employers. In the case of Guiana, the government offered no institutional support for sharecropping. There was no system to encourage or to authorize written labor contracts, largely because municipal government did not exist. Whereas commissars in Martinique and Guadeloupe toured those colonies to speak to workers and to resolve disputes, Pariset did nothing but harp on the need for a large indemnity to compensate slave owners, without which, he claimed, plantation life could not continue.[84] The lack of institutions to mediate labor relations and the threat of random and immediate eviction led freed people in Guiana to exit plantations, never to return.

A positive program accompanied postemancipation efforts by the elite to destroy the Guianese legal subject. The replacement world for Guiana after slavery, as envisaged, was a mechanized civilization of movable bodies that labored and procreated according to administrative directives. Officials and planters hoped to remake the colony into a domain of administrative power where neither private nor public rights could operate. After Guiana's elite learned that transported criminals would be arriving in the colony, plans for a postemancipation system of social control became entangled with the new punishment venture. Imperial officials and local notables hoped to use the convict system to reestablish power over freed people by enclosing them in new zones of repression.

Anne-Marie Javouhey and Pariset defined civilization as the inculcation of savages with piety and laborious habits in a setting that permitted neither private nor public life. On return to France, Pariset helped to write this improving formula into an 1851 bill while serving as a member of a legislative sub-commission on colonization. The accompanying report frequently mentioned Eugène Mélinon, Pariset's protégé, who became the sheriff of Mana when the navy revoked the autonomy of the village in 1847. The bill and report predated Louis-Napoleon's coup d'état and the resulting decree of 8 December 1851 transporting ban-breakers and socialists to Guiana and Algeria. When Pariset and Mélinon later met with the minister of the navy to discuss the settlement of ex-convicts and socialists in Guiana, both men viewed the purge as a chance to promote their development project.

In the 1851 report, Pariset and Mélinon proposed to resurrect Guiana's plantations as villages modeled on Mana, or so they said, where freed people together with European and African immigrants would live in rectilinear agro-Christian life modules under the watchful eye of administrators.[85] The authors wanted to build bourgs on inactive plantations, which the state would expropriate for an indemnity. Freed people who lived on land owned by absentee proprietors would thus be captured and made into inmates of improving towns. The 1851 plan turned on a concession scheme by which aspiring villagers would acquire lots ranging from two to seven hectares after a trial period of five years (34). The delay in conceding land would enable administrators to force adherence to a conduct code embracing all features of life, backed by the threat of expulsion (43). Failure to heed planting instructions would result in removal (42). Settlers who left early would receive nothing (43). Landowners who ceased to work their plots after completing the five-year trial period would lose title to it. "Everywhere public utility confers a right of expropriation" (58).

The bourg scheme placed an extreme emphasis on territorial delimitation and spatial control, while programming movement and interactions among villagers with the same rigidity. The administration would not only design each house on a uniform model but also police the town for crooked lines and unauthorized deviations from building and planting rules. Villagers could not modify their houses or gardens without administrative approval. Social life would consist of what the plan called relations; yet relations (if not a euphemism for procreative sex) seemed to refer to encounters between villagers and administrators. "The concessionaries must not be allowed to isolate themselves. Everything must facilitate religious instruction, primary instruction, relations, neighborliness [*le travail de voisinage*], and administration" (39).

Pariset and Mélinon greeted the purge of socialists and ban-breakers after the December 1851 coup d'état by President Louis-Napoleon as a moment of opportunity. Theodore Ducos, minister of the navy, summoned them on 19 and 20 December 1851 to confer on the settlement of deportees. At that confidential gathering, General Defitte insisted that men would die by epidemic disease if sent all at once. In reply, Mélinon found a solution in the building of new hamlets. "[One could] avoid this if the men were settled in villages and not barracks." When Ducos mentioned sending six thousand men at once, Pariset saw no danger. "The garrison at Cayenne has a low mortality." Captain Saint Quentin, a Guianese planter, then "struggled above all against the idea of colonization" and observed: "The example of the soldiers proves nothing."[86]

In France, advocates for convict transportation had long emphasized the need to isolate prisoners and liberated felons from free society. In February 1852, when the Ducos made public the government's plans for French Guiana, he underscored the closed nature of the future convict settlement. "The deportees must not be allowed to have any free communication with the rest of French Guiana."[87] Under the pressure of local men in Guiana, however, the navy abandoned the original model for the project. In September 1852, Ducos urged that local vagabonds be put to work clearing land and building prisons. "It would tarnish the honor of France to liberate thirteen thousand slaves in Guiana only to let them degenerate to a state of barbarism comparable to that of a population in Africa."[88] Ducos cited a recent sanitary report by Guiana's chief physician, Dr. Laure. The report claimed that blacks in Guiana had become sickly since the abolition of slavery through their ignorance of how to correctly manipulate, and hence maintain, their own bodies.[89] Laure's solution, the repression of vagabondage, reveals what he understood by hygiene: the bodies were not wasting away but being put to waste.

Guiana's elite understood the penal colony as an apparatus that would enclose freed people and transported criminals. Colonial notables put forward a variety of unwholesome schemes for hybrid punishment enclaves as members of a commission convened by Guiana's governor in early 1852 to discuss sites for new prisons. The commission met four times between 17 February and 10 April; participants learned for the first time in March 1852 that hard labor convicts would be coming to the colony.[90]

In 1852, the commission swiftly agreed to a settlement principle for socialists. The government would sprinkle them into a number of different plantations that it would reconstitute as agricultural prisons. The socialists would couple with local women and sire a new race. "This measure . . . would facilitate alliances between deportees and women of the colony and the race they engender would become a powerful element of colonization."[91] For the plantations to function as breeding centers, freed people would need to be enclosed within them. How else would the socialists meet the women they were supposed to couple with?

The envisaged scheme looked back to an 1842 colonial plan that Victor Schoelcher had denounced as "odious juggling."[92] The earlier project began with the Saint Simonian Jules Lechevalier; planters in Guiana made it their own. They proposed to transfer their property to the government on behalf of a putatively philanthropic goal: gradual emancipation. The state would recreate the land from the swamps of Kaw to the Oyapock River as an exceptional jurisdiction where slaves became subject to a fifteen-year work requirement and a new conduct code. The state would sponsor the immigration of poor whites from France to mix with the freed people. The sponsor of the bill, the Comte de Tascher, also submitted a petition to the Chamber of Peers seeking the deportation of *forçats libérés;* perhaps he had white ex-convicts in mind for the breeding experiment. Lechevalier, the Saint Simonian who first conceived the project, had wanted to found a school in Cayenne for the children of non-slaves modeled after La Mettray, the French agricultural youth prison.[93]

Members of the local commission proposed further hybrid schemes for the western frontier. They voted to settle ex-convict ban-breakers at Mana, which the ordonnateur touted for its remoteness, salubrity, ease of surveillance and "a great stretch of cleared land suited for agriculture."[94] The Mana region figured in this discussion as a vacant land of abundance with the natural character of a prison. The aim of planters since the founding of the village had been to seize and reenslave the occupants. The enclosure of the Africans in a new punishment zone for pariahs was the planters' final stroke. Next, in March 1852, when the notables learned that thousands of hard labor prisoners would be coming to Guiana, they chose a rumored mountain range up the Maroni River for the prisoners. On 29 March, Governor Octave-Pierre-Antoine Chabannes wrote to the navy about preparations for a Maroni exploratory mission headed by Vidal de Lingendes, the prosecutor-general, in search of high plateaus.[95] While the mountains remained undiscovered, the region's inhabitants—the Boni tribe—were certainly known to the prosecutor and to notables on the commission, who included Boudaud, onetime sheriff of the Oyapock, and the planter Ronmy, a military engineer, who built the Casfesoca fort on the Oyapock to secure the region against incursions by the tribe. In both the case of the Mana Village and of Maroon territory, the commission did not mention the occupants of land they designated for convict settlement.

Mélinon, Pariset's protégé and the sheriff of Mana, became superior commandant of penitentiaries on the Maroni River in the late 1850s.[96] In 1852, he envisaged the western frontier as a zone for integrated forms of coercion involving convicts, Maroons, and Mana villagers. At the time of the first convicts' arrival to the colony, he began reorienting life at Mana around the new prison system. By September 1852, 1,259 hard labor convicts, 193 ban-breakers, and 168 politicals had reached Guiana, sort of, in being stranded on islands off the coast of Kourou. Mana villagers, under the direction of their sheriff, became a timber gang for the new prison depositories. That month, Mélinon announced his desire to link the nuns' village to the new prisons even more directly by settling convicts on the western frontier. It was "a moment when a considerable population will be thrown on the Maroni" (he hoped). The African village "will be extended by relations with the establishments on that river and through moderate immigration by the families of transportees."[97] Mélinon wanted European convicts to live on the Maroni River while their wives and children lived at Mana.

Mélinon's plan for the African village in the era of the penal colony developed from his earlier subjugation schemes. On becoming sheriff of Mana in 1847, he had ordered villagers to work at a corvée on land they thought they owned, which sparked a revolt—details are scarce—that ended when troops arrived from Cayenne.[98] The 1851 colonial plan, which quoted Mélinon frequently, proposed grandiose changes to the nuns' village that bore the mark of his imagination. The 1851 plan proposed to remake Mana into a vast state sugar plantation with a martial allure; to enlarge the workforce beyond the existing seven hundred inhabitants of the region, the plan recommended that the government ship over another three hundred immigrants from Africa and France. "Since public works are habitually undertaken in France and Algeria by the state, it should be the same in Guiana, beginning with Mana."[99] The 1851 plan presumed that existing Mana villagers, stripped of their freedom plots, would labor in the mangroves as inmates of the new demesne.

The hitching of Mana to Maroni prison life was an accomplished fact by the end of 1852 despite the absence of convicts in the region. Five years elapsed before any arrived. The penal colony began without them. On 4 September, Mélinon announced his intention to begin immediate construction on a Maroni convict site; Mana Africans would build the prison and lay a road from their village to the new establishment.[100] In mid-December he was on the Maroni at the site of an evacuated Indian village. Forty Mana workers were building a rustic circular thing called Camp Louis-Napoleon Bonaparte.[101] There were ten huts around a central one, the eleventh, for the commandant. Mélinon planned two more huts as "lodgings for the officers." Days later, on 17 December 1852, he described preparations for the next timber shipment. "I will show the same care with the materials I receive on my return to the Maroni, where I am going to give a final helping hand and fetch the workers."[102] Mana timber workers built and lived in the circular camp. Six were there in mid-January raising walls and putting windows on the officer cabins.[103] A month had passed since the local government had opted to begin mainland settlement on the Oyapock, at the opposite end of the colony.[104]

The Maroni became the chief site of mainland convict settlement in the late 1850s and remained so for a century. When local notables addressed the settlement of prisoners on the western frontier, they maneuvered to destroy two loathed groups by using the state as their proxy. Mélinon had other aims. In 1853, Governor Léon-Martin Fourichon offered Mélinon one hundred ex-convicts transported for surveillance infractions. Mélinon refused. They would be "the death blow to the small colony."[105] He did not want to destroy the Mana village through the penal colony but to perfect it. Even Camp Louis-Napoleon Bonaparte had no room for men beyond reform.

CHAPTER 7

The Enormous Room

IN THE SPRING OF 1852 the navy shipped fifteen hundred tablespoons with an equal number of forks, goblets, and plates to Guiana, along with planks, empty mattress covers, 190 bathrobes, assorted reparative potions, hammers, hatchets, carpentry tools, paving shovels, and saws.[1] Law also traveled to the colony as part of the navy's assembly kit for a new convict society.[2]

The 1852 decree that emptied the port prisons into Guiana intended the legal apparatus of felonry to move with the men overseas. The navy sent procedural instructions about the special maritime tribunal that had long judged convicts in the ports. It sent copies of letters explaining the application and metric length of the whip.[3] It sketched the meaning of legal interdiction, civic degradation, and civil death, which defined the status of transported men in the colony.[4]

Officials puzzled over the ex-convict at the beginning of this enterprise. Governors who varied widely in character refused to countenance the release of liberated men into colonial society. To accomplish this required administrators to efface all remaining legal rights attached to nominally free yet repellent beings. The systematical confinement of liberated men would unhinge this venture from modern French criminal punishment so completely as to drive the venture toward a new ferocity. The unusual style of governance that came to define Guiana's convict system can only be understood in light of efforts to enclose ex-convicts within militarized zones of punishment unendingly.

Although domestic law provided the germ of this endeavor, the convict system developed structural curiosities that cannot be traced back to metropolitan France. The mode of colonial rule that applied to Guiana in the postemancipation period played a vital role in shaping the convict system. On 3 May 1854, the colony became subject to rule by decree, as did all the other colonies except for Martinique, Guadeloupe, and Réunion; the new legal arrangement assured that imperial rule in Guiana would be quite distinct from what existed in other French colonies of emancipated slaves.

Underlying rule by decree was the notion that unconstrained administrative power would assure the rapid success of any undertaking by permitting the use of any tool counseled by any circumstance. The legal framework of colonial rule during the Second Empire draws attention to an intriguing contradiction that remained central to Guiana's convict system from the moment of its invention in 1852 to its dismantling nearly a century later. The extension of the legal apparatus of felonry to Guiana seemed to define the colony as a continuation of metropolitan soil; yet the guiding framework for imperial rule during the Second Empire and afterward emphasized rupture.

A style of imperial rule that aimed to make anything possible could not confer a specific shape on this or any enterprise. The particular character of Guiana's convict system derived from practices and conceptions that administrators culled from the existing colony of Guiana and from elsewhere in the empire. The Mana Village of Madame Javouhey and the unrealized 1851 colonial plan for Guiana inspired administrators of the convict system as exemplary vacuums where administrative power could fully substitute for legal personhood.

Notions of the imperial foe that arose during the principal phase of Algerian conquest (1830–1847), along with the military style of French rule in Algeria, also shaped the convict venture. In Guiana during the Second Empire, the felon (and the liberated felon most especially) came to be viewed as a permanent enemy against whom the French state was obliged to wage an unending war. Administrators looked to domestic and colonial tactics of military subjugation when fashioning the convict system. They drew inspiration from the state of siege, a means for suppressing domestic insurrection, and from the Algerian military sector, a framework for pacifying indigenous peoples. The Guianese colonial prison during the reign of Napoleon III became a site where the permanent state of siege merged with the colonial frontier war zone.

The normal colony of Guiana influenced the convict system because of severe limits to expressive, civic, and bodily freedom in Guiana after 1848. Transported felons could not be accorded more privileges than the law of the land allowed to ordinary inhabitants. The postemancipation context for this endeavor constrained the life possibilities of transported men before they had reached the shore.

During the 1850s the convict system enveloped freed slaves, immigrant workers, and members of the colored elite whose freedom predated 1848. The nearly two thousand African immigrants who came to French Guiana from 1854 to 1859 became another category of forced laborer. Administrators viewed them as slaves, employed them inside and around prisons, outfitted them as convicts, and hunted them down when they fled.[5] Petty criminals from Guiana wound up in hard labor prisons. Yet the status of emancipated slaves as persons under French civil law, which distinguished them from African immigrants, led their encounter with the convict system to depart considerably from what local notables had anticipated.

Michel Foucault's account of the ineradicable doubleness of human identity is of use to understanding the predicament of freed slaves in the era of the penal colony. "There are two meanings of the word 'subject': subject to another by control and dependence and tied to one's own identity by an awareness or knowledge of the self."[6] In Foucault's account, power relations animate the subject as a creature with a sense of its own distinctiveness and a capacity to act on the world. Yet the same system that enlivens the self is also an apparatus of subjugation. Relations of power invent the human "I" as a divided being, who is both a subject—an agent with inner awareness—and an object—a being who is acted on.

The convict system had the paradoxical effect of empowering freed slaves and their descendants as private persons while causing them to live as noncitizens under permanent dictatorship, encircled by forces of order in an institutional void. This curious effect of the new prisons resulted from the legal framework of life in the New Regime. At the beginning of the nineteenth century, French private (or civil) law and public law became separate domains. Public law then and now concerns the public or sovereign will and encompasses the constitution as well as laws relating to public institutions and to the exercise of citizenship. Private or civil law relates chiefly to acts of the private will, such as buying, selling, willing, giving, marrying, and adopting. With the cleaving of private from public law, it became theoretically possible for French people to be in full possession of their private rights without enjoying any public rights and without having access to a single public institution. In Guiana, private rights coexisted with public nothingness as a permanent state of affairs for the whole of the Second Empire. The colony emerged as a nearly perfect realization of the cleaved city.[7]

Many of the rights accorded to persons in civil law are tied to buying, selling, transmitting, bestowing, and receiving property. These are legal capacities that might appear to be of scarce practical relevance to the lives of poor people. Yet in Guiana during the Second Empire, the penal colony had the curious effect of helping emancipated slaves to access rights that might otherwise have been beyond the reach of people rising from slavery. The arrival of convicts resulted in the flight of whites who could afford to leave; the new prisons provided local people with a market for local products and a source of salaried work. By promoting the rapid redistribution of abandoned land at rock-bottom prices and by allowing freed people to accumulate capital, the convict system helped to turn former slaves from squatters into landed proprietors and shielded them from punishment under postemancipation work decrees.

By prompting white flight, the convict system, in conjunction with the abolition of slavery, rendered Guiana a colony without a master class whose chief inhabitants—a highly African population of freed people— lived outside any formal structure of private or public coercion. With the dwindling of the old master class and the end of the plantation, imperial officials came to regard the colony as too black for French law. The very circumstance that helped to constitute black freed people as proprietors and hence as active legal subjects under the Civil Code also made it necessary to retain Guiana as an institutional vacuum under the dictatorship of military governors. Rule by decree turned Guiana into a monstrosity among postemancipation societies. During the Second Empire, Guiana had no form of local government at the village or municipal level anywhere, including Cayenne, and further lacked an elected council of notables. Rule by decree, which set Guiana apart from nearby Martinique and Guadeloupe, would not have been imposed there in the absence of the penal colony; nonetheless, this regime targeted local people as well as convicts from its inception.

The dupe of the ministry in 1852, Louis-Napoleon Sarda Garriga (no relation), had been commissar-general of Réunion in 1848, where he emancipated the slaves. The navy gave him the same title in Guiana, leading him to picture transported men as awaiting deliverance by his hand. During his brief stint in the colony, Sarda Garriga staged simulations of slave emancipation both within the normal colony of Guiana and among convicts. After the freedom spectacles, Sarda Garriga shunted the very people he claimed to liberate into new spaces of confinement.[8]

Sarda Garriga addressed an acrid letter to the people of Cayenne on 15 August 1852, the anniversary of Napoleon's birthday. To mark the national holiday, he had chosen to unchain the chain gang that cleaned the streets of the colonial capital. "Let them await the day they will no longer see the mark of crime pass beneath their windows as they have ceased to hear the sound of chains, which once flattered their ears."[9] Sarda Garriga replied to the rumored joy of townspeople at the clank of chains by unshackling prisoners pending their deliverance from Cayenne altogether. He planned to move the gang to the insular Montagne d'Argent, an overgrown coffee plantation at the mouth of the Oyapock River. Sarda Garriga acquired the property for the princely sum of 63,995 francs.[10] Far from being a site of freedom, however, that estate was poised to become a hard labor prison for French felons. Sarda Garriga intended black convicts to prepare the ground for Europeans who had yet to move from the islands to the shore.

Among the convicts, too, Sarda-Garriga staged a version of slave emancipation that ended with confinement. On Royal Island, convicts celebrated the new national holiday belatedly, on 22 August 1852. Disembarking there, Sarda Garriga met a brigade of thirty men holding banners marked CONFIDENCE, HOPE, WORK, and RECOGNITION. This event resembled the Festival of Labor, a crude invention of the Second Republic to commemorate the liberation of the slaves. In his speech to the men, Sarda-Garriga promised "to conduct the most meritorious very soon to terra firma. It is this they desire and it will be for them a great recompense."[11]

The men of Royal Island expected free life to begin the moment they reached the mainland. While feeding their expectations, Sarda Garriga developed a settlement scheme that began with trial confinement at the Montagne d'Argent and ended with exile to a yet more remote location on the Oyapock. He intended to settle an elite of zealous laborers at the southern limit of colonial settlement below the first *saut* (rapids). There they would live on small, equal-sized land concessions that would not belong to them. To repay the government for that favor, they would build a land road alongside the rapids into the hideaway of the Indians and toward an imaginary sierra that hung somewhere in the distance.[12] While displacing liberty onto a mobile imperial frontier, Sarda Garriga's plan also conflated deliverance with interdiction. The government of Cayenne forbade local people to cross the rapids by a decree of 1849, which revived an earlier prohibition that had aimed to limit contact between colonists and Indians and to obstruct contact between slaves and Boni tribespeople. Under the 1849 decree, no one could cross the rapids without a government permit.[13]

The commissar's blueprint for an inaccessible, mobile, and indefinitely deferred country for the free man expressed an ideological occlusion that marked his understanding both of punishment and of slave liberation: he could not think beyond unending servitude. After Sarda Garriga left the colony in disgrace, the envisaged town below the rapids became a place where punishment, slavery, and impossible deliverance intersected less abstractly. At the edge of French settlement on the Oyapock, the navy created Saint Georges, a prison for colonial convicts.

In 1853 the imperial administration together with Guiana's new governor, Admiral Fourichon, sought to transform the colony into a circum-Atlantic depository for black convicts. Fourichon hoped to direct as many such black people as he could find into the new colonial prisons. Judicial convictions offered an expedient for laying hold of them, one he would readily have dispensed with. His decree of 31 March 1853 required all local offenders to perform hard labor "inside or outside prison"; outside the prison, in this case, referred to the penal colony.[14] In reply to appeals from Fourichon to the navy for black workers, the French Council of State issued a decree on 20 August 1853 routing nonwhite convicts from Martinique, Guadeloupe, and Guiana itself with sentences to hard labor or to reclusion (prison with light labor) into the penal colony.[15] It is likely that more than one thousand convicts of color alongside an unknown number of local petty offenders passed through Saint Georges during its decade of existence (1853–1862).

In a brief account of Saint Georges that is likely to date from the late 1850s, the Jesuit Father Girré observed: "One has rarely seen so varied a group concentrated at so small a place. Blacks from Africa, Bourbon, Martinique, Guadeloupe, Barbados, Chinese, coolies, mulattoes, Indians, Creoles, Europeans, it is the Tower of Babel and the conflation of languages." The prisoners were mainly black and Father Girré could not tell them apart. "All these lovely ebony faces merge into a single one."[16] This penal cosmopolis at the world's end broke loose from the martial apparatus of punishment that distinguished other convict sites and became embedded in local life. The elevated rate of sickness and death at Saint Georges caused the evacuation of white soldiers and guards. In November 1856, there remained "a gendarme brigade and a detachment of guards, the latter chosen from among blacks of the country."[17] The commandant and the physician were men of color. What began as a timber atelier for prison supply became a sugar plantation. Sixteen men turned a sugar mill meant for mules in 1856, until a new steam engine arrived after the harvest.[18] Soon the prison became the regional center for sugar processing and a marketplace for local food staples.[19] By 1860, Saint Georges seemed poised to become "the bourg of the region."[20]

Before convicts arrived in Guiana, planters and local officials had hoped to gather European prisoners, immigrants, and former slaves in hybrid facilities. Saint Georges was a monument to that early ambition. Yet the envelopment of postemancipation society by the penal colony did not need to entail the reduction of freed slaves to inmates. At Saint Georges, the imperial administration resurrected slavery in the era of

freedom and built it into postemancipation society. The lives of freedmen on the Oyapock became interlaced with the practice of punishment.

The career of Babeau, the Saint Georges commandant, offers a glimpse
of the interplay between choice and necessity that shaped the lives of
men who worked in the convict system. In 1850, while director of the interior in Basse-Terre, Babeau was driven from Guadeloupe for his imagined or real ties to insurrectionary groups.[21] In Guiana, he became bureau
chief at the direction of the interior until a plantation arsonist in Guadeloupe denounced him.[22] Expelled from Guiana's local service, he built a
career in the penal colony, beginning at the lowly post of "agent of colonization in the Bureau of Transportation."[23] At the marriage of Babeau's
daughter in 1862, her trousseau included the most expensive household
appointment in Guiana during the Second Empire: a pianoforte (1,200
francs).[24] That year, perhaps with an eye to duplicating his success at
the black prison, Babeau purchased the Pactole sugar estate outside Cayenne with a group that included local merchants and a convict guard.[25]
The merging of the penal colony with local life was not an Oyapock particularity.

With Babeau's social ascent came the backlash. The administration
seized his workers, dismantled his refinery, and transformed Saint
Georges into a depository for "evildoers of the colony convicted by the
Cayenne Assize Court" and "invalid transportees of the black race."[26] After 1863, Babeau did the work that no one wished to. He became "very
useful in rather difficult circumstances" as the jailer of ex-convicts. In
1865, Babeau assumed command of the prison on Saint Joseph Island
designated for men whom the government transported for surveillance
infractions.[27] Soon afterward he became commandant of Saint Pierre, a
penal settlement for ex-convicts on the Maroni River. In 1868 Babeau was
tried and acquitted in Cayenne for embezzling "products from diverse
concessions to the prejudice of the state or the succession of transportees." He had been tending and selling the abandoned crops of ex-convicts
at Saint Pierre who died or disappeared.[28]

In 1854, a mere two years after the first convicts arrived in Guiana, the
ex-convict became a special class of inmate. With the annexation of

the liberated man to the colonial prison, convict transportation to Guiana became a machine of unending punishment. The reduction of liberated men to inmates began as a bold experiment that required considerable technical art. Both unconventional architectural elements and innovative legal tools enabled their confinement. Soon, however, the absorption of ex-convicts by the military work camp became an unremarkable, enduring norm of Guiana's convict system.

The inventor of permanent enclosure, Governor Louis-Adolphe Bonard, embraced a blueprint for convict settlement that resembled the Oyapock scheme of Sarda Garriga. Bonard, too, pictured a mobile front line of convicts pushing into the forest. To speed their advance, the admiral, an engineer with a degree from the elite École Polytechnique, designed portable prison barracks. The navy indulged his fancy by ordering hundreds of these—mobile iron huts with zinc roofs—to be manufactured and shipped to Cayenne.[29] The Comté River, a region with many abandoned plantations, became the setting for Bonard's experiment in jungle conquest. The ailing governor left Guiana after only two years (in an armchair). Yet he shaped the convict system so profoundly that the Comté might be called the primal scene from which the whole endeavor unfolded.

Bonard intended that convicts, after clearing the land, would build a chain of prisons. Alfred de Saint Quentin, the local official in Guiana responsible for Bridges and Paths, described Bonard's blueprint for convict settlements as a "complete system of colonization" that began with the construction of a "normal penitentiary." He added, "We will restrict ourselves in the first constructions to the general rules of isolation as they pertain to penitentiaries, to modify those rules in a future more or less distant." According to Hamélin, minister of the navy, Bonard's plan involved the construction of "a first provisional penitentiary" from which convicts would advance to create "a second penitentiary" and then a third.[30]

What Saint Quentin called a normal penitentiary struck Captain Armand Jusselain as an eccentric, unwieldy structure with an Algerian motif. Of the first prison to be built on the Comté, called Sainte Marie, Jusselain recalled:

> Rocks from a local quarry served to build the foundations of four
> blockhouses at the angles of the camp. The carpentry for the first of

these blockhouses had just been sent to us from Cayenne. With its walls of bullet-proof hardwood, its openings in the form of ship portals, its crenelations and machicoulis, this construction, which might have rendered service against the Bedouins, was the heaviest, the most inconvenient . . . that could be raised in these forests.[31]

During the phase of Algerian pacification, which largely ended with the defeat of Abd-el-Kadr in 1847, the French blockhouse was a lookout tower at the outer limit of the imperial frontier.[32] The version of this building concocted by Bonard fused the ship and the medieval tower in its design, while seeming African in purpose. Elsewhere Jusselain wrote of "blockhouses as in Africa."[33]

Bonard had been a captive in Algeria as a young man. At the age of twenty-six, just out of school, he survived the shipwreck of the *Silène* during the 1830 invasion of Algiers. In a dictated memoir of his Algerian adventure—a simulated monologue over cigars—Bonard claimed to have survived his first encounter with Arabs by outsavaging the savages. He accomplished this by chewing on the feathery body of a mostly dead chicken that he salvaged from the ship and then by waving the rotting carcass around his captors. "In addition to the protection supplied me by my marabout (who almost abandoned me at a critical moment) I had a fetish that I discovered by accident, which made the Arabs recoil in horror when I exhibited it."[34]

Bonard's inward-pointing watchtowers reveal a structural peculiarity of the frontier that played so large a role in his colonization scheme. His frontier divided civilization from savagery. Yet it was the prisoners, not the forest, who embodied barbarism beyond the line. The frontier lived inside them and moved where they did. As the men felled trees and advanced into the clearings, the size of the unconquered zone of the enemy (and hence the number of frontier watchtowers) would increase.

Bonard meant to use ex-convicts, who were physically the weakest men available, as an expendable front line of prison builders. Several groups of ex-convicts then existed in the colony because of street-sweeping measures by the government after Louis-Napoleon's coup d'état. By mid-July 1853, 335 ex-convicts had reached the colony in execution of the decree of 8 December 1851, which authorized the roundup of criminals with surveillance infractions. The ministry of the interior also packed off an uncertain number of so-called volunteers to Guiana. They were ex-convicts who had supposedly elected to resettle in the colony on exiting French prisons. It is far more likely that the government veiled compulsion as choice, using the same device it employed when assigning surveyed people to locations in France.[35]

At the time of Bonard's arrival, the volunteers languished on Îlet la Mère, a former leprosarium off the coast of Cayenne. The governor made a cynical appeal to these men by reviving the ghost of Sarda Garriga's incremental colonial scheme, involving transfer to the continent and eventual resettlement in a town for somewhat free men. On 18 July 1854, he notified the minister of the navy that sixty ex-convicts would immediately begin preparatory work on the Comté. In reward, "as they belong to the category of liberated men [*libérés*], I made it known that those who conduct themselves without reproach and show unflagging zeal on terra firma would be put to the trial of surveyed liberty in the environs of a penitentiary."[36]

Days before announcing his new plan for liberated men, Bonard contrived a legal framework for ex-convict life on the Comté that made freedom unattainable by anyone, no matter how exemplary his conduct. On 14 July 1854, Bonard enacted a decree laying out procedures for applying surveillance of the high police in French Guiana.[37] On 15 July he declared a state of siege on a sector of the Comté River of unspecified size. The besieged region included the military post of Cacao, a timber workshop created in May 1854 using local prison labor, which became the site of the Sainte Marie prison.

> The Division Chief, Governor of French Guiana, in view of article 4 of the law of 9 August 1849 on the state of siege; considering that the military post of Cacao, placed outside all centers of population, is destined to become a penitentiary; and that it is necessary to concentrate two ateliers there, one for *repris de justice,* the other for men placed under police surveillance. . . .
>
> Article 1. Effective on the 18th of July, the military post of Cacao and the terrain comprised in the plan deposited with the Direction of the Interior is declared in a state of siege. In consequence, at the

establishment called Cacao, all individuals whatever their status, are and remain subject to the dispositions of article 7 of the law of 9 August.[38]

Through the decree of 14 July relevant to surveillance of the high police and that of 15 July declaring a state of siege on the Comté, Bonard constructed a legal space that would seem unprecedented in French history. Bonard fused police surveillance and siege rule in order to affix ex-convicts to the grounds of a prison and retain them there under the jurisdiction of military courts.[39]

Bonard's Comté campaign departed in crucial spatial and temporal respects from the framework of siege rule on domestic territory. Whether responding to a rebellion or to the unwelcome future prospect of one, the state of siege took effect on domestic soil over a clearly defined, circumscribed region, which naturally contained the very people whose behavior disturbed the authorities.[40] Bonard, in contrast, justified his declaration of siege by announcing that the pertinent region was empty of civilians ("outside all centers of population"), while the people who threatened security were elsewhere. In Bonard's Comté campaign, the besieged region was the destination point, not the origin point, of undesirables. His decree also broke with the French tradition of siege rule from a temporal standpoint. He justified siege rule on the Comté by referring to the categories of men whom the government intended to settle there ("considering that it is necessary to concentrate two ateliers there, one for *repris de justice* [i.e., ban-breakers], the other for men placed under police surveillance"). The danger posed by ex-convicts on the Comté inhered to all people of their type. Because the peril they posed could never subside, the siege could never be lifted.

Through Bonard's temporal and spatial experiment, Guiana came to resemble North Africa in a legal sense. Decrees of 9 and 16 December 1848 divided Algeria into civil and military territories, with the former designed on the model of French departments. The military territories fell under the control of the governor general and an administrative hierarchy of army officers while remaining largely empty of civilian institutions.[41] Bonard reconfigured a region of Guiana as an Algerian-style military zone by means of indefinite siege rule.

There were nearer colonial examples of extended siege rule. Guadeloupe had been subject to the state of siege for much of the Second Republic under the auspices of Bonard's friend Admiral Bruat. (Bruat had been with Bonard during the conquest of Algiers as a fellow captive from the shipwrecked *Silène*.)[42] Nearer still, Admiral Fourichon declared a state of siege on Îlet la Mère in Guiana on 22 July 1853 to repress a rebellion of newly arrived political prisoners on the island.[43] It is uncertain whether Fourichon ever lifted that state of siege. Bonard's decree of 15 July 1854 arose from an imperial culture that tolerated, even encouraged, prolonged suspensions of the law overseas.

Bonard's July 1854 decrees for the Comté can equally be read as a response to the sénatus-consulte of 3 May 1854 placing Guiana and all other colonies (except for Martinique, Guadeloupe, and Réunion) under decree rule. That imperial regime licensed administrators to abandon French legal norms on imperial soil. The 1854 decision may have nerved the governor, emboldening him to toy with unusual legal concoctions.

In September 1854, three months after grouping ex-convicts on the Comté, Bonard informed the ministry of his general plan for a future ex-convict settlement. Four kilometers upriver from the Sainte Marie prison, the *libérés* would build their own village, Saint Augustin, which Bonard named after Christianity's most famous penitent. Yet Bonard also intended Saint Augustin to be a fort-like prison in common with its predecessor. In March 1855, he reported that "the blockhouse of Saint Augustin is up; we are going to begin work on the entrenchment that shall serve as a reduct."[44]

In November 1854, Bonard attributed the continued residence of ex-convicts at Sainte Marie to the delayed arrival of the iron huts. There were other causes for that delay. Ex-convicts had not yet built the church, the hospital, the ovens or the storehouses of the Sainte Marie prison; they had not yet laid the road from Sainte Marie to Saint Augustin; finally, they had not yet produced the quantity of bricks needed "not only for the penitentiary under construction, but to satisfy all the needs of Saint Augustin . . . an entire village to be raised for six hundred *libérés* or banbreakers [*repris de justice*] in surveyed liberty."[45]

Both Sainte Marie and Saint Augustin were built of wood, with each building supported by elevated brick foundations; over time Bonard imagined brick buildings would replace the wood ones. Massive brick output served no immediate construction need on the Comté River. In contrast, bricks were in high demand on Royal Island during Bonard's tenure in the colony. Here is an 1857 description of Royal Island by Admiral Baudin, Bonard's successor: "Time was wasted on a project that was truly gigantic, but magnificent, to put the free personnel out of reach of attacks by transportees."[46] Baudin referred to the enormous brick rampart that inmates on Royal Island built in order to protect soldiers who lived on the other side. Captain Jusselain compared the Royal Island wall to the wall of China. It was Guiana's most spectacular architectural feature. "On ascending to the plateau of the transportees, we crossed a crenellated wall that is situated at the edge of the large hill and stretches parallel to the ravine across the whole width of the island."[47] The wall revealed the contradiction that lay at the heart of Bonard's colonial system. He envisaged rapid advancement in space yet required unending confinement. Rising higher and growing thicker while ex-convicts on the Comté made new bricks, the rampart also embodied the threshold separating imprisonment from free life that no inmate could be allowed to cross.

Bonard's lasting contribution to the convict system came in the form of an 1855 imperial decree, issued at his instructions, which would shape Guiana's transportation system for nearly a century. Through the new decree, the jurisdiction of the military prison over free men became a permanent state of affairs. The siege became affixed to ex-convicts as a matter of their personal status.

The new decree aimed to resolve a problem that arose after an ex-convict volunteer protested his detention and disputed the power of a military court to judge him, especially as a court of last resort. The volunteer called Archenault was sentenced to death in absentia by a Comté military tribunal for killing a comrade during a failed escape attempt. Archenault insisted that French jurisprudence allowed civilians sentenced by courts-martial to appeal those judgments to the Court of Cassation. In fall 1854, Bonard demanded a new imperial decree that would eliminate such challenges in the future. He wanted all transported people, including ex-convicts, to be assimilated to soldiers under the jurisdiction of courts-martial and the Code des bagnes—the old royal edicts for galley slaves. He further demanded a revision of the May 1854 transportation law so that future escapists of all categories, including ex-convicts, would be punished as soldiers fleeing to the enemy and shot in the back. The enemy was themselves. "The convict who flees with arms, is he not armed against his country as much as a soldier who passes to the enemy?"[48]

In reply to Bonard's request, the decree of 29 August 1855 adjusted the status of inmates in Guiana by drawing an explicit connection between the Guianese prison and Algeria. Problems might arise, noted the minister of the navy, Admiral Hamelin, should "the establishments of transportation not be englobed by the regime of military zones," by which he meant the new military sectors of Algeria.[49] The 1855 decree did not transform prisons in Guiana into Algerian-style military sectors, however. Instead the body of an inmate became a martial zone as a matter of personal status. The 1855 decree was the final engineering feat of the Bonard era. By an act of law, the governor's massive rampart and the war zone it contained became weightless and portable. A jurisdiction that lived on the man could move. It traveled wherever he did. In this sense, the predicament of convicts in Guiana resembled that of Algerian natives, who remained under the jurisdiction of military courts even when they lived outside military sectors.[50]

Through the new decree, the penal colony became a special jurisdiction that differed profoundly from what had encompassed hard labor prisoners in France. The novelty of this jurisdiction resulted from its arrangements for ex-convicts, which transformed the predicament of everyone else.

> Article 1. All individuals undergoing transportation under whatever title in penitentiary colonies overseas are obliged to work and subject to military discipline and subordination.
>
> They are justiciable by councils of war; military laws are applicable to them.
>
> Article 2. The dispositions in the second paragraph of the preceding article are applicable to *libérés* and to ex-convicts required to reside in the colony.[51]

All transported people, including liberated men, became subject to councils of war and to military laws by this decree. Yet ex-convicts remained exempt from military discipline and subordination. These terms held a particular significance in Guiana's prison system. In the penal colony, the phrase "council of war" did not refer to a normal court-martial, nor did "military laws" refer to laws that applied to sailors and soldiers. For prisoners in Guiana, the so-called council of war was a special maritime tribunal that had long judged hard labor convicts in the navy's prisons, which the decree of 27 March 1852 and the law of 30 May 1854 perpetuated in Guiana. The unusual nature of the forum that went by the name "council of war" in the 1855 decree meant that military law, too, had an unusual significance. It referred to the law of the naval prison.

The 1855 decree greatly increased the violence of this system because of the way the text (1) flattened the distinction between convicts and ex-convicts, and (2) resurrected the liberated man after demolishing him by introducing an unusual distinction between convicts and ex-convicts. By the 1855 decree, ex-convicts became subject to "military law"; in plain terms, they became subject to prison law in common with all other inmates.

While the 1855 decree annexed the ex-convict to the naval prison as a matter of personal status, the text exempted liberated men from "military discipline and subordination." Above all, this phrase referred to corporal punishment. Through the new decree, the beating of convicts by navy officials ceased to be a form of legal violence and became a form of disciplinary power about which the law (in this case, special military prison law) needed to remain silent. The special maritime tribunal that judged hard labor prisoners in France had dispensed blows of the cord as criminal sentences. Duplicate copies of trial documents that were sent by the navy to Guiana in 1852 underscored the importance of the cord as a judicial weapon of repression. To the ministry of the navy, corporal punishment remained legal in Guiana by virtue of the French Criminal Code, which conferred validity on the law of the naval prison. Yet corporal punishment became unmentionable by the special law of Guiana's prisons after 1855. All corporal punishment thereafter became a tool of correction to be dispensed at the discretion of prison commandants, which the special maritime tribunal did not control.[52] To the Jesuit chaplain Verdière, corporal punishment after 1855 lay "outside the common law and the regulations."[53] It is expressive of the world that Guiana became in the years after this decree that this priest should use the phrase "common law"—roughly equivalent here to the law of the land—when referring to the special law of the military prison.

In 1856, a Jesuit traveling along the Comté found "quite a particular population. First, it is entirely black; there is only one white inhabitant in the whole quarter."[54] The banks of the Comté, "distant from any center of population," were scarcely that when Bonard placed a region of unspecified size under a state of siege or afterward. Captain Jusselain writes of his surprise at discovering the number of people who still lived there: "We were surprised at the decision to throw the transportation project into the forest, in a deserted part of the country ... (I did not know then that the Roura quarter, which includes the basins of the Oyac, the Comté, and the Orapu had 1,739 inhabitants in 1857)."[55]

The Roura quarter was not empty of people in 1857 but of plantations. It had become an arresting spectacle of ruins. It was also a region known for political militancy. When, during the Second Republic, the parish priest had sought to sway Roura voters during his sermon, "all negroes and some negresses walked out of the church murmuring, 'They are always talking about the election, they must take us for fools,' and other words I [the gendarme Thouronde] could not hear."[56] On election day in 1849, voters marched to the polling station armed with canes in single file. Soon they rushed the voting urn, canes in the air, when a literate leader cried fraud.[57]

In Second Empire Guiana the single white resident of the Comté, Michel Favard, director of the interior, managed to encircle his indocile neighbors with prisoners and prison guards. The fracas at the polling station in 1849 had been at Favard's huge estate, La Caroline. The choice of the Comté for Bonard's jungle conquest scheme draws attention to the use of prisons by stragglers from among the old elite as weapons against freed people.

In Guiana during the 1850s, on the Comté as elsewhere, the penal colony enveloped African immigrants and former slaves. Both groups tended to be confounded with convicts, although there were nuances. Administrators viewed immigrants less as felons than as slave-like, all-purpose laborers to be rented, swapped, mixed into prisons, and attached to convict road gangs.[58] Emancipated slaves, including people born in Africa, stood for something else. The metropolitan decree of emancipation violated every social and legal principle that planters considered valid. The elite looked on ex-slaves as confiscated property, refractory tools—bodies that refused to be used—and instigators of personal ruin. The emancipated slave's unauthorized exit from bondage constituted his deviance.

In November 1854, the *Cinq Frères,* the first African immigrant ship, reached Guiana with 237 passengers. Bonard claimed one hundred men for the Penitentiary Administration. Nearly everyone aboard belonged to the Kru, a maritime people from the Grain Coast who had long been employed as sailors aboard British naval and commercial vessels. In Guiana they worked in prisons, as auxiliaries to the convict road gang, and as sailors on boats that moved men and supplies to and from convict sites.[59] The Africans wore the costumes of convicts, which meant one wool shirt, one toile smock, one set of toile pants, one white toile chemise, one toile work cap, and one hat in straw or felt per year (art. 5). Bonard fixed their wage at 50 centimes per diem—equal to that of inmates of the Cayenne jail. What distinguished them as immigrants were the letters E. A. (*émigrant africain*), followed by a number, stamped on every article in their trousseau.[60]

For Bonard, the advantage of new Africans lay in what might be done to them or withheld from them that could not be attempted with emancipated slaves for legal reasons. The status of non-European colonial immigrants resembled that of both slaves and convicts. The immigration decree of 27 March 1852 defined non-European immigrants merely as bodies to be numbered and annotated in a roll book (*registre matricule).*[61] These were administrative practices appropriate to a group that would be discussed at the high imperial and the local level as *bras,* arms whose value lay in their robustness and their quantity. Long in use for prison inmates in France, the *registre matricule* became an imperial commonplace with the invention of the slave census. Because they did not exist as legal persons to French civil law, non-European immigrants could not even marry. Later, beginning in 1861, they could wed with the prior consent of the governor, which meant he could refuse them. In 1865, Guiana's privy council discussed the second marriage petition of the Kru boatswain John Edwin, age twenty-six, and Esther Bondy, age forty-eight, a Cayenne laundress born in Africa. The immigration commissioner had refused their first request, noting the bride's age (twenty-two years older than the groom). The governor and his council approved the second petition. Yet the couple soon separated. John Edwin became a hard labor convict in the penal colony.[62]

Immigrants collided with the convict system and the ghost of chattel slavery, often at once, whether or not they became inmates or E.A. The original director of the Saint Georges prison, Bouché, left that post to become an overseer for the Company of the Approuague, a state-supported venture that combined gold mining with sugar planting by immigrant peons on the Approuague River, a region favored by the old planter elite. In 1857 at the sugar plantation called Jamaique, owned by the Approuague Company, Bouché became notorious for his brutality to immigrants. He was "excessively hard and scarcely able to figure to himself that the blacks are free and must be treated as human creatures."[63]

Refractory workers from the Approuague wound up as convicts in the road gang of Cayenne under Michel Favard, director of the interior and Comté magnate; they worked alongside E.A. whom Favard borrowed like slaves from the convict system. In 1856, when Kru began fleeing in large numbers to British Guiana, Favard demanded a fresh supply of workers. "There will be no need, I think, for new transportees if, as you led me to expect, the penitentiary service can cede a certain number of Krouman to the local service."[64]

Confronted with mass immigrant flight, Bonard's successor, Admiral Baudin, demanded the extradition of the Africans from British Guiana as criminal fugitives. They "can be assimilated to thieves, since they steal the sum paid for their passage from Africa to America, which they are supposed to reimburse by work."[65] Governors in Martinique and Guadeloupe responded to recalcitrant immigrants by scavenging from slave law.[66] Baudin looked to the penal colony. He knew the labor contracts of immigrants were fraudulent.[67] Yet he defined them as thieves who stole their labor by leaving. When the British refused to turn over the Africans,

Baudin, who had once patrolled the African coast for illegal slave ships, devised an alert system for hunting the Africans down.[68]

When requesting African immigrants in February 1854, Bonard foresaw a future for Guiana in which "this territory, which might still be usefully exploited by metropolitan interests, is entirely delivered to members of the African race, who will reestablish their native customs." For the governor, Guiana's new prisons were there to keep the colony French. Yet Bonard worried that the exodus of white Creoles and the rise of a landowning black peasantry would tarnish the reputation of the penal colony. People would accuse the navy's new venture of "having destroyed the old colony of Guiana, of having brought about the expatriation and misery of the inhabitants." To the extent that Bonard voiced concern about rural people, he depicted them as a blot on the prisons in their midst.[69]

Bonard's jungle conquest scheme helped to create an unusual class of black proprietors on the Comté in fall 1854, when the river became the epicenter of a yellow fever epidemic. In their marriage contract of 12 October 1854, the African-born couple Auguste Eckessan and Corine Arnola each owned half of Saint Auguste, a plantation named after the groom (not to be confused with Saint Augustin, the ex-convict jail town on that river).[70] The Cayenne office of the notary Joseph Dechamp, who drafted the marriage contract, was then a frequent stopping place for residents of the Oyac (the lower Comté). In September and October 1854, Dechamp sold off enormous waterfront land parcels near or adjoining the property of the married pair.

The specificity of these Comté transactions becomes evident when they are compared with land sales in other parts of Guiana from the same year. For instance, on 27 March 1854, Césaire Guillaumont, Sabine Estanisien, Héloise Estanisien, and Jean-Pierre Lis (acting for himself and his son Charles Estanisien) together purchased a two-hectare (five-acre) parcel of the Sainte Elisabeth plantation in the Tour de l'Ile neighborhood of Cayenne Island.[71] On 2 July, Lucile Chapou and Thérèse Phosphore, acting for themselves and their husbands, jointly purchased a four-hectare parcel of the same plantation.[72] That August, a man called Jean Baptiste Tarrier purchased a hut on a one-hectare lot in the Montsinéry quarter.[73] People on the Comté River, by contrast, acquired ten, thirteen, eighteen, twenty-five, even fifty-five hectares at a time in September and October 1854. In a further distinction from other proprietors, they acquired these tracts of waterfront property with no money down. In the case of Charles Fantaisie, Louis Brutus, Lovelace Moricot, Candide Bonny, Césaire Sainte Croix, Louis Polycarpe, and Demoiselle Doris Anemone, "the acquirer will have the option to pay either in money or in clean, fresh, dry rocou seeds."[74]

The ease with which rural people became proprietors in the 1850s led decrees that regulated plantation work to become inexecutable in Guiana, whether on the Comté or elsewhere. When former slaves became proprietors, they engaged landless people on their plots as sharecroppers. An agricultural bulletin of February 1861 complained that at Roura, "no one works except occasionally; their vagabondage is protected under the inviolable system of association."[75] Association, or sharecropping, meant that landowners did not need to pay salaries, while their workers became exempt from the fixed daily task system that applied to rural wage earners. The exodus of planters in the era of the penal colony helped former slaves to avoid becoming prisoners themselves for labor infractions. The E.A. who filled out Favard's convict road gang were needed to take the place of missing locals.

In their nearness to freed people, the prisons of the Comté expressed an ideological conflation of black liberty with criminal deviance. If locals had failed to comprehend that message, they got a reminder after convicts left their river. In 1860, following the closure of the prisons, Guiana's privy council voted to fund a primary school in the Roura village. Already a small number of children attended a makeshift parish school. Students whose parents lived at distant points on the Comté slept at Roura during the week; boys slept at the home of the curate, and girls stayed with the schoolmistress, a sister of Saint Joseph de Cluny. The founding of a permanent school required sleeping quarters for a larger number of students. In reply, Guiana's privy council offered a mobile iron hut to Roura for use as a child dormitory.[76] In a colony devoid of municipal government, where the budget functioned by gubernatorial decree, the shelter invented by Bonard to advance convicts through the wilderness became the substitute for civic architecture. In a thickly forested colony with no shortage of local carpenters, Roura students were left to board in a metal prison hangar.

Nearly a decade earlier, in 1851, the colony's apostolic prefect had warned the navy about spoiling former slaves for field work with lessons in geography and mathematics.[77] Imperial administrators sought to keep people out of the classroom altogether. In May 1853 Governor Fourichon, who later became minister of the navy, forbade teachers to receive students above the age of fourteen; he denounced the Brothers of Ploermel for admitting "young men who by their age are subject to *livrets* [worker passports] and work engagements."[78] Opposition to rural education survived the demise of the Guianese plantation, as the dormitory affair reveals. What began as a policy that officials defended with the future of the plantation in mind assumed another significance; to oppose rural institutions, or to undermine them symbolically, became a racial doctrine. The iron barrack designated the people of the Comté as uneducable savages and outcasts; it expressed the punitive isolation of black children from the French nation, despite their formal status under the Civil Code.

In 1871, at the founding of the Third Republic, a group of penal colony employees consisting of local men submitted a legislative petition that depicted Guianese people as unfit for French political rights. The petitioners (perhaps under compulsion by the governor) described people "of the African race" as isolated squatters in the domanial forest who languished in "primitive ignorance" and had yet to be "initiated to social life" or even to discover Cayenne, the dwelling place of "the white race and the colored race who alone enjoyed the benefits of civilization."[79] This fantastical rendering of Creole life is chiefly of interest for what it mystifies about the interaction between rural communities and the administration embodied by signatories of this document. The isolation of people in the forest, which the petitioners evoked as a mark of native barbarism, instead resulted from the formal structure of imperial rule. Rule by decree enabled administrators to keep rural districts empty of civilian institutions while tossing prisons on top of independent black communities whenever the occasion arose and enveloping black people in vaguely delimited (ergo unlimited) jurisdictions under siege rule. To the extent that people lived in a state of nature in Guiana, this was a contrivance of law and a form of punitive abandonment.

Cayenne in the 1850s was a kinetic town with a drowsy exterior where people, objects, and bits of turf began to move at a quickened pace. On the Rue du Port, dogs, mules, harnesses, bags of onions, cauldrons, featherbeds, armoires, and used containers of every sort went up for auction at death, legal seizure, and departure.[80] As the debris of an extinct commodity culture, the empty jars, bare cupboards, and secondhand weighing machines all referred back to a single vanished substance, which was slavery. During this heyday of liquidation sales, emancipated people moved between town and country to arrange their affairs and often resettled in Cayenne. Favard called the trend "immigration of a new type."[81]

Emancipated slaves knew Cayenne as the seat of the law. It was the one place in the colony with courts and notaries. It was there they went to create their futures, whether by land purchase or marriage contract, and to create their pasts by recognizing children before notaries. Yet the problem of envelopment by the convict system affected newcomers to town as acutely as it affected people on the Comté. Prisoners and prison guards began thronging to Cayenne at the same moment that freed people began to cluster in the capital.

In 1856 Governor Baudin attempted to resettle convicts in and around Cayenne in supposed mimicry of the British colonial model in Australia. The experiment centered on an elite of men under sentence who would live "outside the penitentiaries in a half-liberty that is the highest good for the transportees, which they fear losing more than anything in the world."[82] Baudin proved quite reticent about loosing convicts on the town. According to a table of January 1857, there were 426 convicts, including nine Antillean women, working "outside the penitentiaries." Of these, 246 worked for the state. Most convicts, though not the women, slept on a pontoon in the harbor.[83] At the time, there were 3,771 men living in prisons, of whom 1,800 lived on the islands.[84]

A new civic discourse arose in Guiana during Baudin's efforts to settle convicts in Cayenne. The mayor, an official appointed by the governor, together with his appointed associates, launched this municipal protest as "organs of the inhabitants of the city," a title they assumed in January 1857.[85] The campaign ended when Jerome Bonaparte, minister of Algeria and colonies, sided with the locals in November 1858 and ordered Baudin to expel all inmates in private employ from the town and island of Cayenne.

This civic protest is puzzling due to the narrowness (even non-existence) of the city in Second Empire Guiana, and because of the mysterious identity of the people whom the councillors hoped to run out of town. In January 1857 Favard observed: "The Municipal Council . . . does not participate at all in the administration of the city, because until now the diverse interests that inspired the organization of the commune in France have never existed here."[86] The council had no budget and no governing functions as a result of maneuvers since 1848 to close freed slaves and men who spoke for them out of politics.[87] The council, which met once a year, had no mandate from the public. Worse, it existed to palliate the refusal of administrators to allow freed slaves a voice in public affairs.

The council, which did not speak for the people, also did not speak for the interests of its members. The group included not only Merlet, mayor since the time of slavery, but also men who made a living off the convict system. The councillor Célestin Lalanne was a *fournisseur,* a middleman who supplied beef—Venezuelan cows—to men on naval rations, including soldiers, guards, and prisoners. The councillor Lheurre, from an old Creole family of color, supplied the prisoners and their keepers by procuring salted cod, salted pork, salted beef, dry beans, tobacco, and flour from North America.[88]

To Guiana's elite, the city was not a political structure but an ideal space that came into being through the removal of undesirables from town and their exclusion from urban livelihoods. Measures that defined the city after slavery aimed to invent a place as empty as possible.

As a municipal mindset and a plan of action, the empty city originated with ruined planters who lingered in Guiana, surviving on administrative sinecures, and with governors who embraced their cause. This municipal program aimed to rebuild social, spatial, and legal boundaries that emancipation destroyed. Nearly all legislation in Guiana for the control of work, markets, and movement during the 1850s can be traced to an 1819 municipal decree that cracked down on tolerant masters and slaves living in de facto liberty in the town.[89] The documentary procedures—matricular registers, numbered plaques, and *livrets* signed by the mayor—that tracked vendors, day laborers, and fishermen after 1848 duplicated methods that had once tracked enslaved workers.

By decree of 10 March 1853, Governor Fourichon struck at the "number of individuals under the name of day laborers who live in a state of vagabondage" by fixing the combined number of boatswains, porters, and day laborers in town at sixty. Each boatswain would receive a white iron plaque and working papers marked with a number.[90] The town of sixty boatswains of good character was also a town of eighty vendors, who needed to carry numbered *livrets* and slips from the mayor in case of random checks by gendarmes (art. 19). Next came the decree limiting the number of town fishermen to 150 and of fishing canoe captains to fifty. There would be forty professional canoes for the town (forty canoes, fifty captains), each with a plaque marked "Fishing Canoe" followed by a number. There would be registers to record the departure of canoes and registers to record their arrival. Failure to fish four times a week meant losing one's license as a professional.[91]

The colonial elite understood the boundaries of the city in both physical and symbolic terms. While referring to Cayenne, the city was also a legal space called forth by identity-related inscriptions that hooked people to the family of man (in its local rendition) through their surnames and lineages. The ideology of the empty city drove efforts to deface and indeed to scramble the freed people's legal selves. On 8 December 1848, André Pariset, commissar-general of Guiana, had sealed the freedmen's rolls.[92] After that date, emancipated people omitted from the list needed to apply for patronymics. In 1854, an elderly Cayenne townswoman, "Rosalie, age seventy-four, having belonged to Monsieur *Pierre* ROMAIN, proprietor in Cayenne," requested a surname from the local government. She received the name MAINRO, an anagram scrambling the name of her former master. The master was not white (note the italics and capital letters, which function as racial glyphs). He may have been her son.[93]

Anagrams linked two or more people and also separated them. Names of this kind, which were commonplace under slavery, announced the existence of a bond that law could not recognize or resist insinuating. As a form of exclusion, anagrams marked the freed people as beings that lacked lineages and rose out of nothingness. In April 1848, before the emancipation decree had reached the colony, "Adolphe called Eydoux" sponsored the manumission of Jean-François Lodaf. Also that month, two young girls, Magdelaine-Marie-Marguerite, age five, and Rose-Christine, age two, became free with the sponsorship of Raphael-Philippe. They received the patronymic "Phirap."[94] "Lodaf" and "Phirap" identified freed children as bound to their sponsors by ties the law refused to acknowledge. "Mainro" folded the enslaved past of Rosalie into her life as a free woman and marked her as unfit to take her master's name (or nearest kin's name), while expressing a further disavowal: anagrams bestowed on freed slaves after 1848 defined them as bastards of what Rousseau called the *moi collectif*—the family-like French body politic.[95]

In 1857, the year Cayenne's municipality began protesting in the name of the city, the minister of the navy rebuked Baudin for the way patronymics were being handled in Cayenne. On the advice of the privy council, Baudin had refused to grant the surname Amiel to Reine, a former plantation domestic.

> At first . . . you refused to receive her request on the grounds that Amiel was the name of the clerk at Sinnamary, but you reversed yourself and accorded the name when the functionary in question produced a certificate demonstrating that he was not in the least opposed to granting this name to REINE . . . the decree of emancipation placed former slaves under the regime of the common law. This new situation has been so well understood in Martinique and Guadeloupe that since 1848 there has not been a single decree conceding patronymics. In contrast, in Guiana one has constant recourse to the legal procedure for changing names.[96]

The affair over Reine's name revealed the gap that had opened between Guiana and the other former slave colonies in the era of the penal colony. The sénatus-consulte of 3 May 1854 placing Guiana under rule by decree helped practices from the era of slavery that vanished from Martinique and Guadeloupe to endure there. Amiel, the clerk at Sinnamary, and Reine, age forty-two, who moved to Sinnamary as a free woman, knew each other quite well. The minister did not reveal what sort of certificate the man produced to show his enthusiastic consent to her name change. He may have been her father. After 1854, parents granted children explicit permission to use the family surname when recognizing them before notaries.

With the arrival of Governor Louis-Marie de Tardy de Montravel, the municipal council knew its moment had come. He was an adoptive son of the colony. As a young lieutenant in the 1840s he had come to Guiana to explore the Amazon and relaunch the French claim to that river. He accomplished this by persuading the Brazilian governor of Para to authorize what he described as a scientific voyage, on which he and perhaps Alfred, his teenage brother, would have been the scientists.[97] The trip killed Alfred and brought about the marriage of Montravel to Mademoiselle Albert, whose father commanded the marine infantry troops stationed in the colony.[98]

At the end of December 1859, the councillors congratulated Montravel for his "scrupulous execution of the ministerial decision to distance transportees from the town and the island of Cayenne."[99] A slow five-minute walk from Montravel's door to the top of Ceperou Hill, which obscures the port from the town, would have revealed hundreds of men in straw hats unloading and reloading supplies commissioned by the town's first citizens. During Montravel's term as governor, there were more convicts than ever working portside for the navy; they slept aboard two pontoons, the *Gardien* and the *Proserpine.* Montravel repeatedly asked for permission—unsuccessfully—to evacuate the pontoons and replace them with a prison on the shore. As of October 1863, "the floating penitentiaries . . . will evidently be insufficient to contain all the men who are needed by the services of artillery, engineering, Bridges and Paths."[100]

In view of the councillors' uncharacteristic glee in December 1859, one can assume that Montravel's conduct during his first months in office answered their wishes exactly. He struck against town undesirables, as he defined them. Within weeks of arriving in the colony, Montravel decreed a general requisition on the roads from Cayenne east to the Approuague and west along the coast.[101] He expelled unsupervised youngsters from the town in July.[102] He initiated a crackdown on vagabondage in November. The same plan of urban renewal inspired Montravel, in September 1860, to revive the old municipal ban on drumming and dancing that had lapsed at the time of emancipation.[103]

In November 1859, before a crowd of administrators, Montravel opened a new session of Guiana's Imperial Court with a speech attacking "that class of parasites living in a state of disguised vagabondage, either in the middle of the forests, or on the ruins of the old plantations, or in the town of Cayenne, next to us."[104] The parasites whom Montravel wanted to evict from town, or to hook to the gang that cleaned its streets, turned out to be irremovable. They were the townspeople. The failure of Montravel to realize the ambitions of the ruined planter class resulted from changes to the colony that preceded his arrival, which even his considerable administrative power could not reverse.

The purchase of vacant lots by former slaves, together with marriage contracts, deeds of child recognition, testaments, acts of gift, and acts of barter created the town that Montravel, alighting in 1859, had hoped to erase. The parasites he wanted to drive out of town would have included people like Zénobie called Gellin, who in 1854 hired Azor, a master carpenter, to build her a house 6.66 meters long and 5.33 meters wide on the Rue Voltaire; in payment she gave him half her lot and permission to board in her new house while he built a house next door. Yet the new town of Cayenne was not simply the result of pluck by the gatecrashers. Epidemic disease caused land to move at remarkable speed during the 1850s. The acts of people as they lay dying and the death they could not escape made Cayenne what it was after slavery. On 16 June, the notary Dechamp headed to a backyard shack on the Rue de Provence where John Nalanne called Lalanne, a freedman and a fisherman, dictated his final testament. It began with a curious and often-repeated legal formula: "I was born in Africa and I have neither antecedents nor descendents." Because Nalanne/Lalanne had no lineage in civil law, there were no legal claimants to his property at death. Lalanne, who could not sign his name, gave his wife, Catherine Virins, usufruct of "a little unfinished house on the Rue Voltaire," while conferring title on her two children, Pierre Louis and Cecilia.[105]

The relationship of the black city to the penal colony was not merely a question of accidental overlap—a matter of living in the wrong place at the wrong time. As in the countryside, so in Cayenne, but more so. The convict system helped freed people to purchase land in and around the capital. As the convict system expanded, the navy offered emancipated slaves virtually the only marketplace for local products and the only opportunity for salaried work. In 1856, Favard noted the changed character of the local economy. Out of twelve thousand freed people, "No more than six thousand are seriously growing export crops. The others subsist on their own plots, or work as domestics in town, or are employed by the diverse industries that supply the transportation system."[106] Four years later, Montravel conceded that the economic future of Guiana lay with the prison, not the plantation. In March 1860, he noted that a rising number of townspeople wanted to employ convict workers, "yet agriculture is not destined to profit. Nearly all the transportees are employed cutting timber and making bricks."[107]

The convict system undermined the restorative municipal program of Guiana's ruined elite by helping freed people to conquer Cayenne. It is noteworthy, however, that the exodus of former slaves from the countryside coincided with the launch of Governor Baudin's neo-Australia experiment. The settlement of convicts in Cayenne transformed new migrants to the colonial capital into the inmates of a jail town. They lived under a style of police rule that resembled the state of siege in its effects. When convicts "outside the penitentiaries" removed their uniforms— toile pants and blouses stamped with a number—they were said to "dissimulate their condition" in an act of concealment that only the guards could see through. The guards, however, patrolled the town ("between whom the streets of the town have been divided"). Baudin split Cayenne into surveillance districts. The small group of convicts who slept in the town were subject to an evening lock-in. Baudin wrote of "men subject to transportation, who must no longer circulate after the cannon shot signaling the curfew at pain of being immediately imprisoned if they are found outside their domiciles." To assure compliance with the measure, the guards would call on convicts at unfixed hours of the night.[108]

Freed people began moving to town just as European ex-convicts became undesirables of the colonial capital. Racism prevented white officials from distinguishing black ex-convicts from other black people: there was no honor or civic body for crime to deface. As for Europeans, their unfitness for town life meant more than municipal expulsion. Baudin arranged convict life in Cayenne so that only a supremely meritorious group of inmates could be allowed to live there. It also seemed crucial that he be able to extract any of these experimental townsmen and return them to the military prisons where they began. The governor did not consider deactivating the jurisdiction that lived on all the convicts. In consequence of these principles, Baudin turned Cayenne into a simulacrum of free life without allowing any convict or ex-convict to exit the convict system. What privileged inmates experienced under the name of half liberty was simply an extended recess in a jail yard—a spacious annex to the facilities from which they came and to which they might return at any instant. The duration of the recess depended on their continued ability or willingness to meet the standard of model inmates.

Baudin could not bring himself to settle European ex-convicts in Cayenne. The eighty-six liberated men whom he listed as half-free on his January 1857 list all resided at Montjoly, a cattle depot outside Cayenne, under the watch of a gendarme brigade. Unlike felons under sentence, ex-convicts could not be held in check by "fear of reintegration." They did not fear the removal of freedom but chafed at its absence. Prison guards felt powerless to repress "infractions that lie outside the repression of civil tribunals such as laziness, drunkenness, and insolence toward employees of the establishment."[109] They were measured against convicts, expected to abide by the same conduct code, and subject to the authority of prison guards, but they could not be beaten for indiscipline. Aloof to the painful instruments of convict moral virtue, ex-convicts languished at the depot. Baudin's attempt to create New South Wales revealed the ex-convict to be a pariah within the prison that forbade his release. That problem, which became ever more pronounced in years to come, opened the question of where to put this undesired, surplus category in the order of law and the space of life.

CHAPTER 8

Metastasis

IN THE FALL OF 1863, Jacques Modeste Vathonne left Guiana for France to resettle as a surveyed man in his home department of Eure-et-Loir. The prefect of Paris assigned him to the village of Pinthières, his birthplace. The mayor of that village, where no one knew him, could expect to identify this average looking man—mouse-haired, balding, of middling stature (5 feet 7 inches)—by his pallor, the dimple on his chin, and the image of a trophy tattooed on his left arm.[1]

Vathonne was a rarity in the 1860s. At the time of his homecoming, more than twelve thousand people had left for Guiana, mainly from France. Just over one thousand people had returned (see Tables 1 and 2). The mere fact of the file on Vathonne defines the man as trophy-worthy. His feat was leaving.

Convicted of burglary and attempted burglary by the Versailles Assize Court on 22 February 1851, he was sentenced to twenty years of forced labor. The emperor reduced his sentence in 1853 by ten years. Yet Vathonne owed his departure from Guiana to more than a sentence remittance. According to the 1852 decree and the 1854 law creating the penal colony, all men with sentences of eight or more years were to remain there in lifelong exile as ex-convicts. Had those texts applied to Vathonne, he could not have left Guiana except as a fugitive.

Originally the navy assumed that legislation creating the penal colony

190

would be retroactive in effect. Guiana's governor in 1856, Admiral Baudin, defied that principle. He advanced a legal doctrine that rid him of men he wished neither to free nor to destroy. On 15 March 1856, after a visit to Saint Augustin, he remarked that ex-convicts "have all asked to benefit from the right one accords them to return to France"—a right that no previous administrator had imagined to exist.[2] The navy retreated from its earlier policy.[3] Men convicted before the transportation law of 30 May 1854 became eligible for repatriation at state expense. The new protocol had the virtue of postponing the ex-convict problem to 1859, when the first men subject to the exile provisions of the 1854 law would reach the end of their sentences.[4]

In the first years of transportation, administrators in Guiana were obliged to ponder the fate of liberated men when confronted with hundreds and soon thousands whom they expected to remain and who seemed to embody the future. Their reply to that challenge was permanent enclosure. The situation of the ex-convict in Guiana at the end of the 1850s was quite different from what it had been eight years before. Men whose sentences expired no longer stood for the future. They were the remainder.

The Jesuit chaplain Montfort observed: "The *libérés* are not liberated from anything."[5] The remaking of liberated men into inmates of the military prison did not cause the distinction between men serving sentences and ex-convicts to disappear. Special ex-convict facilities began to multiply after the legal difference between a liberated man and a man serving time, with respect to the rights they enjoyed, had vanished. Administrators became ever more unsettled by the ex-convict's particularity. Governor Baudin, who viewed such people as a placeless residue, responded by sending them out of the colony. In later years, the expulsion of liberated men became a process internal to the convict system and unfolded within the limits of Guiana.

The predicament of liberated felons in Guiana worsened in step with changes to the relationship between the convict system and Guiana in general. In earlier years, Baudin's neo-Australia experiment caused the convict system to merge with postemancipation life in the colonial capital. Normal inhabitants of the town became subject to a version of perpetual siege rule. The settlement of convicts "outside the penitentiary" (Baudin's phrase) prompted the instant absorption of Cayenne by the military prison. This problem became ever more pronounced in Guiana during the 1860s, when the center of convict settlement shifted to the Maroni River. In a forest peopled by Maroons and Indians, convicts laid the foundations of what became Saint Laurent, Guiana's second city and the eventual seat of the convict bureaucracy. With the creation of Saint Laurent on the western frontier, the prison devoured the world and military prison law became the law of the land.

A version of the same phenomenon that became manifest on the Maroni River affected all of Guiana during the 1860s. The Penitentiary Administration became an insidious and expanding apparatus that rewired legal space, remade the world of work, and generated new understandings of community, authority, and institutions. Whether on the Maroni River, in the colonial capital, or in the backcountry around Cayenne, it became impossible to know where the world was and where the prison ended.

At the beginning of the convict era, the attraction of the Maroni lay in its remoteness from Cayenne and its proximity to independent black communities—Maroons and Mana villagers—whom local notables hoped to destroy. Other motives inspired the ministry of the navy in 1857 to approve plans for a tiny convict village on the Maroni under the direction of Jesuit priests and Eugène Mélinon, onetime commandant of Mana. Ministerial interest in the settlement resulted from concern about the future of ex-convicts, whose numbers would soon explode, whom no one imagined treating as free people, and who were obliged to live in temporary or permanent exile in Guiana.

The arrival of Baudin, a pious man by all accounts, emboldened the Jesuits, who had returned to Guiana after nearly a century for the purpose of curing the souls of convicts there. A combination of religious zealotry and disgust for the violent excesses of martinets brought them into continuous conflict with officials under Bonard. The chaplains' distaste for the military regime of the prisons and for the world, in equal measure, inspired plans for a new style of Jesuit reduction.

Father Beigner, the head of the Jesuit mission, wanted to settle what he called parishes with recent converts—Catholics of conviction. The other men would remain "in separate establishments, in establishments currently in existence, or in similar ones." The Jesuit plan required that military prisons loom over settlers as threats while collecting the backsliders and otherwise shielding the new settlement from harmful influences. Unworthy men could expect to be removed. "The great punishment inflicted on the guilty would be momentary or perpetual reintegration into a penitentiary establishment."[6]

The Maroni parish plan harked back to the 1851 colonial plan of Pariset and to the original Javouhey project at Mana. Eugène Mélinon had ruled Mana after the nuns and knew something of the village's origins. As Pariset's protégé, Mélinon had also shaped the 1851 colonial scheme, which centered on the construction of model hamlets under police rule. When describing the Maroni, Mélinon enthused about the unlimited nature of administrative power in the region, "because the place is isolated from all agglomeration and from all free society, because all the land belongs to the state."[7]

Work began at Camp Louis-Napoleon Bonaparte in August 1857. A group of ten African workers, four gendarmes, fifteen infantrymen, and ten convicts were joined in September by forty more inmates whom the Jesuits picked from the islands. In the chaos of a forest construction project, the men discovered that the system they had hoped to escape would follow them everywhere. Village evictions began before the village went up. The Jesuit superior recommended: "Purge, purge, much severity in the beginnings is rigorously necessary."[8] A blockhouse arrived by boat from Cayenne. The Jesuit Jardinier recalled the incident in an unpublished history of the early years. "The hideous but necessary blockhouse needed to come; its arrival caused stupefaction. The commandant responded: "*It is here because you wanted it!* Now it is for you not to use it!"[9] Mélinon's speech, as recorded by his adoring amanuensis, leaves no mystery as to where the idea of resurrecting Bonard's crenellated prison tower came from. After the blockhouse, in September, came the guards, in small number. The response of the villagers was "The hole is made, the head is through, the body will come." It was an ironic allusion to a man digging his way out of prison. The guards were summoned when men began throwing themselves into the woods. Mélinon, "the hospitable man par excellence, who treads on stupid prejudices," made room for the head guard and his wife in the hut of the commandant.[10]

The Jesuits, like Mélinon, hoped to create villages full of families, despite the provisional tenancy of parish men. The brides needed to be white convict women. They could not be black, mainly though not entirely because they could not be free. "Women of the black race who have no habits of order, of work, of decency, no notion of the sanctity of marriage, *whom one could not subject to any tests, whom one could not thus study, know, and instruct,* would only have a disastrous influence on our transportees." The point was not that white convict women had superior habits but that they could be made to have them, by locking them up in a "vast establishment, closed by walls, directed by nuns"—the very sort of place that had retained African girls in the Javouhey village of Mana during the 1830s. Like Javouhey's brides in waiting, the convict women would be distributed to male settlers once the men performed some final ordeal proving them worthy of the privilege.[11]

On one crucial point, the Jesuit marriage scheme differed utterly from the earlier system at Mana. While nuns in the African village had a cache of girls at the ready, Mélinon and the Jesuits promised brides to settlers without having any women on hand. The future brides had yet to be collected from the prisons of France and shipped to the colony. The scarcity of women would soon discredit the priests in the eyes of the settlers.[12] "Many do not believe any longer in the realization of the marriages and think we are toying with them."[13]

The era of imperial matchmaking began in March 1859, with the long-awaited arrival of thirty-six convict women, who began sobbing uncontrollably as their steamship turned up the Maroni. On learning that their long trip ended in a forest, they became convinced their keepers had planned all along to kill them by dumping them into the woods. To Baudin, who watched, their fright was a great relief, proof that "all good sentiment was not extinguished in the women carried by the *Loire*."[14]

It was the navy that oversaw the shipment of women. It became the navy's task to decide which women—or rather which category of women—the men could pair with. Marriage was the only civil right the government ever considered returning to men on the Maroni. A man's eligibility for that privilege, however, required the future union to meet departmental criteria. In a letter to Governor Montravel of January 1862, Prosper de Chasseloup-Laubbat, minister of the navy, observed: "I believe it is necessary to remind you . . . that the administration and the law cannot authorize the union *between transportees* except when the future spouses are both obliged to remain in Guiana for life."[15] To keep the Maroni household from coming to pieces if the men left for France, convicts with short sentences should not be allowed to marry in the first place. Banished women could only pair with men who would never desert them. The minister claimed that convict women needed to remain fastened to the domiciles of their husbands. According to the Civil Code, "the wife is obliged to live with her husband and to go wherever he chooses to reside; the husband is obliged to receive her, and to furnish her with all necessities of life, according to his means" (art. 214).[16] Women whose spouses returned to France would require imperial pardons to fulfill their legal duty as wives to accompany their husbands. Civil marriage would negate criminal justice.[17]

On 30 June 1862 Chasseloup-Laubat tweaked the marriage policy. Earlier the minister had depicted Guiana as a prison that convict women could not be allowed to exit prematurely. Now he evoked the colony as the elective domicile of convict husbands and hence the obligatory domicile of wives according to article 214 of the Civil Code. By the new standards, concessionaires with sentences of eight or more years to hard labor, who were to remain in lifelong exile in the colony, could marry any sort of convict woman; all concessionaires could marry free women; and wives could join their settler husbands.[18] The new internment policy with regard to brides meant that women who left France to join their husbands on the Maroni, no less than wives with expired sentences, would become inmates of Saint Laurent. This was not illegal detention, according to the minister, but a conventional result of the marriage bond.[19]

A total of 244 women traveled from France to Guiana from 1861 to 1869 (see Table 2). Each woman carried the bundle of documents she would need for a civil marriage: notarized parental consent to any future union, a birth certificate, the death certificate of a past spouse. For Rosalie Béridot, age twenty-five, a native of Gordes (Vaucluse), those documents had a direct link to her crime. She had poisoned her husband Théophile on Christmas Eve, 1861.[20] The *Cormoran*, which carried Rosalie and thirty-five other girls, became the scene of nocturnal appointments, possibly rapes, with "men of the crew having relations with the women with the aid of double keys to their cabins." After the vessel reached Guiana in June 1865 the governor at the time, General Agathon Hennique, complained that "venereal diseases *contracted in France and not aboard ship* became intensely pronounced upon the disembarkation of the women" (it being impossible to doubt the hygiene of the sailors).[21] For women on the Maroni, life resembled the Atlantic crossing of the *Cormoran* in its essentials. They were inmates of a stag province full of soldiers, gendarmes, and guards. Their husbands could offer them nothing. The Jesuits, who soon regretted these unions, began spying on the wives and reporting their assignations to the governor.[22]

The model parish scheme of Mélinon and the Jesuits hinged on the provisional nature of land concessions. Essential to the development of the village was the ease of retracting concessions at the whim of the commandant, the chaplain, or the governor. When a concessionaire died, the land and the house passed to the state. "Because the land was conceded provisionally, the state evidently will take over the lot. Since the house was built with materials that belong to the state . . . it seems equitable that [the administration] should take possession of all the real estate."[23] The structure of property in Saint Laurent turned the settlement into a place for short-term occupancy, as new men replaced the sick, wayward, and dead in government-issued, removable homes. Legal interdiction prohibited all convicts under sentence from acquiring or selling property. The law of 30 May 1854 on convict transportation traced a future regime of land concessions that emphasized the enduring effects of legal interdiction on colonial soil. Land grants "will not become definitive until after the liberation of the convict."[24] On the Maroni River, however, the navy exercised a degree of control over the land that amplified the powerlessness of convicts. By imperial decree of 30 May 1860, "the part of territory of French Guiana bordered to the west by the Maroni River and to the east by an imaginary line from north to south, dividing into equal portions the surface between the Maroni and the Mana Rivers is exclusively reserved for the needs of transportation."[25] The founding of the special Maroni dominion gave navy officials new license to grant and retract plots at will while also allowing them to exclude free inhabitants of Guiana from the region.

The problem was not simply the ease of losing one's land but the difficulty of receiving a patch in the first place, which was the only way of getting a woman. In order for a man to seek a wife in Guiana, or for his existing wife to join him, he needed to be a concessionaire.[26] Although there were 560 men at Saint Laurent in 1860, only 150 were settled on plots, and their number was shrinking.

The Jesuits' model parish had split in two, with most occupants grouped at a place called the camp of trial (*camp d'épreuve*).[27] In principle, the camp was meant to test the mettle of future settlers. Yet the camp grew ever more independent from the parish and closed to it. Fear about the moral contamination of parishioners by men from the camp shaped the urban design of Saint Laurent, which was the work-in-progress of camp men. The marketplace of Saint Laurent was built to thwart the unsupervised movement of convict grocery shoppers. A Jesuit wrote to his superior in August 1860: "One is going to establish a market in order to remove from men in the camp the possibility of walking through the concessions on the pretext of buying an egg."[28] By November 1860, fifteen days in the blockhouse of Saint Laurent punished the camp man who crossed "however little the limits of the concessions."[29]

The requirement that men in the camp of trial raise a jail town around themselves stalled their progress onto plots of their own. The sole industry of Saint Laurent was building Saint Laurent. In practice this meant tending to the builders—punishing and feeding them, ministering to the sick and dying, reading their mail—and tending to the personnel who tended the builders. Governor Montravel explained in September 1863: "We cannot allow vacancies in the camp of trial for fear of stopping the work, except when spots are filled by ... men who meet the standards for acceptance into the camp of trial."[30] Saint Laurent became a town of unpaid noncitizen construction workers, who needed to be kept working, and of employees attached to the prison apparatus that trailed the workers. A promotional description of Saint Laurent of 1865 by Léon Rivière, the director of Guiana's bank, mentioned only two convict shops by name, Falconetti and Lascombe, the booter and the barber, who shod and coiffed the prison master class. As the system chased its tail, the town grew. The hospital was large. The dormitory for the hospital staff was elegant by relative standards. "The house of the health officers, two stories high, and the yet unfinished military hospital, three stories high with an attic, have vast galleries by which air penetrates and circulates in all the rooms." These were the only "public edifices worthy of being mentioned" in Rivière's sketch of Saint Laurent. He gestured to the camp of trial in passing as among the town's "many large barracks with portholes, mounted on pillars in masonry."[31]

The Maroni parish was supposed to be geographically separate from the military prisons; but the Jesuits required the prisons to absorb the bad men and to frighten remaining parishioners as a possible fate. It had not dawned on Father Beigner when pitching the scheme that a purge site for village rejects might arise at the foot of his Maroni project. In 1859 the chaplains learned with dismay that parish expellees were returning to the river as the inmates of a new penal settlement beside their own, called Saint Louis.[32]

Saint Louis was the project of Montravel, who became governor in 1859 after Baudin resigned in a huff when the ministry opposed his settlement of convicts in Cayenne.[33] At Saint Louis, Montravel and a clique of officers, some drawn from the ruins of white Creole society, attempted to inject military dash into the Jesuit settlement, to conquer the Maroni, and to subjugate the Boni Maroons.

The Jesuits drifted into irrelevance. Montravel took control of the Saint Laurent purge lists. The priests ceased to determine who lived and remained in their village.[34] Among the concessionaires in 1866 was Etienne Chantelouve, a former corporal from a punitive colonial regiment, the Troisième Bataillon d'Afrique, with a tattoo on his left arm that read "The past tricked me, the present torments me, and the future disgusts me." Chantelouve came to Guiana from Algeria in 1861 with a conviction to five years of hard labor by a council of war for stealing from the personal accounts of soldiers.[35] The arrival of Chantelouve to the Maroni coincided with dramatic changes to the criteria for becoming a settler. The ravages of tropical disease and the transfer of purge authority to the governor meant that a man's ability to receive a plot or retain one depended on official judgments about his biological fitness. It was no longer Christian virtue but now the physical organism that mattered most.[36] The parish of Saint Laurent turned out the men who grew sick while clearing their plots and building on them, for which the evicted settlers received no compensation whatsoever. In June 1860, Montravel gave instructions for the removal of "sixty invalids, used-up men, among whom I am not sad to see certain men who have neither religion nor honesty," remarked Father Nicou. In exchange the governor promised to "send us other men who are stronger and more vigorous."[37]

Saint Louis was an enclave of punishment unhinged from any system of justice. Commandants of the governor's prison circumvented the special maritime tribunal that sat in Cayenne, opting to have the men beaten instead.[38] The violence of Saint Louis transformed the Maroni into a scene of continuous brigandage by escapists. The road from Saint Laurent to Saint Louis become a corridor of convict flights and military patrols.

The Jesuits became spiritual apologists for Saint Louis. In February 1861, Father Nicou remarked: "Evasion is in a state of epidemic at Saint Louis; only blows of the martinet can cure this illness."[39] After a man from Saint Louis was shot while plundering the Saint Laurent butchery, a chaplain declined to grant him a burial in holy ground. The priest meant "to protest against this folly of evasions that puts the future of Saint Laurent in great danger."[40]

With the founding of Saint Louis, the spirit of the military prison overtook the village of Saint Laurent to the point that the church bell beside the father's hut became a timekeeping device for the camp of trial.[41] The Jesuit church of Saint Laurent became an eyesore. The collapsing grange stood alone on the denuded riverbank, left behind by the town.[42] The replacement church of 1868 had the look of a camp appendage. "We are just finishing with painting the bars on the windows in gray," wrote Father Garnier.[43] The jail town so eradicated the Jesuit vision of a rustic Christian enclave that no trace of nature or patch of shade remained. The only trees in Saint Laurent were, according to the banker Rivière, "a lovely allée of coconut palms, at the extremity of which is the house of the superior commandant."[44] In 1868, the demolition of the Jesuit project climaxed when prison guards—so-called officers—replaced the gendarmes posted among the concessionaires. The settlers were "put under the regime of transportation and in a sense of the camp."[45] The chaplains adjusted to this as to earlier developments. "The guards are radiant, superb to see at their functions."[46]

The spatial history of Saint Laurent's transformation as recorded by priests in snatches makes it possible to visualize the evolving relationship between land and law in the Maroni settlement. Where a church bell marks the hours of a military prison camp; where that camp has become a town; and where the town rests on a dominion "reserved for the needs of transportation," the law of the land is military prison law and its companion piece, "military discipline and subordination." The transformation of military prison law and anomic brutality into the law of the land had loomed as a likely outcome as early as 1857 when convicts moved to the Maroni trailed by a blockhouse. The founding of the camp of trial and its metamorphosis into a stationary reservoir of town builders, combined with the advent of Saint Louis and the creation of the special Maroni zone, turned likelihood into fact.

The legal character of that colonial space became quite manifest in the report of a commission created in 1862 by Montravel that sought to "grant to this region apart and to its entirely special population a system of legislation appropriate to its destination and needs."[47] The centerpiece of the new legal system, as envisaged, was a tribunal headed by the Maroni commandant that would decide civil, commercial, and criminal matters. When judging crimes or misdemeanors, it became a tribunal of last resort. The jurisdiction of this court was rather flexible. Convicts and ex-convicts who did not occupy concessions would remain under the jurisdiction of courts-martial in criminal matters. It remained for the governor to decide whether people on concessions should pass before the new court or instead face trial by special maritime tribunals like the other men. Conversely, no decision of the governor could place one of the military men—the camp officials—under the jurisdiction of the new court. Finally, any free person who happened to stumble into the special dominion, whether they were Maroons, relatives of concessionaires, or Mana villagers, would fall under the jurisdiction of this tribunal.[48]

Reviewing the commission's unfinished work in 1865, the new head of the judiciary services, Paulinier, wrote with amazement: "Everywhere the legislator has attempted to divide administrative from judicial matters. . . . In defiance of that principle, the commission names the superior commandant of the penitentiaries to the head of the court that will, as a correctional tribunal, judge all infractions and misdemeanors committed on the territory reserved for transportation by nonmilitary individuals. Thus it will judge the ordinary inhabitants of the region as well as the transportees and its judgments are of last resort." To Paulinier, the problem began with the commission's mistaken understanding of the 1860 decree that created the Maroni as a special dominion. "The commission believed from the decree of 30 May 1860 that the territory of the Maroni was detached from the colony of French Guiana, that it comprised a separate colony."[49]

The problem with the report had little to do with the commission's perception of the special dominion's legal autonomy from Cayenne (which was not a mistake). The trouble lay elsewhere: the prison so engulfed the Maroni region that it became impossible to conceive of people living outside the walls or to picture institutions arising extramurally. There were no walls around the Maroni dominion, of course. The boundaries there were legal in character. On the western frontier, the martial jurisdiction of the colonial prison, which enveloped the men as an effect of their status, colonized a patch of earth and drove out the possibility of civil society. In retrospect, the wall of Bonard looks quaint in comparison to what occurred after his departure. The curiosity of the commission report did not lie in its failure to divide administrative and judicial matters. Instead, the report had failed to divide the prison from the world.

A structure similar to permanent siege rule, yet with sharper teeth, engulfed any land occupied by convicts because of the power of the jurisdiction that traveled on their persons to restructure space and experience. The movement of a very large number of people enveloped by this jurisdiction to an otherwise sparsely inhabited patch of earth rezoned that land as a static war zone organized around the subjugation and pursuit of the total enemy. That the convict signified the total enemy is plain from the fact that unarmed fugitives were killed for pilfering food and their bodies discarded like animal carcasses.

What is most striking about this undertaking (apart from the violence) is the limited vision of the project from the beginning. No one had sought to create a society of colonists who could exist on their own, marry, and reproduce without the hand of the colonial state moving the levers. The Jesuits, local officials, and administrators in Paris acted to assure that men could not buy and sell things, own land, move around, or licitly couple with women without approval from the minister of the navy. The monstrosity that crowned that enterprise was Saint Laurent, the city without citizens.

The idea of detaining ex-convicts in pseudo villages was as old as the transportation system. Yet the founding of Saint Laurent and the drift of the convict enterprise to the Maroni River altered the character of later ex-convict settlements. In France and even under Governor Bonard, the ex-convict had been defined against the norm of the citizen. That changed in Guiana with the implementation of the Jesuit scheme. Thereafter imperial officials envisaged a convict's integration into the model parish as the measure of colonial success. When Saint Laurent became the center of the convict enterprise, the liberated felon ceased to be defined by his unfitness for metropolitan or even for colonial society. The ex-convict emerged as a pariah in a place where the military prison had become the world.

A 1923 exposé of Guiana's convict system by the former war correspondent Albert Londres evoked shoeless, shirtless, starving ex-convicts who slept in the immaculate streets of Saint Laurent; a small number of similar people slept in the market of Cayenne. The motto of ex-convicts in Londres's interwar account was "the prison [bagne] begins at liberation."[50] The refashioning of an inmate's putative release into a threshold of denial, whereupon the man lost the right to food and clothes yet remained under martial rule, subject to residential assignment, and in permanent exile—the hands of the state ever upon him—began under Minister Chasseloup-Laubbat and Governor Montravel; that system nonetheless acquired new intensity of purpose under Montravel's successor, Governor Hennique (1865–1870).

In developing a regime for the ex-convict, Montravel scavenged measures from the normal colony of Guiana that had sought, unsuccessfully, to retain former slaves in plantation agriculture. Ex-convicts experienced the quadruple effect of surveillance, the military prison, postemancipation work decrees, and the lack of a nearby community of sympathizers—or even a remote one. It is unlikely that many letters got through. The journalist Charles Delescluze, who spent five years in French prisons before reaching Guiana in 1858, noted the unusual handling of letters there. In other prisons, it was normal practice for inmates to submit letters in unsealed envelopes. In Guiana, a convict was required "(1) Not to use an envelope; (2) to leave a margin one-third the page width blank; (3) to indicate his name at the top adding the word transportee and the category and section number to which he belonged."[51] Relatives of convicts who lacked news and hoped to move on—wives to remarry, daughters to marry—corresponded with the navy to obtain substitute death certificates.[52]

The administration could not abide landed ex-convicts who were free to work or not as masters of their bodies and time. Ex-convicts on concessions at Saint Laurent needed (as men under sentence did not) to engage themselves as workers or face disciplinary measures for vagabondage. The only employer in the Maroni region was the penitentiary administration. The men on concessions resisted the rule, which led to their eviction. In October 1860, Father Nicou found that rural Saint Laurent had "changed a bit since my departure. Its population has diminished considerably . . . we are losing another 16 concessionaires whom the CASABLANCA will remove. The cause of their departure is sickness, feebleness, and their refusal to seek an engagement for the period after their liberation, which will take place within the year."[53]

Ex-convicts felt trapped in a prison where they did not belong. To administrators, they were contaminants of a prison they could not be allowed to exit. Father Houdouin called them "the residuum of transportation."[54] The minister of the navy, Chasseloup-Laubbat, observed in May 1862: "It is liberation and not detention that has made transportation into a problem." They seemed a useless expenditure. "I think it would be preferable not to credit the opinion that the state owes the gift of provisions to those whom liberty has placed under the law."[55] He approved two years of rations with reluctance.

This 1862 dispatch, which ordered the cutting of rations to men whom "liberty has placed under the law," also approved a new use of law with regard to ex-convicts. Chasseloup-Laubbat authorized the framework that Montravel had earlier proposed for new ex-convict detention centers. "This internment is necessary for the security of the colony in order to force hardened criminals to submit to the law of work. It is perfectly justified, according to you, by [local] legislation on vagabondage, the policing of work and surveillance of the high police." Colonial work decrees required freed people to seek engagements as servile workers and punished the vagabond with forced labor.[56] Among normal residents of Guiana, administrators were unable to act preemptively to enforce these decrees; the courts could only respond to attested infractions. Montravel proposed to avoid this inconvenience with regard to ex-convicts. Since it was liberation that constituted the former inmate as a vagabond idler, it would be liberation that unleashed preventive antivagabond measures. The ex-convict, subject to surveillance of the high police, would be grouped with other men of his type at an assigned place and forced to work as long as his exile endured; yet, at the urging of Chasseloup-Laubbat, the food would stop in two years. This structure combined preemptive internment, forced labor, residential assignment, and animal deprivation.

Montravel did not wait for ministerial approval to undertake the experiment. In January 1862, he activated the project of isolating men at internment centers after their sentences expired. The result, at first attempt, was an extinction park for humans at the edge of the penal city. In view of the legal predicament of the ex-convict in Guiana since Bonard, the new experiment is of interest in revealing what still remained to be removed.

In January 1862, the now-blind Mélinon arranged to send a tailor from Ypres, a Parisian bookshop assistant, a Breton ragpicker, a Tunisian farmer, a charcoal merchant from Lyon, and a sculptor—or was he a notary clerk?—downriver from Saint Laurent with a few dozen other burglars, all bachelors in their twenties, to an abandoned timber atelier on Maipouri Creek. The new settlement, called Saint Pierre, was the first dedicated ex-convict site on the Maroni River. The men received saws and a ration of lard and beans. They were supposed to be woodsmen and to subsist on the crops they grew in the clearings for the next five, maybe six years, when they could return to France, if they were from France. The tailor from Ypres had already been expelled from France. After the Belgian government declined to receive him, the French sent him to Algeria. He came to Guiana from Oran.

The blockhouse of Saint Pierre went up in 1864. The village came to center on a camp for men who did not want or did not have the strength to work the land and live scattered, in groups of five, in clearings in the woods. Together the settlers on their corvée and the camp men laid a road ten meters wide—as wide as possible—through the forest from Saint Pierre to Saint Laurent, the jail town they were unfit to live in.[57]

The settlers at Saint Pierre were not subsistence farmers. The energetic men cleared the land, hunted, sold the timber, and sold the shacks they built in the clearings to the old men, the invalids, and the men who wished to be left alone. The enterprising men moved onto new patches. The men called anemics and the old men "eat their rations waiting for the two years to pass. He who will live will see."[58]

The decree of 1855 that subjected ex-convicts to military law and courts-martial of an implicitly special kind also exempted them from military discipline, which meant (among other things) that they could not be beaten with a cord, did not need to shave their beards, and did not need to wear uniforms.[59] Exemption from military discipline, from another perspective, meant the men could be denied uniforms. The agreement at Saint Pierre was for two years of rations. No one had mentioned clothing. "I have seen them dressed as savages. What to say to them? They say that no one gives them clothes. I would believe it." Father Montfort found, in December 1865, that the rations did not always come. "I myself was left for a few days without food, a few days without fresh meat. . . . I conclude that if I, who can so easily complain to the commandant, have to suffer such errors, they cannot be absent for these poor people lost in the middle of the woods."[60]

In July 1869, the men on allotments were holed up in their huts, hiding from the guards who had replaced the gendarmes. They were afraid to abandon the little they had to starving ex-villagers who were on the loose in the forest.[61] Twenty-five men lost their rations that July. Thirty more would lose them in December. The new device of Governor Hennique beginning in April 1869 was incremental starvation: half rations followed by quarter rations of dry bread, followed by no food and removal to a point "distant on the Upper Maroni."[62] It is not obvious that there was dry bread. "Some live on nothing! . . . And with that still no baker at Saint Pierre" (Father Beaumont, 26 July 1869).[63]

Though enclosed by a web of strange legal structures, ex-convicts on the Maroni inhabited the wooded banks of an international border surrounded by ample raft-making materials. Many escaped only to find that an ineradicable interdict chased them everywhere. In the case of unlucky Arnoult, sentenced to five years of hard labor for attempted burglary "with the aid of a ladder" (no previous convictions), the man toured the Atlantic world after his first flight attempt, in 1865, as a liberated man.[64] In a boat made by master carpenters, he sailed with comrades to Berbice; the British sent them to Paramaribo (Dutch Guiana); the Dutch sent them to Barbados, where the fugitives separated. Arnoult traveled to Demerary, New York, Pernambuco, Hamburg, England, and finally to Rouen, where on 1 October 1867 he was nabbed, "not having papers."

Arnoult's return voyage to Guiana reveals the importance of ex-convicts to the administrative circuitry linking France to the penal colony. Arnoult sailed on the *Amazone,* a convoy that left Toulon on 11 Dec. 1867 and reached Guiana on 9 January 1868. Also aboard were two more ex-convict fugitives; eight men with sentences to forced labor, all escapists from Guiana; and forty-nine ex-convicts with surveillance infractions, who were being transported for ten years in execution of the decree of 8 December 1851, the text that launched the roundup after Louis-Napoleon's coup d'état. Nearly every prisoner aboard the ship was an ex-convict being punished for a motion offense.[65]

In the 1860s the frontiers of European states and empires seemed to close on the liberated felon. Quite a few ex-convicts with the right to leave found themselves on the wrong side of impassable frontiers. England took back the English. The Netherlands took the Dutch.[66] In contrast, the Swiss would not accept anyone who had been convicted of theft, begging, or vagabondage.[67] Neither the Prussians nor the Russians took back the Poles. Poland did not exist.[68] As for French colonies, nearly all were closed to men from the penal colony (Martinique took back the Martiniquans).The navy closed national frontiers to French ex-convicts by sleight of hand. In September 1868, the state ceased to pay for the re-patriation of ex-convicts who completed their terms of exile. Even men with the funds to leave required an exit pass from the governor, which meant he could refuse them.[69] The new policy coincided with a change in the function of Guiana's convict system. In 1867, with the founding of a penal colony in New Caledonia, the navy began routing European con-victs to the Pacific while designating Guiana for colonial convicts, espe-cially North Africans. Beginning in 1869, ex-convicts who could not leave Guiana after completing their terms of exile, whether because they lacked the funds or gubernatorial assent, remained there under a new official rubric: volunteer residents.[70]

In the final year of the Second Empire, ex-convicts departed for France from a transit depot on Devil's Island. In 1863 Montravel had pitched the new site as an expression of his concern for their health. He had hoped to shield ex-convicts from diseases that might befall them before returning to France.[71] It was then, or soon became, the other way around. Devil's Island served in the late 1860s as an isolation site for unusual punishment brigades and for infected ships. In April 1869 General Hennique, Montra-vel's successor, offered this sketch of the island: "Sterile rock, inhabited by a few men serving disciplinary punishments and by the small number of transportees having the right to their repatriation ... when the *Cérès* transport ship arrived on the islands with an epidemic of smallpox, which required the ship to be quarantined, and the contaminated personnel to be transferred to this rock, we experienced considerable difficulty in sheltering the sick from the heat and the extreme humidity."[72] The fortunate ex-convict at the end of the second decade of transportation lived on a quarantined island for incurables.

The spread of the convict system throughout the colony had dramatic consequences for postemancipation society in French Guiana, as did the reduction of liberated men to inmates. During the 1860s, the curtain between the normal colony and the penal colony disintegrated. The convict system devoured Guiana just as it seemed to draw farther away. It was after the founding of the special Maroni dominion, which lay far from the colony centered at Cayenne, that the prison really started to travel.

During the 1860s, as before, the ex-convict acted as the involuntary catalyst for every significant spatio-legal metamorphosis in Guiana. In these years, black liberated people from the convict system became fixtures in normal Guianese industries, where they often worked alongside knockoff versions of themselves—released petty offenders under surveillance of the high police. The new prominence of black liberated convicts in private industry shaped the Penitentiary Administration into an authority that presided over the whole of Guiana.

The ideal worker in Guiana during the Liberal Empire of Napoleon III was someone whose will lacked significance and whose labor was not contractual. When it came to black people, colonial administrators sought to create a worker with whom anything could be done yet who counted as a nonslave in the sense that he or she could not be liberated. There was nothing left to abolish.

Elite notions of the ideal laborer in postemancipation Guiana did not hark back to the slave past. Slavery, as a present condition, still organized labor relations in the colony; it was the unavowed enabler of Guianese private industry. In 1858 the immigrant recruiter Chevalier filled out his fourth African convoy, the *Orion,* with people he redeemed (bought) on the Mano River east of Sierra Leone. All 573 people who came to Guiana aboard his next two convoys, the *Méridien* and the *Phénix,* were slaves redeemed in Gabon.[73] So, too, were the 140 Africans who traveled on a private vessel, the *Joseph,* commissioned by Monsieur Franconie for the Society of Approuague Mines in 1859.[74] In 1860, when Chevalier could not make good on his 1858 contract to supply French Guiana with another two thousand immigrants, the navy annulled the contract.[75] British opposition to the redemption of slaves forced the French to abandon the practice. In exchange, by treaty of July 1861, Britain opened India to French recruiters.[76]

In Guiana, the number of Africans who came to the colony as immigrants after 1848 shrank due to mass flight, an extremely high death rate, and the repatriation of survivors beginning in 1860. Faced with a diminishing supply of immigrants from Africa, administrators sought substitute black workers who shared the immigrants' legal disadvantages. Employers and administrators in Guiana did not want the thousands of South Asians who began pouring into the colony.[77] They did not want the hundred or so Chinese who came to the colony in 1860 as an unhappy and ultimately lethal experiment.[78] They hankered after Africans, or people who looked like Africans. They had their eye on freedmen from the United States.[79]

The African immigrant shortage crisis unfolded against the backdrop of a colony full of Africans. Many Creoles in their late teens and twenties were the children of two African parents. During the Second Empire and Third Republic, emancipated people were still known by their African ethnicity. The protagonist of the Creole-language novel *Atipa* (1885) calls his friend Jean-Gaillard "an Arada negro" and also refers to "Mayombé, a Mana negro, a Foulard."[80]

To be young, male, black, and landless, the child of Africans, or a thirty-something African did not suffice. The only dark-skinned people who mattered needed to have robust legal disadvantages. In principle, they needed to come from outside. Yet law, which created the African immigrant shortage, seemed to promise a solution. In 1860, the administration launched the project of creating another country inside Guiana. With assistance from the emperor, the navy rewired the colony so that it might become its own Africa, manufacture its own immigrants, and then inject the virtual Africans—propitiously disadvantaged black people—back into itself. This new idea for a continent did not require much technical wizardry. There simply needed to be an anomalous jurisdiction—a special box—and a group of black people who lived inside. The people: the Boni Maroons. The zone: the Maroni dominion. The special dominion may or may not have been created for the unique goal of producing virtual African immigrants, but it certainly took shape with that purpose in mind.

Camp Saint Louis, the iniquitous prison, served as the chief site of encounter between Frenchmen and Maroons under its commandant, Lieutenant Ronmy, a desperado from one of Guiana's first families (cousin by marriage to Montravel). On 8 September 1861, the Jesuit chaplain at Saint Louis exchanged pleasantries with a group of Boni who happened to be sojourning there (yes, inside the prison camp) in a hut they built beside the house of the commandant. Speaking through an interpreter, Ronmy "had them told in my presence that if they sent their children we would teach them everything we teach to whites, which seemed to please them." After the prison fused with the world, where did schools belong? "I would not be surprised if there were a Boni school at Saint Louis next year."[81]

It was not enough to invent a new colony by choreographing its legal limits. In 1860 the French could not navigate the rapids on the Maroni dividing them from the tribe. The tribe could not reach the French. The Boni lived on the Lawa River, an influent of the Maroni, in tense isolation from the Auka, who controlled passage on the Maroni and blocked the Boni from descending to the coast. As an imperfect solution to these difficulties, the penal colony issued a declaration of rights. In September 1860, four months after the emperor created the special dominion, the head of Montravel's general staff, Lieutenant Sibour, signed a treaty with the Dutch governor in Surinam granting river inhabitants free passage up and down the Maroni and its influents, thus stripping the Auka of river sovereignty.

The 1860 treaty was surely not a "watershed event that gave lasting recognition to the de facto freedom the Aluku [Boni] had won long before," in the startling words of a modern ethnographer.[82] Montravel had long nursed the goal of subjugating the Boni by stealth. In 1847, before the abolition of slavery, yet with a view to its demise, he noted the time had come for "conquest and moralization of these peoples" by suasion; "through a violent approach . . . one deprives oneself forever of hands [*bras*] that one might have been able to use."[83] The French signatory of the Franco-Dutch accord, Lieutenant Sibour, called it an immigration treaty. "If we do not have to fear emancipation any longer, we have much to do to rebuild the ruins with which this humanitarian act has covered the soil of Guiana. We go very far away, at great expense, to recruit the

Chinese and the Hindus; it would be profitable to draw toward us the Indians and the Bosh."[84] That was also the view of Lieutenant Ronmy, the commandant of Saint Louis. In November 1860, on the official Franco-Dutch mission to spread news of the agreement, Ronmy acted as a recruiter for Guianese entrepreneurs. On return, he reported to the prison chaplain that forty men would leave shortly for the Approuague (it is not clear what happened next).[85] Twenty Boni did descend that November with the French frontiersman called Tollinche, who directed a timber atelier on the Sparouine Creek near Saint Louis.[86]

For the Maroni to become a site of virtual immigrant extraction, a tribe of people who lived only for bodily freedom and self-rule would need to desert their ancestral homes and confide their futures to prison commandants. The lieutenants and presumably Montravel hoped to surmount this glaring defect in the scheme by using force to keep the Boni who descended from leaving.

In his first-person account of Maroni diplomacy, Sibour vaunts his secret accord with Byman, the Auka paramount chief, for the violent constraint of Boni on the lower river. Sibour calls this accord a "treaty in six articles." (The treaty with the Dutch, not the Auka, had five.) He also calls it a "verbal engagement." He concedes that Byman "wanted to slow down the redaction of this clause." He also claims to have informed *Byman*, in the presence of the Dutch governor, that France did not recognize him or any Maroon as a party in diplomacy. "The grand man is strangely mistaken about the nature of our mutual relationship."[87] All that remains steady amid the flicker and whirl is Sibour's hope that a death threat would keep the Boni from leaving.

In this authoritative account of Maroni diplomacy—vetted by the navy, published by the navy, written by the head of the governor's general staff— the author (who cannot maintain self-consistency from line to line) reports meeting with Byman at Camp Saint Louis on 11 September 1860, three days after the signing of the Franco-Dutch accord. New arrangements emerge out of that meeting that contradict the earlier accord. The Boni are to enjoy free circulation on the Maroni in only one direction. The Boni who descend the river cannot go up again. The Auka are supposed to kill them the instant they cross the rapids. "Once the Boni are *chez nous,* which is to say, once they are within our circle of administrative action, those who would not have known to ally themselves with us, or who would not have desired to, will be retained by the fear of vengeance from the Auka."[88] Sibour claims to have suggested, during the Saint Louis roundtable, that Commandant Ronmy go and round up the Boni from their villages in early October 1860.

Ultimately the Boni confronted a different lethal challenge. Entering the special dominion proved to be more dangerous than leaving it. In 1861, the Boni who worked at Tollinche's timber atelier fled, along with a group of Wayana Indians, to escape diseases that raged in the penal colony.[89] Only eight Boni remained on the lower river four years later.[90]

For the Boni to substitute for immigrants required them to be struck with comparable legal disadvantages. "The Boni, I continued, are on French soil in the opinion of the governor of Paramaribo, and consequently no treaty can separate them from us, nor can they be subject to anyone but us."[91] Because the Boni resided on French soil, Sibour insisted they could not be recognized by foreign powers as a public person—a sovereign nation. While lacking any independent legal status, the Boni were not private persons according to French civil law and hence did not count as French nationals. As public and private nonentities, their status resembled that of French colonial subjects in the Second Empire. Yet the Boni, unlike the so-called *indigènes* (natives) of Africa, Oceania, and Asia, did not even have a customary law; they enjoyed no form of collective acknowledgment. Moreover, Sibour defined them as people who could be killed with impunity for southward exit attempts. He understood their legal status to be indistinguishable from that of inmates of the penal colony. The gunning down of unarmed escapists became commonplace under Governor Bonard and persisted thereafter.[92]

This effort to reduce the Boni to slavery soon vanished from memory. Yet the effort during the 1860s to engineer virtual Africans—black forced laborers for local use—proved a resounding success, which the penal colony made possible. The convict system became a machine of immigrant creation, in the sense that it produced black people struck with immigrant-like disadvantages who filled immigrant vacancies in private employ.

Surveillance of the high police, which entered the colony through the convict system, proved essential to the manufacture of virtual African immigrants during the 1860s. In France, surveillance scattered ex-convicts in random villages and prevented them from working. On the Maroni, surveillance enabled the open-ended detention of ex-convict undesirables. Yet surveillance, when turned against black people, assumed another function altogether. This mechanism made it possible to bond black liberated convicts to the land of their employers; they might even be assigned to those employers by the government. A black Creole or African-born freedman could now be treated just like non-European immigrants to the colony.

The end of African immigration turned an existing tendency to new purposes. Surveillance of the high police went into local use during the 1850s as a measure against petty offenders. In that earlier period, however, administrators used surveillance against black ex-convicts of all descriptions in mimicry of Governor Bonard's experiment on the Comté River (where he assigned European ex-convicts to a military prison under siege rule). In March 1858, the director of the interior, Favard, wrote to Baudin about six Africans who would soon be joining the local road gang. They were former employees of Alexandre Franconie, president of the administrative council of Approuague mines. In January 1858, they received sentences of one month in prison and two years of surveillance for exhibiting rebellious tendencies. They worked in Favard's convict road gang during their one month as prisoners and continued there as free men. Their assigned residence was probably the jail of Cayenne.[93] The next year, in August 1859, Governor Montravel began interning black ex-convicts from the Antilles at Saint Georges, the penal farm for colonials on the Oyapock.[94]

Beginning in 1860, when the government canceled its treaty with Chevalier for African immigrants, black male ex-convicts became immigrant substitutes. In July of that year, the Approuague planter Constant Bar asked Favard for "negro prisoners, men and women, whom I will assume the obligation of feeding and paying according to the usages of the colony."[95] To justify this request, Bar explained that the ten African immigrants he employed on the Maroni had become drunks (which does not explain why he needed convicts for his estate, Le Collège, on the Approuague). Favard wrote Montravel that the law forbade him to distribute minor criminals to private employers. To reward Bar for his perseverance as a planter, "I assured him that the administration . . . would not fail to direct to the Approuague all the surveyed people leaving prison and to intern them there. I will research whether there are Antillean *repris de justice* at the penitentiary depots of Montjoly and Saint Georges who could be usefully placed at his disposition."[96]

Bar's region, the Approuague River, the home of influential planters, stood apart from all other parts of the colony; it was among the few rivers in the colony to remain free of military prisons. The region relied on immigrants (Africans mainly) in gold mining concerns and on plantations during the 1850s. In 1864, Minister Chasseloup-Laubat, instructed Governor Montravel to supply Franconie with "(1) liberated blacks constrained to reside in the colony, who finding themselves under surveillance . . . could be interned at the localities where there are operations of the company; (2) convicts of the black race, *originating from Guiana.*"[97]

Note that the inflexible legal precept stated by Favard in 1860, which forbade him to distribute local prisoners to private employers, had either ceased to apply three years later or else could be suspended (and inverted) by ministerial whim at any instant. Note, moreover, that two opposite and discretely absurd peon distribution principles were active on the Approuague next to one another, turning that river into a neofeudal zone for workers who included (1) black liberated felons sentenced in either the Antilles or Guiana who had yet to complete periods of exile in the colony; (2) black petty offenders sentenced by courts in Cayenne; (3) liberated petty offenders under surveillance who were originally sentenced in Cayenne; and (4) indentured immigrants from Africa and Asia. What no one cared to mention when prescribing this or that category of inmate for use on the Approuague was that workers in the region consisted principally of Africans and South Asians.

Which local liberated black men might Favard have sent to his friend Bar on the Approuague? Speculatively, as one skims the local court blotter, excellent candidates include Frédéric Lisis, age seventeen, apprentice mason, sentenced for theft to "one year and one day of prison and ten years of surveillance of the high police" (16 December 1857).[98] Also at Favard's disposal in 1860 was Saturnin Barrit, age nineteen, carpenter, living in Cayenne, sentenced for theft to "fifteen months of imprisonment and five years of surveillance of the high police" (13 January 1858).[99] While scanning the newspaper court blotters, one cannot help but remark that magistrates tended to apply surveillance of the high police to petty criminals who seemed most suited to plantation work.

Black liberated men from the penal colony carried the dust of the convict system on their persons and extended the reach of that system wherever they went. The labor disputes, crimes, and motion-related offenses of these people fell under the jurisdiction of the special maritime tribunal that judged transportees, including liberated men. The Guadeloupean ex-convict Jean-Baptiste Morinan appeared before Cayenne's special maritime tribunal in February 1868 on charges of breaking his ban and stealing two chickens, eighteen francs, and two dogs. His elderly employer, Pactole (named after a large plantation), denounced Morinan as a thief and shirker. Disgruntled by his treatment, Morinan had broken his ban without leaving the premises. "I stayed nearby the house of Pactole and every night I went to sleep in my old lodgings. In the morning I left before he could see me."[100] He moved with the dogs between his old shack and the forest for a month. The interest of the case begins, but does not end, with the fact that a black liberated felon should face court martial for fleeing from the home of a freed slave. More significant is the role the convict system had assumed in the life of Pactole. The Penitentiary Administration was the agency to which he took his troubles. It functioned as a simulacrum of municipal government. The prison court-martial was the tribunal to which Pactole looked for redress. Institutionally, the convict system became the form in which local people encountered the French state.

The special maritime tribunal eventually withdrew from the life of liberated felons. Ex-convicts who completed their exile terms and chose (or were obliged) to remain in Guiana fell under the normal court system. Had the prison lifted its hand? Of course not. By 1863 there ceased to be any real distinction between the thing called Guiana and the thing called the convict system. The two merged most explicitly in a 10 May 1863 decree concerned with liberated men who had completed their mandatory exile terms and wished to remain in Guiana as free residents. The text mapped the journey of these virtual immigrants, aspiring settlers, along an administrative bridge leading from one world into another.

Ex-convicts who remained in Guiana after completing their terms of exile were said to be members of the fourth category, second section. They did not have numbered dossiers in the colonial archive, however, because people in this group were not, in principle, supposed to exist to the Penitentiary Administration. With the decree concerning free settlement by ex-convicts in Guiana, the forbidden archive for fourth category, second section people began to take shape. After May 1863 every definitively free ex-convict settler to be "removed from the control of the transportation system," had a dossier with the colonial authorities that began with "an extract from the matricules [numbered registers] of the transportation system" detailing his crimes, previous convict numbers, physical characteristics, disciplinary infractions, and punishments while an inmate.[101]

Every time an ex-convict moved across a threshold, picturing that limit as deliverance, the system attached itself to him, moved, and enveloped the place he went. It was through the liberated man that the convict system extended itself: he always stood at the outer limit of its authority. More or less exactly at the time that local officials began to manufacture an inmate archive for the fourth category, second section, they developed a passion for referring to free people by number who had no formal link to the convict system. Court blotters published in the official and only newspaper, *La Feuille de la Guyane*, began listing immigrants, for the first time, by their *numéro matricule* in July 1863, as though these people had arrived in Guiana as convicts. Because of this change, the blotter of Guiana's normal criminal court mimicked a line-up of convicts before the special court-martial that convened in Cayenne to judge the inmates.

2 March. Mouttin, Indian immigrant, *numéro matricule* 1528, age 17, domestic, living in Cayenne, declared guilty of theft and sentenced with attenuating circumstances to 3 months in prison.

2 March. Rangassamy, Indian immigrant, *numéro matricule* 518, age 19, domestic in Cayenne, declared guilty of theft and convicted with attenuating circumstances to three months in prison.

16 March. Jean-François, transportee of the 4th category, 2nd section, age 27, born in Martinique, cultivator at Macouria, sentenced for death threats to 15 days in prison.

23 March. Solomengué called Remicie, African immigrant, *numéro matricule* 1586, age 16, domestic on Ile de Cayenne, declared guilty of theft, sentenced to fifteen days of prison.

7 May. Madavin. Indian immigrant, *numéro matricule* 1455, age 12, domestic in Cayenne, declared guilty of theft, having acted with calculation, and sentenced to three months of prison.

7 May. Hyppolite Charles, transportee of the 4th category, 2nd section, age 24, born Martinique, living Cayenne, declared guilty of theft and sentenced as a recidivist to five years in prison.[102]

By referring to people by their numbers and indicating members of the ghost class (fourth category, second section), *La Feuille de la Guyane* represented the local correctional court in a manner that called into question the nature of that legal forum, the status of the immigrants, and even the law of the land.

The remaking of the law of the land by the convict system became most pronounced in a security plan of 27 September 1870 that dates from the collapse of the Second Empire. The inspiration for this plan might or might not have been a rumored conspiracy by the small number of European ex-convicts then living in Cayenne.[103] Mixed squads of marine infantry, gendarmes, prison guards, and volunteer snipers were to patrol the streets at all hours—three squads by day, three by night.[104] At 10 p.m. the bell of Fort Ceperou would clang the hour of the ex-convict lock-in. Night squads would round up people under surveillance of the high police who failed to comply with the curfew. At all hours, ex-convicts could be arrested for anything. "The police will arrest all ex-convicts guilty of misconduct, vagabondage, or an attitude contrary to public order." The security plan further charged the squads with searching ex-convict lodgings and removing their firearms to a new depot for confiscated weapons.[105]

The new emergency plan drove ex-convicts out of town, while turning everyone else into a suspect under round-the-clock scrutiny by prison guards functioning as beat police. The squads that hunted for ex-convicts would also enforce the new closing hour of coffee shops (11 p.m.) and taverns (8 p.m.); they would check working papers and internal passports to enforce all decrees on urban employment and travel since 1852. After the arrest of illegal city dwellers and workers, "Individuals who are not subject to surveillance of the high police will be judged summarily by the police according to the common law." The very regime that Admiral Baudin invented in 1856 for convicts living "outside the penitentiary" had become the regime for everyone—the common law.

The advent of the Third Republic rattled administrators in Guiana, who mistook the revival of politics after a twenty-two-year hiatus for a threat to the convict system and its squires. In 1871, when locals rejected the state candidate in favor of the republican Victor Schoelcher (who opted instead to represent Martinique), Governor Loubère, a former director of the Penitentiary Administration, responded by finagling the colony's disenfranchisement.[106] Guiana recovered its seat in the national legislature when republican electoral success in 1879 drove the regnant French political class into retirement.[107]

Victor Schoelcher called for governing the colonies as extensions of France, which would have required ending decree rule and destroying the convict system. The gentlemen Freemasons in Guiana's republican movement adapted that program to suit their commercial interests. Their leader was the socialist tycoon, Alexandre Franconie, who ruled an empire of black peons on the Approuague. In 1864, the same year he submitted a request for convict and ex-convict black workers to the ministry of the navy, he sponsored the production of illegal pamphlets (soon suppressed) calling for an end to "the permanent dictatorship" of military governors. The republican opposition in Guiana wanted national representatives, civic institutions, and an elected general council. They also wanted the citizenry to rule the penal colony in the navy's stead.[108] There is no reason to doubt the sincerity of Franconie's socialist convictions. Yet rule by legal exception proved central to his notion of Guiana as a republican polity. He wanted self-government to include local control over voiceless laboring bodies. He envisaged Guiana as two quite distinct places. One was for citizens and the other was for slaves.

Ernst Renan famously defined the nation as a union of spirits enacted by "daily plebiscite"—the persistent and simultaneous action of individual wills. Instead, in France of Renan's day, the bond of a Frenchman to the nation endured after his will lost all significance. Formally, a person's national status remained in tact after his private and public rights disappeared. At the close of the Franco-Prussian War, this feature of the French legal order became manifest in obscure provisions of the Treaty of Frankfurt (1871). According to the treaty, the inhabitants of annexed Alsace-Lorraine were allowed to choose whether they wished to remain French—with two exceptions. By article 6, the inmates of lunatic asylums and of "penitentiary establishments in France or the colonies" who originated in the ceded provinces "will be directed to the town closest to the frontier and remitted to the German authorities."[109]

In November 1872, a reporter for *Le Toulonnais* observed the transfer of convicts through Toulon to the Germans. "Until this day, it had seemed that by losing their civil rights the convicts were forbidden to vote. It appears that the question of nationality is an exception to the rule."[110] The handover of convicts to the occupying troops struck the journalist as an enactment of the social compact in the wrong direction. Through the transfer, which *Le Toulonnais* took for a sort of national election, the convict merged with the citizen at the instant he forsook the country. It seemed that a man prohibited from voting, testifying, signing, marrying, earning, buying, selling, bestowing, receiving, and even complaining still retained one final and extraordinary right: that of voting not to be French and handing himself to the German authorities. The mad people were also supposed to be exchanged. It sufficed to have a birth certificate in the archives of the annexed land. The criminals and the insane were the people who could say nothing.

At the beginning of the Third Republic, the aspirations of people in Guiana took them along paths that met and diverged near the Maroni jail town, Saint Laurent. Ex-convicts on the Maroni thought of nothing but fleeing across the river toward deliverance (they hoped) on Dutch soil. After "declaring themselves liberated of all punishment" to Dutch officials, however, many were returned to Guiana.[111] The Dutch extradited ex-convicts capriciously and intermittently. The Maroons faced a different sort of nonrecognition at the foot of the penal city. Trading parties that descended the Maroni to the coast found themselves banned from French soil. They "stood on the beach beside their canoes, seeming to wait for a long time to receive passes to advance."[112] For local republicans, Saint Laurent embodied the power of the French state. The new Maroni town beckoned to the free residents of French Guiana as a symbol of their unachieved sovereignty. Summarizing restorative efforts in the town, a 1994 internal report of the Department of Cultural Affairs in French Guiana signaled the need "to return to Saint Laurent the architectural and urban reputation that was hers during the convict years, which gave the town the nickname, 'Little Paris.' "[113]

Conclusion

I N 1947, FRENCH GUIANA became a department of France—an appendage of the metropolitan state. Robert Vignon, the first civilian prefect, viewed the former colony as land that civilization had overlooked. He became known locally for his expeditions, by plane and canoe, to visit the so-called *populations primitives.* These were Maroons and the few hundred Indians of the Wayana and Emerillon tribes who survived in the interior. "Maintaining the Indians artificially in medieval conditions, cut off from all evolution, is criminal and genocidal, because it is the disappearance of an ethnicity that is at stake," he wrote.[1] For Vignon, the Indians were threatened with extinction because of their lack of contact with French administrators. Vignon seemed unable to detect any trace of four hundred years of French colonial presence there.

With the end of the colonial era came a version of the age of discovery.[2] In 1956, a team from the Institute of Geography arrived with radio equipment for ground-to-air communication and cameras for taking aerial photographs.[3] Eight years later, in 1964, Prime Minister Georges Pompidou chose French Guiana over places ranging from Roussillon to Mogadishu as the future location of a French space station. French Guiana has since become Europe's Cape Canaveral.[4]

In 1947, the French government did not discover Guiana. Instead, with the end of the colonial era, the convict system ceased to exist. At the vanishing of a regime founded on violence, silence, and untruth, the land became a worthy object of knowledge. Yet the power that summoned the mapping team was in a sense the same that had allowed this land to subsist as an enigma before then.

The bureaucratization of violence and dereliction in the convict system arose through the convergence and novel synthesis of legal structures that hovered at the edges of the postrevolutionary state. Civil death, civic degradation, legal interdiction, siege rule, surveillance of the high police, the exceptional jurisdiction of the naval prison, and the *régime d'exception* of colonial government came together in an isolated setting and fused into a new means of exercising power over individuals.

The treatment of marginal groups in France and French Guiana during the eighteenth, nineteenth, and twentieth centuries cannot be described as a violation of the Declaration of the Rights of Man and Citizen. During the Revolution, the political elite reinterpreted the 1789 Declaration to make room for the proscription of revolutionary enemies and the perpetuation of slavery in the empire. The convict system did not violate the natural rights of anyone, either, because natural law disappeared from France as a viable form of moral appeal after 1804. No constitution in the nineteenth century included the Declaration in its preamble. The charters of 1814 and 1830 accorded personal, press, and religious freedom as donations from the sovereign; both documents specified that they did not apply in the slave colonies under the same heading: "particular rights guaranteed by the state."[5] The 1848 constitution included a distinctly modern declaration of rights; the constitution of the second empire "recognized, confirmed, and guaranteed the great principles proclaimed in 1789" without using the word "right" (except in reference to Napoleon III) or mentioning which principles.[6] The constitution of the third republic "made no reference to the Declaration of Rights of 1789."[7]

The history of marginal groups in France, and of felons especially, calls into question the distinction between legal norms and exceptional practices. Transportation to French Guiana began in 1852 with a decree by a sovereign who then commanded dictatorial emergency powers. Two years later, the same practice became a normal punishment through the revision of the Criminal Code. Transportation to French Guiana was part of normal penal law. But French Guiana was also a place where *libérés* starved to death under open-ended siege rule.

The advent of the convict transportation system turned French courts and the apparently normal laws they applied into a mode for transferring men into no-exit enclaves of executive power. This had been the case before the era of transportation, because hard labor convicts on metropolitan soil lived within special martial jurisdictions. But in 1852 the special jurisdiction of the work camp ceased to be a small and circumscribed punitive zone on domestic territory; it swallowed all of French Guiana and absorbed ex-convicts as an inferior class of inmate.

In metropolitan France, modes of repression that first afflicted convicts and ex-convicts routinely shifted their targets. During the eighteenth and the nineteenth centuries, the political elite defined enemies of state by drawing on concepts and practices they otherwise used for traditional sorts of deviants. In the 1790s, revolutionaries conflated nonjuring priests and émigrés with the *homme sans aveu,* the brigand without a domicile or a passport who lived under interdict wherever he went in the country. In later years, pundits and administrators depicted socialists as ex-convicts to the effect of worsening the predicament of both common and political criminals during the crackdown that followed the 1851 coup d'état .

Beginning in the late eighteenth century, a new sort of historical subject assumed prominence on French territory, both in the empire and at home. This was someone called free who was neither a foreigner nor a citizen, who lived with considerable legal incapacities and was struck by policing mechanisms that narrowed the difference between slavery and freedom. In French Guiana, Africans of the Mana Village, Boni Maroons, people subject to surveillance of the high police, and immigrants to the colony after 1848 from Africa and Asia all diversely embodied this figure. A new set of practices replaced slavery and civil death in the modern period while poaching from the past. Ex-convicts experienced a form of legal violence that exceeded civil death in its effects. No one had ever proposed to withhold sustenance systematically and as a matter of principle from civilly dead prisoners.

The problem of the liberated man in Guiana should not be mistaken for a local peculiarity. Perceptions of ex-convicts and legal structures affecting them arose from within French society. The metropolitan crisis over liberated men created the convict system in the first place. As the nineteenth century wore on, the ex-convict came ever more to the fore of French and international concern; learned cosmopolitans and imperial administrators spread themselves on "the crisis of liberation."[8] Soon after the founding of the convict settlement in New Caledonia (1867–1895), officials discovered ex-convicts to be a toxic by-product of the new system that they hoped to exile to the Panama Canal, or to some future reserve in the Pacific. "The annexation of the New Hebrides," observed one administrator, "would be the solution to the social question of ex-convicts in New Caledonia."[9]

In domestic France, the law of 27 May 1885 abolished surveillance of the high police and replaced it with "prohibition to appear at sites whose interdiction will be made known to [the convict] at the time of his liberation" (art. 19). The new law did not actually abolish surveillance (just as the 1854 law abolishing civil death did not abolish civil death). The system that went by the name of surveillance of the high police from 1832 to 1851—the use of forbidden zones to control suspect movement—became a substitute for surveillance of the high police in 1885 under a new name, *interdiction de séjour*. The 1885 law toughened the predicament of ex-convicts and worsened the administrative measure it claimed to destroy. It empowered the government to ban released petty offenders from the entirety of metropolitan France while assigning them residence to overseas territory. The same mindset and the same power that constituted the prison for liberated men in Guiana during the Second Empire enabled the "perpetual internment on colonial territory" of liberated riffraff, including vagabonds and minor crooks: 15,600 such people, called *rélégués*, came to Guiana from France, the Antilles, and Algeria during the Third Republic.[10] In the late nineteenth century, liberated people became inmates of colonial prisons as an effect of ordinary French law. Once more, the exception became the rule.[11]

In a 1994 essay commissioned by the Caisse nationale des monuments historiques et sites (Bureau of National Monuments and Sites), the Martiniquan novelist Patrick Chamoiseau described the overgrown ruins of the prisons in French Guiana. These became transhistorical symbols of colonial violence that secreted tales of resistance by Indians and slaves as well as prisoners. "The trajectory of these people unfolded silently . . . without statues, without monuments, without documents."[12] At the close of his essay, Chamoiseau opposed restoring the prisons. The work was already under way. The ruins were classified as historical monuments in 1987. Restoration began in 1992.[13] Many of the old prison hangars are now municipal buildings. They have been restored to their original hue, an earthy pink, from a paint made from the laterite soil of the region.[14] There are still bars on the windows. Apart from gendarmes, soldiers, and occasional tourists, the people who frequent Saint Laurent are Maroons.

To Chamoiseau, the collapsing prisons stood for the decay of structures, both physical and symbolic, that had dominated colonial land and silenced the people there. In French Guiana, the exuberance of the forest, especially near the coast, is also a poignant reminder of what is not there, even as ruins. Missing from the postcolony is any trace of life as it might have developed outside the walls for more than seventy thousand people.

To Robert Vignon, the density of the forest in French Guiana suggested that the hand of the colonizer had yet to extend there. This was hardly the case. The convict system was an enterprise that centered on prohibitions against having a house, working a trade, selling, buying, and settling down with a woman. The equivalent of a slave shack became a retractable reward for supreme penitents. The forest that impressed the new prefect was not a wilderness awaiting civilization, as he supposed. It was civilization as it reached this colony that turned a populous forest into a wilderness.

Appendix

Table 1, "General statistics for convicts, 1852–1869," describes the movement of convicts to the penal colony (from France, Senegal, the Antilles, Guiana) and what became of them after arrival. The column marked *rayés* refers to people who were "removed from the controls of transportation." For more information on this term, see Chapter 8.

The column headings for Table 2, "Convict arrivals by ship from France, 1852–1870," are those used by the Penitentiary Administration, and they appear in the Jesuit table that I reproduce here. The abbreviation "cat." stands for category and the abbreviation "sec." stands for section.

1st cat. refers to convicts serving hard labor sentences.

2nd cat. refers to convicts with sentences to reclusion rather than forced labor; this heading includes two quite different sort of prisoners: (a) prisoners from the Antilles or Guiana who were incorporated into the penal colony in spite of not being sentenced to hard labor and (b) women from France.

3rd cat. refers to prisoners of two different types who were transported by virtue of the imperial decree of 8 Dec. 1851. Those in the first section were ban-breakers who were transported for surveillance infractions. Those in the second section were transported as "members of secret societies." An uncertain number of political transportees arrived in Guiana as "3rd. cat., sec. 1." The correspondence of Sarda Garriga includes complaints by the head of the colony about the miscategorization of politicals.

After the amnesty of August 1859, no further "members of secret societies" (3rd cat., 2nd sec.) arrived, at least not under that designation. In contrast, a few hundred women from France came in this period. The total number of French women sent between 1852 and 1869, according to the available statistics, is 281 (40 arrived in Guiana between 1852 and early 1859). Although this is a table of convoys to Guiana from metropolitan France, this does not mean that the convicts originated there. Convoys 63–69 on this table carried prisoners from Algeria who were routed through Toulon to French Guiana along with a small number of captured escapists. Details on those convoys are in the H (bagne) series at the Centre des Archives d'Outre Mer (Aix-en-Provence).

Table 1. *General statistics for convicts, 1852–1869*

Year	1 Jan.	From France	From Antilles	From Senegal	From Guyane	Total arrivals	Escaped/disappeared	Recaptured	Rayés	Died	To France	To Antilles	To other places
1852		1,929	76		28	2,033	32		4	79	2		
1853	1,916	928	68		21	1,017	26		1	522	9	1	
1854	2,372	649	37		5	691	21			247			
1855	2,771	1,151	40		33	1,224	47		11	769	18		4
1856	3,146	1,945	60		2	2,007	106	4	23	912	334	8	3
1857	3,771	1,005	33		2	1,040	127	106		1,332	119	29	
1858	4,296	958	38		4	1,000	110	88		386	105	29	2
1859	4,753	1,210	31		4	1,245	165	127	45	537	154	18	3
1860	5,203	799	48		1	848	180	109	2	476	105	17	
1861	5,380	1,407	86		8	1,501	338	248	3	535	114	15	13
1862	6,111	495	59	6	6	566	281	181	2	486	69	8	4
1863	6,002	1,026	38		4	1,068	357	248	80	394	246	6	22
1864	6,213	1,526	59	13	13	1,611	499	329	36	300	70	5	9
1865	7,231	1,068	72		11	1,151	593	461	39	428	119	15	7
1866	7,642	989	32		19	1,040	635	432	41	616	212	15	13
1867	7,582	514	39	5	7	565	381	268	19	586	128	19	4
1868	7,182	406	81	3	4	494	430	253	7	432	271	12	1
1869	6,742	323	15		3	341	560	365	9	350	191	12	18
Total		18,328	912	27	175	19,442	4,888	3,219	322	9,387	2,266	209	103

Source: Fonds Guyane 20, Archives jésuites, Vanves.

Table 2. *Convict arrivals by ship from France, 1852–1870*

Convoy no.	Date of arrival	Ship	1st cat.	2nd cat.	3rd cat./1st sec.	3rd cat./2nd sec.	3rd cat./2nd Women	Other	Per ship	Per year
1	11 May 1852	*Allier*	298			3			301	
2	20 May 1852	*Forte*	347		36	16			399	
3	29 June 1852	*Erigone*	161		96	144	1		401	
4	25 Aug. 1852	*Duguesclin*	453		61	5			519	
5	30 Oct. 1852	*Fortune*	302		1	6			309	1,929
6	21 Jan. 1853	*Egérie*	178		125				303	
7	6 July 1853	*Allier*	182		17	99			298	
8	1 Sept. 1853	*Fortune*	62		254	10	3		327	928
9	29 Jan. 1854	*Armide*		23					23	
10	6 May 1854	*Armide*	300						300	
11	31 Aug. 1854	*Armide*	300		6				306	
12	29 Nov. 1854	*Rapide*			20				20	649
13	13 Feb. 1855	*Gardien*	304	2					306	
14	23 Mar. 1855	*Erigone*	298						298	
15	20 July 1855	*Fortune*	248						248	
16	27 Sept. 1855	*Armide*	299						299	1,151
17	1 Jan. 1856	*Erigone*	300						300	
18	7 Feb. 1856	*Fortune*	179		37	32			248	
19	7 Mar. 1856	*Egérie*	194		53	2			249	
20	1 July 1856	*Armide*	262		36				298	
21	14 July 1856	*Africaine*	300			3			303	
22	22 Nov. 1856	*Egérie*	219		25	3			247	
23	2 Dec. 1856	*Africaine*	286		14				300	1,945
24	14 May 1857	*Adour*	467		30	3			500	

No.	Date	Ship								
25	10 Sept. 1857	*Seine*			7				7	
26	9 Dec. 1857	*Adour*	480		18				498	1,005
27	23 May 1858	*Adour*			12	1			13	
28	9 July 1858	*Loire*			10				10	
29	15 Oct. 1858	*Seine*	398		36	1			435	
30	11 Dec. 1858	*Adour*	464		36				500	958
31	24 Jan. 1859	*Loire*	36				36		36	
32	12 Apr. 1859	*Seine*	349		100				449	
33	24 June 1859	*Amazone*			524	1			525	
34	15 Nov. 1859	*Cérès*	33		167				200	1,210
35	6 Feb. 1860	*Amazone*	226		65			9 expelled foreigners	300	
36	24 Sept. 1860	*Amazone*	303		196				499	799
37	16 Feb. 1861	*Amazone*	300		73				373	
38	31 May 1861	*Cérès*	417		83				500	
39	22 Aug. 1861	*Amazone*	455		45				500	
40	9 Oct. 1861	*Cacique*	34				34		34	1,407
41	21 May 1862	*Cérès*	396		99				495	495
42	9 Feb. 1863	*Amazone*	498						498	
43	9 July 1863	*Amazone*	398		100				498	
44	26 Nov. 1863	*Africaine* (W)	24	6			30	1 expelled foreigner	30	1,026
45	20 Apr. 1864	*Amazone*	397		98				495	
46	1 Aug. 1864	*Cormoran* (W)	27	8			35		35	
47	3 Sept. 1864	*Amazone*	401		99				500	
48	17 Sept. 1864	*Achéron*	39	28			1		67	
49	23 Dec. 1864	*Cérès*	398		100				498	1,595
50	26 Apr. 1865	*Amazone*	438	1	59		2		498	

Table 2. Convict arrivals by ship from France, 1852–1870 (continued)

Convoy no.	Date of arrival	Ship	1st cat.	2nd cat.	3rd cat./1st sec.	3rd cat./2nd sec.	3rd cat./2nd Women	Other	Per ship	Per year
51	5 June 1865	Cormoran	15	6	15		36		36	
52	30 Aug. 1865	Cérès	448		44				492	
53	17 Oct. 1865	Cacique	24	3	13		40		40	1066
54	14 Feb. 1866	Cérès	457	1	38			3 correctional convicts	499	
55	25 June 1866	Casablanca	22	10			2		32	
56	5 Oct. 1866	Cérès	445	3	41		16		489	1,020
57	25 Feb. 1867	Titan	30	9			2		39	
58	8 Mar. 1867	Amazone	422		76		1		498	
59	31 July 1867	Amazone	12	4	5		16		21	558
60	9 Jan. 1868	Amazone	2		48		2		50	
61	29 Feb. 1868	Achéron	23	19			4		42	
62	1 Sept. 1868	Amazone			35				35	
63	6 Sept. 1868	Cérès	150						150	
64	25 Nov. 1868	Alecton	151		20				171	
65	16 Dec. 1868	Cérès	150						150	598
66	30 Jan. 1869	Amazone	150						150	
67	9 June 1869	Amazone	151				1		151	
68	22 Aug. 1869	Cérès	17	1	4		22		22	
69	24 Apr. 1870	Cérès	148						148	323
Total			15,267	125	3076	329	284	13	18,810	

Source: Fonds Guyane 20, Archives jésuites, Vanves.

Notes

AD	Archives départementales
ADGuy	Archives départementales de la Guyane française (Cayenne)
AN	Archives nationales (Paris)
AP	*Archives parlémentaires de 1787 à 1860: recueil complet des débats législatifs et politiques des chambres françaises*
B. Guy.	*Bulletin officiel de la Guyane française.* Cayenne: Imprimerie du gouvernement.
B. L.	*Bulletin des lois de la République française*
CAOM	Centre des archives d'outre mer (Aix-en-Provence)
Feuille	*Feuille de la Guyane française* (Cayenne: Imprimerie royale, 1819–)
FGu AJ	Fonds Guyane, Archives Jésuites (Vanves)
JP	*Journal du Palais: contenant les jugemens du Tribunal de cassation, et des tribunaux d'appel de Paris et des départemens, dans les principales causes et questions que les lois nouvelles rendent douteuses et difficiles*
SHM	Services historiques de la Marine

INTRODUCTION

1. Marc Bloch, *Apologie pour l'histoire ou métier d'historien* (Paris: Armand Colin, 1993).
2. Pierre-Victor Malouet, "Voyage dans les forêts et les rivières de la Guyane," in *Mélanges de littérature*, ed. Jean-Baptiste Suard, vol. 1 (Paris, 1803), 188.
3. Robert Vignon, *Gran Man Baka* (n.p.: Editions Davol, 1985), 56.

4. Marc de Villiers, "Journal inédit du voyage du sergent La Haye de Cayenne aux chutes de Yari, 1728–1729," *Journal de la société des américanistes de Paris* 12 (1920): 115–126.

5. Jean Hurault, *Français et Indiens en Guyane* (Paris: Union général d'éditions, 1972), 74–80, 92, and 111.

6. "Rebel Village in French Guiana: A Captive's Description," in *Maroon Societies*, ed. Richard Price, 3rd ed. (Baltimore: The Johns Hopkins University Press, 1996), 312–319.

7. Serge Mam Lam Fouck, "La résistance au rétablissement de l'esclavage en Guyane: 1604–1972 française: Traces et regards 1802–1822," in *Rétablissement de l'esclavage dans les colonies françaises: aux origines de Haïti*, ed. Yves Bénot and Marcel Dorigny (Paris: Maisonneuve and Larose, 2003), 251–268.

8. Armand Jusselain, *Un déporté à Cayenne: la Californie française, nouvelle édition* (Paris: Calmann Lévy, 1878), 137. This is a narrative by a prison commandant, not a prisoner.

9. Michel de Certeau, "Psychoanalysis and History," in de Certeau, *Heterologies*, trans. Brian Massumi (Minneapolis: University of Minnesota Press, 2000), 4; "Writing the Sea: Jules Verne," in ibid., 144.

10. Peter Redfield, *Space in the Tropics: From Convicts to Rockets in French Guiana* (Berkeley: University of California Press, 2000), 20 and 104.

11. Henri Lefebvre, *The Production of Space*, trans. Donald Nicholson-Smith (Cambridge, Mass.: Blackwell, 1991), 7, 16, 160.

12. Bloch, *Apologie pour l'histoire*, 51.

13. Bloch, *Apologie pour l'histoire*, 61.

14. Ibid.

15. On land and law, see Christopher L. Tomlins, "The Legal Cartography of Coloniza- tion, the Legal Polyphony of Settlement: English Intrusions on the American Main- land in the Seventeenth Century," *Law and Social Inquiry* 26, no. 2 (Spring 2001): 315–372; on personal status and law, see Lauren Benton, *Law and Colonial Cultures: Legal Regimes in World History 1400–1900* (Cambridge: Cambridge University Press, 2002). On personal and territorial identity in French history, see Peter Sahlins, *Boundaries: The Making of France and Spain in the Pyrenees* (Berkeley: University of California Press, 1989).

16. Albert Memmi, *Portrait du colonisé précédé de portrait du colonisateur* (Paris: Galli- mard Folio, 1985), 111.

17. George Kateb, "Fiction as Poison," in *Thinking in Dark Times: Hannah Arendt on Ethics and Politics,* ed. Roger Berkowitz, Jeffrey Katz, and Thomas Keenan (New York: Fordham University Press, 2010), 30–31.

18. Hannah Arendt, *The Human Condition*, 2nd ed. (Chicago: University of Chicago Press, 1998), 198.

19. Arendt, *Human Condition*, 177; see Peg Birmingham, "Heidegger and Arendt: The Birth of Political Action and Speech," in *Heidegger and Practical Philosophy*, ed. Fran- çois Raffoul and David Pettigrew (Albany: State University of New York, 2001), 190–202.

20. Hannah Arendt, *On Revolution* (New York: Penguin, 2006), 97.

21. Hannah Arendt, *On Totalitarianism* (New York: Harvest Harcourt Brace Jovanovich, 1979), 300.

22. Arendt, *Human Condition*, 176.

23. Arendt, *Human Condition*, 180.

24. Arendt, *On Totalitarianism*, 287.

25. Samuel Beckett, *The Unnamable*, in *Samuel Beckett Trilogy*, Everyman's Library 236 (New York: Knopf, 1997), 476.

26. Gerard Noiriel, "The Identification of the Citizen: The Birth of Republican Civil Status in France," in *Documenting Individual Identity: The Development of State Practices in the Modern World*, ed. Jane Caplan and John Torpey (Princeton: Princeton University Press, 2001), 29–30.

27. Albert Mathiez, *Les conséquences religieuses de la journée du 10 août 1792: la déportation des prêtres et la sécularisation de l'état civil* (Paris: E. Leroux, 1911), 1.

28. Maurice Blanchot, *Le très haut* (Paris: Gallimard, 1975), 26, 32, 47.

29. Kwame Anthony Appiah, *Cosmopolitanism: Ethics in a World of Strangers* (New York: Norton, 2006).

30. Michel Foucault, *Discipline and Punish: The Birth of the Prison*, trans. Alan Sheridan, 2nd ed. (New York: Vintage, 1995), 297.

31. On the permanent state of war, see Michel Foucault, "Cours du 21 janvier 1976," *"Il faut défendre la société": cours au Collège de France 1975–1976*, ed. François Ewald et al. (Paris: Seuil, 1997), 37–53.

32. On the plagued city, see Michel Foucault, "Cours du 15 janvier 1975," *Les anormaux: Cours au Collège de France (1974–1975)*, ed. François Ewald et al. (Paris: Seuil, 1999), 41–44; "La naissance de la médecine sociale" (1977), in Foucault, *Dit et écrits*, vol. 2 (Paris: Quarto Gallimard, 2001), esp. 217–220; *Discipline and Punish*, 195–200.

33. *Discipline and Punish*, 301.

34. Michel Foucault, "Désormais la sécurité est au-dessus des lois," *Le Matin*, 18 Nov. 1977, reprinted in *Dits et écrits*, vol. 2, 367.

35. Michel Foucault, "La sécurité et l'État," *Tribune socialiste*, 24–30 Nov. 1977, reprinted in *Dits et écrits*, vol. 2, 385.

36. Michel Foucault, *"Society Must Be Defended": Lectures at the Collège de France 1975–1976*, trans. David Macey (New York: Picador, 2003), 256.

37. Michel Foucault, "Truth and Juridical Forms" (1974), in Foucault, *Power*, trans. Robert Hurley et al., ed. James D. Faublon (New York: New Press, 2000), 55.

38. Gordon Wright, *Between the Guillotine and Liberty: Two Centuries of the Crime Problem in France* (New York: Oxford University Press, 1983), 138.

39. André Zysberg, "Politiques du bagne 1820–1850," *Annales historiques de la Révolution française* 2 (July–Sept. 1974): 304.

40. Carl Schmitt, *La Dictature* (1921), L'Ordre philosophique, ed. Alain Badiou and Barbara Cassin (Paris: Seuil, 2000), 141–142.

41. Carl Schmitt, *Political Theology: Four Chapters on the Concept of Sovereignty*, trans. George Schwab (Chicago: University of Chicago Press, 1985), 5.

42. Schmitt, *Political Theology*, 23.

43. Josep M. Fradera, "L'esclavage et la logique constitutionnelle des empires," *Annales Histoire, Sciences Sociales* 63, no. 3 (May–June 2008): 533–560.

44. Nasser Hussain, *The Jurisprudence of Emergency* (Ann Arbor: University of Michigan Press, 2003).

45. Walter Benjamin, *Illuminations*, trans. Harry Zohn (New York: Schocken Books, 1968), 257.

46. Giorgio Agamben, "The Messiah and the Sovereign: The Problem of Law in Walter Benjamin," in *Potentialities: Collected Essays in Philosophy*, trans. Daniel Heller-Roazen (Stanford: Stanford University Press, 1999), 160–174.

47. Giorgio Agamben, *Homo Sacer: Sovereign Power and Bare Life*, trans. Daniel Heller-Roazen (Stanford: Stanford University Press, 1998), 20.

1. LEAVING THE REPUBLIC

1. Louis-Ange Pitou, *Le Chanteur parisien, recueil des chansons de L.A. Pitou, avec un almanach-tablette des grands évènements depuis 1787 jusqu'a 1808, chaque fait place a son rang de date et de jour, ou calendrier éphéméride pour l'année* (Paris, L. A. Pitou, 1808), 5.

2. Louis-Ange Pitou, *Analyse de mes malheurs et de mes persécutions depuis 26 ans* (Paris: L. A. Pitou, 1816).

3. Louis-Ange Pitou, *Les déportés de fructidor: Journal d'Ange Pitou annoté d'après les documents d'archives et les mémoires*, ed. Albert Savine, Collection Historique Illustrée (Paris: Louis Michaud, 1909), 53.

4. *Moniteur universel*, 9 Sept. 1797, 808.

5. *Moniteur universel*, 6 Sept. 1797, 796.

6. Ordonn. to Min., 8 thermidor V (26 July 1797), 1E 498, p. 254, SHM (Rochefort).

7. Maurice Barbotin, *Conamama: Camp de la mort en Guyane pour les prêtres et les religieux en 1798* (Paris: l'Harmattan, 1995), 125.

8. Commissaire des Armes to Min., "La prise de La Décade," 3 brumaire VI (24 Oct. 1798), no. 873, 1A 126, SHM (Rochefort).

9. Commandant des Armes to Min., "L'arrivée de la Bayonnaise et le détail de son combat avec la frégate anglaise," 19 Dec. 1798, no. 932, 1A 126, SHM (Rochefort).

10. *Le Grand Robert de la langue française* (1985), s.v. "déportation."

11. Brigitte Borgmann, "Mors civilis: Die Bildung des Begriffs im Mittelalter und sein Fortleben im Französischen Recht der Neuzeit," IUS COMMUNE 4 (1972): 123–126. See also Kim Lane Scheppele, "Facing Facts in Legal Interpretation: Questions of Law and Questions of Fact," *Representations* 30 (Spring 1990): 42–77.

12. Victor Molinier, "Observations sur la proposition d'abolir la mort civile," *Revue de droit français et étranger* 7 (1850): 374.

13. André-Jean Arnaud, *Les origines doctrinales du Code civil français*, Bibliothèque de philosophie du droit (Paris: Librarie générale de droit et de jurisprudence, 1969), 15.

14. Hugo Grotius, *The Rights of War and Peace Including the Law of Nature and of Nations* (1625), trans. A. C. Campbell, Universal Classics Library (Washington, D.C.: M. Walter Dunne, 1901), pt. 2, bk. 20, par. 40.

15. François Richer, *Traité de la mort civile tant celle qui résulte des condamnations pour cause de crime, que celle qui résulte des vœux en religion* (Paris: Durand, 1755), 3.

16. Richer, *Traité de la mort civile*, 159.

17. David A. Bell, *The Cult of the Nation in France: Inventing Nationalism 1680–1800* (Cambridge, Mass.: Harvard University Press, 2001), 60 and 76.

18. Marcel Roncayolo, "Le département," in *Lieux de mémoire*, vol. 2, ed. Pierre Nora (Paris: Quarto Gallimard, 1997), 29–40.

19. Lynn Hunt, *Politics, Culture, and Class in the French Revolution* (Berkeley: University of Calif. Press, 1984), 59.

20. Mona Ozouf, *Festivals and the French Revolution*, trans. Alan Sheridan (Cambridge, Mass.: Harvard University Press, 1988), 126.

21. Michel Vovelle, *The Revolution against the Church: From Reason to the Supreme Being*, trans. Alan José (Cambridge: Polity, 1991), 31, 46–47, 55–57.

22. Ordonnance of Louis-le-Hutin (1315), M. F. Laferrière, *Histoire du droit français*, vol. 1 (Paris: Joubert, 1838), 441; Sue Peabody, *"There Are No Slaves in France": The Political Culture of Race and Slavery in the Ancien Regime* (New York: Oxford University Press, 1996), 118.

23. Soc. pop. Longwy, 24 ventôse II (14 March 1794), pièce 7b, AP, 1st ser., 89: 45. All further citations in this chapter to volumes in the AP are from the 1st series.

24. Soc. pop. Loudon, 24 ventôse II (14 March 1794), pièce 7a, ibid.

25. Société pop. La Rochelle, 25 germinal II (14 Apr. 1794), pièce 20, AP 88: 546.

26. Société pop. Josselin, 4 prairial II (23 May 1794), AP 91: 237.

27. Soc. pop. Oradour-sur-Vayres, 17 messidor II (5 July 1794), AP 92: 409.

28. Louis-Michel Le Peletier de Saint Fargeau, Rapport sur le projet du Code pénal fait au nom des Comités de Constitution et de Législation criminelle (22–23 May 1791) in Pierre Lenoël, Pierre Lascoumes and Pierrette Poncela, *Au nom de l'ordre: Une histoire politique du Code pénal* (Paris: Hachette, 1989), 338 (italics in the original).

29. Ibid., 351. This was the formula for men only; women (like foreigners) were not subject to *dégradation civique*. In their case, the formula was simply "Votre pays vous a trouvée convaincu d'une action infâme."

30. C. Pén. (1791), tit. I, art. 28.

31. C. Pén. (1791), tit. IV, art. 3.

32. Isser Woloch, "Political Participation: The First Wave," in *The New Regime: Transformations of the French Civic Order 1789–1820s* (New York: Norton, 1995), 66–7.

33. Camille Desmoulins, "Discours sur la situation politique de la nation à l'ouverture de la seconde session de l'Assemblée Nationale prononcé à la société des amis de la constitution dans la séance du 21 octobre [1791]," in François-Alphonse Aulard, ed., *Société des Jacobins: recueil de documents pour l'histoire du club des Jacobins de Paris,*

vol. 3, Collection de documents relatifs à l'histoire de Paris pendant la Révolution française (Paris: Librairie Jouaust, 1889–1897), 214.

34. Le Peletier de Saint Fargeau, Rapport, 336.

35. Olwen H. Hufton, *The Poor of Eighteenth-Century France 1750–1789* (Oxford: Clarendon, 1974), 221 and 228–229.

36. Frédérique Joannic-Seta, *Le Bagne de Brest 1749–1800: L'émergence d'une institution carcérale au siècle des lumières* (Rennes: Presses universitaires de Rennes, 2000), 308–309, 312–314.

37. "Domicile (Jurisprudence)," in *Encyclopédie ou Dictionnaire des arts et métiers*, vol. 5, ed. Dénis Diderot and Jean le Rond d'Alembert (Paris, 1755), 31.

38. Projet d'ordonnance au sujet de forçats libérés (1718), Ms. Joly de Fleury 12, fol. 208, Manuscrits occidentaux, Bibliothèque nationale, Paris.

39. Ordonnance de police concernant des forçats libérés (1777), Ms. Joly de Fleury 491, fol. 72, Manuscrits occidentaux, Bibliothèque nationale.

40. Charles-Antoine-Joseph Leclerc de Montlinot, "Essai sur la mendicité (1786)," *Un Observateur des misères sociales: Leclerc de Montlinot (1732–1801)*, ed. Guy Thuiller (Paris: Comité d'histoire de la sécurité sociale, 2001), 224.

41. André Zysberg, *Les Galériens: Vies et destins de 60,000 forçats sur les galères de France 1680–1748*, Univers historique (Paris: Seuil, 1987), 368–370; Yves Roumajon, *Enfants perdus, enfants punis: Histoire de la jeunesse délinquante en France: Huit siècles de controversées*, Collection Pluriel (Paris: Robert Laffon, 1989), 106–111.

42. AP 26: 724 (3 June 1791).

43. Ibid.

44. AP 27: 4 (6 June 1791).

45. Isser Woloch, *The New Regime*, 243.

46. Min. Justice to Min. Navy, 17 July 1798, BB³ 143, AN.

47. Rapport à sa majesté impériale, Bureau des bâtiments civils et prisons, 10 Jan. 1807, F¹⁶ 120, AN.

48. AP 34: 350 (22 Oct. 1791), 404–405 (25 Oct. 1791), 474–475 (28 Oct. 1791).

49. Stéphane Rials, *La Déclaration des droits de l'homme et du citoyen*, Collection Pluriel (Paris: Hachette, 1988), 22.

50. AP 34: 320 (20 Oct. 1791). Compare with [Charles-Louis de Secondat, Baron de] Montesquieu, *The Spirit of Laws*, ed. David Wallace Carrithers, bk. 12, ch. 19, 224.

51. AP 34: 399 (25 Oct. 1791).

52. Denise Roughol-Valdeyron, *Recherches sur l'absence en droit français, Travaux et recherches de la Faculté du droit et des sciences économiques de Paris* (Paris: Presses universitaires de France, 1970), 9.

53. AP 34: 699 (8 Nov. 1791).

54. AP 34: 542 (31 Oct. 1791).

55. Décret relatif aux formalités à observer pour les paiemens dans les différentes caisses nationales, no. 1452 of 13–17 Dec. 1791, *Code des émigrés, condamnés et déportés ou recueil des décrets rendus par les Assemblées Constituante, Législative et Convention-*

nelle concernant la poursuite et le jugement des émigrés, condamnés et déportés, le séquestre, la vente et l'administration de leurs biens (Paris: Imprimerie du dépôt des lois, an II), 6–7.

56. Décret relatif au séquestre des biens des émigrés, no. 1523 of 9–12 Feb. 1792, *Code des émigrés*, 7.

57. AP 47: 225–226 (28 July 1792).

58. Décret qui ordonne le bannissement à perpétuité des émigrés français, 23–25 Oct. 1792, no. 96, *Code des émigrés*, 28.

59. Décret qui ordonne la proclamation et l'exécution des articles du décret sur les émigrés, relatifs aux Emigrés rentrés dans le territoire de la République, et à ceux qui sont détenus dans les villes frontières ou dans l'intérieur de la France, no. 181 of 26 Nov. 1792, *Code des émigrés*, 31.

60. Art. 5, Décret relatif aux certificats de résidence, no. 269 of 20–25 Dec. 1792, *Code des émigrés*, 33.

61. Sec. 3, art. 6, Décret contre les émigrés, no. 742 of 28 Mar.–15 Apr. 1793, *Code des émigrés*, 50.

62. Arts. 76 and 78, Décret contre les émigrés, no. 742 of 28 Mar.–15 Apr. 1793, *Code des émigrés*, 62.

63. AP 35: 110 (17 Nov. 1791).

64. AP 43: 24 (5 May 1792).

65. AP 44: 66 (24 May 1792).

66. AP 43: 313 (13 May 1792).

67. AP 44: 69 (24 May 1792).

68. AP 44: 168 (27 May 1792).

69. AP 65: 67 (24 May 1792). Jean-Jacques Rousseau, "De la religion civile," in *Du contrat social*, bk. 4, ch 8.

70. AP 69: 438 (24 July 1793).

71. AP 69: 439 (24 July 1793).

72. AP 60: 298 (18 Mar. 1793).

73. AP 88: 55. (n.d.).

74. Wilfred B. Kerr, *The Reign of Terror 1793–4* (Toronto: University of Toronto, 1927), 292.

75. *Journal d'Ange Pitou*, 23.

76. Gamas, *Les émigrés aux terres australes, ou le dernier chapitre d'une grande révolution, comédie en 1 acte, et en prose, Amis de la Patrie, 24 Nov. 1792* (Paris: Mme Tourbon, 1794).

77. According to Victor Pierre, 943 clerks were deported to Ré Island, including 246 Belgians; 192 were deported to Oléron Island, including 126 Belgians. Victor Pierre, *La déportation ecclésiastique sous le Directoire: documents inédits recueillis et publiés pour la société d'histoire contemporaine* (Paris: Alphonse Picard, 1896), xxxii.

78. Victor Pierre, "La déportation à la Guyane après fructidor," *Revue des questions historiques* 31 (April 1882): 510.

79. Bernard Saugier, *Pichegru: Histoire d'un suicide* (Bourg-en-Bresse: Les Éditions provincials, 1992), 220.

80. François Barthélemy, *Mémoires de Barthélemy*, ed. Jacques de Dampierre (Paris: Plon, 1914), 258–261.
81. [François Barbé de Marbois], *Journal d'un déporté non jugé ou déportation en violation des lois, décrétée le 18 fructidor V*, vol. 1 (Paris: Chatet & Fournier, 1835), 57.
82. *Moniteur universel*, 13 Sept. 1797, 814.
83. Jean-Henri Rouchon, *Conseil des Cinq Cents: Discours de Rouchon, prononcé à la séance du 14 brumaire an VII, sur le projet, présenté par Poulain-Grandpré, relativement à la confiscation proposée des biens des individus condamnés à la déportation* (Paris: n.p. an VII [1798]); Théodore Chabert, *Conseil des Cinq Cents: Opinion sur le projet de résolution présenté par Poullain-Grandprey, au nom d'une Commission spéciale, sur les peines à infliger aux individus condamnés à la déportation, qui se sont évadés ou qui sont soustraits, séance du 16 brumaire an VII* (Paris, n.p., an VII [1798]); Pierre-Joseph Briot, *Conseil des Cinq Cents: Rapport présenté par Briot (du Doubs) au nom d'une Commission spéciale sur la législation relative aux ecclésiastiques sujets à la déportation, et les mesures à prendre à leur égard, séance du 21 brumaire an VII* (Paris: Imprimerie nationale, brumaire VII [1798]); Michel Marvaud-Baudet, *Conseil des Cinq Cents: Quelques observations du citoyen Marvaud sur l'opposition du citoyen Rouchon, à l'admission du projet de résolution concernant les peines à appliquer aux individus condamnés à la déportation, qui ne l'auroient point subie ou qui s'y seroient soustraits* (Paris: Lemaire, brumaire VII [1798]).

2. STRANGE DOMINION

1. Laurent Dubois, *A Colony of Citizens: Revolution and Slave Emancipation in the French Caribbean 1787–1804* (Chapel Hill: University of North Carolina Press, 2004), 5, 317, and 172.
2. Bernard Gainot, "The Constitutionalization of General Freedom under the Directory," in *The Abolitions of Slavery from L. F. Sonthonax to Victor Schoelcher: 1793, 1794, 1848*, ed. Marcel Dorigny (New York: Berghahn/UNESCO, 2003), 182.
3. Arthur Girault, *Principes de colonisation et de legislation coloniale*, 3rd ed. (Paris: L. Larose and L. Tenin, 1907), 204–205.
4. Art. 6–7, constitution du 5 fructidor an III (22 Aug. 1795), in *Les constitutions de la France depuis 1789*, ed. Jacques Godechot (Paris: Garnier-Flammarion, 1970), 104.
5. On the abolition of slavery in Saint Domingue, see Jeremy D. Popkin, *You Are All Free: The Haitan Revolution and the Abolition of Slavery* (New York: Cambridge University Press, 2010); see also Laurent Dubois, *Avengers of the New World* (Cambridge, Mass.: Harvard University Press, 2004), 152–170.
6. Claude Wanquet, *La France et la première abolition de l'esclavage 1794–1802: le cas des colonies orientales, Île de France (Maurice) et Réunion* (Paris: Karthala, 1998), 41; Claude Wanquet, "Un 'Jacobin' esclavagiste: Benoît Gouly," *Annales historiques de la Révolution française* 65, nos. 293–294 (July–Dec. 1993): 445–468.

7. Jules-François Saintoyant, *Les évènements coloniaux*, vol. 2, *La colonisation française pendant la Révolution* (Paris: La Renaissance du Livre, 1930), 221–247.

8. David Barry Caspar, "La Guerre des Bois: Revolution, War and Slavery in Saint Lucia, 1793–1838," in *A Turbulent Time: The French Revolution and the Greater Caribbean* (Bloomington: Indiana University Press, 1997), 102–130.

9. On Hugues's refusal to promulgate the constitution, see Dubois, *A Colony of Citizens*, 281. A new Guadeloupean envoy, General Edme-Étienne-Borne Défourneaux, applied the 1795 constitution to that colony on 25 Feb. 1799 after declaring a state of siege on the colony on 4 Dec. 1798. Since the state of siege was a mechanism for suspending the constitution, it does not seem possible to argue that the document applied in Guade-loupe except in the form of a suspended law. See Frédéric Régent, *Esclavage, métis-sage, liberté* (Paris: Karthala, 2004), 289.

10. AP 1st ser. 26: 60 (13 May 1791).

11. On the rights campaign of free men of color, see Valerie Quinney, "The Problem of Civil Rights for Free Men of Color in the Early French Revolution," *French Historical Studies* 7, no. 4 (Autumn 1972): 544–557; David Geggus, "Racial Equality, Slavery, and Colonial Secession during the Constituent Assembly," *American Historical Review* 94, no. 5 (Dec. 1989): 1290–1308; John Garrigus, "Opportunist or Patriot: Julien Rai-mond (1744–1801) and the Haitian Revolution," *Slavery and Abolition* 28, no. 1 (April 2007): 1–21. For a gendered reading of Old Regime miscegenation concerns, see Doris Garraway, *The Libertine Colony: Creolization in the Early French Caribbean* (Durham, N.C.: Duke University Press, 2005).

12. AP 1st ser. 31: 274 (24 Sept. 1791).

13. Robespierre, "Rapport fait au nom du Comité de Salut Public sur la situation poli-tique de la République" (27 brumaire, year II, 17 Nov. 1793), *Oeuvres complètes,* ed. Marc Bouloiseau and Albert Soboul, vol. 10 (Paris: PUF, 1967), 173–174.

14. AP 1st ser. 24: 639 (7 May 1791). For similar remarks of Malouet see AP 1st ser. 25: 752 (11 May 1791).

15. Here I disagree with the interpretation of Louis Sala Molins. See his "Sous l'éclat des lumières, l'inexistence du droit des noirs à l'existence," *L'héritage philosophique de la Déclaration des Droits de l'Homme et du Citoyen de 1789: signification pour le Caraïbe* (Paris: L'Harmattan, 2002), 84–107, and *Dark Side of the Light: Slavery and the French Enlightenment,* trans. John Conteh-Morgan (Minneapolis: University of Minnesota Press, 2006), 54–66.

16. AP 1st ser. 8: 165, 189 (27 June and 4 July 1789); Malick Ghachem, "The 'Trap' of Representation," *Historical Reflections/Réflexions historiques* 29, no. 1 (Spring 2003): 123–144.

17. Honoré-Gabriel Riqueti, Comte de Mirabeau, *Les Bières flottantes des negrières, un discours non-prononcé sur l'abolition de la traite des Noirs (nov. 1789–mars 1790),* ed. Marcel Dorigny (Saint Etienne, France: 1999), 42 n. 14; for the activities of La Roche-foucauld at sessions of the Society of Friends of the Blacks, see Marcel Dorigny and Bernard Gainot, *La Société des Amis des Noirs* (Paris: Éditions UNESCO, 1998), 119, 124, 127, 145, 152, 170, 178, 180, 194.

18. AP 1st ser. 31: 301 (24 Sept. 1791, annex).

19. Michel Troper, "La Déclaration des droits de l'homme et du citoyen en 1789," in *La Déclaration des droits de l'homme et du citoyen et la jurisprudence* (Paris: PUF, 1989), 13–33; Georges Vedel, "Place de la déclaration dans le 'bloc de constitutionnalité,'" ibid., 35–73.

20. Letter of 11 January 1790, *Correspondance sécrète des députés de Saint Domingue avec les comités de cette isle* (Paris, L'an de la liberté I), 29.

21. Gabriel Debien, *Les colons de Saint Domingue et la Révolution: essai sur le Club Massiac, août 1789–août 1792* (Paris, 1953), 64–65 and 80–81; letter of Jean-Baptiste Nairac to La Rochelle Chamber of Commerce, 22 August 1789, Jean-Michel Deveau, *Le commerce Rochelais face à la Révolution: Correspondance de Jean-Baptiste Nairac 1789–1790* (La Rochelle: Rumeur des Ages, 1989), 131–132.

22. AP 1st ser. 12: 71 (8 Mar. 1790).

23. AP 1st ser. 12: 72 (8 Mar. 1790).

24. Nairac, letter of 23 Feb. 1790, in Deveau, *Le commerce Rochelais face à la Révolution*, 192.

25. *Le Patriote française*, 9 March 1790, 3.

26. Const. 1791, title 7, art. 8, in Godechot, *Les Constitutions de la France*, 67.

27. See Valerie Quinney, "The Problem of Civil Rights for Free Men of Color in the Early French Revolution," *French Historical Studies* 7, no. 4 (Autumn 1972): 544–557; David Geggus, "Racial Equality, Slavery, and Colonial Secession during the Constituent Assembly," *American Historical Review* 94, no. 5 (Dec. 1989): 1290–1308; Garrigus, *Before Haiti*, 236–241.

28. Décret abrogeant la législation coloniale de la Constituante et la remplaçant par des articles constitutionnels, 24 Sept. 1791, J. Saintoyant, vol. 1, *La Colonisation française pendant la Révolution* (Paris: La Renaissance du Livre, 1930), 398.

29. AP 1st ser. 34: 327 (30 Oct. 1791); AP 1st ser. 35: 475 (1 Dec. 1791).

30. AP 1st ser. 35: 631 (7 Dec. 1791).

31. Saintoyant, *La colonisation française pendant la Révolution*, vol. 2, 85–115 and 199–203. The decrees of the Constituent Assembly defining powers of the first commissars date from 27 Nov. 1790 (Martinique) and 1 Feb. 1791 (Saint Domingue); Saintoyant, *La colonisation française pendant la Révolution*, vol. 1, 389–392.

32. AP 1st ser. 40: 452 (24 Mar. 1792).

33. AP 1st ser. 40: 453 (24 Mar. 1792).

34. AP 1st ser. 45: 218 (14 June 1792).

35. Décret additionnel à la loi relative à l'envoi des commissaires civils à Saint Domingue (Décret du 28 Mars 1792), 15 June 1792, in Saintoyant, *La colonisation française pendant la Révolution*, vol. 1, 411.

36. Art. 18, Déclaration des droits de l'homme et du citoyen, constitution de 1793 ou de l'un I, in Godechot, *Les Constitutions de la France*, 81.

37. Quoted in Yves Bénot, "Comment la Convention a-t-elle voté l'abolition de l'esclavage?," *Annales historiques de la Révolution française* 3–4 (1993): 355; Bénot, "La constitution de l'an I et les colonies," *La constitution du 24 juin 1793: L'utopie dans le droit public français?*, ed. Jean Bart (Dijon: Éditions de l'université de Dijon, 1997), 195–199.

38. Session of 3 June 1793, in François-Alphonse Aulard, *La Société des Jacobins*, vol. 5, 227. Compare with Florence Gauthier, "The Role of the Saint Domingue Deputation in the Abolition of Slavery," *The Abolitions of Slavery from Léger Félicité Sonthonax to Victor Schoelcher*, ed. Marcel Dorigny (New York: Berghahn, 2003), 169. For an earlier instance of François Chabot's opposition to slavery, see AP 1st ser. 48: 361 (18 Aug. 1792).

39. Session of 3 June 1793, *Journal de la Montagne*, 6 June 1793, 38.

40. AP 1st ser. 66: 57 (4 June 1793); see Alyssa Goldstein Sepinwall, *The Abbé Grégoire and the French Revolution: The Making of Modern Universalism* (Berkeley: University of California Press, 2005).

41. Quoted in Yves Bénot, "Un anti-esclavagiste kleptomane?: En marge de l'affaire Milscent," *Dix-Huitième Siècle* 22 (1990): 296. On Milscent, see Yves Bénot, "L'Affaire Milscent (1794)," *Dix-huitième siècle* 21 (1989): 311–327; Jean-Daniel Piquet, "Le Créole patriote, apôtre de l'insurrection de Saint Domingue," *Annales historiques de la Révolution française* 3–4 (1993), 519–521.

42. George Rudé, *The Crowd in the French Revolution* (New York: Oxford University Press, 1959), 120–124.

43. "Commune de Paris: Conseil-général révolutionnaire," *Moniteur universel,* 12 June 1793: 606–607 (session of 8 June).

44. "Commune de Paris, Conseil-général révolutionnaire," *Moniteur universel,* 15 June 1793, 630 (session of 12 June).

45. Nicole Bottu, *Chaumette: Porte-Parole des Sans-Culottes* (Paris: Éditions du Commission d'Histoire de la Révolution Française, 1998), 308.

46. Florence Gauthier, *Triomphe et mort du droit naturel en révolution: 1789–1795–1802* (Paris, PUF, 1992), 220.

47. Robert Palmer, *Twelve Who Ruled: The Year of the Terror in the French Revolution* (Princeton: Princeton University Press, 1969), 256–257.

48. Denis Richet, "Enragés," *Dictionnaire critique de la Révolution française: Acteurs* (Paris: Flammarion, 1992), 338.

49. Palmer, *Twelve Who Ruled,* 291–295; Wanquet, *La France et la première abolition,* 176.

50. AP 1st ser. 76: 312 (10 Oct. 1793). As both Olivier Jouanjean and Michel de Guillenschmidt observe, this decree formalized a political goal that deputies of the Mountain sought since August 1793. See Olivier Jouanjean, "La suspension de la Constitution de 1793," *La Constitution du 24 Juin 1793: utopie dans le droit public français?,* ed. Jean Bart et al. (Dijon: Editions de l'Université de Dijon, 1997, 164; Michel de Guillenschmidt, *Histoire constitutionnelle de la France depuis 1789* (Paris: Economica, 2000), 20.

51. Of the representative Jean-Baptiste (Mars) Belley, a freed slave in the Saint Domingue deputation, see Georges Jean-Charles, "Belley," *Dictionnaire historique de la Révolution haïtienne* (1789–1804), ed. Claude Moïse and others (Montreal: Éditions images, 2003), 52–53; on the portrait of Belley by Anne-Louis Girodet, see Helen Weston, "Representing the Right to Represent: The Portrait of Citizen Belley, Ex-representative of the Colonies by Girodet," *Res* 26 (Autumn 1994): 83–99. For details about other

Saint Domingue deputies including Jean-Baptiste Mills, Louis Dufay, and alternates Étienne Bussières Laforest and Pierre-Nicolas Garnot, see A. Kuscinski, *Dictionnaire des conventionnels* (Paris: Société de l'histoire de la Révolution française, 1916).

52. On the admission of colonial deputies to the Convention, see remarks by Merlet in AP 1st ser. 48: 358–361 (18 Aug. 1792) and AP 1st ser. 50: 656–659 (annex).

53. AP 1st ser. 84: 283–284 (4 Feb. 1794).

54. *Journal de la Montagne,* 5 Feb. 1794, 672.

55. The *Moniteur universel* refers to "some debates relating to the drafting of the decree" following the speech by Danton; the *Procès verbal* refers to "some discussions on the different redactions" following the unattributed speech by "a member" (unmistakably Danton). See AP 1st ser. 84: 284 (4 Feb. 1794).

56. Here is the earlier draft proposed by the deputy Jean-François Delacroix: "The National Convention decrees that slavery is abolished over the whole extent of the territory of the Republic; in consequence, all men without distinction of color will enjoy the rights of French citizens." AP 1st ser. 84: 283.

57. AP 1st ser. 84: 326–327 (5 Feb. 1794). The first to speak in this session was Marie-Benoît-Louis Gouly, deputy for the East Indies to the Convention, member of the Jacobin Club (elected club secretary on 7 July 1794), and vigorous opponent of emancipation. Copies of his two drafts of the emancipation decree—neither of which would have freed the slaves—are in the papers of the Colonial Committee. See "Projet de rédaction du décret rendu le 16 pluviôse de l'an II de la République française une et indivisible, concernant l'abolition de l'esclavage," and "Autre projet de rédaction," DXXV/57, dossier. 565, AN. On his political opportunism, see Wanquet, "Benoît Gouly," 445–466.

58. On the denunciation of Saint Domingue commissars by Jeanbon Saint André, see Marcel Dorigny, "Sonthonax et Brissot: le cheminement d'une filiation politique," in Marcel Dorigny, ed., *Léger-Félicité Sonthonax:La première abolition de l'esclavage. La Révolution française et la Révolution de Saint Domingue* (Saint Denis: Société d'histoire d'outre mer, 1997), 38; on the opposition of Jeanbon Saint André to abolition, see Bénot, "Un anti-esclavagiste kleptomane?" 298; on Prieur de la Marne and the question of colonial representation, see AP 1st ser. 8: 164 (27 June 1789); on the tie between Collot d'Herbois and proslavery Saint Domingue lobbyists, see Bénot, *La Révolution française et la fin des colonies: essai* (Paris: La Découverte, 1987), 164.

59. For the denunciation on 25–28 Apr. 1793 of Roume and Saint Léger, Saint Domingue commissars, by Hugues and the lobbyists Page and Brulley, see "Pièces remises au Comité concernant le nommé Cambefort, et les commissaries civils Roume et Saint Léger, traduits au tribunal révolutionnaire," DXXV/56, AN. Hugues is denounced in a letter of 6 ventôse year II by the elected deputies from Saint Domingue to the Committee of Public Safety as "attached to the Assembly of Saint Marc, and sent by them to England, to Jamaica, and on diverse missions of confidence. He came from Saint Domingue aboard the Léopard, with all the Léopardins." See Florence Gauthier, "Inédits de Belley, Mills et Dufay, députés de Saint Domingue, de Roume et du Comité de Salut Public, concernant le démantèlement du réseau du lobby esclavagiste en France Février-Mars 1794," *Annales historiques de la Révolution française* 67, no. 302 (1995): 607–611.

60. Commissaires du 4 avril, domiciliés à Bordeaux, auprès de la Convention nationale, to Comité du Salut Public, 27 Mar. 1794, F1A-343, AN.

61. Florence Gauthier, "Inédits de Belley, Mills et Dufay," *Annales historiques de la Révolution française* 67: 610. See also Yves Bénot, *La Révolution française et la fin des colonies,* 186.

62. "Projet de Constitution pour la République française présenté par la Commission des Onze dans la séance du 5 messidor an III (23 June 1795)," ADXVIIIc 267, no. 1, AN.

63. Jacques Defermon, *Moniteur universel,* 9 Aug. 1795: 1298 (speech of 23 July 1795).

64. This power of appointment did not apply to Réunion and Ile de France (present Mauritius). Const. 1795, arts. 155–156.

65. Jacques Godechot, *Les institutions de la France sous la Révolution et l'Empire,* 409–410; Loi qui autorise le Directoire exécutif à nommer les members qui composeront jusqu'au premier thermidor prochain les administrations municipales de Bordeaux, Lyon, Marseille et Paris, no. 133 of 4 pluviose IV (24 Jan. 1796), *B. L.,* no. 21, p. 3.

66. *Moniteur universel,* 23 thermidor III (10 Aug. 1795), 1300.

67. Const. 1795, art. 17.

68. Note the exclusion of colonies from the law voted after this constitution, which fixed the location of every institution in France, including courts and administrations in France. See art. 41, Loi sur la division du territoire de la République, le placement et l'organisation des autorités administratives et judiciaires, no. 1160 of 19 vendémiaire year IV (11 Oct. 1795), *B. L.,* no. 194.

69. Godechot, *Les institutions de la France sous la Révolution et l'Empire,* 405.

70. "Conseil des Cinq Cents: Suite du Rapport d'Isouard," *Moniteur universel,* 6 frimaire V (26 Nov. 1796), no. 66: 262.

71. The insults directed at people in Saint Domingue was omitted from the transcript published in the newspaper. For the complete text, see Izoard, *Corps législatif, Conseil des Cinq-Cents: Rapport fait au nom d'une commission spéciale, sur une nomination de députés au Corps législatif, faite à Cayenne le 20 prairial de l'an IV, Séance du 28 brumaire an V* [18 Nov. 1796] (Paris: Imprimerie nationale, 1795).

72. François-Antoine Boissy d'Anglas, *Moniteur universel,* 10 June 1797, 1049 (session of 4 June 1797). See earlier remarks of Boissy about the nonapplication of the constitution to the colonies in *Moniteur universel,* 6 Jan. 1797, 427 (session of 2 Jan. 1797).

73. Villaret-Joyeuse, Discours sur l'importance des colonies et les moyens de les pacifier, 12 prairial V (1 June 1797), quoted in Jouda Guetata, "Le refus d'application de la constitution de l'an III à Saint Domingue 1795-1797," in *Périssent les colonies plutôt qu'un principe! Contributions à l'histoire de l'abolition de l'esclavage,* ed. Florence Gauthier (Paris: Société des études robespierristes, 2002), 89. See also Kenneth Gregory Johnson, "Louis-Thomas Villaret de Joyeuse: Admiral and Colonial Administrator (1747–1812)" (Ph.D. diss., Florida State University, 2006).

74. Marcel Dorigny, "La Révolution française et la question coloniale: esquisse d'un bilan historiographique," in *Recherches sur la Révolution,* ed. Michel Vovelle and Antoine de Baecque, Société des études robespierristes (Paris: La Découverte, 1991), 421.

75. Jouda Guetata, "Le refus de l'application de la constitution de l'an III," 89.

76. Loi contenant division du territoire des colonies occidentales, no. 1563 of 4 brumaire year VI (26 Oct. 1797), *B.L.*, no. 160, pp. 1–10; loi concernant l'organisation constitutionnelle des colonies, no. 1659 of 12 nivôse year VI (1 Jan. 1798), *B.L.*, no. 177, pp. 1–22.

77. Arts. 15 and 18, Loi concernant l'organisation constitutionnelle des colonies, *B.L.*, no. 177, p. 4.

78. Louis-Antoine-Esprit Rallier, *Corps legislatif, Conseil des Anciens: Opinion de Rallier sur la resolution du 28 brumaire an VI, relative à l'organisation de la Constitution dans les colonies, séance du 11 nivôse an VI* (Paris: Imprimerie nationale, an VI).

79. Fick, *The Making of Haiti,* 198–201; Ardouin, *Études,* vol. 3, chs. 14–16; Antoine Michel, *La Mission du Général Hédouville en Saint Domingue* (Port-au-Prince, 1929). On the state of siege as employed by Hédouville in France, see Howard G. Brown, *Ending the French Revolution: Violence, Justice, and Repression from the Terror to Napoleon* (Charlottesville: University of Virginia Press, 2006), esp. 200–210.

80. Constitution de l'an VIII (13 Dec. 1799), art. 91, in Godechot, *Constitutions de la France,* 161.

81. Const. 1799, art. 92.

82. Théodore Reinach, *De l'état de siège: Étude historique et juridique* (Paris: Librairie Cotillon, 1885), 96–97. For a legislative review of siege power, see Jean-Baptiste Jourdan (de la Haute Vienne), *Corps législatif, Conseil des Cinq Cents: Rapport fait par Jourdan (de la Haute Vienne) au nom d'une commission composée des représentants du peuple Mayeuvre, Siméon, Vasse, Chabaud et Jourdan, chargée d'examiner si la mise en état de siège est une mesure qui puisse concorder avec l'esprit et les principes de la Constitution, séance du 21 thermidor an V* (Paris, 1797).

83. Arthur Girault, *Principes de colonisation et de législation coloniale,* 1st ed. (Paris: Recueil Sirey, 1895), 186–187.

84. Sénatus-consulte organique de la Constitution, title 3, 16 thermidor X (4 Aug. 1802).

85. Conseil d'État, AP 2nd ser. 7: 449–450 (24 Feb. 1803).

86. Discussion du projet de Code civil, Conseil d'Etat, AP 2nd ser. 7: 236 (22 Aug. 1801).

87. Conseil d'État, AP 2nd ser. 7: 237 (22 Aug. 1801).

3. FREE SOIL

1. Jeannet-Oudin, 15 Apr. 1793, C^{14} 71, fol. 18, AN (microfilm).

2. For his later career, see Rafe Blaufarb, *Bonapartists in the Borderlands: French Exiles and Refugees on the Gulf Coast 1815–1835* (Tuscaloosa: University of Alabama, 2005), 88–89, 163, 207.

3. Ciro Flammarion Cardoso, *La Guyane française (1715–1817): aspects économiques et sociaux* (Petit-Bourg, Guadeloupe, 1999), 335.

4. Lettres Patentes du Roi, qui accordent à l'Isle de Cayenne & la Guyane françoise la liberté de commerce avec toute les Nations pendant douze ans, no. 1778, May 1768, in *Acts of French Royal Administration Concerning Canada, Guiana, the West Indies, and Louisiana, Prior to 1791,* ed. Lawrence C. Wroth and Gertrude L. Annan (New York: New York Public Library, 1930).

5. D'Alais, Compte rendu des habitations du Roy, Voyage à Approuague, 27 Jan. 1789, C^{14} 63, fol. 8v.

6. Léon Levavasseur (Seine-Inférieur), Rapport sur l'île de Cayenne et la Guyane française, 14 June 1792, AP 1st ser. 45: 213–219.

7. Flávio Gomes, "Other Black Atlantic Borders: Escape Routes, *Mocambos,* and Fears of Sedition in Brazil in French Guiana (Eighteenth and Nineteenth Centuries)," *New West Indian Guide/Nieuwe West-Indische Guids* 77, nos. 3–4 (2003): 273.

8. For municipal law, see Établissement et organisation de la municipalité tant pour la ville que pour la campagne arrêtés et décrêtés par l'Assemblée Coloniale de la Guyane française dans la séance du 15 octobre de la matinée 1790 en observant qu'il a été fait des changements sur plusieurs articles dans les séances du 22 décembre 1790 et 12 janvier 1791, C^{14} 66, fol. 257 ; for constitution, see Organisation de la Guyane française, 5–10 décembre 1792 [promulgated 19 Dec.], with D'Alais to Min., Compte rendu, 1 Jan. 1793, C^{14} 70, fol. 18v.

9. Organisation de la Guyane française, C^{14} 70, fol. 18v.

10. Pierre-Samuel Dupont de Nemours, Exposé des motifs des décrets des 13 et 15 mai 1791 sur l'état des personnes aux colonies, 29 May 1791, in Jules-François Saintoyant, *Les assemblées révolutionnaires et les colonies*, vol. 1, *La colonisation française pendant la Révolution*, 392–393.

11. Adolphe Cabon, "Le Clergé de la Guyane sous la Révolution," *Revue d'histoire des colonies* 37 (3rd trim. 1950): 181.

12. Proclamation de [Frédéric-Joseph] Guillot, 24 Sept. 1792, C^{14} 69, fol. 8.

13. Guillaume-Thomas Raynal, *Histoire philosophique et politique des établissements et du commerce des européens dans les deux Indes*, vol. 6 (Geneva: n.p., 1781), 182–183; Sankar Muthu, *Enlightenment against Empire* (Princeton: Princeton University Press, 2003), 72–121; for the book's reception during the Revolution, see Yves Bénot, "Traces de l'*Histoire des deux Indes* chez les anti-esclavagistes sous la Révolution," *Studies on Voltaire and the Eighteenth Century* 286: 141–154.

14. In 1789, French officials reported the beginnings of what became the second Boni Maroon War. Bourgon to Luzerne, Min. Navy, 28 Nov. 1789, C^{14} 63, fol. 31; Wim Hoogbergen, *The Boni Maroon Wars in Suriname* (Leiden: Brill, 1990), 129–156. For the first war, see John Gabriel Stedman, *Narrative of a Five Years Expedition against the Revolted Negroes of Surinam* (Baltimore: The Johns Hopkins University Press, 1988). On the eighteenth-century Guianas, see *Maroon Societies: Rebel Slave Communities in the Americas,* ed. Richard Price (Baltimore: The Johns Hopkins University Press, 1996), 292–311.

15. Villebois to Min., 4 Oct. 1787, C^{14} 67, fol. 42; see Alvin O. Thompson, *The Berbice Revolt 1763–64* (Georgetown, Guyana: Free Press, 1999).

16. Gov. to Min., 2 April 1790, C^{14} 66, fol. 51. Of the revolt, see Yves Bénot, "The Chain of Slave Insurrections," *The Abolitions of Slavery from L. F. Sonthonax to Victor Schoelcher,* ed. Marcel Dorigny (New York: Berghahn, 2003), 150–151.

17. Henri Benoist, Observations adressés à l'assemblée coloniale le 9 février [1791] sur la nécessité de conserver l'enceinte de la ville de Cayenne, C^{14} 67, fol. 40–41.

18. Moranville, Président de l'Assemblée coloniale, to Min., 14 Jan. 1794, C^{14} 70, fol. 210–211.

19. Extrait des informations faites contre les nègres révoltés d'Approuague, Déposition de la Dame Saint Marcel, C^{14} 66, fol. 90.

20. MM les officiers, bas-officiers, et soldats des troupes de lignes, détachement à Approuague, 7 Jan. 1791, C^{14} 67, fol. 222.

21. André Pomme, *Convention nationale: observations d'A. Pomme, l'Américain, sur le mode d'exécution de la déportation en Guyane, imprimées par ordre du Comité des Finances* (Imprimerie nationale, n.d.).

22. Yves Bénot, *La Guyane sous la Révolution française, ou l'impasse de la révolution pacifique* (Kourou, Guyane française: Ibis Rouge, 1997), 114.

23. Ibid., 164–165.

24. Georges-Nicolas Jeannet-Oudin, Mémoire sur les colonies en général et sur la Guyane en particulier présenté au Premier Consul Bonaparte [24 Oct. 1801], C^{14} 79, fol. 104v.

25. Cabon, "Le Clergé de la Guyane sous la Révolution," 178.

26. Promulgation of assembly's decree dated 15 Sept. 1791 concerning refractory priests, 17 Sept. 1791, C^{14} 67 fol.185.

27. Cabon, "Le Clergé de la Guyane sous la Révolution," 182.

28. D'Alais to Jacquemin, 1 Apr. 1793, C^{14} 70 fol. 79.

29. Cardoso, *La Guyane française,* 195; Compagnie de Jésus, *Mission de Cayenne et de la Guyane française* (Paris: Julien, Lanier & Cosnard, 1857), 361–366.

30. André Pomme and Bertrand Bajon, Demande et observations qu'ont l'honneur de présenter des députés de Cayenne et Guiane française à M. Monge, Ministre de la Marine, 31 Aug. 1792, C^{14} 69 fol. 98v; Pomme, *Observations.* Internal evidence and references to this report in the *Archives parlémentaires* in July 1793 suggest this was published in late June.

31. Pomme and Bajon, Demande et observations qu'ont l'honneur de présenter des députés de Cayenne et Guiane française à M. Monge, Ministre de la Marine, 31 Aug. 1792, C^{14} 69 fol. 98v.

32. Gov. Fitz-Maurice, Mémoire concernant la situation actuelle de la Guyane française, 31 Mar. 1787, C^{14} 61 fol. 10v. Biographical details in A. Kuscinski, *Dictionnaire des conventionnels* (Paris: Société de l'histoire de la Révolution française, 1916).

33. Pomme, *Observations,* 4.

34. Pomme, *Observations,* 5.

35. Pomme, *Observations,* 9, 11–12.

36. De la gendarmerie nationale, Organisation de la Guyane française, C^{14} 70 fol. 21r.

37. C^{14} 70 fol. 21v.

38. C^{14} 70 fol. 21r.

39. C^{14} 70 fol. 21v.

40. Pomme, *Observations,* 9.

41. Georges-René Pléville le Pelley to Jeannet-Oudin, Paris, 20 fructidor V (6 Sept. 1797), B 239, AN.

42. Bernard Saugier, *Pichegru: Histoire d'un suicide* (Bourg-en-Bresse: Éditions provinciales, 1992), 234; Jeannet-Oudin, Affaire du curé Hochard, 8 Dec. 1793, C^{14} 91.

43. Sinnamary: Naissances, Mariages et Décès (IV–XI), ANSOM 119, CAOM. The term Bambara referred to the Bamana, "a self-conscious ethnic group exported from Greater

Senegambian ports, mainly Gorée and along the Gambia River." Congo was a broad designation for West Central Africans that may refer to people from the Bight of Biafra. See Gwendolyn Midlo Hall, *Slavery and African Ethnicities in the Americas: Restoring the Links* (Chapel Hill: University of North Carolina Press, 2005), 35, 65, 75, 96. Vogel was probably a survivor of the ill-fated Kourou expedition. For biographical details, see his marriage on 14 prairial IV (2 June 1796), Sinnamary: Naissances, Mariages et Décès IV–XI (1795–1802), ANSOM 119, CAOM. On the Kourou disaster, see Marion E. Godfroy-Tayart de Borms, "La guerre de sept ans et ses conséquences atlantiques: Kourou ou l'apparition d'un nouveau système colonial, *French Historical Studies* 32, no. 2 (Spring 2009): 167–191; Emma Rothschild, "A Horrible Tragedy in the French Atlantic," *Past & Present* 192, no. 1 (Aug. 2006): 67–108; Jacques Michel, *La Guyane sous l'ancien régime: Le désastre de Kourou et ses scandaleuses suites judiciaries* (Paris: L'Harmattan, 1989).

44. Bénot, *La Guyane sous la Révolution,* 123.
45. [François Barbé de Marbois], *Journal d'un déporté non jugé, ou déportation en violation des lois,* vol. 1 (Paris: Chatet & Fournier, 1834), 151.
46. Laffon-Ladébat, 15 nivôse VI (4 Jan. 1798), *Journal de ma déportation à la Guyane française* (Paris: Ollendorff, 1912), 232–233.
47. Louis-Ange Pitou, *Les déportés de fructidor,* 94.
48. Laffon-Ladébat, 8 frimaire VIII (29 Nov. 1799), *Journal,* 359; on advisory role, see entries of vendémiaire–nivôse VIII (Oct. 1799–Jan. 1800), 356–368.
49. François-Maurice Cointet, Proclamation, 6 ventôse III (24 Feb. 1795), DXXV/130, AN.
50. Regulation of 28 frimaire IV (17 Dec. 1796). Bénot, *La Guyane sous la Révolution,* 98.
51. Bénot, *La Guyane sous la Révolution,* 102–109.
52. Decree of 1 Messidor IV (19 June 1796), quoted in Bénot, *La Guyane sous la Révolution,* 112–114.
53. Jeannet-Oudin to Min., 13 thermidor V (31 July 1797), C^{14} 75, fol. 32.
54. Barbotin, *Conamama,* 123.
55. Pléville to Jeannet-Oudin, 25 ventôse VI (15 Mar. 1798), C^{14} 76, fol. 04.
56. Jeannet-Oudin to Min. 10 messidor VI (28 June 1798), C^{14} 76, fol. 35.
57. André-Daniel Laffon-Ladébat, 15 nivôse VI (4 Jan. 1798), *Journal,* 243.
58. Barbotin, *Conamama,* 161–162.
59. No. 107, 1 pluviôse VII (20 Jan. 1799), DPPC Not. Guy 130 (Paguenault), CAOM. Of Leroy, see Barbotin, *Conamama,* Annex II.
60. Pitou, *Les déportés de fructidor,* 85.
61. AP 1st ser. 31: 438–443 (28 Sept. 1791).
62. Flávio Gomes, "Other Black Atlantic Borders," *New West Indian Guide/Niewe West-Indische Guids* 77, nos. 3–4 (2003): 253–287. On the earlier handling of slave refugees in French Guiana, see C. Laroche, *L'esclavage en Guyane française sous l'ancien régime: Extrait de la Revue française d'histoire d'outre mer* (Paris: RFHO, 1960), 52–55.
63. Extrait des registres de délibérations du conseil de guerre (25–27 Oct. 1794), C^{14} 73, fol. 36–fol. 37.

64. L'agent particulier du Directoire exécutif au Gouverneur Général de Surinam, 26 fructidor VI (12 Sept. 1798), C^{14} 76, fol. 62–63; title 3, art. 18, loi concernant l'organisation constitutionnelle des colonies, no. 1659 of 12 nivôse VI (1 Jan. 1798), *B. L.,* no. 177.

65. Jeannet-Oudin to Truguet, 12 vendémiaire V (3 Oct. 1796), C^{14} 74, fol. 122v–123.

66. Bénot, *Guyane sous la Révolution,* 89–102 and 107.

67. Voyages. 2010. *Voyages: The Trans-Atlantic Slave Trade Database.* http://slavevoyages .org/tast/database/search.faces?yearFrom=1795&yearTo=1800&mjslptimp=36200 (accessed 1 June 2011).

68. Laurent Dubois, *A Colony of Citizens: Revolution and Slave Emancipation in the French Caribbean 1787–1804* (Chapel Hill: University of North Carolina Press, 2004), 298–299.

69. Voyages. 2010. *Voyages: The Trans-Atlantic Slave Trade Database* http://slavevoyages .org/tast/database/search.faces?yearFrom=1794&yearTo=1797&mjslptimp=36200.36300 (accessed 1 June 2011).

70. This statistic is based on a voyage search for Saint Domingue excluding Port-au-Prince. Voyages. 2010. *Voyages: The Trans-Atlantic Slave Trade Database.* http:// slavevoyages.org/tast/database/search.faces?yearFrom=1794&yearTo=1798&mjslptimp= 36401.36402.36403.36404.36405.36406.36407.36408.36409.36410.36411.36414.36499 (accessed 1 June 2010).

71. Dupont de Nemours, Exposé des motifs des décrets des 13 et 15 mai 1791 sur l'état des personnes aux colonies, in Saintoyant, *La Colonisation française pendant la Révolution,* vol. 1, 392–393.

72. Claude Wanquet, "La première abolition française de l'esclavage fut-elle une mystification? Le cas Daniel Lescallier," in *Esclavage, résistances, et abolitions,* ed. Marcel Dorigny, Congrès national des sociétés historiques et scientifiques (Paris : Comité des travaux historiques et scientifiques, 1999), 253–268; for another text addressing the status of these captives, see Mémoires et projets par le Capitaine de Vaisseau Jacques-Joseph Eyriès (1795), C^{14} 73, fol. 215v–216.

73. Cointet to Commission de Marine et des Colonies, 1 vendémiaire IV (23 Sept. 1795), C^{14} 73, fol. 12–13; Discours prononcé par le Citoyen Gouverneur au Conseil de Guerre, 5 germinal III (25 March 1795), C^{14} 73, fol. 14; Proclamation, 22 floréal III (20 Apr. 1795), C^{14} 73, fol. 65; Proclamation, 18 germinal III (7 Apr. 1795), C^{14} 73, fol. 67.

74. Jeannet-Oudin to Min., 13 fructidor IV (30 Aug. 1796), C^{14} 76, fol. 113–118; Burnel to Min., 17 frimaire VII (7 Dec. 1798), C^{14} 76, fol. 97.

75. Burnel to Min., 17 frimaire VII (7 Dec. 1798), C^{14} 76, fol. 101v.

76. For draft language concerning Africans from seized slave ships, see C^{14} 80, fol. 30–30v, fol. 35, fol. 39v.

77. Administration départementale de la Guyane française to Min., 19 prairial V (7 June 1797), C^{14} 75, fol. 168.

78. On the enforcement of the July 1802 decree, see Michael D. Sibalis, "Les Noirs en France sous Napoléon: L'enquête de 1807," in *Rétablissement de l'esclavage dans les colonies françaises,* ed. Yves Bénot and Marcel Dorigny (Paris: Maisonneuve et Larose, 2003), 95–107. On Victor Hugues's anticipatory efforts to limit travel by black

and colored people, see Hugues to Min., 20 vendémiaire XI (12 Oct. 1802), C¹⁴ 80, fol. 100.

79. Sue Peabody, *"There Are No Slaves in France": The Political Culture of Race and Slavery in the Ancien Régime* (New York: Oxford, 1996), 55, 117–136.

80. Cointet, Proclamation, 6 ventôse III (24 Feb. 1795), DXXV/130, AN.

81. Jeannet-Oudin, Proclamation, 23 messidor V (11 July 1797), C¹⁴ 75, fol. 36.

82. Dubois, *Colony of Citizens*, 203.

83. On Hugues's appointment, see Rapport aux consuls de la République, 13 frimaire VIII (4 Dec. 1799), C¹⁴ 77, fol. 188.

84. Art. 26, title II, regulation, 5 floréal XI (25 April 1803), C¹⁴ 82, fol. 58v.

85. Victor Hugues to Min., 23 vendémiaire XII (15 Oct. 1804), C¹⁴ 83, fol. 86v.

86. Hugues to Min. 20 vendémiaire X (12 Oct. 1802), C¹⁴ 80, fol. 130.

87. Observations sur le projet d'arrêté tendant à établir à Cayenne et dans la Guyane française un esclavage plein pour certains noirs et une simple conscription rurale pour les autres [30 Nov. 1802], C¹⁴ 80, fol. 26v.

88. Hugues to Min. ["pour lui seul"], 20 vendémiaire XI (12 Oct. 1802), C¹⁴ 80, fol. 124–134.

89. On the gradual return of slavery, see declarations of 15 germinal X (5 April 1802) and 9 frimaire XI (30 Nov. 1802) by Marie-Catherine Duquesne de Lambrun regarding her slave Jeannette, registered on 1 pluviôse XI (21 pluviôse 1803), État civil: actes d'affranchissement 1802–1803, ANSOM 39, CAOM.

90. 2 messidor IX (21 June 1801), no. 211, DPPC Not. Guy 131 (Paguenault), CAOM.

91. 3 thermidor IX (22 July 1801), no. 219, DPPC Not. Guy 131, CAOM.

92. 4 fructidor X (22 August 1802), no. 365, DPPC Not. Guy 132, CAOM.

93. 10 fructidor X (28 Aug. 1802), DPPC Not. Guy 132, CAOM.

94. 20 fructidor X (15 Sept. 1802), no. 381, DPPC Not. Guy 132, CAOM.

95. Both women eventually secured their freedom by producing a suspicious manumission deed dated 13 June 1794, one day before the emancipation decree went into effect in Guiana. For their manumission, see no. 7, État Civil: actes d'affranchissement 1802–1803, ANSOM 39, CAOM; for their later acquisition of Rondeau's land, see no. 393, 20 thermidor XI (8 Aug. 1803), no. 663, Not. Guy 132, CAOM.

96. See 15 vendémiaire XI (7 Oct. 1802) no. 393, 20 thermidor XI (8 Aug. 1803), no. 663, Not. Guy 132, CAOM.

97. See Nos. 323 and 418 of 18 vendémiaire xi (10 Oct. 1802), DPPC, Not. Guy 132.

98. Hugues to Min., 20 vendémiaire XI (12 Oct. 1802), C¹⁴ 80, fol. 124–fol. 134.

99. On changes in October 1802, see Laroche narrative of 20 nivôse year XI (10 Jan. 1803), no. 437, DPPC Not. Guy 133 (Paguenault), CAOM.

100. Arrêté relatif à la traite des noirs et au régime des noirs en Guyane française, C¹⁴ 80, fol. 42.

101. Monique Pouliquen, "L'esclavage subi, aboli, rétabli en Guyane de 1789 à 1809," in *L'esclavage et les plantations: De l'établissement de la servitude à son abolition, un hommage à Pierre Pluchon* (Rennes: Presses Universitaires de Rennes, 2008), 258.

102. Cardoso, *La Guyane française*, 395.

103. No. 205, État Civil: actes d'affranchissement 1802–1803, ANSOM 39, CAOM.

104. Hugues to Min., 10 brumaire XI (1 Nov. 1802), C¹⁴ 80, fol. 135–fol. 138, and 18 nivôse XI (8 Jan. 1803), C¹⁴ 82, fol. 30–31.

105. Victor Hugues, A son excellence M. le Comte de Cessac, Min. de l'État, Président, Monsieur le Général Comte Hullin, et Monsieur l'Amiral Rosilly, C¹⁴ 87, fol. 111. For an account of the defeat, see Jean Soublin, *Cayenne 1809: La conquête de la Guyane par les portugais de Brésil* (Paris: Karthala, 2003); see also Baron Carra de Vaux, "Documents sur la perte et la retrocession de la Guyane française (1809–1817)," *Revue de l'histoire des colonies* (3rd trim. 1913): 333–368.

4. MISSING PERSONS

1. Dezalier to Min. Justice, 3 Oct. 1827; Dezalier to Min. Intérieur, 28 Sept. 1828; Préfet de Police to Min. Intérieur, 22 Jan. 1828; Préfet Aisne to Min. Intérieur, 27 Dec. 1827. All in Desalliers (*sic*) file, F⁷ 12239, AN.

2. André-Jean-Simon Nougarède de Fayet, AP 2nd ser. 10: 618 (20 Feb. 1810).

3. Min. Intérieur, Passeport Pierre-Emmanuel Vié, Chaîne de Brest, 4ème jour complémentaire VII (20 Sept. 1799), F¹⁶ 474A, AN.

4. Chaîne role and report, Paris, 1 pluviôse year III (20 Jan. 1795), F¹⁶ 474A, AN.

5. Rapport en exécution des ordres de la commission des administrations civiles, polices, et tribunaux, 6 brumaire year IV (28 Oct. 1795), F¹⁶ 474A, AN. On convict deaths during the march, see Min. Marine to Min. Intérieur, 26 Dec. 1808, F¹⁶ 474A, AN.

6. [Antoine-Claire Thibaudeau], *Mémoires sur le Consulat, 1799 à 1804, par un ancien conseiller d'état* (Paris: Ponthieu, 1827), 97.

7. Conseil d'état, AP 2nd ser. 7: 452, 5 ventôse an XI (24 Feb. 1803).

8. Tribunat, AP 2nd ser. 3: 191–192 (20 Dec. 1801).

9. Of new effects of civil death, see Jean Maleville, Conseil d'État, AP 2nd ser. 7: 236 (14 Aug. 1801).

10. Conseil d'État, AP 2nd ser., 7: 216–218, 16 thermidor year IX (4 Aug. 1801); Tribunal d'appel séant à Paris, Pierre-Antoine Fenet. *Recueil complet des travaux préparatoires du Code civil* (Paris: Videcoq, 1836), 5: 102.

11. On émigré marriages and nineteenth-century courts, see Cour de Cassation [hereafter Cass.], 10 Aug. 1842, *JP* (1842), vol. 2, 577–578; Cass., 13 Feb. 1849, *JP* (1849), vol. 1, 442–444. On the dissolution of marriage after the code, see Cour royale de Toulouse, 26 May 1837, *JP* (1837), vol. 2, 185–186; of amnesty, see Cass., 21 July 1850, *JP* (1850), vol. 2, 275–276. For an excellent discussion of these matters, see Jennifer Ngaire Heuer, *The Family and the Nation: Gender and Citizenship in Revolutionary France 1789–1830* (Ithaca: Cornell University Press, 2005), esp. 41–42, 134, 155.

12. De la jouissance et de la privation des droits civils, première discussion du Conseil d'état, 4 fructidor year IX (22 Aug. 1801), Fenet, *Recueil complet des travaux préparatoires du Code civil*, 7: 133–134.

13. Quoted in [Thibaudeau], *Mémoires sur le Consulat*, 427.

14. Philippe-Antoine Merlin, *Répertoire universel et raisonné de jurisprudence,* 5th ed. (Brussels, 1828), s.v. "flétrissure." On the branding of forgers see Régnier to Tribunate, AP 2nd ser. 3: 237 (24 Dec. 1801). Of the brand as deportation, see Trophime Gérard de Lally-Tollendal, *Opinion de M. le Marquis de Lally-Tollendal sur la proposition faite à la chambre par Monsieur de Marquis de Marbois, et tendant à faire substituer à la peine de la déportation une autre peine proportionnée à la nature et à la gravité des crimes,* Chambre des Pairs de France, Session of 1818, Séance of 1 May 1819 (Paris: P. Didot, aîné, n.d.).

15. Jean-Claude Vimont, *La Prison politique en France: Genèse d'un mode d'incarcération spécifique XVIIIe–XXe siècles* (Paris: Anthropos, 1993); Merlin, *Répertoire universel,* 5th ed. (1828), s.v. "mort civile," sec. 1, art. 5, p. 436; Cour Royale d'Orléans, 5 Feb. 1847, *JP* (1847), vol. 1, 400–402.

16. C. Pén. 1791, tit. IV, art. 2.

17. C. Pén. 1810, art. 29.

18. Adolphe Chauveau and Faustin Hélie, vol. 1, *Théorie du Code pénal,* ed. Edmond Villey and E. Mesnard, 6th ed. (Paris: Imprimerie et Librairie générale de Jurisprudence, 1908), ch. 7, 185–186; see also Ernest Nusse, *Étude sur les droits civils des condamnés aux peines du grand criminel* (Paris: Cotillon, 1876), 25 and 53.

19. On the three schools of thought concerning legal interdiction, see Gustave-Amédée Humbert, *Les conséquences des condamnations pénales relativement à la capacité des personnes en droit romain et en droit français* (Paris: Durand, 1855), 350–353.

20. Nusse, *Étude sur les droits civils des condamnés,* 20.

21. Jean Carbonnier, vol. 1, *Droit civil: Introduction, Personnes,* 8th ed., Collection Thémis, ed. Maurice Duverger (Paris: PUF, 1969), 55.

22. Of the legal sex change, see Jan. M. Broekman, *Droit et anthropologie* (Paris and Brussels: Librairie générale de droit et de jurisprudence, 1993), 76.

23. Noiseux to Min., Pont Chartrain, 1e jour complémentaire IV (17 Sept. 1796), F[16] 474A, AN.

24. Noiseux to Min., Dreux, 2e jour complémentaire IV (18 Sept. 1796), F[16] 474A, AN.

25. Noiseux to Min., Port Brieux, 12 vendémiaire year V, F[16] 474A, AN.

26. AP 2nd ser. 3: 237 (24 Dec. 1801).

27. Isser Woloch, "Napoleonic Conscription: State Power and Civil Society," *Past and Present* 111 (May 1986): 101–129; Alan Forrest, *Conscripts and Deserters: The Army and French Society during the Revolution and Empire* (New York: Oxford University Press, 1989).

28. Comm.-Gén. to Min. Intérieur, Boulogne, 20 Jan. 1813, F[7] 3034, AN.

29. Projet de décret sur la police et la justice dans les ports et arsenaux, title 3, art. 16, AP 1st ser. 31: 101.

30. C. Pén. 1810, art. 484.

31. Merlin, *Répertoire universel,* 5th ed. (1828), s.v. "forçat," 28: 286. Here Merlin quotes from his own remarks before the Court of Cassation on 28 messidor XII.

32. Nougarède, AP 2nd ser. 10: 618 (20 Feb. 1810).

33. Rapport au Ministre, 4 Aug. 1836, sent as enclosure C with Min. Marine to Gov., 3 Oct. 1852, 1M50*, ADGuy.

34. Cass., 18 July 1833, *JP* (1833), vol. 25, 695; Cass., 2 Jan. 1845, *JP* (1845), vol. 2, 567–568.
35. Cass., 9 Dec. 1842, *Bull. ch. crim.,* no. 320.
36. Regulation of 1 Apr. 1749, art. 86, superseded by Ordinance of 2 Jan. 1817, art. 2, "Code des bagnes," O-107, SHM Toulon.
37. Cass., 14 Mar. 1845, *JP* (1845), vol. 2, 568.
38. "Départ de la chaîne," *Gazette des tribunaux,* 11 Apr. 1832, 595.
39. "Chaîne des forçats," *Gazette des tribunaux,* 26 Oct. 1826, 2.
40. "Lettre d'Hippolyte Raynal sur la Chaîne des Forçats," *Gazette des tribunaux,* 16 Oct. 1830, 1147.
41. "Arrivée de la chaîne des forçats à Toulon," *Gazette des tribunaux,* 27 May 1831, 707.
42. Commissaire de la chaîne to Min. Intérieur, 29 Sept 1835, F[16] 507–508, AN.
43. "Suppression de la chaîne des forçats," in *Recueil administratif du département de la Seine* (Paris: Bureau de l'Administration, 1837), vol. 1, 453; vol. 2, 124.
44. The original decree of 19 ventôse XIII (10 March 1805) responded to complaint by the préfet of Bas-Rhin. See Ministère de la Police Générale, Rapport au Conseil, 1 ventôse year XIII (20 Feb. 1805), F[7] 9934, AN.
45. Decree of 18 July 1806, arts. 6 and 10, in Merlin, *Répertoire universel,* 5th ed. (1828), s.v. "forçat."
46. See Ordres de fourniture for Bernard Vanier, Gilles Baroche, and Charles Pierson of 16 Aug., 30 Aug., and 30 Sept. 1816, département d'Ille et Vilaine, Place de Montaubon, transports des prisonniers civils et criminels, F[7] 10225b, AN.
47. H. Forneron, *Histoire des émigrés,* vol. 2 (Paris: Plon, 1884), 373.
48. Préfet Aisne to Maire Laon, 10 April 1810; Arrêté par le Maire de Laon, 4 May 1810, 2i.112, Archives communales de Laon, AD Aisne (Laon).
49. C. Pén. 1810, art. 44.
50. C. Pén. 1810, art. 271.
51. Alfred Giraud, *De la surveillance de la haute police et de la réhabilitation* (Paris: Durand, 1862), 10.
52. Decision of 4 Aug. 1812, approved 20 Sept. 1812, Désiré Dalloz, *Répertoire méthodique et alphabétique de législation, de doctrine et de jurisprudence en matière de droit civil, commercial, criminel, administratif, de droits des gens et de droit public* (Paris: Bureau de la jurisprudence générale, 1846–1870), s.v. "peines," no. 673.
53. C. Pén. 1810, art. 45.
54. Guy-Jean-Baptiste Target, "Observations sur le projet de Code criminel (1804)," in Adolphe Chauveau, *Étude de législation pénale comparée, Code français de 1810 avec les motifs, les discussions au Conseil d'état et les dispositions correspondantes des codes de 1791 et de l'an IV, Code révisé de 1832* (Brussels: Meline, 1851), 9.
55. Préfet Allier to Min. Police Général, with marginalia, 17 Sept. 1810, F[7] 9934, AN.
56. Séance du 8 août 1820, Extrait des registres des délibérations du conseil général du département des Landes, F[7] 9932, AN.
57. Notes sur 8 forçats à libérer le 3e trimestre de 1830, F[7] 9932, AN.
58. Notes sur plusieurs forçats du bagne de Brest à libérer dans le courant du 2e trimestre de 1830, F[7] 9332, AN.
59. Directeur Gén. Police to Sous-Préfet Toulon, 7 Dec. 1821, F[7] 9934, AN.

60. Préfet Seine-Inférieure to Min. Intérieur, 19 Aug. 1826, 4M 2729, AD Seine Maritime (Rouen).

61. Notes sur plusieurs forçats du bagne de Toulon à libérer dans le courrant du 2ᵉ trimestre de 1830, F⁷ 9932, AN.

62. Directeur Gén. Police to Sous-Préfet Toulon, 10 Jan. 1822, F⁷ 9934, AN.

63. Congé de forçat, Antoine-Nicolas Landeux; Min. Intérieur to Maire Laon, 19 Dec. 1817; of Landeux's disappearance, see Préfet Aisne to Maire Laon, 16 May 1818, and response of 18 May 1818, which includes physical details. All from 2.i.113, Archives communales de Laon, AD Aisne (Laon).

64. Préfet Police (Paris) to Maire Laon, 22 Apr. 1819; about his arrest and return that summer, see Préfet Police to Maire Laon, 2 June 1819, and Gendarmerie royale, Ordre de conduite de Bicêtre, 6 June 1819; of his administrative detention, see Préfet Police to Maire Laon, 20 Apr. 1820; of detention in poorhouse, see Préfet Aisne to Maire Laon, 11 Feb. 1822. For later detentions in Paris, see Préfet Police to Maire Laon, 30 June 1823; Gendarmerie royale, Ordre de conduite de Bicêtre, 2 July 1823 (signalement de Landeux. dit Cartouche); Préfet Aisne to Maire Laon, 31 July 1823; extrait du registre du 31 juillet 1823; and Préfet Police to Maire Laon, 3 June 1824. All in 2.i.113, Archives communales de Laon, AD Aisne (Laon).

65. Circ. Min., no. 61, 22 Nov. 1825, F⁷ 9931, AN.

66. Préfet Eure-et-Loir to Maire Gallardon, 4 Oct. 1825; Préfet Eure-et-Loir to Préfet Mayenne, 4 Oct. 1825; Préfet Mayenne to Préfet Eure-et-Loir, 27 Sept. 1825; Min. Intérieur to Préfet Eure-et-Loir, 18 Jan. 1823, 4 M P art. 675, AD Eure-et-Loir (Chartres).

67. Directeur, Maison Central de Détention de Gaillon, to Préfet Eure, 21 Aug. 1830, F⁷ 9931, AN.

68. Maire Chartres to Préfet Eure-et-Loir, 24 Dec. 1824; Police Report, 3 Jan. 1825; Préfet Eure-et-Loir to Min. Intérieur, 12 Jan. 1825; Commissaire de Police to Maire Chartres, 13 Dec. 1825; Maire Chartres to Préfet Eure-et-Loir, 15 Dec. 1825; Min. Intérieur to Préfet Eure-et-Loir, 25 Dec. 1825, 4 M P art. 675, AD Eure-et-Loir (Chartres).

69. Laussat, Gov. Fr. Guiana to Portal d'Albarèdes, Min. Marine, Cayenne, 30 Dec. 1819; Portal to Siméon, Min. Intérieur, Paris, 4 Aug. 1820. Both in H1, CAOM.

70. Conseil général Loiret, Session Aug. 1821, F⁷ 9751, AN.

71. Excerpted 1828 registers of Conseils généraux for Nord, Seine, Dordogne, and Loire-Inférieure in F⁷ 9752, AN.

72. Excerpt, 1834 register, Finistère; Excerpt, 8 Sept. 1829, Nord, F⁷ 9752, AN.

73. Comte de Tascher, Président du Comité des pétitions, to Min. Marine, 12 Jan. 1841, H1, CAOM.

74. Circ. Min., 18 July 1833, quoted in François Joseph Bourrier, *De l'interdiction de l'eau et du feu et de la relégation en droit romain, de la surveillance de la haute police en droit français* (Paris: Arthur Rousseau, 1883), 109.

75. Circ. Min., no. 61, 22 Nov. 1825, F⁷ 9931, AN.

76. Circ. Min., 22 June 1819, quoted in Circ. Min., 18 July 1833, F⁷ 9931, AN.

77. Circ. Min., 18 July 1833 and 25 Oct. 1833, F⁷ 9931, AN.

78. Circ. Min., no. 7 (Police gén.), 1 Apr. 1841, 4 M 441, AD Rhône (Lyon).

79. Circ. Min., no. 25, 18 July 1833, F⁷ 9930, AN.

80. Préfet Rhône to Min. Intérieur, 19 Sept. 1835, and to Procureur-Gén., 4 M 655, AD Rhône (Lyon).

81. Préfet Aisne to Maire Laon, 4 July 1836, 2i 115, Archives communales de Laon, AD Aisne (Laon).

82. Décision Min., 9 May 1840, 4 M 655, AD Rhône (Lyon).

83. Circ. Min., no. 7bis, 7 May 1841, F^1 A64, AN.

84. Décision Min., 22 Apr. 1846, 4 M 655; Maire Lyon to Préfet Rhône, 28 Apr. 1846, 4 M 441. Both from AD Rhône (Lyon).

85. See for example the request of the municipality of Elbeuf in letter of Préfet Seine-Inférieure to Min. Interior, 19 March 1845, 4 M 2729, AD Seine Maritime.

86. Chambre de Commerce du Havre à Son Excellence, Monsieur le Ministre de l'Agriculture et du Commerce, 9 April 1845, 4 M 2729, AD Seine Maritime.

87. *Procès des accusés des 12 et 13 mai devant la Cour des Pairs* (Paris: Pagnerre, 1839), 14–15. Maurice Dommanget, *Auguste Blanqui: Des origines à la revolution de 1848, premiers combats et premières prisons* (Paris: Mouton, 1969), 163–171; Roger Merle, *Armand Barbès: Un révolutionnaire romantique* (Toulouse: Privat, 1977), 65–81.

88. *Procès des accusés des 12 et 13 mai devant la Cour des Pairs,* 325–326; Alfred Villeroy, *Histoire de 1840: Annuaire historique et politique* (Paris: Paulin, 1841), 68–69.

89. See cases of Joseph-Théodore Hugon and Marc-Étienne Reverchon in *Gazette des tribunaux,* 23 July 1837, 3704; 9 Aug. 1837, 3718; and 3 Sept. 1837, 3740.

90. Quoted in Dommanget, *Auguste Blanqui,* 334.

91. AP 86: 693 (25 Feb. 1834).

92. Lamartine, AP 87: 425–6 (13 Mar. 1834); Isambert, AP 88: 603 and 88: 12 (19 and 24 Mar. 1834); Laurence, AP 88: 14 (24 Mar. 1834).

93. "Chronique: Départements," *Gazette des tribunaux,* 22 Sept. 1836, 1065; "Détention d'un condamné après l'expiration de sa peine: Affaire du sieur Rixain, question grave," *Gazette des tribunaux,* 23 Sept. 1836, 1066; "Chronique: Départemens," *Gazette des tribunaux,* 28 Oct. 1836, 1169; "Justice criminelle: Tribunal correctionnel de Troyes, Audience du 27 octobre 1836, Affaire Rixain," *Gazette des tribunaux* 1 Nov. 1836, 2.

94. Patron to Loiseau, Nemours, 12 Oct. 1836, in Patron file, F^7 12240, AN.

95. Préfet Nord to Min. Intérieur, 26 Feb. 1838, Patron file, F^7 12240, AN.

96. Maison d'arrêt de la Force, 27 Mar. 1845, Patron file, F^7 12240, AN.

97. Patron to Loiseau, Nemours, 12 Oct. 1836; the letter includes an itinerary. Patron file, F^7 12240, AN.

98. Min. Intérieur to Commissaire provisoire Seine-Inférieure, 25 March 1848, 4 M 2729, AD Seine Maritime (Rouen).

99. Préfet Seine-Inférieure to Min. Intérieur, 5 June 1848; Min. Intérieur to Pref. Seine-Inférieure, 15 June 1848; Préfet Seine-Inférieure to Min. Intérieur, 7 July 1848, 4 M 2729, AD Seine Maritime (Rouen).

100. Maire Rouen to Préfet Seine-Inférieure, 30 June 1848, 4 M 2729, AD Seine Maritime (Rouen).

101. Préfet Seine-Inférieure to Directeur des prisons de Rouen, 30 Oct. 1848, 4 M 2729, AD Seine Maritime (Rouen).

102. Préfet Seine-Inférieure to Maire Le Havre, 10 Nov. 1848, 4 M 2729, AD Seine Maritime Rouen.

103. *Compte général de l'administration de la justice criminelle en France pendant l'année 1850* (Paris: Imprimerie nationale, 1852), lxiv. It is not possible from this source to determine how many of these were political offenses.

104. For military divisions of France during the Second Republic, see no. 291 of 28 Apr. 1848, *B. L.,* no. 31, pp. 313–316; for changes to divisions after the coup, see no. 3473 of 26 Dec. 1851, *B. L.,* no. 475, pp. 1254–1258. For use of the state of siege in Paris and Lyon, see no. 1357 of 13 June 1849, *B. L.,* no. 169, p. 549, and no. 1379 of 15 June 1849, *B. L.,* no. 169, p. 565.

105. No. 3259 of 12 Sept. 1851 for Ardèche, *B. L.,* no. 444, p. 531; no. 3331 of 21 Oct. 1851 for Cher and Nièvre, *B. L.,* no. 454, p. 889.

106. For uses of the state of siege before and after the coup d'état, see Ted Margadant, *French Peasants in Revolt: The Insurrection of 1851* (Princeton: Princeton University Press, 1979); John Merriman, *The Agony of the Republic: The Repression of the Left in Revolutionary France 1848–1851* (New Haven: Yale University Press, 1978).

107. For declarations of siege connected with the coup d'état, see no. 3378 of 2 Dec. 1851 for Paris and 1st mil. division, *B. L.,* no. 465, p. 987; no. 3400 of 5 Dec. 1851 for Allier, *B. L.,* no. 467, pp. 1028–1029; no. 3399 of 5 Dec. 1851 for Saône-et-Loire, *B. L.,* no. 467, p. 1028; no. 3402 of 7 Dec. 1851 for Hérault and Gard, *B. L.,* no. 467, pp. 1029–1030; no. 3419 of 9 Dec. 1851 for Basses Alpes, *B. L.,* no. 469, p. 1074; no. 3420 of 10 Dec. 1851 for Gers, Vars, Lot, and Lot-et-Garonne, *B. L.,* no. 469, pp. 1074–1075; no. 3426 of 15 Dec. 1851, for Aveyron and Vaucluse, *B. L.,* no. 469, pp. 1089–1090; no. 3465 of 17 Dec. 1851 for Jura, *B. L.,* no. 475, p. 1248; no. 3556 of 4 Jan. 1852 for Hautes-Alpes, *B. L.,* no. 482, pp. 117–118. For statistics on arrests, see Vincent Wright, "The Coup d'état of December 1851: Repression and the Limits of Repression," in *Revolution and Reaction: 1848 and the Second French Republic,* ed. Roger Price (New York: Barnes and Noble Books, 1975), 303–333; of the impact of this repression on the political mindset of the peasantry, see Margadant, *French Peasants in Revolt,* 302–335.

108. Min. Intérieur to Préfet Aisne, 9 May 1851, and Préfet Aisne to Maire, 23 Dec. 1851, 2.i.115, AC Laon, AD Aisne (Laon).

109. *Courrier du Havre* 95 (5 July 1848): 1. This editorial follows demands by General Council of Seine-Inférieure in 1848 session. See 4 M 2729, AD Seine Maritime (Rouen).

110. Margadant, *French Peasants in Revolt,* 312–313.

111. Art. 7, no. 3403 of 8 Dec. 1851, *B. L.,* no. 467, p. 1031.

112. For these statistics, see Margadant, *French Peasants in Revolt,* 320; Wright, "Coup d'état of December 1851," 326; and *État numérique des convois de transportés venus de France depuis le 11 mai 1852 jusqu'au 1er janvier 1860,* and *Etat numérique . . . depuis le 1er janvier 1860,* Fonds Guyane 20, Archives jésuites, Vanves. For Jesuit statistics on the penal colony during the first two decades, see the appendix. The number of political prisoners sent to Cayenne indicated by the ministry of general police does not accord with the number indicated by Jesuit priests in French Guiana, who tallied the

people in this category per convoy. The number of transported political prisoners to Cayenne, according to the former source, was 239; the number given by the Jesuits was 329.

113. See *État numérique . . . depuis le 1er janvier 1860,* Fonds Guyane 20, AJ FGu 20, app.

114. Antoine Blanche, vol. 1, *Études pratiques sur le Code pénal* (Paris: Librairie général de jurisprudence, 1861), 226.

115. Henri Pascaud, *Étude sur la surveillance de la haute police, ce qu'elle a été–ce qu'elle est ce qu'elle devrait être* (Paris: Cotillon, 1865), 10.

5. IDEA FOR A CONTINENT

1. Pierre-Jean-Georges Cabanis, "De l'influence des tempéraments sur la formation des idées et des affections morales," vol. 3, *Rapports du physique et du moral de l'homme* (Paris: Rosanges frères, 1824), 434.

2. On the Institut national, see Jean-Luc Chappey, *La Société des Observateurs de l'homme: des anthropologues au temps de Bonaparte (1799–1804)* (Paris: Société des études robes-pierristes, 2002); see also George W. Stocking, Jr., "French Anthropology in 1800," *Isis* 55 (1964): 134–150, and Elizabeth A. Williams, "The Science of Man: Anthropological Thought and Institutions in Nineteenth-Century France" (Ph.D. Diss., Indiana University, 1983).

3. Christine Cornell, *Questions Relating to Nicolas Baudin's Australian Expedition 1800–1804* (Adelaide: Libraries Board of South Australia, 1965), 24.

4. Roger Ageorges, *Ile de Ré, terres australes: Les voyages du capitaine Baudin, marin et naturaliste* (La Rochelle: Imprimerie de l'Ouest, 1994), 133. On French geographical interest in Australia, see Leslie R. Marchant, *France Australe: The French Search for the Southland and Subsequent Explorations and Plans to Found a Penal Colony and Strategic Base in South Western Australia 1503–1826* (Perth: Scott Four Colour Print, 1998).

5. François Péron, "Tableau général des colonies angloises aux terres australes en 1802," *Voyage de découvertes aux terres australes, exécuté sur les corvettes le Géographe, le Naturaliste, et la goëlette le Casuarina, pendant les années 1800, 1801, 1802, 1803 et 1804; sous le commandement du capitaine de vaisseau N. Baudin. Publié par ordre de son excellence le Ministre de la Marine et des Colonies; et rédigé par M. Louis Freycinet, capitaine de frégate, chevalier de Saint Louis et de la Légion d'honneur, correspondant de l'Institut de France, et de la Société des Sciences, Belles-Lettres et Arts de Rochefort, &c.; Commandant du Casuarina pendant l'expédition,* vol. 2 (Paris: Imprimerie royale, 1815), 414.

6. Report of 9 June 1806, quoted in Ernest Scott, *Terre Napoleon: A History of French Explorations and Projects in Australia* (London: Methuen, 1910), 249–250.

7. Thiessé, 27 frimaire X (18 Dec. 1801), Recueil complet, vol. 7: 193–194.

8. Colin Forster, *France and Botany Bay: The Lure of a Penal Colony* (Melbourne: Melbourne University Press, 1996), 175.

9. Robert Hughes, *The Fatal Shore: The Epic of Australia's Founding* (New York: Vintage, 1986), 118.

10. Bruce Kercher, "Perish or Prosper: The Law and Convict Transportation in the British Empire, 1700–1850," Forum: The "New" Australian Legal History, *Law and History Review* 21, no. 3 (Fall 2003): 536–537.

11. Writing on *terra nullius* in Australia chiefly concerns uses of the doctrine to establish imperial dominion and individual land title at the expense of native inhabitants. See James Simsarian, "The Acquisition of Legal Title to Terra Nullius," *Political Science Quarterly* 52, no. 1 (Mar. 1938): 111–138; Bruce Kercher, "Native Title in the Shadows: The Origins of the Myth of Terra Nullius in Early New South Wales Courts," *Colonialism and the Modern World: Selected Studies,* ed. Gregory Blue et al. (Armonk, N.Y.: M. E. Sharpe, 2002), 100–119; Stuart Banner, "Why Terra Nullius? Anthropology and Property Law in Early Australia," *Law and History Review* 23, no. 1 (Spring 2005): 95–131; Bruce Buchan, "Traffick of Empire: Trade, Treaty, and *Terra Nullius* in Australia and North America 1750–1800," *History Compass* 5, no. 2 (2007): 386–405. For links between the predicament of convicts and aborigines, see Lauren Benton, *Law and Colonial Cultures: Legal Regimes in World History 1400–1900* (New York: Cambridge University Press, 2002), 183–206.

12. C. A. Bayly, *Imperial Meridian: The British Empire and the World 1780–1830* (New York: Longman, 1989), 207; Alan Atkinson, "The Free-born Englishman Transported: Convict Rights as a Measure of Eighteenth-century Empire," *Past and Present* 144 (August 1994): 88–115; David Neal, *The Rule of Law in a Penal Colony: Law and Power in Early New South Wales* (Cambridge: Cambridge University Press, 2002); Bruce Kercher, "Perish or Prosper," 527–584, and "Recovering and Reporting Australia's Early Colonial Case Law: The Macquarie Project," *Law and History Review* 18, no. 3 (Fall 2000): 259–265.

13. William Eden, *The Principles of Penal Law* (London, 1771), quoted in Atkinson, "Free-born Englishman Transported," 92.

14. On martial law as a framework for colonial rule in Australia, see Lauren Benton, *A Search for Sovereignty: Law and Geography in European Empires 1400–1900* (New York: Cambridge Unversity Press, 2010), 187–197.

15. François Barbé de Marbois, *Complot d'Arnold et de Sir Henry Clinton contre les États Unis d'Amérique et contre le général Washington* (Paris, 1816).

16. E. Wilson Lyon, *The Man Who Sold Louisiana: The Career of François Barbé-Marbois* (Norman: University of Oklahoma Press, 1942), 159.

17. Quoted in ibid., 163.

18. Théodore Reinach, *De l'état de siège: Étude historique et juridique* (Paris: Librairie Cotillon, 1885), 98.

19. Quoted in Lyon, *The Man Who Sold Louisiana,* 172–173.

20. François Barbé de Marbois, *Opinion sur la proposition faite à la chambre dans sa séance du 30 mars dernier et tendante à faire substituer à la peine de la déportation une autre peine proportionnée à la nature et à la gravité des crimes,* Chambre des Paris de France, 1818 Session, séance of 27 Apr. 1819, Impressions diverses, no. 63 (Paris: Didot aîné, 1819), 8.

21. Marbois, *Opinion,* 22 and 24.

22. Marbois, *Observations sur les votes de quarante-un conseils généraux de département concernant la déportation des forçats libérés; présentées à Monsieur le Dauphin par un membre de la Société royale pour l'amélioration des prisons* (Paris: Imprimerie Royale, 1828), 5–6.

23. Marbois, *Observations,* 27.

24. Marbois, *Observations,* 7, 48, 57.

25. H. de Basterot, "Observations sur la déportation et sur la réforme des criminels en réponse à l'ouvrage de M. le Marquis de Barbé-Marbois intitulé, 'Observations sur les votes de quarante-un Conseils généraux de département concernant la déportation des forçats libérés' " (1830), pt. 2, H2, CAOM.

26. Michèle Riot-Sarcey, *Le Réel de l'utopie: Essai sur le politique au XIXe siècle,* Bibliothèque Albin Michel Histoire (Paris, 1998); Pierre Rosanvallon, *L'état en France de 1789 à nos jours* (Paris: Seuil, 1990), 114–129.

27. Henri Saint Simon, preface to *Du système industriel,* pt. I (1821), reprinted in *Selected Writings on Science, Industry, and Social Organisation,* trans. and ed. Keith Taylor (London: Croom Helm, 1975).

28. [Auguste Comte], *De la Physiologie appliquée à l'amélioration des institutions sociales,* vol. 5, *Oeuvres de Claude-Henri de Saint Simon* (Paris: Dentu, 1875), 180.

29. Riot-Sarcey, *Le Réel de l'utopie,* 45–46.

30. Armand Rastoul, introduction to *La Ville des Expiations* (Paris: Editions des presses françaises & Société d'Édition Belles Lettres, 1926), lxxii (hereafter *VE*).

31. Gordon Wright, *Between the Guillotine and Liberty: Two Centuries of the Crime Problem in France* (New York: Oxford, 1983), 65–66.

32. *Science against the Unbelievers: The Correspondence of Bonnet and Needham 1760–1780,* ed. Renato G. Mazzolini and Shirley A. Roe (Oxford: Voltaire Foundation, 1986), 63.

33. Pierre Ballanche, *Palingenésie sociale,* vol. 4, *Œuvres* (Paris: Bureau de l'encyclopédie des connaissances utiles, 1833), 80 (hereafter PS; cited in text).

34. Bentzien to Theodore Ducos, Min. Navy, 16 June 1852, H4, CAOM.

35. Eugène Sue, "Le Départ," *Mystères de Paris* (Paris: Jean-Jacques Pouvert, 1963), 108.

36. Jean-Daniel Bentzien, *Mémoire à consulter adressé aux Chambres législatives françaises et étrangères, contenant l'exposition d'un nouveau système pénitentiaire, basé sur la loi naturelle du progrès, précédé de vues et de propositions tendant à faire diminuer les délits et les crimes et surtout les récidives* (Bordeaux: C. Lawalle, neveu, 1846), 44–45.

37. Ibid., 45.

38. Alexis de Tocqueville, *Notes du voyage en Algérie de 1841,* vol. 1, *Œuvres,* Bibliothèque de la Pléiade (Paris: Gallimard, 1991), 686.

39. Admiral Mackau to Chasseloup-Laubat, Paris, 22 June 1851, H3, CAOM.

40. Solutions proposées sur plusieurs hypothèses relatives au système et au régime de la déportation, 7 July 1851, H3, CAOM.

41. Cited in G. A. Humbert, *Des conséquences des condamnations pénales relativement à la capacité des personnes en droit romain et en droit français* (Paris: Durand, 1855), 453.

42. Antoine Marie Demante, Rapport, 13 Novembre 1851, cited in Humbert, *Des conséquences des condamnations pénales*, 458–460.

43. Pierre Rosanvallon, *L'état en France*, 73.

44. Solutions proposées, H3, CAOM.

45. Min. to Maritime Prefect, 19 Jan. 1852, 1 O 49, SHM Toulon.

46. Min. to Maritime Prefect, 5 Feb. 1852, no. 15, 1 O 49, SHM Toulon.

47. Envoi d'une demande de transportation formée par le forçat Van Neuvetz (no. 4215), 28 Aug. 1852, no. 124, 1 O 49, SHM Toulon.

48. Min. to Maritime Prefect Brest, 11 July 1853 (draft), file marked "8ème convoi, La Fortune," H26, CAOM.

49. Mar. Pref. Brest to Min., 29 May 1852, no. 132, file marked "Erigone, 3ème convoi"; Ministerial instructions to Captain of the Armide (draft), 20 Mar. 1854, file marked "Armide, 9ème convoi," H26, CAOM.

50. Résumé 1ère conférence, 19–20 décembre 1851, marked in pencil "à lire confidentiellement par Saint Rémy, Douat, Duchayla, Aigr[illé]," file marked "Déportation: Documens à classer, travaux préparatoires sur l'organisation de la Colonie pénale," H11, CAOM.

51. Loi sur l'exécution de la peine des travaux forcés, no. 1527 of 30 May 1854, art. 2, *B. L.*, 11th ser., no. 178, p. 1439.

52. Law of 30 May 1854, art. 1.

53. Décret concernant les condamnés aux travaux forcés, actuellement détenus dans les bagnes, et qui seront envoyés à la Guyane française pour y subir leur peine, no. 3957 of 27 Mar. 1852, art. 12, *B. L.*, 10th ser., no. 519, p. 1017; italics in original.

54. Decree of 27 Mar. 1852, art. 4.

55. Law of 30 May 1854, art. 1.

56. Hamelin, Min. Navy to Vice-Admiral Baudin, Gov. Fr. Guiana, Paris, 14 Dec. 1855, H11, CAOM. This is from Baudin's instructions before departure.

57. Loi portant abolition de la mort civile, no. 1534 of 2–31 May 1854, *B. L.*, 11th ser., no. 180, pp. 1459–1462; *Feuille de la Guyane française*, 7 Aug. 1858, 2.

58. Bk. 1, ch. 2, sec. 2, C. Civ. 1804.

59. Law of 2–31 May 1854, art. 4.

60. Sénatus-Consulte qui règle la Constitution des Colonies de la Martinique, de la Guadeloupe, et de la Réunion, title 3 (Des autres colonies françaises), art. 18, no. 1382 of 3 May 1854, *B. L.*, 11th ser., no. 166, p. 1163; *Feuille*, 7 Aug. 1858, 1.

61. Arthur Girault, *Principes de colonisation et de législation coloniale* (Paris: Librairie du recueil général des lois et des arrêts, 1895), 324.

62. Decree of 10 Mar. 1855, *Feuille*, 7 Aug. 1858, 1.

63. Decree of 10 Mar. 1855, art 2, no. 2.

64. Jérôme Bonaparte, Min. Algeria and Colonies (24 June 1858–24 Nov. 1860), to Gov. Baudin, 25 Aug. 1858, no. 126, 1M62*, ADGuy.

65. Hamelin to Baudin, 27 Apr. 1858, no. 312, 1M61*, ADGuy.

6. LOCAL ARRANGEMENTS

1. Benjamin Claude Brower, *A Desert Named Peace: The Violence of France's Empire in the Algerian Sahara, 1844–1902* (New York: Columbia University Press, 2009), 23–25.

2. Olivier Le Cour Grandmaison, *Coloniser, Exterminer: Sur la guerre et l'état colonial* (Paris: Fayard, 2005).

3. Loi concernant le régime législatif des colonies of 28 Apr. 1833, in Duvergier, *Collection complète des lois, décrets, ordonnances, réglemens et avis du Conseil d'état* 33 (1833): 74.

4. Jean Carbonnier, "L'esclavage sous le régime du Code civil," *Annales de la faculté de droit de Liège* (1957): 53–63.

5. La Charte constitutionnelle du 14 August 1830, art. 14, in *Les constitutions de la France depuis 1789*, ed. Jacques Godechot (Paris: Garnier-Flammarion, 1970), 248.

6. Yvan Debbasch, *Couleur et liberté: Le jeu du critère ethnique dans un ordre juridique esclavagiste* (Paris: Dalloz, 1967), 287–288.

7. Ira Berlin, *Slaves without Masters* (New York: New Press, 1974), 89.

8. *Neither Slave nor Free: The Freedmen of African Descent in the Slave Societies of the New World*, ed. David W. Cohen and Jack P. Greene (Baltimore: The Johns Hopkins University Press, 1972); Rebecca Scott, *Slave Emancipation in Cuba: The Transition to Free Labor 1860–1899* (Princeton: Princeton University Press, 1985), 70–71.

9. Serge Daget, *La répression de la traite des noirs au XIXe siècle: L'action des croisières françaises sur les côtes occidentales de l'Afrique (1817–1850)* (Paris: Éditions Karthala, 1997), 53–55, 65–66, 68–70, 98–99.

10. Voyages Database. 2010. *Voyages: The Trans-Atlantic Slave Trade Database.* http://www.slavevoyages.org (accessed 1 June 2011). Numerous ships disembarked people in Cayenne that are omitted by the database or incompletely accounted for there. These include *Le Destin* (Oct. 1827), *La Jeune Créole* (May 1828), *La Topaze* (Mar. 1828), *L'Abeille* (Mar. 1828), and *L'Amitié* (July 1830). For references to these ships, see Arrêté qui déclare libres 493 noirs et négresses de traite provenant de saisies antérieures à la loi du 4 mars 1831, no. 124 of 16 June 1831, *B. Guy.* (1838), 120–158.

11. Daget, *La répression de la traite des noirs,* 251, 255, 277.

12. Lavollée, *Projet de loi sur la colonisation de la Guyane: Rapport au nom de la sous-commission* (Paris: Imprimerie nationale, 1851), 109–110.

13. On criteria for membership in the family of nations, see Henri Wheaton, "De la nature du droit des gens en général et de l'ouvrage intitulé 'Droit des gens actuel de l'Europe' par M. Heffter," *Revue de droit français et étranger* 1 (1844): 955–966; on legal nonrecognition of imperial subjects, see Antony Anghie, *Imperialism, Sovereignty, and the Making of International Law* (Cambridge: Cambridge University Press, 2004).

14. Serge Mam-Lam-Fouck, *La Guyane française au temps de l'esclavage, de l'or et de la francisation 1802–1946* (Petit-Bourg, Guadeloupe: Ibis Rouge, 1999), 140–152, 153.

15. Auguste Duport, *Des épaves maritimes* (Meulan: Auguste Rety, 1897), 46.

16. Pierre B. Boucher, *Institution du droit maritime* (Paris: Levrault, 1803), 708–724.

17. Guyane française, Conseil du Gouvernement et d'Administration, Procès-verbal d'une séance du 19 March 1822, FM/SG Guy 101, dossier K3 (101), CAOM.

18. Lagotellerie to Freycinet, 17 Mar. 1827, X/153, ADGuy.

19. Loi concernant la répression de la traite des noirs, arts. 2–3 and 11, no. 87 of 4 Mar. 1831, *B. L.*, 9th ser., no. 22, pt. 1, pp. 35–36.

20. For the implementation of this law in Cayenne, see Arrêté qui déclare libres 493 noirs et négresses de traite provenant de saisies antérieures à la loi du 4 mars 1831, no 124 of 16 June 1831; Arrêté de promulgation des arrêtés rendus à Cayenne le 16 juin 1831 et, à la Guadeloupe, le 23 juillet suivant, lesquels déclarent libres les noirs de traite y dé-nommés, no. 123 of 19 May 1838; Arrêté portant libération définitive de 22 négresses de traite ayant accompli leur temps d'engagement envers le gouvernement, no. 126 of 19 May 1838; Arrêté portant libération définitive du 16 négresses de traite ayant accom-pli leur temps d'engagement envers le Gouvernement, no. 127 of 21 May 1838; Arrêté portant libération définitive de 147 noirs et négresses de traite ayant accompli leur temps d'engagement envers le Gouvernement, no. 128 of 21 May 1838. All documents from *B. Guy.* (1838), 119–167.

21. To Duperré, 10 April 1838, in Anne-Marie Javouhey, *Correspondance* (herafter AMJ), ed. Jen Hébert and Marie-Cécile de Segonzac, vol. 2 (Paris: Éditions du Cerf, 1994), 242.

22. Art. 12, Arrêté rendu par M. le Ministre de la Marine et des Colonies, no. 38 of 18 Sept. 1835, *B. Guy.* (1836), 37.

23. Geneviève Lecuir-Nemo, *Anne-Marie Javouhey: Fondatrice de la Congrégation des Soeurs de Saint Joseph de Cluny (1779–1851)* (Paris: Éditions Karthala, 2001), 22–24.

24. Lecuir-Nemo, *Anne-Marie Javouhey*, 36–47.

25. To M. de Mauduit, Directeur des Colonies, Saint Louis, 25 Nov. 1822, no. 67, in Anne-Marie Javouhey, *Correspondance*, vol. 1 [hereafter AMJ], ed. Jean Hébert and Marie-Cécile de Segonzac (Paris: Éditions du Cerf, 1994), 135.

26. Lecuir-Nemo, *Anne-Marie Javouhey*, 113.

27. Philippe Delisle, "Colonisation, christianisation, et émancipation: les soeurs de Saint Joseph de Cluny à Mana (Guyane française) 1828–1846," *Revue française d'histoire d'outre mer* 85, no. 320 (1998): 21–27.

28. Laurens, Chef du bureau du Domaine, to Ordonnateur, *Rapport,* 27 June 1838, X/160, ADGuy.

29. Laurens, *Rapport* (1838).

30. This is a paraphrase by Delisle. Ordonnateur to Gov., 21 Mar. 1838, FM/SG Guy, 61, dossier 20, CAOM, quoted in Delisle, "Colonisation, christianisation, et émancipa-tion," 23.

31. Augustin Cochin, *L'abolition de l'esclavage*, vol. 1 (Paris: Jacques Lecoffre, 1861), 49.

32. Kenneth Bilby, "Swearing by the Past, Swearing to the Future: Sacred Oaths, Alli-ances, and Treaties among the Guianese and Jamaican Maroons," *Ethnohistory* 44, no. 4 (autumn 1997), 665–666; Hoogbergen, *The Boni Maroon Wars in Suriname*, 187–190.

33. The term "Djuka" is often used by scholars to refer to this group. I have chosen to fol-low nineteenth-century archives, which employ the term "Auka" or "Aukanier." In Su-riname, the word Djuka/Dyuka has become an ethnic slur in the town of Paramaribo. The name for this group following the wishes of its present members is "Aukaner," which is similar to Auka. Roy Tjin and Els Schellekens, *The Guide to Suriname,* trans. Judi and Henk Reichart (n.p., Brassa, 1999), 37.

34. Privy council minutes of 30 Dec. 1836 and 8 Mai 1837; Charles Couy to Gov., Oy-apock, 11 Jan. 1839; Lieut. Durand to Gov., Casfesoca Post, 12 Jan. 1839; Lieut. Ferrer to

Governor, Casfesoca Post, 7 June 1839; and Lieut. Couder, Fort Malouet, 7 July 1841. All from FM/SG Guy 10, dossier A3 (02), CAOM. The experience of the naturalist Couy is summarized in Hoogbergen, *The Boni Maroon Wars,* 193.

35. Emerich de Vattel, *Le droit des gens ou principe de la loi naturelle appliqués à la conduite et aux affaires des nations et des souverains* (1758; Washington, D.C.: Carnegie Institute, 1916), Préliminaires, secs. 1–2.

36. Gov. to Min., 12 Jan. 1837, FM/SG Guy 31, dossier D11 (03), CAOM.

37. Copie des instructions données à M. Faivre, Lieutenant, Commandant de détachement dans l'Oyapock, 20 April 1837 and Rapport au Roi, Bureau de personnel, 18 July 1838, FM/SG Guy 10, dossier A3 (02), CAOM.

38. Gov. to Min., 22 June 1839, FM/SG Guy 10, dossier A3 (02), CAOM.

39. Copie d'une lettre du Gouvernement de Surinam, Paramaribo, 12 June 1837, with Gov. to Min., 2 July 1837, FM/SG Guy 31, dossier D11 (03), CAOM.

40. Privy council minutes, 18 Feb. 1839, FM/SG Guy 10, dossier A3 (02), CAOM.

41. Privy council minutes, 18 Feb. 1839.

42. Lieut. Couder to Gov., Fort Malouet, 7 July 1841; Interrogatoire de la négresse Adouba, 15 July 1841; both in FM/SG Guy 10, dossier A 3 (02), CAOM.

43. To Rosalie Javouhey, 17 Aug. 1838, no. 387, AMJ II: 258.

44. To Admiral Rosamel, 29 July 1840, no. 429, AMJ II: 329–330.

45. To Admiral Duperré, 10 April 1838, no. 384, AMJ II: 246.

46. To Admiral Duperré, 1 March 1841, no. 446, AMJ II: 371.

47. To Admiral Duperré, 10 April 1838, no. 384, AMJ II: 247.

48. Exposé sur l'état de Mana, premiers mois de 1838, no. 383, AMJ II: 239.

49. To Admiral Duperré, 4 juillet 1838, no. 386, AMJ II: 254; to Admiral Rosamel, 29 July 1840, no. 429, AMJ II: 333. On land arrangements, see Arrêté rendu par M. le Ministre de la marine et des colonies, art. 5, no. 38 of 18 Sept. 1835, *B. Guy.* (1836), 34–39.

50. Pariset to Min., 1 Dec. 1847, FM/SG Guy 170/3, CAOM.

51. Two acts of 27 April 1848 defined the powers of commissars. See Décret portant suppression des conseils coloniaux and Décret sur les pouvoirs extraordinaires des commissaires-généraux de la République, in *Abolitionnistes de l'esclavage et réformateurs des colonies 1820–1851: Analyse et documents,* ed. Nelly Schmidt (Paris: Karthala, 2000), 1001.

52. Josette Falloppe, *Esclaves et colons: les noirs à la Guadeloupe au XIXᵉ siècle dans le processus de résistance et d'intégration (1802–1910)* (Basse-Terre: Société d'Histoire de la Guadeloupe, 1992), 383; *Journal du Conseiller Garnier à la Martinique en 1848,* ed. Gabriel Debien (Fort de France: Société d'histoire de la Martinique, 1969), 65.

53. État résumé des votes électoraux de la Guyane française pour la nomination d'un représentant titulaire et d'un représentant suppleant à l'Assemblée nationale (élections du 4 mars 1849), FM/SG Guy 15, dossier B40 (03), CAOM.

54. Extrait d'une lettre du Gouverneur de la Guyane du 29 août 1848 rendant compte des dispositions qu'il a prises pour l'inscription des noms des noirs affranchis, FM/SG Guy 15, dossier B40 (03), CAOM.

55. Privy council minutes, 21 Oct. 1848, FM/SG Guy 1, dossier A 10 (16), CAOM.

56. Of the July election, see "Partie officielle," *Feuille*, no. 19, 12 May 1849, Supplément, 1–4; Commissaire-gén. to Min., 18 July 1849 and 31 July 1849, FM/SG Guy 15 dossier B40 (03), CAOM.

57. *Journal du Conseiller Garnier*, 80; *Sugar and Slavery, Family and Race: The Letters and Diary of Pierre Dessalles, Planter in Martinique 1808–1856*, ed. and trans. Elborg Forster and Robert Forster (Baltimore: The Johns Hopkins University Press, 1996), 232 and 243.

58. Mélinon to Pariset, 4 March 1849, Mana, no. 12 (copie), FM/SG Guy 15, dossier B 40 (03).

59. Copie d'une lettre adressé à l'Ordonnateur sous la date du 16 mars 1849 par le Sieur Jouven, commissaire de police à Kourou," FM/SG Guy 15, dossier B 40 (03), CAOM.

60. Vidal de Lingendes to Pariset, Cayenne, 15 March 1849, FM/SG Guy 15, dossier B 40 (03).

61. Const. 1848, art. 109.

62. A. Bonnefoy-Sibour, *Le pouvoir législatif aux colonies: essai historique sur le droit de légiférer en matière coloniale* (Dijon: Imprimerie régionale, 1908), 105–112.

63. Const. 1848, arts. 19–20 and arts. 40–42.

64. Const. 1848, arts. 49 and 56–59.

65. Arrêté portant organisation provisoire du conseil municipal de Cayenne, no. 345 of 2 Aug. 1848, *B. Guy.* (1848), 448–449.

66. Gov. to Min., 25 May 1848, FM/SG Guy 106, dossier K5 (16), CAOM.

67. Commissaire-gén. to Min., 30 Aug. 1848, FM/SG Guy 1, dossier A10 (16), CAOM.

68. Philidor Barthélemy to Réprésentant [Jouannet], 4 March 1850, FM/SG Guy 15, dossier B40 (03), CAOM.

69. Commissaire-gén. to Min.,17 April 1849, FM/SG Guy 15, dossier B 40 (03), CAOM.

70. Arrêté pour la répression des menaces non prévues par le Code pénal, no. 95 of 4 April 1849; Arrêté qui rend exécutoires à la Guyane française, les dispositions de la loi des 19 et 22 juillet 1791, et du Code du 3 brumaire an IV (25 octobre 1795) sur les voies de fait et violences légères, no. 98 of 4 April 1849, *B. Guy.* (1849), 144–145 and 148–149.

71. Arrêté concernant le port d'armes quelconques, no. 96 of 4 April 1848; arrêté qui promulgue à la Guyane les actes de la legislation métropolitaine relatifs à la prohibition des armes à feu et de munitions de guerre, no. 102 of 4 April 1849, followed by Ordonnance de 1669, titre XXX, concernant les armes de chasse (no. 103), Déclaration du 23 mars 1728 concernant les armes prohibées (no. 104), Décret du 15 décembre 1805 qui interdit l'usage et le port des fusils et pistolets à vent (no. 105), loi du 13 fructidor an V (no. 106), Ordonnance du roi relative aux armes de guerre (no. 107), Loi du 24 mai 1834 contre les détenteurs d'armes ou de munitions de guerre (no. 108), Ordonnance du 25 février 1837 sur les pistolets de poche (no. 109), *B. Guy.* (1849), 145–146 and 154–163.

72. Arrêté portant repression des faits séparés dont l'ensemble constitue le vagabondage, no. 97 of 4 April 1849, *B. Guy.* (1849), 146–147.

73. Arrêté concernant la vente et le colportage des bois et autres produits du sol, no. 151 of 3 May 1849, *B. Guy.* (1849), 222–223.

74. Arrêté qui punit d'une amende tous individus rencontrés sans être vêtus, no. 149 of 3 May 1849, *B. Guy.* (1849), 218–219. This decree revives a measure from the slavery period.

75. Arrêté pour la tutelle des enfants trouvés et abandonnés, et les enfants pauvres, no. 101 of 4 April 1849, and Arrêté sur les enfants trouvés, abandonnés, ou orphelins placés à la Gabrielle, no. 165 of 23 May 1849. All from *B. Guy.* (1849), 150–153 and 269–272.

76. Rapport du préfet apostolique (18 Sept. 1849), FM/SG Guy 141, dossier R5 (12), CAOM.

77. Art. 2, Decree of 8 Dec. 1848, "Partie officielle," *Feuille de la Guyane,* 23 Dec. 1848, 1, FM/SG Guy 111 dossier K9 (10), CAOM.

78. Vidal de Lingendes to Min., 15 April 1830, "Au sujet de l'arrêt de la chambre d'accusation de la Cour Royale rendu en faveur du Sieur Prus, susceptible d'être attaqué par voie de Cassation," FM/SG Guy 107, d. K7 (06), CAOM; Jean-Baptiste Renouvellat de Cussac, *Situation des esclaves dans les colonies françaises: urgence de leur emancipation* (Paris: Pagnerre, 1845), 133–134.

79. Vidal de Lingendes (interim governor) to Min., 23 April 1851, FM/SG Guy 111, dossier K9 (11), CAOM.

80. "L'affranchissement d'un enfant impubère doît aussi bien que tout autre moyen d'aliénation profiter à la mere de cet enfant" (edit de mars 1685, art. 47), no. 53 of 16 Apr. 1845, Cass., *JP* (1845), 47: 133–134.

81. Yvan Debbasch, *Couleur et liberté,* 293, fn4.

82. Dépôt du testament de Vidal de Lingendes, no. 28 of 19 Oct. 1857, DPPC Not. Guy 113 (Marck, 1857–9), CAOM.

83. For the contrasting case of Martinique, see *Sugar and Slavery,* 219–224.

84. Pariset to Min., 12 June, 30 June, and 13 Aug. 1848, FM/SG Guy 1, dossier A10 (16), CAOM.

85. Lavollée, *Projet de loi sur la colonisation de la Guyane: Rapport au nom de la sous-commission* (Paris: Imprimerie nationale, 1851); parenthetical page numbers in the text refer to this 1851 report.

86. Minutes, première conférence sur la déportation à Cayenne, 19 Dec. 1851, H11, CAOM. For a discussion of this meeting and of Ducos's conduct at the time of the purge, see Chapter 5.

87. Théodore Ducos, "Rapport au Prince Président de la République française," *Le Moniteur* 52 (21 Feb. 1852): 1–2.

88. Min. to Commissaire-gén., 18 Sept. 1852, no. 497, 1 M 50, ADGuy.

89. Min. to Commissaire-gén. 15 May 1852, 1 M 49, ADGuy.

90. Procès verbaux de la commission chargée par arrêté de M. le Gouverneur du 31 janvier 1852 de donner son avis sur le choix des lieux où pourraient être placées les établissements pénitentiaires destinés aux déportés. Séances des 17 février, 1 et 26 mars et 10 avril 1852 présidées par l'Ordonnateur de la Colonie, H19, CAOM.

91. Procès verbaux de la commission, 1ère séance (17 Feb. 1852), H19, CAOM.

92. Mam-Lam-Fouck, *La Guyane française au temps de l'esclavage,* 187–188.

93. Jules Lechevalier, *Projet d'une colonisation agricole et industrielle à fonder à la Guyane française comme moyenne d'affranchissement progressif* (Paris: Vichon, 1843); Jack Hayward, "From Utopian Socialism, via Abolitionism to the Colonization of French Guiana: Jules Lechevalier's West Indian Fiasco 1833–1844," in *De la traite à l'esclavage:*

Actes du colloque international sur la traite des noirs, ed. Serge Daget (Paris: Société française d'histoire d'outre mer, 1985), 603–626.

94. Procès-verbaux de la commission, 1ère séance (17 Feb. 1852), H19, CAOM.

95. Gov. to Min., 29 Mar. 1852, no. 131, Register (1852), ADGuy.

96. Of Mélinon's first career as a tropical gardener, see Cordier, Director, Muséum d'histoire naturelle to Min. Navy, Paris, 18 Dec. 1839, FM/SG Guy 64, dossier 63 (08), CAOM; on his later activities in the penal colony see Chapter 8.

97. Mélinon to Sarda Garriga, Mana, 16 Dec. 1852, X/160, ADGuy.

98. Lavollée, *Rapport,* 99.

99. Lavollée, *Rapport,* 103–104.

100. Mélinon to Sarda Garriga, 4 Sept. 1852, X/160, ADGuy.

101. Mélinon to Sarda Garriga, 13 Dec. 1852, X/160, ADGuy.

102. Mélinon to Sarda Garriga, 17 Dec. 1852, X/160, ADGuy.

103. Mélinon to Sarda Garriga, 19 Jan. 1853, X/160, ADGuy.

104. Commissaire-gén. to Min., Cayenne, 18 Dec. 1852, Montagne d'Argent file, H14, CAOM.

105. Gov. to Min., 8 Apr. 1853, Register (1853), ADGuy.

7. THE ENORMOUS ROOM

1. Lists with ministerial dispatch to governor, 3 June 1852, no. 282, 1M49*, ADGuy.

2. For first mention of special maritime tribunal, see Min. to Gov., 30 April 1852, 1 M49*, ADGuy.

3. See Min. to Commissaire-Gén., 3 Oct. 1852, 1M50*, ADGuy.

4. Min. to Commissaire-Gén., 27 Oct. 1852, 1M50*, ADGuy.

5. For tables concerning the first four convoys, the *Cinq Frères* (11 Nov. 1854), *Diane* 1 (6 Jan. 1856), *Diane* 2 (20 June 1856), and *L'Orion* (20 Nov. 1857), see Monica Schuler, "Kru Emigration to British and French Guiana 1841–1857," *Africans in Bondage: Studies in Slavery and the Slave Trade,* ed. Paul Lovejoy (Madison: University of Wisconsin Press, 1986), 175–176.

6. Michel Foucault, "The Subject and Power" (1982), in *Power,* ed. James D. Faubion, vol. 3 of *The Essential Works of Foucault 1954–1984,* ser. ed. Paul Rabinow (New York: New Press, 2000), 331; "Le sujet et le pouvoir," vol. 2, *Dits et écrits 1976–1988,* ed. Daniel Defert, François Ewald, and Jacques Lagrange (Paris: Quarto/Gallimard, 2001), 1046. I have modified the English translation.

7. This split proved influential to the young Marx. See Donald R. Kelley, *Historians and the Law in Postrevolutionary France* (Princeton: Princeton University Press, 1984).

8. On Sarda-Garriga's earlier activities, see Françoise Vergès, *Monsters and Revolutionaries: Colonial Family Romance and Métissage* (Durham: Duke University Press, 1999), 58–62.

9. *Feuille,* 21 Aug. 1852, 2.

10. *Feuille,* 24 July 1852, 1–2; Tableau des propriétés achetées à la Guyane de 1852 à 1856, H19, CAOM.

11. Commissaire-Gén. to Min., 3 Sept. 1852, no. 229, Register (1852), ADGuy.

12. Commissaire-Gén. to Min., 17 Sept. 1852, H14, CAOM.

13. Arrêté édictant des pénalités contre les individus qui, sans autorisation, passeraient les sauts d'Oyapock, no. 31 of 15 Feb. 1849, *B. Guy.* (1849), 45.

14. Decree of 31 March 1853, *Feuille,* 2 April 1853, 1.

15. The text of 20 August 1853 was a decree of the Conseil d'état; the original date, 26 July 1853, is struck and replaced by the date 20 August in the draft preserved in H45, CAOM. This decree does not appear in *Le Bulletin des lois* for 1853 or 1854.

16. Récit d'un voyage du P. Girre à Saint Georges (n.d.), FGu 88, AJ.

17. Gov. to Min., 18 Nov. 1856, H14, CAOM.

18. Gov. to Min., 17 Jan 1856, H14, CAOM; Baudinto Min., 18 Nov. 1856, H14, CAOM; Gov. to Min., 26 April 1856, no. 454, Register (1856), ADGuy.

19. Gov. to Min., 12 Dec. 1857, no. 1053, Register (1857), ADGuy; "Bulletin de l'agriculture et du commerce," *Feuille* 11 May 1861, 3.

20. Abbé Puech to Révérend Père, Saint Georges, 15 Oct. 1860, FGu 88, AJ.

21. Fallope, *Esclaves et colons,* 393; Oruno D. Lara, *De l'Oubli à l'histoire: Espace et identité caraïbes* (Paris: Maisonneuve et Larose, 1998), 158.

22. Gov. Guadeloupe to Gov. Guiana, 20 February 1851, X/228, ADGuy.

23. Gov. to Min., 17 Aug. 1856, no. 845, Register (1856), ADGuy.

24. "Mariage de M. Ragmey et Mlle Barbeau," no. 78 of 20 March 1862, DPPC Not. Guy 115 (Marck 1862–1863), CAOM.

25. "Vente par Abstoul à Barbeau," no. 232 of 17 Oct. 1862, DPPC, Not. Guy 115 (Marck, 1862–1863), CAOM.

26. Gov. to Min., 16 Oct. 1863, H24, CAOM.

27. Gov. to Min., 14 March 1865, H14, CAOM.

28. Note sur l'Affaire Babeau, Direction, Ministère de la Marine et des Colonies, April 1868, H1851, CAOM.

29. Min. to Gov., 14 Dec. 1855, H11, CAOM.

30. Min. to Gov., 14 Dec. 1855, H11, CAOM.

31. Jusselain, *Un déporté à Cayenne,* 241.

32. Tocqueville, Œuvres 1, 686.

33. Jusselain, *Un déporté à Cayenne,* 37.

34. A. Lomon, *Souvenirs de l'Algérie: Captivité de l'Amiral Bonard et de l'Amiral Bruat,* with an introduction by L. Rigault (Paris: Hetzel, n.d.), 47.

35. On volunteers, see Charles Verdière, SJ, "Comment on justifie le décret du 27 mars 1852, et la loi du mois du mai 1854: Observations," ch. 2 in "Notes pour servir a l'histoire de la transportation à la Guyane française" (hereafter Verdière), 39–40, Ms. FGu 55, AJ.

36. Gov. to Min., 18 July 1854, H47, CAOM.

37. Arrêté qui détermine les formalités propres à constater la présence continue des condamnés dans le lieu de leur internement, no. 367 of 14 July 1854, *B. Guy.* (1854), 270–271.

38. Arrêté qui déclare en état de siège le poste militaire de Cacao, no. 369 of 15 July 1854, *B. Guy.* (1854), 280.

39. "Discussion du projet de loi organique sur l'état de siège," *Moniteur universel,* 10 Aug. 1849, 2650–2655.

40. "Assemblée législative, Séance du 28 juillet," *Moniteur universel,* 29 July 1849, 2521.

41. Charles-André Julien, vol. 1, *Histoire de l'Algérie Contemporaine* (Paris: Presses universitaires de France, 1964), 353–354.

42. Loi relative à la mise en état de siege en Guadeloupe, no. 2278, 11 July 1850, *B. L.,* 10th ser., no. 285, p. 25.

43. For state of siege on Îlet la Mère, see Partie officielle, *Feuille* 6 Aug. 1853, 1; of political prisoners aboard *Allier,* see *Allier* file, H26, CAOM; about their revolt and its repression, see Gov. to Min., 4 Aug. 1853 and 27 Aug. 1853, Register (1853), ADGuy. Prisoners convicted in Cayenne after revolt included Tassilier, Hollet, and Angélieaune. For Tassilier's file, see H579, CAOM.

44. Gov. to Min., 15 March 1855, no. 195, H9, CAOM.

45. Gov. to Min., 18 Nov. 1854, H9, CAOM.

46. Gov. to Min., 9 Apr. 1857, Register (1857), ADGuy.

47. Jusselain, *Un déporté à Cayenne,* 36–37.

48. Privy council minutes, 20 Nov. 1854, H11, CAOM.

49. Rapport de l'Amiral Hamelin, Ministre de la Marine et des colonies, à l'Empereur, sur la manière dont devaient être traités les individus envoyés en Guyane à divers titres, quoted in Verdière, ch. 8, Ms. FGu 55, AJ.

50. Décret imperial portant qu'en Algérie, dans le resort des justices de paix établies en territoire militaire, la connaissance des crimes et délits commis par les Indigènes appartient aux Conseils de guerre, no. 1400 of 29 April 1854, *B. L.,* no. 166, pp. 1169–1170.

51. In Verdière, ch. 8, notebook B13, FGu 55, AJ.

52. On circumvention of this court in favor of corporal punishment, see Min. to Gov., 15 April 1865, no. 161, 1M75*, ADGuy.

53. Décision relative aux transportés de la 1er catégorie, 18 August 1856, in FGu 20, AJ. Gov. to Min., 19 Aug. 1856, no. 853, Register (1856), ADGuy; Verdière, 52–53, Ms. FGu 55, AJ. For ministerial views about the legality of physical abuse, see Min. to Gov., 14 Feb. 1861, no. 59, 1M67*, ADGuy.

54. F. J. Léroy to Révérend Père, 26 Jan. 1856, FGu 87, AJ.

55. Jusselain, *Un déporté à Cayenne,* 106–107.

56. Copie d'une lettre adressé à M. le Commissaire général sous la date du 27 février 1849 par M. Thouronde, Lieutenant commandant la Gendarmerie coloniale, FM/SG Guy 15, dossier B40 (03), CAOM.

57. Arrêté portant désignation des lieux de réunion des assemblées électorales, Cayenne, 9 Feb. 1849; for a list of election officers, see Arrêté of 1 Feb. 1849, in *Arrêtés concernant les elections pour l'année 1849* (Cayenne: Imprimerie du Gouvernement, 1849); for details on the electoral assembly, see Extrait du rapport de la Gendarmerie coloniale du 8 Mars 1849, signed Thouronde, FM/SG Guy 15, dossier B 40 (03), CAOM.

58. Favard, Dir. Interior, to Gov., 11 Dec. 1856, X/236, ADGuy.

59. Masset, military commandant, to Min., 20 Jan. 1856, Cayenne, Register (1856), ADGuy.

60. Arrêté portant règlement sur les salaires, les vivres, et l'habillement des engagés africains affectés aux divers services de la colonie pénitentiaire, no. 592 of 23 Nov. 1854, *B. Guy.* (1854), 433.

61. Décret sur l'émigration d'Europe et hors d'Europe à destination des colonies françaises, no. 3958 of 27 Mar. 1852, *B. L.,* 10th ser., no. 519, p. 1018 ; for promulgation in French Guiana, see "Partie officielle," *Feuille,* 1 June 1852, 1.

62. Extrait du registre des procès-verbaux des délibérations du Conseil privé de la Guyane française, 24 May 1865, FM/SG 52 dossier F2 (07), CAOM; Relevé nominatif et signalétique des immigrants africains introduits dans la Guyane française par les navires Les Cinq Frères, Diane, 1er voyage, Diane, 2e voyage, et L'Orion, du 11 novembre 1854 au 20 novembre 1857, FM/SG Guy 53, dossier F2 (22), CAOM.

63. Gov. to Min., 8 Aug. 1857, no. 657, Register (1857), ADGuy.

64. Favard to Gov., 11 Dec. 1856, X/236, ADGuy.

65. Gov. to Min., 17 Feb. 1857, FM/SG Guy 52, dossier F2 (07), CAOM.

66. On the question of special legal arrangements for their punishment, see Min. Navy to Min. Justice, Paris, 7 Jan. 1862, and reply by Min. Justice, 12 Feb. 1862; for accounts of the crisis, see Gov. Martinique to Min., 10 July 1861; Procureur-Impérial of Fort-de-France to Procureur-Général Martinique, 29 Oct. 1861; all from H31, CAOM.

67. Gov. to Min., 4 Nov. 1856, FM/SG Guy 52, dossier F2 (10), CAOM.

68. This system included firing off cannons whenever immigrants fled. He also invented a coastal patrol. Gov. to Min., 15 Nov. 1857, FM/SG Guy 52, dossier F2 (10), CAOM. On the earlier career of Baudin, see Daget, *La Répression de la traite des noirs,* 431–443.

69. Gov. to Min., 17 Feb. 1854, FM/SG Guy 129, dossier P2 (04).

70. No. 408 of 12 Oct. 1854, DPPC Not. Guy 62 (Dechamp, 1854), CAOM.

71. No. 83 of 27 March 1854, ibid.

72. No. 218 of 2 July 1854, ibid.

73. No. 320 of 26 Aug. 1854, ibid.

74. For the parceling of Urbain Flotte's estate Saint François into adjacent plots at 130 francs per hectare, see sale of thirteen hectares to Louis Brutus, no. 334 of 9 Sept. 1854; of thirteen hectares to Candide Bonny, no. 345 of 9 Sept. 1854; of ten hectares to Lovelace Moricot, no. 346 of 9 Sept. 1854; of twenty-five hectares to Césaire Sainte Croix, no. 391 of 1 Oct. 1854; of thirteen hectares to Charles Fantaisie, no. 394 of 4 Oct. 1854; of fifty-five hectares to Pierre-Louis Polycarpe and Doris Anémone, no. 395 of 4 Oct. 1854; of twenty-five hectares to Guillaume Granmaré, no. 439 of 10 Nov. 1854; of eighteen hectares to Catherine Maba, no. 442 of 11 Nov. 1854; all in DPPC Not. Guy 62 (Dechamp, 1854), CAOM.

75. "Bulletin de l'agriculture et du commerce: Roura," *Feuille,* 23 Feb. 1861, 2; see also "Bulletin de l'agriculture et du commerce: Tour de l'île," *Feuille,* 16 Aug. 1862, 174.

76. Privy council minutes, 27 March 1860, FM/SG Guy 139, dossier R1 (02), CAOM.

77. Abbé Dossat to Min., Rapport du Préfet Apostolique, 19 Nov. 1851, p. 7, FM/SG Guy 141, d. R5 (16), CAOM.

78. Gov. to Min., 3 May 1853, FM/SG Guy 52, d. F2 (07), CAOM. On the activities of the Brothers of Ploermel in Guiana before and after emancipation, see Philippe Delille, *Histoire réligieuse des Antilles et de la Guyane françaises* (Paris: Éditions Karthala, 2000), 105, 112–114, 174–176.

79. Petition adressé à Messieurs les deputes par les habitants de la Guyane, 14 Sept. 1871, FM/SG Guy 1, d. A 10 (19), CAOM; for a refutation, see Gustave Marck, Note sur la pétition adressée à l'Assemblée nationale contre le suffrage universel à la Guyane par suite des élections qui ont eu lieu les 2 avril et 27 août 1871 pour l'élection du député de cette colonie, FM/SG Guy 171, dossier 2 (supp.), CAOM.

80. See for instance "Avis et annonces," *Feuille,* 27 Nov. 1852, 10.

81. Favard, Rapport en Conseil Privé, 4 Feb. 1858, X/236, ADGuy.

82. Gov. to Min., 18 Aug. 1858, no. 853, Register (1858), ADGuy.

83. Transportation hors pénitenciers, Année 1856 (mois de décembre), with Gov. to Min., 15 Jan. 1857, H47, CAOM.

84. Établissements pénitentiaires: statistique général des transportés de toutes catégories depuis le 1er mai 1852, FGu 20, AJ.

85. Conseil municipal, Session of 11 Jan. 1856, X/236, ADGuy.

86. Favard, Rapport sur la situation du service de la Direction de l'Intérieur [annual report for 1856], 22 Mar. 1857, X/236, ADGuy.

87. Pariset to Min., 17 April 1849. FM/SG Guy 15, d. B40 (03), CAOM. Arrêté qui maintien provisoirement les nominations du conseil municipal de Cayenne, des maire et adjoints, telles qu'elles ont été réglées par l'arrêté du 2 août 1848, 30 July 1851, *B. Guy.* (1851), 258–259.

88. On Lheurre, see "Nouvelles maritimes," *Feuille* 30 Oct. 1852, 4; 23 July 1853, 4.

89. Arrêté municipal, 16 Sept. 1819, in *Code de la Guyane française*, vol. 2 (Cayenne: Imprimerie du Roi, 1824), 536.

90. Decree of 10 Mar. 1853, *Feuille,* 12 Mar. 1853, 2–4.

91. Arrêté concernant l'exercice de la profession de marin ou de pêcheur à la Guyane, no. 318, 17 June 1854, *B. Guy.* (1854), 226–229.

92. Art. 2, Arrêté qui règle l'établissement des registres de l'état civil de la population affranchis par le décret du 27 avril 1848, et la délivrance des extraits de ces registres constatant l'identité et la liberté des affranchis, Cayenne, no. 518 of 8 Dec. 1848, *B. Guy.* (1848), 657; see also Arrêté complémentaire de celui du 8 décembre 1848, relatif à la clôture des registres constatant l'état de la population affranchie par le décret du 27 avril 1848 la délivrance des extraits de ces registres et le mode d'attribution des noms patronymiques aux nouveaux libres, Cayenne, no. 22 of 23 Jan. 1851, *B. Guy.* (1851), 40–42.

93. Arrêté qui confère des noms patronymiques à divers individus, no. 366 of 14 July 1854, *B. Guy.* (1854), 269.

94. Arrêté portant affranchissement de 30 personnes qui ont satisfait aux dispositions des lois et ordonnances sur les affranchissements, Cayenne, no. 101 of 10 Mar. 1848, *B. Guy.* (1848), 87.

95. See Françoise Vergès, *Monsters and Revolutionaries,* esp. 62–63; on the politics of illegitimacy in Indochina, including naming practices, see Emanuelle Saada, *Les enfants de la colonie: Les métis de l'empire française entre sujétion et citoyenneté* (Paris: La Découverte, 2007).

96. Observations relatives à un arrêté local qui a autorisé la nommée REINE à prendre le nom patronymique d'Amiel (1857), *B. Guy.* (1857), 412–413.

97. Tardy de Montravel, "Considérations générales sur la délimitation, l'étude et la colonisation de la Guyane française," *Revue coloniale* 12 (Aug. 1847): 408–434.

98. On the still-extant fountain to commemorate Montravel, see Decision of 4 June 1868, *B. Guy.* (1868), 240.

99. Favard to Montravel, 20 March 1860, Résumé of Minutes of the Conseil Municipal, Session of 31 Dec. 1859, X/236, ADGuy.

100. Gov. to Min., 16 Oct. 1863, H24, CAOM.

101. Arrêté portant qu'un atelier de travailleurs à requérir dans les quartiers de l'Ile-de-Cayenne, du Tour-de-l'Ile, de Roura, et de Kaw, sera employé sur les routes de Cayenne à Approuague, 13 June 1859, *Feuille,* 18 June 1859, 2.

102. Arrêté of 27 July 1859, mentioned in Favard to Montravel, 20 March 1860, Résumé of the Minutes of the Conseil Municipal (30 Dec. 1859), X/236, ADGuy.

103. Arrêté concernant les danses au tambour ou au tambourin dans les campagnes, no. 627 of 20 Sept. 1860, *B. Guy.* (1860), 400–401.

104. "Cour impériale de la Guyane, Audience solennelle de rentrée," *Feuille,* 12 Nov. 1859, 3.

105. No. 182 of 16 June 1854, DPPC Not. Guy 62, CAOM.

106. Favard, Rapport, 28 février 1856, X/236, ADGuy.

107. Gov. to Min., 16 Mar. 1860, no. 257, H47, CAOM.

108. Gov. to Min., 17 Sept. 1857, H47, CAOM.

109. Ibid.

8. METASTASIS

1. See Préfet Police to Préfet Eure-et-Loir, 23 Oct. 1863; Renseignements demandé à M. le Maire de la Commune de Pinthières sur le nommé Vathonne (et Mocquet), 9 Nov. 1863; Renseignements demandé à M. le Maire de la commune de Boutigny sur le nommé Vathonne, 19 Dec. 1863; Préfet Seine-et-Oise to Préfet Eure-et-Loir, 27 July 1864; and Préfet Police to Préfet Eure-et-Loir, 10 Nov. 1864; all from 4 M P art. 675, AD Eure-et-Loir (Chartres).

2. Gov. to Min., 15 March 1856, no. 269, Register (1856), ADGuy.

3. Min. to Gov., 25 April 1856, no. 308, and 29 April 1856, no. 331, 1M57*, ADGuy.

4. Gov. to Min., 18 May 1856, H47, CAOM.

5. Montfort to Révérend Père (hereafter RP), Saint Laurent, 25 April 1862, FGu 101, AJ.

6. Benjamin Beigner, Réponse aux questions posées dans une dépêche ministérielle du 16 janvier 1857 relative à la transportation à la Guyane, marked "transmise par l'Amiral à Paris le 7 mars 1857," FGu 20, AJ.

7. Quoted in [Emile Jardinier], "Notes pour servir à l'histoire de Saint Laurent (1862)," 35, MS FGu 95, AJ [hereafter Hist. St. Laurent]. I am attributing this text on the basis of internal evidence. It is listed without an author in the Jesuit catalog.

8. Hist. St. Laurent, 27.

9. Hist. St. Laurent, 66.

10. Hist. St. Laurent, 73.

11. Beigner, Réponse, FGu 20, AJ; italics added.

12. "Premier mariage célébré le 23 octobre 1859 à l'établissement agricole et pénitentiaire de Saint Laurent du Maroni," Partie Non Officielle, *Feuille* 5 Nov. 1859, 3. On the first couple, see Danielle Donet-Vincent, *De soleil et de silences: Histoire des bagnes de la Guyane* (Paris: Bibliothèque de l'Histoire, 2003), 178.

13. Nicou to RP, 25 March 1860, FGu 101, AJ.

14. Gov. to Min., 2 Feb. 1859, H33, CAOM.

15. Min. to Gov., 29 Jan. 1862, 1M69*, ADGuy.

16. Bk. 1, ch. 6, art. 214, C. Civil, in Gaston Griolet and Charles Vergé, *Code Civil noté d'après la doctrine et la jurisprudence* (Paris: Bureau de Jurisprudence générale, 1906), 61; François Laurent, *Principes de droit civil*, vol. 2, 4th ed. (Paris and Brussels: Bruylant-Christophe/Maresq, 1887), 114–115.

17. Min. to Gov., 27 June 1862, no. 320, 1M69*, ADGuy.

18. Min. to Gov., 30 June 1862, no. 325, 1M69*, ADGuy.

19. Min. to Gov., 30 June 1862, no. 325, 1M69*, ADGuy. On wives who joined convict husbands, see Danielle Donet-Vincent, *De soleil et de silences,* 179–181.

20. Matricule for Rosalie Marguerite Fortunée Béridot, H33, CAOM.

21. Min. to Gov., 9 Oct. 1865, no. 466, 1M76*, ADGuy.

22. Chateau to RP, 10 Aug. 1860, FGu 101, AJ.

23. Gov. to Min., 15 March 1863, no. 273, Register (1863), ADGuy.

24. Loi sur l'exécution de la peine des travaux forcés, no. 1527 of 30 May 1854, *B. L.*, no. 178, pp. 1439–1442.

25. Quoted in Paulinier, Rapport en Conseil privé, 16 Oct. 1866, H14, CAOM.

26. Odile Krakovitch, *Les femmes bagnardes* (Paris: Olivier Orban, 1990), 163.

27. Situation des établissements pénitentiaires de la Guyane française en 1860, lettre annuelle, FGu 41, AJ.

28. Chateau to RP, 31 Aug. 1860, FGu 101, AJ.

29. [Gaudré], 21 Nov. 1860, FGu 101, AJ.

30. Gov. to Min., 26 Sept. 1863, no. 551, Register (1863), ADGuy.

31. Léon Rivière, *La Guyane française en 1865: Aperçu géographique, historique, législatif, agricole, industriel et commercial* (Cayenne: Imprimerie du Gouvernement, 1866), 204–205.

32. Situation des établissements pénitentiaires de la Guyane française en 1860, Lettre annuelle, FGu 41, AJ.

33. Gov. to Min., 5 Jan. 1859, no. 1, Register (1859), ADGuy; Min. Navy to Min. Algeria and Colonies, 3 Jan. 1859, personnel file, Louis-François-Marie Tardy de Montravel, CC^7 2334, SHM (Vincennes).

34. Nicou to RP, 10 Feb. 1861, FGu 101, AJ.

35. On Etienne Chantelouve (4th cat., 1st sect., no. 1745) and his failed escape of 5 August 1867, see TMS file (1868), H4880, CAOM. Chantelouve's tattoo was probably a motto

of the Bataillons d'Afrique. Albert Londres noted a convict in Guiana with the same tattoo in 1923. See Albert Londres, *Au bagne* (Paris: Arléa, 1997), 26.

36. Min. to Gov., 28 March 1860, no. 54, 1M65*, ADGuy.

37. Nicou to RP, 23 June 1860, FGu 101, AJ.

38. Gaudré to RP, 24 Sept. 1860, FGu 101, AJ.

39. Nicou to RP, 10 Feb. 1861, FGu 101, AJ.

40. [Chateau?] to RP, 10 Dec. 1862, FGu 101, AJ.

41. Chateau to RP, 24 Oct. 1860, and Nicou, 25 March and 23 June 1860, FGu 101, AJ.

42. Nicou to RP, 9 Oct. 1860, FGu 101, AJ.

43. Garnier to RP, 20 Feb. 1868, FGu 101, AJ.

44. Rivière, *La Guyane en 1865,* 204.

45. Garnier to RP, 20 Feb. 1868, FGu 101, AJ.

46. Begin to RP, 20 Feb. 1868, FGu 101, AJ.

47. Paulinier, Rapport en Conseil privé, 16 Oct. 1866, H14, CAOM.

48. Projet du Code civil, H14, CAOM.

49. Paulinier, Rapport en Conseil privé, 16 Oct. 1866, H14, CAOM.

50. Londres, *Au bagne*, 131.

51. Charles Delescluze, *De Paris à Cayenne* (Paris: Lechevalier, 1872), 280.

52. See files of Louis Jules Bizet (d. 29 April 1856), François-Pierre Beurneau (d. 5 Jan. 1874), and Jean Barraud (d. 8 Feb. 1862) in H265, CAOM.

53. Nicou to RP, 9 Oct. 1860, FGu 101, AJ.

54. Houdouin to RP, 11 Dec. 1862, FGu 120, AJ.

55. Min. to Gov., 16 May 1862, no. 246, 1M69*, ADGuy.

56. Decree of 13 Feb. 1852, Title IV, art. 22, *Feuille* supp., 6 Apr. 1852, 6.

57. Petit résumé sommaire, Diarum Saint Pierre du Maroni, FGu 111, AJ.

58. Montfort to RP, 20 Dec. 1865, FGu 120, AJ.

59. Verdière, "Notes pour servir à l'histoire," p. 57 of B1, MS, FGu 55, AJ.

60. Montfort to RP, 20 Dec. 1865, FGu 120, AJ.

61. Houdouin, De la Pentecôte à la Toussaint (13 May 1869–20 Oct. 1869), FGu 120, AJ.

62. Hennique, Tournée d'Inspection, 22 Apr. 1869, no. 242, H24, CAOM.

63. Beaumont to RP, Saint Pierre, 26 July 1869, FGu 120, AJ.

64. Arnoult, Paul-Firmin (4th cat., 1st sec., no. 896), TMS file (1868), H4880, CAOM.

65. Liste nominative de 8 transportés de la 1ère catégorie évadés des pénitenciers de Cayenne and Liste nominative de 49 transportés de la 3e catégorie, 1ère section, *Amazone* file, H29, CAOM.

66. On Brakel (3rd cat., 1st sec., no. 1347), Min. to Gov., 31 Jan. 1861, no. 41, 1M67*, ADGuy.

67. Min. Interior to Min. Navy, 7 June 1859, H52, CAOM.

68. On Edouard Baczinski, Min. to Gov., 16 March 1861, no. 35, 1M67*, ADGuy.

69. Hennique, Tournée d'Inspection, 22 Apr. 1869, H24, CAOM.

70. Décision réglant l'état, à la Guyane, des transportés libérés non astreints à la résidence, condamnés sous l'empire de la loi de 30 mai 1854, 3 Feb. 1869, *B. Guy.,* 52.

71. Min. to Gov., 26 Sept. 1863, no. 551, Register (1863), ADGuy.

72. Hennique, Tournée d'Inspection, 22 Apr. 1869, no. 242, H24, CAOM.

73. On the use of rachat [the redemptive purchase of slaves], see Monica Schuler, "Kru Emigration to British and French Guiana 1841–1857," in *Africans in Bondage: Studies in Slavery and the Slave Trade,* ed. Paul Lovejoy (Madison: University of Wisconsin Press, 1986), 178; on the earlier British recruitment of slaves in Africa to fill out immigrant convoys, see 173; Lawrence C. Jennings, "French Reactions to the 'Disguised British Slave Trade': France and British African Emigration Projects 1840–1864," *Cahiers d'étude africaine* 18, nos. 69–70 (1978): 201–213.

74. For remarks on *Phénix, Méridien,* and *Le Joseph,* see Privy council minutes, 13 Dec. 1859, and Gov. to Min., 16 April 1860; both in FM/SG Guy 52, dossier F2 (07), CAOM.

75. For the contract see Arrêté pour l'exécution d'un traité conclu entre le département de la marine et le capitaine Chevalier, sous la date du 30 juin 1858, pour l'introduction de 2000 immigrants africains à la Guyane (7 Sept. 1858), *Feuille,* 11 Sept. 1858, 2; on nullification, see Min. to Gov., 29 Feb. 1860, 1M65*, ADGuy.

76. Décret impérial portant promulgation de la convention conclue le 1er juillet 1861 entre la France et la Grande Bretagne, pour régler l'immigration de travailleurs indiens dans les colonies françaises, no. 9415 of 10 Aug. 1861, *B. L.,* 11th ser., no. 959, pp. 345–351; on French implementation of the convention, see Min. to Gov., 26 March 1862, 1M69*, ADGuy. French implementation of the treaty locally entailed greater ministerial oversight of immigrant working conditions than had earlier been the case for either Africans or Indians in Guiana.

77. Min. to Gov., 15 May 1860, no. 167, 1M65*, ADGuy; on the South Asian immigrant experience, see Singaravelou, *Les Indiens de la Caraïbe* (Paris: L'Harmattan, 1987).

78. Gov. to Min., 19 Feb. 1862, 1M69*, ADGuy.

79. Min. to Gov., 13 Nov. 1862, no. 554, 1M70*, ADGuy.

80. Alfred Parépou [pseud.], *Atipa: Roman Guyanais,* trans. Marguerite Fauquenoy (Paris: Editions Harmattan, 1987), 159 and 175.

81. Berriaud to RP, Saint Louis, 19 Sept. 1861, FGu 103, AJ.

82. Bilby, "Swearing by the Past," 666.

83. Report of 21 Sept. 1847, quoted in Tristan Bellardie, "Diplomatie et politique coloniale aux marges de la Guyane française: La France et le Maroni (1848–1892)," *Revue française d'histoire d'outre mer* 84, no. 315 (1997): 87.

84. Sibour, "Nos Relations avec les nègres et les indiens du Haut Maroni (Guyane française)," *Feuille,* 16 May 1861, 5.

85. Ronmy, "Excursion dans le haut Maroni," *Revue maritime et coloniale* 1 (June 1861): 779–796.

86. Berriaud to RP, Saint Louis, 8 Dec. 1860, FGu 103, AJ.

87. Sibour, "Nos Relations avec les nègres et les indiens du Haut Maroni (Guyane française)," *Feuille,* 16 May 1861, 5.

88. Ibid., 4.

89. Berriaud to RP, Saint Louis, 9 May 1862, FGu 103, AJ.

90. Jardinier, "Voyage au premier saut (3 November 1866)," Diarum 1866–67: Chantiers du Haut Maroni, FGu 133, AJ.

91. Sibour, "Nos Relations," 5.

92. On bounties, see Verdière, p. 83 of B2, FGu 55, AJ. On killings, see Verdière, pp. 383–384 of B9, FGu 55, AJ.

93. Favard to Baudin, 26 Mar. 1858, X/236, ADGuy.

94. Montravel to Jérôme Bonaparte, 16 Aug. 1859, H4, CAOM. Favard refers to this depot in his letter about Constant Bar to Montravel of 17 July 1860, X/236, ADGuy.

95. Constant Bar to Montravel, n.d., attached to Favard, Rapport au Gouverneur, 17 July 1860, X/236, ADGuy.

96. Favard to Montravel, Rapport, 17 July 1860, X/236, ADGuy.

97. Gov. to Min., Paris, 12 Aug. 1864, no. 377, 1M74*, ADGuy; italicized passage underlined in original.

98. "Condamnations prononcées par la Cour impériale de la Guyane française, pendant sa session correctionnelle du mois de décembre 1857," *Feuille,* 27 Feb. 1858, 2.

99. "Condamnations prononcées par la Cour impériale de la Guyane française, pendant sa session correctionnelle du mois de janvier 1858," *Feuille,* 6 March 1858, 4.

100. Jean-Baptiste Morinan called Cognio (4th cat., 1st sec., no. 2287), TMS file (1868), H4880, CAOM.

101. Decree of 10 May 1863, *Feuille,* 16 May 1863, 1.

102. "Condamnations prononcées par la Cour impériale de la Guyane française pendant sa session correctionnelle du mois de mars 1863," *Feuille,* 4 July 1863, 140; "Condamnations pronounces par la cour impériale de la Guyane française pendant sa session correctionnelle du mois de mai 1863," *Feuille,* 25 July 1863, 154.

103. Quintrie, Dir. Interior, to Loubère, Gov. (1870–1877), 1 Oct. 1870, X/279, ADGuy.

104. The snipers were local men. Parépou, *Atipa,* 29.

105. Résumé d'une commission instituée par le Gouverneur, le 27 septembre 1870, en vue de diverses dispositions d'ordre public à adopter à Cayenne, approuvée par le gouverneur le 28 septembre 1870, *B. Guy.,* 327.

106. Gov. to Min., 11 Sept. 1871, FM/SG Guy 1, file A 10 (19), CAOM. On colonial representation and the 1875 constitution, see Nelly Schmidt, *Victor Schoelcher et l'abolition de l'esclavage,* 209; see also Loi du 24 février 1875 relative à l'organisation du Sénat, arts. 2 and 4, in *Constitutions de la France,* ed. Jacques Godechot (Paris: Garnier-Flamarrion, 1970), 333. On ministerial support for disenfranchisement, see Note sur la représentation au Sénégal et à la Guyane, June 1875, FM/SG Guy 171, dossier 2 (supplément), CAOM.

107. Loi qui rétablit la représentation des colonies de la Guyane et du Sénégal à la Chambre des Députés, no. 7891 of 8 April 1879, *B. L.,* 12th ser., vol. 18, no. 437, pp. 463–464; Décret qui convoque les collèges électoraux de la Guyane et du Sénégal à l'effet d'élire un député pour chacune des colonies, no. 7999 of 12 April 1879, *B. L.,* 12th ser., vol. 18, no. 442, p. 634.

108. For details on the production of these texts, see Gov. to Min., 16 June 1865, no. 394, and Note annexe à la lettre no. 394 contenant des renseignements fournis par la police locale; for the pamphlets, see FM/SG Guy 10, dossier A4 (08).

109. Jules Faure, Min. Affaires Étrangères, Versailles, 26 July 1871, H1834, CAOM.

110. *Toulonnais: Gazette de Provence,* 10 Nov. 1872, 2.

111. This observation is based on data for 1868. François Bourdiaux (4th cat., 1st sec.) fled on 21 Oct. 1867, returned on 17 Dec. 1867, convicted by Tribunal Maritime Spécial on 27 Feb. 1868 with Marie-Marc-François Rolland (4th cat., 1st sec., no. 2032), Paul-Léon Garin (4th cat., 1st sec., no. 2105), and Barthélemy Pollero (4th cat., 1st sec., no. 2013). See remarks of Pollero from interrogatoire in group file, H4880, all in CAOM.

112. Min. to Gov., 26 July 1878 (copy), in folder marked "relation avec les noirs Bonis," FM/SG Guy 10, dossier A3 (05), CAOM.

113. Bernard Castieu et al., *Commune de Saint Laurent du Maroni, Département de la Guyane, Patrimoine architectural et urbain, DRAC Guyane, Office du Tourisme, Saint Laurent* (June 1994), 1.

CONCLUSION

1. Robert Vignon, *Gran Man Baka*, 218.

2. In 1972, there were 27,800 Indians in British Guiana (now Guyana) and 4,400 Indians in Dutch Guiana (now Surinam). In contrast, there were 1,200 Indians in all of French Guiana, including the 800 Caribs who lived on the coast. Hurault, *Français et Indiens en Guyane*, 22.

3. Jean-Marcel Hurault, *Institut géographique national: mission de délimitation de la frontière Guyane française-Brésil Frontière Sud, bassin du Maroni, octobre 1956-février 1957: Rapport de fin de mission par Jean Hurault* (n.p., n.d.), 101–112.

4. Peter Redfield, *Space in the Tropics: From Convicts to Rockets in French Guiana* (Berkeley: University of California Press, 2000), 125–128.

5. Charter 1814, art. 73; Charter 1830, art. 64. In Pierre Rosanvallon, *La Monarchie impossible: Les Chartes de 1814 et de 1830* (Paris: Fayard, 1994), 257 and 355.

6. Const. 14 Jan. 1852, art. 1.

7. Philippe Raynaud, "The 'Rights of Man and Citizen' in the French Constitutional Tradition," in *The Legacy of the French Revolution,* ed. Ralph C. Hancock and L. Gary Lambert (Lanham, Md.: Rowman and Littlefield, 1996), 211; Claude Nicolet, *L'idée républicaine en France 1789–1924: essai d'histoire critique* (Paris: Gallimard, 1982), 342–356.

8. Quoted from *Revue internationale de droit pénal* (1930) in Albert Rauzy, *De l'interdiction de séjour* (Toulouse: Imprimerie régionale, 1935), 9.

9. Isabelle Merle, *Expériences coloniales: la Nouvelle Calédonie 1853–1920* (Paris: Belin, 1995), 222–223.

10. Sylvie Clair, Odile Krakovitch, and Jean Préteux, *Établissements pénitentiaires coloniaux 1792–1952, série Colonies H: répertoire numérique* (Paris: Archives nationales, 1990), 15.

11. Robert Badinter, *La prison républicaine* (Paris: Fayard 1992), 160–174. On the Martiniquan *rélégué* Médard Aribot, see Richard Price, *The Convict and the Colonel: A Story of Colonialism and Resistance in the Caribbean* (Boston: Beacon Press, 1998).

12. Patrick Chamoiseau and Ralph Hammadi, *Guyane: Traces-mémoires du bagne* (Paris: Caisse nationale des monuments historiques et sites, 1994), 14.

13. Arnaud de Saint Jouan, "Le camp de la Transportation à Saint Laurent du Maroni," *Monumental: Revue scientifique et technique de la Sous-direction des Monuments historiques* 12 (March 1996): 78.

14. Arnaud de Saint Jouan, "Les Chantiers de restauration des monuments historiques de Guyane: Les objectifs," *Monumental* 13 (June 1996): 73.

Acknowledgments

I HAVE RELIED OFTEN on the help of archivists in France and French Guiana, without whom this book would not have been possible. Myriam Pauillac and her wonderful family made me feel welcome in Cayenne while helping me to explore the riches of French Guiana's document collection. Thanks to Elizabeth Martinez at the Centre des Archives d'Outre Mer in Aix-en-Provence, I had the good luck to discover uncatalogued registers in the archive storehouse that unlocked the story of reenslavement in Guiana. Those documents proved indispensable to Chapter 3 ("Free Soil"), which I would like to dedicate to her.

The Social Science Research Council made possible the research in France and French Guiana on which much of this book is based. I am thankful to Kim Lane Scheppele and to Kwame Anthony Appiah for making possible my year at the Princeton University Center for Human Values, which enabled me to conduct additional research while rewriting portions of the manuscript. The College of Social and Behavior Sciences at the University of Arizona allowed me time away from teaching to conduct final revisions. I am grateful to my chair, Professor Kevin Gosner, for his commitment to this project.

The anonymous readers for Harvard University Press helped me to develop a more nuanced approach to Guiana after slavery. Stephen Burt,

Howard Brown, John Garrigus, David Geggus, Rafe Blaufarb, and Gary Wilder were generous with their time in reading and commenting on draft chapters. I am grateful for the incisive commentary that I received from Jeremy Popkin, David Bell, Frederick Cooper, and Darrin McMahon during the crafting of the manuscript. I wish to thank Rebecca Spang in particular for her saintly forbearance and gifts as a reader. Daniel Heller-Roazen, who guided me to the work of Giorgio Agamben during a chance meeting in Paris years ago, has been a source of encouragement and inspiration throughout the revision process.

Simon Schama gave me the courage to attempt a book on French Guiana in the first place. He has shaped this work in incalculable ways, rescued me, kept my spirits up, and reminded me of what was important without mentioning it. He helped me to see my way through a project that proved to be much sadder and stranger than either of us had imagined possible. Isser Woloch first led me to explore political institutions as a framework for human freedom, which later emerged as central themes of my research. David Armitage stirred my interest in law, political theory, and imperial legal regimes. His sensible guidance, friendship, and support over the years are humbling to think about; this book would not be what it is without him. I am further indebted to Laurie Benton, whose wide-angled view of imperial history has led me to discover new worlds of law and to rediscover French history. I also wish to thank my friend and colleague Julia Clancy-Smith for the gift of time she did not have: I was lucky to have a reader of draft chapters with a legal perspective rooted in North Africa.

I am indebted to Lois Kain for her brilliant map of Surveillance of the High Police. Benjamin Spieler, my brother, drew the map of Guiana for this book, which my sister Cassie Spieler transformed into a computerized image. Most of all, I am grateful to my siblings Ben, Cassie, and Abby for the pleasure I take in simply knowing that they exist.

Throughout the writing of this book, Christopher Schmidt-Nowara has been a teacher, a guide, and the truest friend.

Index